Outdoor Gas Griddle
Cookbook for Beginners

Tasty & Affordable Outdoor Gas Griddle Recipes for Beginners and Advanced Users

Debbie Person

© Copyright 2022 – All rights reserved.

The content contained within this book may not be reproduced, duplicated or transmitted without direct written permission from the author or the publisher.

Under no circumstances will any blame or legal responsibility be held against the publisher, or author, for any damages, reparation, or monetary loss due to the information contained within this book, either directly or indirectly.

▶ Legal Notice:

This book is copyright protected. It is only for personal use. You cannot amend, distribute, sell, use, quote or paraphrase any part, or the content within this book, without the consent of the author or publisher.

▶ Disclaimer Notice:

Please note the information contained within this document is for educational and entertainment purposes only. All effort has been executed to present accurate, up to date, reliable, complete information. No warranties of any kind are declared or implied. Readers acknowledge that the author is not engaged in the rendering of legal, financial, medical or professional advice. The content within this book has been derived from various sources. Please consult a licensed professional before attempting any techniques outlined in this book.

By reading this document, the reader agrees that under no circumstances is the author responsible for any losses, direct or indirect, that are incurred as a result of the use of the information contained within this document, including, but not limited to, errors, omissions, or inaccuracies.

Table of Contents

Introduction 1

Fundamentals of Outdoor Gas Griddle 2

What Is Outdoor Gas Griddle? 2
Functions of Outdoor Gas Griddle 2
Benefits of Using this Outdoor Gas Griddle 2
Preparation and Maintenance 3
How It Works 3

4-Week Meal Plan 4

Chapter 1 Breakfast Recipes 6

Simple Almond Pancakes 6
Cinnamon Chocolate Pancake 6
Cauliflower Patties 6
Easy Pumpkin Pancake 6
Scrambled Egg with Tomato 6
Fluffy Blueberry Pancakes with Maple Syrup 6
Cherry Tomato Omelet with Mozzarella Cheese 7
French Crepes 7
Easy-to-Make Broccoli Omelet 7
Cinnamon Cheese Pancakes 7
Cheese Butter Sandwich 7
Banana Pancakes 7
Typical Denver Omelet 7
Spinach Pepper Egg Scramble 8
Vanilla Toast Sticks 8
Cheese Omelet with Olives 8
Bacon Burrito 8
Almond Vanilla Pancakes 8
Cheese Kale Omelet 8
Cinnamon Toast Sticks 8
Broccoli Omelet 8
Simple French Crepes 9
Coconut Spinach Pancakes 9
Homemade Cheese Omelet 9
Cheese Cauliflower Patties 9
Cheese Ham Omelet 9
Parmesan Cauliflower Hash Browns 9
Seasoned Sirloin Pieces and Eggs 9
Scallion Cauliflower Pancakes 10
Cheesy Potato Hash Brown 10
Potatoes Hash Browns 10
Cinnamon Pumpkin Pancakes 10
Scrambled Eggs with Spinach and Mushroom 10
Bacon Omelet with Gruyere 10
Cheese Tomato Omelet 10
Bacon Egg Sandwich with Cheese Slices 11
Yogurt Oatmeal Pancake 11
Simple Omelet with Cheddar Cheese 11
Butter Almond Cauliflower Patties 11
Butter Cheese Sandwiches 11
Herbed Cheese Omelet 11
Cheese Coconut Pancakes 11
Simple Toad in a Hole 12
French Toast with Maple Syrup 12
Spicy Bacon Vegetable Tortillas 12
Crispy Bacon Potato Hash 12
Sausage Scramble Vegetable 12
Bacon, Egg and Cheese Sandwich 12
Scrambled Bean with Cheese 13
Broccoli Onion Hash with Cheddar Cheese 13
Tomato Omelet 13
Soft Blueberry Pancakes 13
Flavored Buttermilk Pancakes 13
Golden Potato Hash Browns 13
Chorizo Scramble Greens 14
Basil Tomato Omelet 14
Fluffy Vanilla Pancakes 14
Scrambled Eggs with Cilantro 14
Egg Scrambled with Tomato and Chili 14
Kale Omelet with Parmesan Cheese 14
Vanilla Oatmeal Pancakes 15
Bacon Gruyere Omelet 15
Garlic Cauliflower and Broccoli Patties 15

Chapter 2 Burger Recipes 16

Garlicky Pork Burgers 16
Mustard Pork Tenderloin Sandwiches 16
Lamb amd Cucumber Burger 16
Pinapple and Ham Sandwich 16
Tasty Bacon Cheese Serrano Wraps 16
Veggie Pesto Flatbread with Mozzarella Cheese 16
Marinated Portobello Cheese Burgers 17
Garlic Parsley Cheese Sandwiches 17
Croque Ham Cheese Buegers 17
Beef & Corn Burgers 17
Bulgur Beet Burgers 17
Cheese and Tomato Burgers 17
Garlic Cheese Pizza 18
Mozzarella Vegetable Pizza 18

Chapter 3 Vegetarian and Sides Recipes 19

Steamed Carrots in Ranch Dressing 19
Zucchini Squash Mix 19
Sautéed Savoury Green Beans 19
Crispy Cooked Potatoes 19
Parmesan Zucchini 19
Fried Green Tomatoes with Parsley 19
Cotija Vegetable Scrable 20
Homemade Caribbean Jerk Vegetables 20
Rosemary Bread 20
Vegetable Fried Rice 20
Fried Brussels Sprouts and Dried Cranberries 20
Asparagus with Butter and Pepper 20
Pita Bread 21
Bacon Brussels Topped with Blue Cheese 21
Sweet Potato Black Bean Burritos 21
Savory Candied Sweet Potatoes 21
Rosemary Potatoes 21
Green Beans Pancetta 21
Mayonnaise Corn Fritters 22
Collards Greens Stew in Chicken Stock 22
Ginger Coleslaw Egg Rolls 22
Delicous Pepper Butternut Squash 22
Sautéed Zucchini and Carrots 22
Cranberry Jalapeño Stuffed Sausage 22
Maple Glazed Green Beans Fried Bacon and Onion 23
Basil Veggie Salad with Cheese 23

Recipe	Page
Herded Broccoli Rice	23
Spicy Onion Patties	23
Radish Bell Pepper	23
Garlic Eggplant	23
Parsley Parmesan Ravioli with Sauce	24
Sweet Yogurt Flatbread	24
Cinnamon Seed Eggplant	24
Thyme Lemon Cabbage	24
Celery Onion Corn Bread	24
Savoury Plantains	24
Cabbage Bacon Pancake	25
Arugula and Mushroom Burgers	25
Grilled Bok Choy	25
Paprika Cheese Ears Corn	25
Lemon Mushrooms	25
Steamed Bell Peppers with Vinaigrette	25
Onion and Tomato Sandwich	26
Healthy Basil Wine Zucchini and Eggplant Salad	26
Basil Tomato and Zucchini Ratatouille	26
Garlic Tofu with Cilantro	26
Carrot Coleslaw	26
Garlic Potato Cubes with Corn and Black Beans	26
Delectable Egg Fried Rice with Green Onion	27
Oregano Vegetable Frittata	27
Garlic Lemon Zucchini Slices with Parsley	27
Grilled Bell Pepper and Zucchini	27
Basil Tomatoes with Cheese	27
Sesame Pineapple Fried Rice	27
Vinegar Coleslaw with Mayo Dressing	27
Grilled Thyme Zucchini	28
Garlicky Tomatoes	28
Garlic Thyme Mushrooms	28
Gold Potato Hobo Packs	28
Rosemary Red Potatoes	28
Cheese Buffalo Turds	28
Grilled Dijon Artichokes	29
Green Beans with Sesame Seed	29
Salty Sweet Potatoes	29
Garlic Cabbage in Soy Sauce	29
Garlic Cauliflower in BBQ Sauce	29
Lemon Pepper Vegetables	29
Paprika Lemon Eggplant	29
Paprika Potatoes	30
Lemon Wilted Spinach	30
Simple Cooked Ears Corn	30
Grilled Squash	30
Cheese Cauliflower Cakes	30

Chapter 4 Snack, Dessert and Appetizer Recipes 31

Recipe	Page
Honey Nectarines Topped with Blackberries	31
Gorgonzola Pear Bowls with Craisins	31
Garlic Cauliflower Skewers	31
S'mores Toast	31
Honey Walnut Figs	31
Cocoa Vanilla Pies	31
Colada Tacos	32
French Fruit Stuffed Toast	32
Sugared Peaches with Ginger Ice Cream	32
Mayonnaise Bacon Patties	32
Banana and Strawberry Pizza	32
Doughnut with Vanilla Ice Cream	33
Golden Banana Coconut Fritters	33
Vanilla Peanut Butter Sundae	33
Raspberry Cobbler	33
Griddle-Baked Stuffed Apple	33
Chocolate Marshmallows Toast	33
Cinnamon Apple Pie	33
Sweet Apple Bowls	34
Fruits Pound Cake	34
Honey Peaches Apricots	34
Chocolate Marshmallows Dip	34
Lime Pineapple with Maple Walnut Ice Cream	34
Cinnamon Pumpkin Seeds	34
Caramel Bananas	34
Peanut Butter Chips with Banana	35
Honey Peaches with Vanilla Ice Cream	35
Crispy Seasoned Eggplant Bites	35
Sweet and Sour Watermelon	35
Vanilla Pineapple Sundae	35
Chocolate Bacon Pecan Pie	35
Creamy Berries Cake	35
Griddle-Cooked Potatoes and Carrots	36
Sausage and Cheese Balls	36
Sweet Chocolate Bread	36
Vanilla Butter Blackberry Pie	36
Pineapple and Strawberry Sundae	36
Vanilla Chocolate Bread Pudding	36
Mozzarella Broccoli Fritters	37
Brioche Apricots with Ice Cream	37
Sweet Apple Cobbler	37
Cauliflower and Zucchini Fritters	37
Rosemary Cauliflower Bites	37
Sweet Cinnamon Peaches	37
Pain Perdu Strawberries	37
Creamy Vanilla Fruit Skewers	38
Tasty Mushrooms with Herbs	38
Golden Zucchini Patties	38
Butter Pumpkin Seeds with Cinnamon	38
Sweet Pear Crisp	38
Coconut Chocolate Brownies	38
Vanilla Chocolate Chip Cookies	38
Jalapeno Corn Cakes	39
Thyme Mushroom Skewers	39
Maple-Glazed Bananas with Vanilla Ice Cream	39
Brioche Toast with Maple Syrup	39
Honey-Glazed Pineapple Slices	39
Herbed Potatoes	39
Oregano Spinach Turkey Burgers	39
Walnut Chocolate Chip Cookies	40
Mayo Potato Skewers	40
Lemon Strawberry Shortcake	40
Cheese Pepperoni Chicken Sandwich	40
Peanut Butter Pancake	40
Rum-Soaked Pineapple with Vanilla Ice Cream	40
Star Fruit Skewers with Orange-Clove Syrup	41
Sweet Potato Pancakes	41
Buttermilk Biscuits	41
Chili Pineapple Slices	41
Sweet Potato Fries	41
Banana Chocolate Peanut Chips	41
Taco-Seasoned Chicken Drumsticks	41
Rosemary Cheese Tomatoes	42
Chicken Burger Patties	42
Mint Five-Spice Oranges	42
Seared Fruits with Berries	42
Delectable Turkey Burger	42
Peach Apple Pie	42

Chapter 5 Fish and Seafood Recipes 43

Recipe	Page
Fried Fish with Cilantro Mixture	43
Seasoned Rainbow Trout	43
Gremolata Swordfish Skewers	43
Cod Fish Fillets	43
Tasty Ceviche	43
Simple Garlic Haddock	43
Lemon Oysters with Spiced Tequila Butter	44
Cajun White Fish Fillets	44
Flavorful Tilapia	44
Dijon Lump Crab Cakes	44
Halibut Fillets with Spinach	44
Simple Grouper	44
Spicy Cod Fillets	44
Delicious Bacon-Wrapped Scallops	45
Savoury Red Snapper Fillets	45

Quick-Cooking Shrimp 45
Tasty Herb-Seasoned Fish 45
Spicy Amberjack Fillets 45
Spicy Squid in Sauce 45
Garlicky Tuna Steaks 45
Sweet Potato Snapper Apple Ceviche 46
Pineapple and Shrimp Skewers 46
Chipotle Salmon Fillets 46
Lobster Tails 46
Honey-Lime Tilapia 46
Spicy Shrimp 46
Garlic Shrimp with Lime Juice 47
Delectable Crab Legs 47
Palatable Cod Patties 47
Delicious Crab Cakes 47
Salmon Patties 47
Lobster Tails with basil Butter 47
Snapper with Mango Salad 47
Pop-Open Clams with Horseradish Sauce 48
Mayo Mussels with Italian Bread 48
Seasoning Salmon Fillets 48
Quick Halibut 48
Golden Zucchini Tuna Patties 48
Scallops with Lemony Salsa Verde 48
Lobster Salad with Vinaigrette 49
Easy Scallops 49
Fennel Clam and Shrimp Bouillabaisse 49
Yummy Jumbo Shrimp 49
Lemon Pepper Scallops 49
Chili Crab Legs 49
Lemon Spinach Halibut 50
Mustard Crab Panko Cakes 50
Butter Salmon Fillets with Broccolini 50
Tomato Crab-stuffed Trout 50
Pepper Shrimp with Parsley 50
Lime Corn Tilapia 50
Shrimp and Pineapple Skewers 51
Boneless Salmon Fillets 51
Lemon Scallops 51
Paprika Shrimp 51
Shrimps with Cherry Tomatoes Asparagus Salad 51
Grilled Teriyaki-glazed Coho Salmon Fillets 51
Paprika Salmon with Parsley 52
Pine Nuts Shrimp 52
Basil Salmon Fillets with Broccolini 52
Paprika Crab Cakes 52
Lemon Seafood Salad 52
Corn Tilapia Fillets 53
Stir-Fried Shrimp and Veggie 53
Swordfish Skewers 53
Mayo Salmon Patties 53
Basil Halibut Fillets 53
Quick Shrimp 53
Lemon Butter Shrimp 53
Halibut Dill with Herbs and Olives 54
Cheese Halibut with Parsley 54
Grilled Soy Salmon 54
Grilled Jumbo Shrimp 54
Salmon Fillets with Broccolini 54
Octopus with Lemon and Oregano 54
Sour and Sweet Shrimp 55
Spice Popcorn Shrimp 55
Rosemary Skinless Salmon 55
Pepper Swordfish 55
Mexican Shrimp 55
Lemon Pepper Salmon 55
Spiced Snapper with Mango Salsa and Lime Wedges ... 56
Salmon Zucchini Patties 56
Oregano Shrimp Skewers 56
Coconut-Rum Shrimp and Pineapple Skewers 56
Lemon Butter Tilapia 56
Pineapple Chunks and Shrimp with Sauce 56
Lemon Trout 56
Bacon Scallops 57

Whitefish with Garlic Mayonnaise 57
Cheese Pistachio Shrimp 57
Blackened Cod 57
Dijon-ginger Glazed Salmon 57
Ginger Salmon 57

Chapter 6 Poultry Recipes 58

Olive BBQ Chicken 58
Stuffed Chicken Breast 58
Marinated Chicken Breast with Salsa Verde 58
Chili Lime Chicken with Sesame Seed 58
Seared Spicy Boneless Chicken Thighs 58
Chili Chicken Wings 58
Oregano Boneless Chicken 59
Chicken Thighs Cooked in Root Beer 59
Gochujang Chicken Wings 59
Glazed Chicken Wings 59
Garlic Chicken Breast on Tortillas 59
Chicken Fritters with Dill 59
Zucchini Basil Crusted Chicken 60
Garlic Chicken Thighs and Vegetable Skewers 60
Hawaiian Chicken Kabob 60
Seasoned Chicken Breast Stuffed with Cheese 60
Marinated Chicken Thighs 60
California Seared Chicken Breast 61
Seasoned Chicken Wings with Buffalo Sauce 61
Herb Roasted Turkey in Chicken Broth 61
Sriracha Chicken Thighs 61
Zucchini Turkey Patties 61
Avocados Chicken Fajitas with Corn Tortillas 61
Garlic Chicken Breast with Kale Caesar Salad 62
Tasty Oregano Chicken Bites 62
Chicken Drumsticks with Sauce 62
Jalapeno Chicken Thighs 62
Coconut Chicken with Almond Butter Sauce 62
Marinated Chicken with Veggie and Brown Rice Bowls 62
Chicken Breasts Fried Rice with Veggies 63
Bacon Chicken Breast with Chipotle 63
Spicy Chicken with Blue cheese 63
Garlic Turkey Patties 63
Stir Fry Chicken Breast and Broccoli 63
Chicken Zucchini Pepper Stir Fry 63
Rosemary Honey Chicken Tenders 63
Flavorful Cornish Hen 64
Turkey Burger Patties 64
Dijon Mustard Chicken Wings 64
Roasted BBQ Hen 64
Tasty Balsamic Chicken 64
Sizzling Chicken Breasts with Tortillas 64
Honey Cornish Hen 64
Spicy Chicken Breasts 65
Curried Chicken Kebabs 65
Mayo Turkey Sandwich 65
Itanlian Seasoning Chicken Breasts 65
Pepper Chicken Breast Fajita 65
Cheddar Chicken Breasts 65
Lemon Chicken with Fruit Salsa 65
Spinach and Garlic Turkey Patties 66
Mayo Turkey Mayo Green Apple 66
Typical BBQ Chicken 66
Soy Chicken Thighs 66
Chili Smoked Turkey Breast 66
Chicken Fried Rice and Corn 66
Savory-Sweet Turkey Legs with Mandrain Glaze 67
Classic Thanksgiving Turkey 67
Smoked Marinated BonelessTurkey Breast 67
Buttery Smoked Turkey 67
Smoked Turkey Tabasco in Sauce 67
Cured Turkey Drumstick 68
Tasty Cornish Game Hen 68
Jalapeno Turkey in Broth 68
Honey-Mustard Chicken 68

Table of Contents | 3

Sambal-Glazed Chicken Thighs 68
Turkey Cooked in Jerky 68
Roast Pineapple and Chicken Skewers 69
Pineapple, Vegetables and Chicken Skewers 69
Spatchcock Turkey 69
Bourbon Turkey 69
Blackened Boneless Chicken Breasts 69
Brine-Marinated Turkey Breast 70
Griddle-Smoked Whole Turkey 70
Balsamic Honey Chicken Thighs 70
Taco Turkey Burger Patties 70
BBQ Boneless Turkey Breast 70
Cheddar Chicken Patties 71
Green Cheese Stuffed Chicken 71
Whole Turkey 71
Cheese Bacon Chicken Burger Patties 71
Easy BBQ Chicken 71
Simple and Delicious Turkey Legs 71
Roast Turkey in Orange Sauce 72
Tailgate Smoked Turkey 72
Herbed Spatchcock Turkey 72
Seared Chicken with Kale Caesar Salad 72
Honey Turkey Breast 72

Chapter 7 Beef, Pork and Lamb Recipes 73

Basic Juicy Strip Steak 73
Delectable Lamb Chops 73
Caprese Mignon Fillets 73
Savoury Lamb Loin (Rib Chops) 73
Flavorful Beef Stew 73
Teppanyaki Beef 73
New York Strip Steak 74
Rib-Eye Steak 74
Gribiche Skirt Steak 74
Moink Ball Skewers 74
Cumin Pork Chops 74
Caprese Flank Steak with Balsamic Glaze 75
Dijon Pork Chops 75
Country Ribs 75
Tuscan-Style Steak and Crispy Potatoes 75
Herbed Pork Tenderloin 75
Texas-Style Beef Brisket 76
Country Spiced Pork Ribs 76
Parmesan Pork Tenderloin Pieces 76
Butter Rib Eye Steak 76
Easy-to-Make Porterhouse Steak 76
Fried Lamb Chops with Mint 76
Beef Fillets with Pineapple Rice 77
Glazed Pork with Fish Sauce 77
Marinated Flank Steak with Yogurt Sauce 77
BBQ Baby Back Ribs 77
Easy Lamb Shoulder Chops 77
Beef and Broccoli Rice 78
Flavorful Pork Chops 78
Lime Pork Paillards 78
Pork Ribs with Low-sugar Ketchup 78
Garlic Lamb Chops 78
Rosemary Flank Steak 78
Lamb Burgers in Sauce with Squash Salad 79
Vegetables and Ham Hock 79
Lamb Chops with Spiced New Potatoes 79
Paprika Pork Chops 79
Tasty Beef Burger Patties 79
Butter Pork Chops 80
Simple Lamb Chops 80
Oyster Sesame Pork Shoulder 80
Rosemary Lamb Chop Slices 80
Rib Roast with Russet Potatoes 80
Mayo Filet Mignon Steaks 80
Pork Loin with Chile and Pineapple Slices 81
Omelet with Smoky Bacon Strips 81
Strip Steak with Worcestershire Sauce 81
Palatable Pork Tenderloins 81
Kielbasa with Jalapeño Chiles 81
Apricot Jam Lamb Kabobs 82
Pork Chops with Pineapple and Bacon 82
Sweet and Sour Pork Chops 82
Oregano Lamb Chops 82
Honey Boneless Pork Chops 82
Pork Chops with Apple and Herbs 82
Mediterranean Pork Tenderloin 83
Lemon Lamb Chops with Apricot 83
Thyme Lamb Racks 83
Seasoned Lamb Patties 83
Dijon Pork Tenderloin 83
Cheese Strip Steak 83
Tangy Masala Lamb Chops 84
BBQ Lamb Chops 84
Tzatziki Lamb Chops 84
Oregano Zucchini and Beef Skewers 84
Lamb Kofta in Yogurt-Garlic Sauce 84
Lamb Kebabs with Lemon Wedges 84
Cayenne Pork Chops in Worcestershire Sauce 85
Griddle-Fried Marinated Flank Steaks 85
Cinnamon Pork Tenderloin with Harissa 85
Garlicky Sirloin Beef with Parmesan 85
Butterflied Lamb Leg 85
Coffee Crusted Steak 85
Buffalo Beef Mozzarella Filets 86
Griddle-Cooked Marinated Pork Chops 86
Basil Grilled Filet Mignon 86
Greek Cheese Lamb Patties 86
Griddled Lamb Steak 86
Green Onion and Beef Burger Patties 86
Pork Chops Fried in Orange Marinade 86
Butter Sirloin Steaks with Vegetables 87
Pork, Mushrooms and Bell Pepper Skewers 87
Bell Pepper and Pork with Chimichurri 87
Fried Montreal Marinade Pork Chops 87
Marinade Citrus Griddle Pork 87
Griddle-Seared Steaks 87
Curry Pork Roast 88
Roasted Beef Sirloin Skewers 88
Coffee Skirt Steak 88
Fried Pork Chops with Apple Compote 88
Vinegar Pork Tenderloin Cubes 88
Palatable Pork Chops with Creole & Parsley 88
Delicious Pepper Pork Chops 88
BBQ Pork Tenderloin Sandwiches 89
Country Ribs in Garlic Sauce 89
Honey Pork Chops 89
Glazed Pork Shoulder Fried in Sauce 89
Smoked Flat Beef Brisket 89
Pork Tenderloin with Creamy Harissa Sauce 89
Vinegar-Marinated Pork Chops 90
Cayenne Pork Chops 90
Rosemary-Coconut Pork Chops 90
Garlicky Pork Chops 90
Roast Cumin Steak 90
Rosemary Pork Chops with Sage Apple 90
Garlic Soy Pork Chops in Soy Sauce 90
Glazed Pork Chops with Pineapple Quarter 91
Vinegar Flank Steak with Oregano 91
Cumin Cuban Pork Chops 91
Herbed Pork Patties 91
Honey Vinegar Boneless Pork Chops 91
Roasted Basil Pork Tenderloin 91

Conclusion 92

Appendix 1 Measurement Conversion Chart 93

Appendix 2 Recipes Index 94

Introduction

Are you a greedy caravan? Do you like to do a back door before the big game? Do you like to cook at friends' houses? Well, the Outdoor Gas Griddle gives you maximum flexibility, allowing you to take your baking sheet with you wherever you need to go. With minimal effort, you can remove the flat top, safely fold and store the legs, and remove the propane tank. Best of all, the skillet comes with industrial-grade wheels so you can roll the pan where you need it.

Fundamentals of Outdoor Gas Griddle

Fundamentals of Griddle Cooking Station are as follows;

What Is Outdoor Gas Griddle?

The Griddle is a propane-powered outdoor cooking device with a flat top surface used to spread heat evenly and consistently. It can prepare foods like pancakes, sausages, bacon, French toasts, home fries, stir-fries, eggs and any other meal made with a frying pan. While the Griddle is commonly used by amateur BBQers, it can also be used by professional chefs. Its flat top surface is made of heavy, cold-rolled steel that does not stick, dent, bruise or rust. The legs of the griddle are fold able; therefore, it easy to transport from location to location. Generally, Griddles make cooking simple, quick, and efficient.

Functions of Outdoor Gas Griddle

The Outdoor Gas Griddle contains everything needed to make excellent meals. Here, I will be discussing all the parts of the griddle and the function of each feature in the griddle. Those features will be explained below.

- **Multiple Powerful Burners**

Cooking with the Outdoor Gas Griddle has been easier and faster because I can cook a variety of items on the burners simultaneously. For example, this griddle allows me to cook pancakes for my kids while making grilled cheese on different burners. The burners on the griddle can produce heat up to 60,000 BTUs.

- **Adjustable Heat Controls**

All burners on the griddle are independently controlled, and I control how much heat I use in cooking a meal. Each burner can produce heat up to 15,000 BTUs for versatile cooking options.

Shelves

Just when I thought I could not look more like a restaurant chef when using the Outdoor griddle, I discovered there was also a bottom shelf and two side shelves that I could also use to prepare and store food. I love how the Outdoor Gas Griddle provides a space where I can keep the gas cylinder instead of leaving it exposed. You can also use the cabinets to keep your cooking boards, spatulas and other accessories.

- **Ignition Button**

One of the reasons I have found it easy to use my Outdoor Gas Grill is that I can start cooking by just pressing a button. The battery powers the button, and once it is on, I can start cooking.

Industrial Strength Wheels

I have always found it easy to move my Outdoor Gas griddle around because it folds up legs and has strong wheels. You can also secure the griddle in the desired location by locking the caster wheels.

- **Garbage Bag Holder**

The Outdoor Gas Griddle is equipped to provide excellent meals with comfort. A readily available makes it convenient to dispose of waste while cooking and after cooking.

- **Paper Towel Holder**

This is used to hold paper towels. Paper towels always come in handy whenever I am cooking, and this provision makes it easy to have them close by.

The features and their functions can improve your experience with this appliance. You will find grilling fun.

Benefits of Using this Outdoor Gas Griddle

There are lots of benefits to cooking your food on a outdoor gas griddle. Let's see all these benefits one by one.

- **Large and Flat Surface Cooking**

One of the main benefits of the gas griddle is its large and flat cooking surface. The large cooking area allows you to cook more food items to cook at once and flip food is easy to compare to a frying pan. You can use the griddle to cook a large quantity of food. The griddle is capable to hold 72 hotdogs, 28 hamburgers, and 16 steaks in a single cooking batch. Due to the large cooking surface, it doesn't hold moisture and gives you a crispy cooking result. It is one of the perfect choices for bigger families who love to enjoy food like eggs, bacon, hotdogs, burgers, and veggies at the same time in backyard parties.

- **Excellent Built Quality**

The gas grills are made up of high-quality stainless steel materials. The main cooking surface is made up of rolled high quality 7 gauge steel. The entire body surface is covered with a black powder coating which protects it from rust.

- **Runs on Propane Gas**

The gas grills use propane gas to cook your food. Compare to charcoal fuel propane gas never creates smoke and harmful gases while cooking food in your backyard. Propane griddles are easy to start all you just need to turn the dial and the burner fired up. The gas griddle is capable to maintain a steady temperature. Your griddle takes less than 15 minutes to reaches its maximum temperature.

- **Versatile**

The gas griddle is one of the versatile outdoor cooking

appliances offers to cook most of the foods over a smooth cooking surface. The gas griddle is equipped with 4 burners which allow you to operate them individually. The griddle is capable to cook different types of food at a different temperature at the same time. You can make pancakes, eggs, waffles, steak, burgers, hot dogs, and more with perfection on gas griddle.

• **Easy to Clean**

To clean the griddle is one of the easy tasks you just need to clean the greasy cooking area. To clean grease you can use a spatula or griddle to scrap up grease. Use a paper towel to wipe the cooking surface and finally give the touch-up with a scouring pad.

Preparation and Maintenance

Regularly clean your grill between uses and especially after extended periods of storage. Ensure that the grill and its components are sufficiently cool before cleaning.
1. Never handle hot parts with unprotected hands.
2. In order to extend and maintain the life and condition of your grill, we strongly recommend that the unit be covered when left outside for any length of time, especially during the winter months.

• **First Seasoning before Use**

The first step in getting the most out of your gas griddle is seasoning, before first use. To proceed you will need:
· A damp cloth
· A paper towel
· Cooking oil

First clean up the surface of your griddle top with the damp cloth. Afterwards switch on the griddle to high and wait 10-15 Minutes. Once the griddle has become darker you can sprinkle with oil. Use a paper towel to spread the oil on the top but also on the hedges, sides and corners. Keep burning high and repeat the process to spread the oil. You can repeat the process many times but after 2 o 3 times the griddle top will be well seasoned. Now you can start cooking!

• **Maintenance**

The proper storage and maintenance are necessary to increase the lifespan of your griddle. The following steps guide you for the storage and maintenance of your griddle.

1. After each use clean your griddle

When you first start using your griddle it will automatically season itself after each use. Cleaning is one of the important steps to keep your griddle clean and hygienic. Use hot water and a paper towel to clean the griddle surface. Do not use soapy water to clean the cooking surface and use scrapper to clean the cooking area. You can clean the greasy surface with clean and dry paper towels.

2. Remove Rust

If you find any rust spot over the griddle then use 40 or 60 low grit sandpaper or you can also use steel wool to remove the rust spot scrub them properly.

3. Coat griddle after cleaning

After finishing the cleaning process give a thin coat of cooking spray over the griddle cooking surface to prevent rusting built up the overcooking surface area of the griddle.

4. Store and Maintain griddle

After finishing all the cleaning steps store your griddle in a cool and dry place. To prevent dust always keep your griddle covered and keep it away from the humid area.

How It Works

The mechanism of operation of the Griddle is similar to the process of traditional griddle-cooking. They both involve the heating of a flat surface, which eventually performs the cooking. But with the Griddle, there is no need to remove the cooking surface from direct heat because it has control valves that regulate the temperature. The Griddle uses propane or butane LPG bottle gas as a fuel source for creating controlled fire. When the griddle is set to a particular temperature with the control valves and switched on with the ignition switch, the inbuilt igniter needles create a fire in the burner tube. The burner tube is positioned below the griddle top and is responsible for heating it to the desired temperature.

Unlike the traditional griddle-cooking, food is prepared directly on the heated Griddle Top. The heat generated allows the griddle to fry, grill, and sear. Here is a step-by-step direction for igniting the Griddle:

1. Check the battery of the ignition switch to ensure it is correctly installed.
2. Release the gas with the control valve on the gas bottle and at the cylinder.
3. Turn the control valves on the griddle until the indicator line points to high.
4. Press the ignition switch quickly. You should hear a click and Preheat the griddle for 3-5 minutes before cooking every meal.

4-Week Meal Plan

Week 1

Day-1:
Breakfast: Bacon Omelet with Gruyere
Lunch: Beef & Corn Burgers
Snack: Garlic Cauliflower Skewers
Dinner: Spicy Amberjack Fillets
Dessert: Cocoa Vanilla Pies

Day-2
Breakfast: Scrambled Eggs with Spinach and Mushroom
Lunch: Lemon Butter Tilapia
Snack: Lemon Wilted Spinach
Dinner: Zucchini Turkey Patties
Dessert: Cinnamon Apple Pie

Day-3
Breakfast: Cheese Butter Sandwich
Lunch: Snapper with Mango Salad
Snack: Colada Tacos
Dinner: BBQ Lamb Chops
Dessert: Brioche Apricots with Ice Cream

Day-4
Breakfast: Sausage Scramble Vegetable
Lunch: Mustard Pork Tenderloin Sandwiches
Snack: Sweet Potato Fries
Dinner: Salmon Fillets with Broccolini
Dessert: Creamy Berries Cake

Day-5
Breakfast: Banana Pancakes
Lunch: Fried Green Tomatoes with Parsley
Snack: Herbed Potatoes
Dinner: Spicy Chicken Breasts
Dessert: Sweet Chocolate Bread

Day-6
Breakfast: Fluffy Blueberry Pancakes with Maple Syrup
Lunch: Spicy Onion Patties
Snack: S'mores Toast
Dinner: Glazed Pork with Fish Sauce
Dessert: Pineapple and Strawberry Sundae

Day-7
Breakfast: French Toast with Maple Syrup
Lunch: Flavorful Tilapia
Snack: Mayonnaise Bacon Patties
Dinner: Gribiche Skirt Steak
Dessert: Sweet Apple Bowls

Week 2

Day-1:
Breakfast: Simple Almond Pancakes
Lunch: Bacon Scallops
Snack: Thyme Mushroom Skewers
Dinner: Delectable Egg Fried Rice with Green Onion
Dessert: Honey Peaches with Vanilla Ice Cream

Day-2
Breakfast: Yogurt Oatmeal Pancake
Lunch: Celery Onion Corn Bread
Snack: French Fruit Stuffed Toast
Dinner: Caprese Flank Steak with Balsamic Glaze
Dessert: Honey-Glazed Pineapple Slices

Day-3
Breakfast: Bacon Burrito
Lunch: Garlicky Pork Burgers
Snack: Crispy Seasoned Eggplant Bites
Dinner: Jalapeno Chicken Thighs
Dessert: Caramel Bananas

Day-4
Breakfast: Crispy Bacon Potato Hash
Lunch: Coconut-Rum Shrimp and Pineapple Skewers
Snack: Mozzarella Broccoli Fritters
Dinner: Chicken Zucchini Pepper Stir Fry
Dessert: Vanilla Butter Blackberry Pie

Day-5
Breakfast: Spinach Pepper Egg Scramble
Lunch: Pinapple and Ham Sandwich
Snack: Banana Chocolate Peanut Chips
Dinner: Lime Corn Tilapia
Dessert: Vanilla Chocolate Chip Cookies

Day-6
Breakfast: Almond Vanilla Pancakes
Lunch: Tasty Bacon Cheese Serrano Wraps
Snack: Golden Banana Coconut Fritters
Dinner: Pepper Swordfish
Dessert: Peanut Butter Chips with Banana

Day-7
Breakfast: Butter Almond Cauliflower Patties
Lunch: Mozzarella Vegetable Pizza
Snack: Golden Zucchini Patties
Dinner: Simple Lamb Chops
Dessert: Vanilla Chocolate Bread Pudding

Week 3

Day-1:
Breakfast: Parmesan Cauliflower Hash Browns
Lunch: Cheese and Tomato Burgers
Snack: Mint Five-Spice Oranges
Dinner: Seasoned Chicken Breast Stuffed with Cheese
Dessert: Fruits Pound Cake

Day-2
Breakfast: Cheese Kale Omelet
Lunch: Beef and Broccoli Rice
Snack: Creamy Vanilla Fruit Skewers
Dinner: Tasty Cornish Game Hen
Dessert: Peach Apple Pie

Day-3
Breakfast: Cinnamon Toast Sticks
Lunch: Lemon Mushrooms
Snack: Cauliflower and Zucchini Fritters
Dinner: Coffee Crusted Steak
Dessert: Walnut Chocolate Chip Cookies

Day-4
Breakfast: Cauliflower Patties
Lunch: Cheese Cauliflower Cakes
Snack: Garlicky Tomatoes
Dinner: Herbed Spatchcock Turkey
Dessert: Chocolate Marshmallows Toast

Day-5
Breakfast: Soft Blueberry Pancakes
Lunch: Croque Ham Cheese Buegers
Snack: Buttermilk Biscuits
Dinner: Seasoned Lamb Patties
Dessert: Vanilla Peanut Butter Sundae

Day-6
Breakfast: Cherry Tomato Omelet with Mozzarella Cheese
Lunch: Stuffed Chicken Breast
Snack: Sweet and Sour Watermelon
Dinner: Cod Fish Fillets
Dessert: Sweet Cinnamon Peaches

Day-7
Breakfast: Cheese Cauliflower Patties
Lunch: Paprika Potatoes
Snack: Delectable Turkey Burger
Dinner: Mayo Turkey Sandwich
Dessert: Brioche Toast with Maple Syrup

Week 4

Day-1:
Breakfast: Vanilla Toast Sticks
Lunch: Lobster Salad with Vinaigrette
Snack: Sweet Pear Crisp
Dinner: Oregano Lamb Chops
Dessert: sugared Peaches with Ginger Ice Cream

Day-2
Breakfast: Scrambled Egg with Tomato
Lunch: Lamb amd Cucumber Burger
Snack: Grilled Bell Pepper and Zucchini
Dinner: Lemon Scallops
Dessert: Honey Nectarines Topped with Blackberries

Day-3
Breakfast: Seasoned Sirloin Pieces and Eggs
Lunch: Garlic Turkey Patties
Snack: Steamed Bell Peppers with Vinaigrette
Dinner: Curry Pork Roast
Dessert: Gorgonzola Pear Bowls with Craisins

Day-4
Breakfast: Easy Pumpkin Pancake
Lunch: Garlic Tofu with Cilantro
Snack: Seared Fruits with Berries
Dinner: Griddle-Cooked Marinated Pork Chops
Dessert: Vanilla Pineapple Sundae

Day-5
Breakfast: Homemade Cheese Omelet
Lunch: Butter Sirloin Steaks with Vegetables
Snack: Onion and Tomato Sandwich
Dinner: Mayo Salmon Patties
Dessert: Banana and Strawberry Pizza

Day-6
Breakfast: Simple French Crepes
Lunch: Turkey Burger Patties
Snack: Carrot Coleslaw
Dinner: Corn Tilapia Fillets
Dessert: Doughnut with Vanilla Ice Cream

Day-7
Breakfast: Cheese Ham Omelet
Lunch: Garlic Cheese Pizza
Snack: Sweet Yogurt Flatbread
Dinner: Whole Turkey
Dessert: Honey Walnut Figs

Chapter 1 Breakfast Recipes

Simple Almond Pancakes

Prep time: 15 minutes | Cook time: 10 minutes | Serves: 2

Ingredients:
1 egg
½ cup almond flour
½ teaspoon baking powder
½ tablespoons heavy whipping cream
1 ½ tablespoons swerve

Preparation:
1. In a suitable bowl, mix almond flour, baking powder, sweetener, and salt.
2. In another bowl, whisk egg and heavy whipping cream.
3. Mix dry ingredients with the wet.
4. Grease the cooking surface of the griddle with cooking spray.
5. Turn on the 4 burners and turn their knobs to medium heat.
6. Let the Griddle preheat for 5 minutes.
7. Drop batter onto the preheated griddle top and then let it cook for 5 minutes per side.
8. Serve.
Per Serving: Calories: 90; Fat: 7 g; Carbs: 13 g; Sugar: 11g; Protein: 4 g; Cholesterol: 87 mg

Cinnamon Chocolate Pancake

Prep time: 15 minutes | Cook time: 15 minutes | Serves: 4

Ingredients:
2 eggs
½ teaspoon baking powder
2 tablespoons erythritol
1 ½ tablespoons cocoa powder
¼ cup ground flaxseed
2 tablespoons water
1 teaspoon nutmeg
1 teaspoon cinnamon
¼ teaspoon salt

Preparation:
1. Grease the cooking surface of the griddle with cooking spray.
2. Turn on the 4 burners and turn their knobs to medium heat.
3. Let the Griddle preheat for 5 minutes.
4. In a suitable bowl, mix ground flaxseed, baking powder, erythritol, cocoa powder, spices, and salt.
5. Add eggs and stir well.
6. Add water and stir until batter is well combined.
7. Pour a large spoonful of batter on a preheated griddle top and make a pancake.
8. Cook pancake for 3-4 minutes on each side.
9. Serve.
Per Serving: Calories: 138; Fat: 12 g; Carbs: 11 g; Sugar: 8 g; Protein: 4.5 g; Cholesterol: 82 mg

Cauliflower Patties

Prep time: 15 minutes | Cook time: 15 minutes | Serves: 6

Ingredients:
2 eggs
1 large head cauliflower, cut into florets
1 tablespoon butter
½ teaspoon turmeric
1 tablespoon nutrition yeast
⅔ cup almond flour
¼ teaspoon black pepper
½ teaspoon salt

Preparation:
1. Grease the cooking surface of the griddle with butter.
2. Turn on the 4 burners and turn their knobs to medium heat.
3. Let the Griddle preheat for 5 minutes.
4. Add cauliflower florets to a suitable pot.
5. Pour enough water to cover the cauliflower florets. Bring to boil for 8-10 minutes.
6. Drain cauliflower well and transfer in food processor and process until it looks like rice.
7. Transfer cauliflower rice into the suitable bowl.
8. Add the rest of the recipe's ingredients except for butter to the bowl and stir to combine.
9. Make small patties from cauliflower mixture and place on preheated griddle top.
10. Cook for almost 3-4 minutes on each side or until lightly golden brown.
11. Serve.
Per Serving: Calories: 155; Fat: 10 g; Carbs: 11.1 g; Sugar: 3.9 g; Protein: 8.1 g; Cholesterol: 60 mg

Easy Pumpkin Pancake

Prep time: 15 minutes | Cook time: 10 minutes | Serves: 4

Ingredients:
4 eggs
½ teaspoon cinnamon
½ cup pumpkin puree
1 cup almond flour
2 teaspoons liquid stevia
1 teaspoon baking powder

Preparation:
1. Grease the cooking surface of the griddle with cooking spray.
2. Turn on the 4 burners and turn their knobs to medium heat.
3. Let the Griddle preheat for 5 minutes.
4. In a suitable bowl, mix almond flour, stevia, baking powder, cinnamon, pumpkin puree, and eggs until well combined.
5. Drop batter onto the preheated griddle top.
6. Cook pancakes until lightly golden brown from both sides.
7. Serve.
Per Serving: Calories: 235; Fat: 18.5 g; Carbs: 9.6 g; Sugar: 2.4 g; Protein: 11.9 g; Cholesterol: 164 mg

Scrambled Egg with Tomato

Prep time: 15 minutes | Cook time: 5 minutes | Serves: 2

Ingredients:
2 eggs, lightly beaten
2 tablespoons fresh basil, chopped
1 tablespoon olive oil
½ tomato, chopped
Black pepper, to taste
Salt, to taste

Preparation:
1. Grease the cooking surface of the griddle with cooking oil.
2. Turn on the 4 burners and turn their knobs to medium heat.
3. Let the Griddle preheat for 5 minutes.
4. Add tomatoes on top of the griddle and then let it cook until softened.
5. Whisk eggs with basil, pepper, and salt.
6. Pour egg mixture on top of tomatoes and then let it cook until eggs are set.
7. Serve.
Per Serving: Calories: 125; Fat: 12 g; Carbs: 1 g; Sugar: 0.8 g; Protein: 5.8 g; Cholesterol: 164 mg

Fluffy Blueberry Pancakes with Maple Syrup

Prep time: 15 minutes | Cook time: 10 minutes | Serves: 2

Ingredients:
1 cup flour
¾ cup milk
2 tablespoons white vinegar
2 tablespoons sugar
1 teaspoon baking powder
½ teaspoon baking soda
½ teaspoon salt
1 egg
2 tablespoons butter, melted
1 cup fresh blueberries
Butter for cooking

Preparation:
1. Grease the cooking surface of the griddle with cooking spray.
2. Turn on the 4 burners and turn their knobs to medium heat.
3. Let the Griddle preheat for 5 minutes.
4. In a suitable bowl, combine the milk and vinegar. Set aside for 2 minutes.
5. In a suitable bowl, combine the flour, sugar, baking powder, baking soda, and salt.
6. Stir in the milk, egg, blueberries, and melted butter.
7. Mix until combined but not totally smooth.
8. Pour the pancakes onto the griddle and then let it cook until one side is golden brown.
9. Flip the pancakes and then let it cook until the other side is golden.
10. Remove the pancakes from the griddle and servings with warm maple syrup.
11. Serve.
Per Serving: Calories: 499; Sodium: 356 mg; Fiber: 3.5g; Fat: 16.5.g; Carbs: 76.2g; Protein: 12.9g

Cherry Tomato Omelet with Mozzarella Cheese

Prep time: 15 minutes | Cook time: 10 minutes | Serves: 2

Ingredients:
- 6 eggs
- 3 oz cherry tomatoes, cut in halves
- 1 tablespoon fresh basil
- 5 oz mozzarella cheese, sliced
- Black pepper, to taste
- Salt, to taste

Preparation:
1. Grease the cooking surface of the griddle with cooking spray.
2. Turn on the 4 burners and turn their knobs to medium heat.
3. Let the Griddle preheat for 5 minutes.
4. Whisk eggs in a suitable bowl with pepper and salt. Stir in basil.
5. Add tomatoes on preheated griddle top and sauté for few minutes.
6. Pour egg mixture on top of tomatoes and wait until eggs are slightly firm.
7. Add mozzarella cheese slices on top and let the omelet set.
8. Serve.

Per Serving: Calories: 515; Fat: 40 g; Carbs: 5.2 g; Sugar: 2.1 g; Protein: 37 g; Cholesterol: 529 mg

French Crepes

Prep time: 15 minutes | Cook time: 15 minutes | Serves: 4

Ingredients:
- 1 ¼ cups flour
- ¾ cup whole milk
- ½ cup water
- 2 eggs
- 3 tablespoons unsalted butter, melted
- 1 teaspoon vanilla
- 2 tablespoon sugar

Preparation:
1. In a suitable bowl, add all the ingredients and mix with a whisk.
2. Grease the cooking surface of the griddle with cooking spray.
3. Turn on the 4 burners and turn their knobs to medium heat.
4. Let the Griddle preheat for 5 minutes.
5. Add about ¼ cup of the prepared batter on top of the griddle.
6. Using a crepe spreading tool, form your crepe and then let it cook for 1-2 minutes.
7. Use your crepe spatula and flip. Cook for another minute.
8. Top with Nutella and strawberries for a sweet crepe.
9. Serve.

Per Serving: Calories: 303; Sodium: 112mg; Fiber: 1.1g; Fat: 12.7g; Carbs: 38.2g; Protein: 8.4g

Easy-to-Make Broccoli Omelet

Prep time: 15 minutes | Cook time: 10 minutes | Serves: 2

Ingredients:
- 4 eggs
- 1 cup broccoli, chopped and then let it cooked
- 1 tablespoon olive oil
- ¼ teaspoon black pepper
- ½ teaspoon salt

Preparation:
1. Grease the cooking surface of the griddle with cooking oil.
2. Turn on the 4 burners and turn their knobs to medium heat.
3. Let the Griddle preheat for 5 minutes.
4. In a suitable bowl, beat eggs with pepper, and salt.
5. Pour broccoli and egg mixture onto the preheated griddle top and then let it cook until set.
6. Flip omelet and then let it cook until lightly golden brown.
7. Serve.

Per Serving: Calories: 203; Fat: 16 g; Carbs: 4 g; Sugar: 1.5 g; Protein: 12 g; Cholesterol: 327 mg

Cinnamon Cheese Pancakes

Prep time: 15 minutes | Cook time: 5 minutes | Serves: 2

Ingredients:
- 2 eggs
- 2 oz cream cheese
- ½ teaspoon cinnamon
- 1 tablespoon erythritol

Preparation:
1. Grease the cooking surface of the griddle with cooking spray.
2. Turn on the 4 burners and turn their knobs to medium heat.
3. Let the Griddle preheat for 5 minutes.
4. Add all the recipe's ingredients into the blender and blend until smooth.
5. Pour ¼ cup of batter on preheated griddle top and then let it cook for 2 minutes.
6. Flip pancake and then let it cook for 1 minute.
7. Serve.

Per Serving: Calories: 163; Fat: 14.3 g; Carbs: 1.6 g; Sugar: 0.4 g; Protein: 7.7 g; Cholesterol: 195 mg

Cheese Butter Sandwich

Prep time: 15 minutes | Cook time: 10 minutes | Serves: 1

Ingredients:
- 2 bread slices
- 2 teaspoon butter
- 2 cheese slices

Preparation:
1. Preheat the griddle to medium-low heat.
2. Grease the cooking surface of the griddle with cooking spray.
3. Turn on the 4 burners and turn their knobs to medium heat.
4. Let the Griddle preheat for 5 minutes.
5. Place cheese slices on top of 1 bread slice and cover cheese with another bread slice.
6. Spread butter on top of both the bread slices.
7. Place sandwich on preheated griddle top and then let it cook until golden brown or until cheese is melted.
8. Serve.

Per Serving: Calories: 340; Fat: 26 g; Carbs: 9.8 g; Sugar: 1 g; Protein: 15.4 g; Cholesterol: 79 mg

Banana Pancakes

Prep time: 15 minutes | Cook time: 10 minutes | Serves: 6

Ingredients:
- 2 eggs
- 2 tablespoons vanilla ; Protein: powder
- 1 large banana, mashed
- ⅛ teaspoon baking powder

Preparation:
1. Grease the cooking surface of the griddle with cooking spray.
2. Turn on the 4 burners and turn their knobs to medium heat.
3. Let the Griddle preheat for 5 minutes.
4. Meanwhile, add all the recipe's ingredients into the bowl and mix well until combined.
5. Pour 3 tablespoons of batter onto preheated griddle top to make a pancake.
6. Cook pancake until lightly browned from both sides.
7. Serve.

Per Serving: Calories: 79; Fat: 1.6 g; Carbs: 5.5 g; Sugar: 3 g; Protein: 11 g; Cholesterol: 55 mg

Typical Denver Omelet

Prep time: 15 minutes | Cook time: 10 minutes | Serves: 2

Ingredients:
- 6 large eggs
- ¼ cup country ham, diced
- ¼ cup yellow onion, chopped
- ¼ cup green bell pepper, chopped
- ⅔ cup cheddar cheese, shredded
- ¼ teaspoon cayenne pepper
- Black pepper and salt, to taste
- 2 tablespoons butter

Preparation:
1. Grease the cooking surface of the griddle with butter.
2. Turn on the 4 burners and turn their knobs to medium heat.
3. Let the Griddle preheat for 5 minutes.
4. Add the ham, onion, and green bell pepper to the griddle and then let it cook until the vegetables have just softened.
5. Beat the eggs in a suitable bowl and add a pinch of salt and the cayenne pepper.
6. Split the vegetables into to portions on the griddle and add ½ of the eggs to each portion.
7. Cook until the eggs have begun to firm up, and then add the cheese to each omelet.
8. Fold the omelets over and remove from the griddle. Season with black pepper.
9. Serve.

Per Serving: Calories: 507; Sodium: 747 mg; Fiber: 0.8g; Fat: 40.5g; Carbs: 4.9g; Protein: 31.5g

Chapter 1 Breakfast Recipes | 7

Spinach Pepper Egg Scramble

Prep time: 5 minutes | Cook time: 10 minutes | Serves: 1

Ingredients:
- 3 eggs, lightly beaten
- 4 mushrooms, chopped
- ½ cup spinach, chopped
- ¼ cup bell peppers, chopped
- ½ teaspoon black pepper
- ½ teaspoon salt

Preparation:
1. Preheat the Griddle by turning all its knob to medium-heat setting.
2. Grease the griddle top with cooking spray.
3. Place chopped vegetables on the hot griddle top and cook until they are softened.
4. Stir in the eggs, pepper, and salt until the eggs are scrambled and set.
5. Serve and enjoy.

Per Serving: Calories: 220; Fat: 13.5 g; Sodium: 1395 mg; Carbs: 6.9g; Fiber: 1.7g; Sugar: 3.8g; Protein: 19.7g

Vanilla Toast Sticks

Prep time: 15 minutes | Cook time: 10 minutes | Serves: 2

Ingredients:
- 2 eggs
- 4 bread slices, sliced
- ⅔ cup milk
- ¼ teaspoon ground cinnamon
- 1 teaspoon vanilla

Preparation:
1. Grease the cooking surface of the griddle with cooking spray.
2. Turn on the 4 burners and turn their knobs to medium heat.
3. Let the Griddle preheat for 5 minutes.
4. In a suitable bowl, whisk eggs with cinnamon, vanilla, and milk.
5. Dip each bread piece into the egg mixture and coat well.
6. Place coated bread pieces onto the preheated griddle top and then let it cook until golden brown from both sides.
7. Serve.

Per Serving: Calories: 166; Fat: 7 g; Carbs: 14 g; Sugar: 5 g; Protein: 10.4 g; Cholesterol: 193 mg

Cheese Omelet with Olives

Prep time: 5 minutes | Cook time: 5 minutes | Serves: 4

Ingredients:
- 4 large eggs
- 2 tablespoons olive oil
- 1 teaspoon herb de Provence
- 2 oz. cheese
- 8 olives, pitted
- ½ teaspoon salt

Preparation:
1. In a suitable mixing bowl, whisk together the eggs, salt, olives, herb de Provence, and olive oil.
2. Preheat the Griddle by turning all its knob to medium-heat setting.
3. Grease the griddle top with cooking spray.
4. Pour the egg mixture onto the hot griddle top
5. Cook for 3 minutes, or until the omelet is light golden brown.
6. Flip the omelet and cook for another 2 minutes.
7. Serve and enjoy.

Per Serving: Calories: 199; Fat: 17.9g; Sodium: 525mg; Carbs: 1.1g; Fiber: 0.3g; Sugar: 0.6g; Protein: 9.9g

Bacon Burrito

Prep time: 5 minutes | Cook time: 20 minutes | Serves: 2

Ingredients:
- 4 eggs
- 4 strips bacon
- 1 large russet potato, peeled and cut into small cubes
- 1 red bell pepper
- ½ yellow onion
- 1 ripe avocado, sliced
- 2 tablespoons hot sauce
- 2 large flour tortillas
- Vegetable oil

Preparation:
1. Preheat the Griddle by turning all its knob to medium-heat setting.
2. Grease the griddle top with cooking spray.
3. Add bacon to one side, and veggies to other side of the griddle.
4. Cook the bacon until crispy then transfer to a plate.
5. Sauté veggies until golden brown.
6. Pour beaten eggs on top, stir and cook for 5 minutes.
7. Divide egg, veggies and bacon over the tortillas.
8. Add rest of the fillings on top then serve warm.

Per Serving: Calories: 825; Fat: 52.1 g; Sodium: 1422 mg; Carbs: 59.9g; Fiber: 13.1g; Sugar: 7.4g; Protein: 33.3g

8 | Chapter 1 Breakfast Recipes

Almond Vanilla Pancakes

Prep time: 10 minutes | Cook time: 10 minutes | Serves: 5

Ingredients:
- 4 eggs
- 2 tablespoons swerve
- 1 tablespoon coconut oil
- ½ cup butter, melted
- 2 cups almond flour
- 1 teaspoon baking powder
- ½ teaspoon vanilla
- ¼ cup of water
- ½ teaspoon of salt

Preparation:
1. In a blender, add all of the ingredients and blend until smooth.
2. Preheat the Griddle by turning all its knob to medium-heat setting.
3. Grease the griddle top with cooking spray.
4. Pour ⅓ cup of pancake batter onto the hot griddle top.
5. Cook for 5 minutes per side.
6. Serve and enjoy.

Per Serving: Calories: 501; Fat: 45.8 g; Sodium: 430 mg; Carbs: 11.2g; Fiber: 4.8g; Sugar: 0.3g; Protein: 14.2g

Cheese Kale Omelet

Prep time: 5 minutes | Cook time: 10 minutes | Serves: 3

Ingredients:
- 4 eggs
- 4 cups kale, chopped
- 1 tablespoon fresh sage, chopped
- ⅓ cup parmesan cheese, grated
- ½ teaspoon black pepper
- ½ teaspoon salt

Preparation:
1. Place kale on the hot griddle top and cook for a few minutes, or until it has wilted.
2. Beat eggs in a suitable mixing bowl, then add parmesan cheese, sage, pepper, and salt.
3. Preheat the Griddle by turning all its knob to medium-heat setting.
4. Grease the griddle top with cooking spray.
5. Pour the egg mixture onto the hot griddle top then cook for 4 minutes per side.
6. Serve and enjoy.

Per Serving: Calories: 161; Fat: 7.9 g; Sodium: 595 mg; Carbs: 10.8g; Fiber: 1.7g; Sugar: 0.5g; Protein: 13.2g

Cinnamon Toast Sticks

Prep time: 10 minutes | Cook time: 10 minutes | Serves: 2

Ingredients:
- 2 eggs
- 4 bread slices, cut each bread slice into 3 pieces vertically
- ⅔ cup milk
- ¼ teaspoon ground cinnamon
- 1 teaspoon vanilla

Preparation:
1. Preheat the Griddle by turning all its knob to medium-heat setting.
2. Grease the griddle top with cooking spray.
3. Whisk together the eggs, cinnamon, vanilla, and milk in a suitable mixing dish.
4. Coat each slice of bread in the egg mixture thoroughly.
5. Place the coated bread pieces on the hot griddle top and cook until both sides are golden brown.
6. Serve and enjoy.

Per Serving: Calories: 179; Fat: 7.5 g; Sodium: 242 mg; Carbs: 16g; Fiber: 0.6g; Sugar: 6.8g; Protein: 10.6g

Broccoli Omelet

Prep time: 10 minutes | Cook time: 10 minutes | Serves: 2

Ingredients:
- 4 eggs
- 1 cup broccoli, chopped and cooked
- 1 tablespoon olive oil
- ¼ teaspoon black pepper
- ½ teaspoon salt

Preparation:
1. In a suitable mixing bowl, whisk together the eggs, pepper, and salt.
2. Preheat the Griddle by turning all its knob to medium-heat setting.
3. Grease the griddle top with cooking spray.
4. Add the broccoli and egg mixture onto the hot griddle top
5. Cook for 10 minutes with stirring.
6. Serve and enjoy.

Per Serving: Calories: 202; Fat: 15.9g; Sodium: 720 mg; Carbs: 3.9g; Fiber: 1.3g; Sugar: 1.6g; Protein: 12.4g

Simple French Crepes

Prep time: 1 hour | Cook time: 15 minutes | Serves: 4

Ingredients:
- 1 ¼ cups flour
- ¾ cup whole milk
- ½ cup water
- 2 eggs
- 3 tablespoons butter, melted
- 1 teaspoon vanilla
- 2 tablespoons sugar

Preparation:
1. Whisk together all of the ingredients in a suitable mixing bowl.
2. Check to see if the batter is smooth. Let stand for 1 hour.
3. Preheat the Griddle by turning all its knob to medium-heat setting.
4. Grease the griddle top with butter.
5. Pour a ladle of the batter onto the hot griddle top, spread it well and cook for 1-2 minutes per side.
6. For a sweet crepe, top with Nutella and strawberries.
7. Serve.

Per Serving: Calories: 303; Fat: 12.7 g; Sodium: 112 mg; Carbs: 38.1g; Fiber: 1.8g; Sugar: 8.8g; Protein: 8.4g

Coconut Spinach Pancakes

Prep time: 15 minutes | Cook time: 10 minutes | Serves: 6

Ingredients:
- 4 eggs
- 1 cup coconut milk
- ¼ cup chia seeds
- 1 cup spinach, chopped
- ½ teaspoon black pepper
- ½ teaspoon ground nutmeg
- 1 teaspoon baking soda
- ½ cup coconut flour
- ½ teaspoon salt

Preparation:
1. Grease the cooking surface of the griddle with cooking spray.
2. Turn on the 4 burners and turn their knobs to medium heat.
3. Let the Griddle preheat for 5 minutes.
4. In a suitable bowl, whisk eggs with coconut milk until frothy.
5. Mix together all the dry recipe's ingredients and add in the egg mixture and whisk until smooth.
6. Add spinach and stir well.
7. Pour 3-4 tablespoons of batter onto the preheated griddle top and make a round pancake.
8. Cook pancake until lightly golden brown from both sides.
9. Serve.

Per Serving: Calories: 111; Fat: 7 g; Carbs: 5 g; Sugar: 0.4 g; Protein: 6.3 g; Cholesterol: 109 mg

Homemade Cheese Omelet

Prep time: 15 minutes | Cook time: 10 minutes | Serves: 2

Ingredients:
- 6 eggs
- 7 oz cheddar cheese, shredded
- 3 oz butter
- Black pepper, to taste
- Salt, to taste

Preparation:
1. Turn on the 4 burners of the Griddle and turn their knobs to medium heat.
2. Let the Griddle preheat for 5 minutes.
3. In a suitable bowl, whisk together eggs, ½ cheese, pepper, and salt.
4. Melt butter on the preheated griddle top.
5. Once butter is melted then pour egg mixture onto the griddle top and then let it cook until set.
6. Add remaining cheese fold and servings.
7. Serve.

Per Serving: Calories: 892; Fat: 80 g; Carbs: 2.4 g; Sugar: 1.6 g; Protein: 41.7 g; Cholesterol: 687 mg

Cheese Cauliflower Patties

Prep time: 5 minutes | Cook time: 10 minutes | Serves: 6

Ingredients:
- 3 eggs
- 3 oz. (85 g) onion, chopped
- 1 pound cauliflower, grated
- ½ cup parmesan cheese, grated
- ½ cup almond flour
- 1 ½ teaspoons lemon pepper
- ½ teaspoon baking powder
- 1 teaspoon salt

Preparation:
1. In a suitable mixing bowl, add all of the ingredients and stir until well blended.
2. Preheat the Griddle by turning all its knob to medium-heat setting.
3. Grease the griddle top with cooking spray.
4. Form patties out of the mixture and cook on the hot griddle top until lightly browned on both sides.
5. Serve and enjoy.

Per Serving: Calories: 122; Fat: 7.5 g; Sodium: 465 mg; Carbs: 9g; Fiber: 3.8g; Sugar: 2.8g; Protein: 7.4g

Cheese Ham Omelet

Prep time: 5 minutes | Cook time: 10 minutes | Serves: 2

Ingredients:
- 6 large eggs
- ¼ cup country ham, diced
- ¼ cup yellow onion, chopped
- ¼ cup green bell pepper, chopped
- ⅔ cup cheddar cheese, shredded
- ¼ teaspoon cayenne pepper
- ½ teaspoon salt and black pepper
- 2 tablespoons butter

Preparation:
1. In a suitable skillet, melt the butter and sauté the ham, onion, and pepper until the veggies are just cooked.
2. In a suitable mixing bowl, whisk together the eggs with a pinch of salt and cayenne pepper.
3. Preheat the Griddle by turning all its knob to medium-heat setting.
4. Grease the griddle top with cooking spray.
5. Divide the veggie mixture on top of griddle into 4 parts.
6. Pour ¼ of the egg mixture on each section of the veggies on the hot griddle top.
7. Cook each omelet for 3-5 minutes per side.
8. Serve warm.

Per Serving: Calories: 508; Fat: 40.5 g; Sodium: 747 mg; Carbs: 5.2g; Fiber: 0.9g; Sugar: 2.8g; Protein: 31.6g

Parmesan Cauliflower Hash Browns

Prep time: 15 minutes | Cook time: 10 minutes | Serves: 12

Ingredients:
- 3 eggs
- 3 oz onion, chopped
- 1 lb. cauliflower, grated
- ½ cup parmesan cheese, grated
- ½ cup almond flour
- 1 ½ teaspoon lemon pepper
- ½ teaspoon baking powder
- 1 teaspoon salt

Preparation:
1. Grease the cooking surface of the griddle with cooking spray.
2. Turn on the 4 burners and turn their knobs to medium heat.
3. Let the Griddle preheat for 5 minutes.
4. Add all the recipe's ingredients into the mixing bowl and mix until well combined.
5. Make patties from mixture and place on preheated griddle top and then let it cook until lightly browned from both sides.
6. Serve.

Per Serving: Calories: 106; Fat: 6.5 g; Carbs: 4 g; Sugar: 1.5 g; Protein: 7.3 g; Cholesterol: 51 mg

Seasoned Sirloin Pieces and Eggs

Prep time: 15 minutes | Cook time: 10 minutes | Serves: 4

Ingredients:
- 1 pound sirloin, cut into 4 ½-inch thick pieces
- 8 large eggs
- 3 tablespoons vegetable oil
- Black pepper and salt, to taste

Preparation:
1. Grease the cooking surface of the griddle with cooking spray.
2. Turn on the 4 burners and turn their knobs to medium heat.
3. Let the Griddle preheat for 5 minutes.
4. Season those steaks with black pepper and salt.
5. Place steaks on the medium high side and then let it cook for 3 minutes and add the oil to the medium heat side.
6. Flip the steaks and crack the eggs onto the medium heat side of the griddle.
7. After 3 minutes remove the steaks from the griddle and allow to rest 5 minutes. Finish cooking the eggs and place 2 eggs and 1 piece of steak on each plate to servings.
8. Season those eggs with a pinch of black pepper and salt.
9. Serve.

Per Serving: Calories: 444; Sodium: 215 mg; Fiber: 0g; Fat: 27.2g; Carbs: 0.8g; Protein: 47g

Scallion Cauliflower Pancakes

Prep time: 15 minutes | Cook time: 10 minutes | Serves: 3

Ingredients:
2 eggs
1 tablespoon flax meal
½ cup scallions, sliced
½ cauliflower head, grated
½ teaspoon pepper
1 ½ teaspoon salt

Preparation:
1. Add grated cauliflower and 1 teaspoon salt in a suitable bowl and mix well. Set aside for 20 minutes.
2. After 20 minutes squeeze out all liquid from cauliflower.
3. Add squeezed cauliflower into a suitable mixing bowl.
4. Add the rest of the recipe's ingredients and mix well.
5. Grease the cooking surface of the griddle with cooking spray.
6. Turn on the 4 burners and turn their knobs to medium heat.
7. Let the Griddle preheat for 5 minutes.
8. Add spoonful of cauliflower mixture on preheated griddle top and flatten out into small pancakes.
9. Cook pancake for almost 2-3 minutes on each side.
10. Serve.

Per Serving: Calories: 197; Fat: 17.9 g; Carbs: 5.2 g; Sugar: 1.7 g; Protein: 5.9 g; Cholesterol: 145 mg

Cheesy Potato Hash Brown

Prep time: 15 minutes | Cook time: 10 minutes | Serves: 4

Ingredients:
2 russet potatoes, shredded, rinsed, and drained
8 eggs, beaten
1 cup cheddar cheese
6 slices bacon, cut into small pieces
⅓ cup green onion, chopped
Vegetable oil

Preparation:
1. Grease the cooking surface of the griddle with cooking spray.
2. Turn on the 4 burners and turn their knobs to medium heat.
3. Let the Griddle preheat for 5 minutes.
4. On one side, place the potatoes on the griddle and spread in a ½ inch thick layer.
5. Cook the potatoes until golden brown and then flip.
6. Add the bacon to the other side of the griddle and then let it cook until the; Fat: has rendered.
7. Add the eggs and cheese to the top of the hash browns and stir in the bacon and green onion.
8. Cook until the cheese has melted and divide equally among 4 plates.
9. Serve.

Per Serving: Calories: 470; Sodium: 965 mg; Fiber: 2.8g; Fat:30.2g; Carbs: 18.8g; Protein: 30.6g

Potatoes Hash Browns

Prep time: 10 minutes | Cook time: 15 minutes | Serves: 4

Ingredients:
3 russet potatoes, peeled
1 tablespoon onion powder
1 tablespoon salt
1 teaspoon black pepper
3 tablespoon vegetable oil

Preparation:
1. Grate the potatoes with a grater then mix with onion powder, salt, and black pepper in a bowl.
2. Preheat the Griddle by turning all its knob to medium-heat setting.
3. Grease the griddle top with cooking oil.
4. Divide the potato mixture on the hot griddle top into hash browns.
5. Cook for 3-5 minutes per side until golden brown.
6. Serve warm.

Per Serving: Calories: 208; Fat: 10.5 g; Sodium: 1755 mg; Carbs: 26.9g; Fiber: 4.1g; Sugar: 2.5g; Protein: 2.9g

Cinnamon Pumpkin Pancakes

Prep time: 10 minutes | Cook time: 10 minutes | Serves: 4

Ingredients:
4 eggs
½ teaspoon cinnamon
½ cup pumpkin puree
1 cup almond flour
2 teaspoons liquid stevia
1 teaspoon baking powder

Preparation:
1. In a suitable mixing bowl, whisk almond flour, stevia, baking powder, cinnamon, pumpkin puree, and eggs.
2. Preheat the Griddle by turning all its knob to medium-heat setting.
3. Grease the griddle top with cooking spray.
4. Pour a ladle of the batter onto the hot griddle top and cook for 5 minutes per side.
5. Serve and enjoy.

Per Serving: Calories: 235; Fat: 18.5 g; Sodium: 64 mg; Carbs: 9.6g; Fiber: 4.1g; Sugar: 2.4g; Protein: 11.9g

Scrambled Eggs with Spinach and Mushroom

Prep time: 15 minutes | Cook time: 10 minutes | Serves: 1

Ingredients:
3 eggs, lightly beaten
4 mushrooms, chopped
½ cup spinach, chopped
¼ cup bell peppers, chopped
Pepper
Salt

Preparation:
1. Grease the cooking surface of the griddle with cooking spray.
2. Turn on the 4 burners and turn their knobs to medium heat.
3. Let the Griddle preheat for 5 minutes.
4. Add chopped vegetables on preheated griddle top and sauté until softened.
5. Add eggs, pepper, and salt and stir until eggs are set and scrambled.
6. Serve.

Per Serving: Calories: 335; Fat: 27 g; Carbs: 6 g; Sugar: 3 g; Protein: 19 g; Cholesterol: 491 mg

Bacon Omelet with Gruyere

Prep time: 15 minutes | Cook time: 15 minutes | Serves: 2

Ingredients:
6 eggs, beaten
6 strips bacon
¼ lb. gruyere, shredded
1 teaspoon black pepper
1 teaspoon salt
1 tablespoon chives, chopped
Vegetable oil

Preparation:
1. Add salt to the beaten eggs and set aside for 10 minutes.
2. Grease the cooking surface of the griddle with cooking spray.
3. Turn on the 4 burners and turn their knobs to medium heat.
4. Let the Griddle preheat for 5 minutes.
5. Add the bacon strips, cook until crispy.
6. Remove the bacon from the griddle and place on paper towels.
7. Once the bacon has drained, chop into small pieces.
8. Add the eggs to the griddle in 2 even pools.
9. Cook until the bottom of the eggs starts to firm up.
10. Add the gruyere to the eggs and then let it cook until the cheese melts.
11. Add the bacon pieces and use a spatula to turn 1 ½ of the omelet onto the other ½.
12. Remove from the griddle, season by adding pepper and chives and servings.
13. Serve.

Per Serving: Calories: 734; Sodium: 855 mg; Fiber: 0.3g; Fat: 55.3g; Carbs: 2.8g; Protein: 54.8g

Cheese Tomato Omelet

Prep time: 15 minutes | Cook time: 5 minutes | Serves: 1

Ingredients:
2 eggs
1 tablespoon water
2 oz mozzarella cheese
1 tomato, cut into thin slices
6 fresh basil leaves
Black pepper, to taste
Salt, to taste

Preparation:
1. Grease the cooking surface of the griddle with cooking spray.
2. Turn on the 4 burners and turn their knobs to medium heat.
3. Let the Griddle preheat for 5 minutes.
4. In a suitable bowl, whisk together eggs and water.
5. Pour egg mixture on preheated griddle top and then let it cook for 30 seconds.
6. Spread tomatoes, basil, and cheese on top of the omelet. Season by adding pepper and salt.
7. Cook for 2 minutes until egg firm.
8. Fold omelet in ½ and then let it cook on low for a minute.
9. Serve.

Per Serving: Calories: 405; Fat: 30.4 g; Carbs: 5.2 g; Sugar: 2.3 g; Protein: 27.8 g; Cholesterol: 388 mg

Bacon Egg Sandwich with Cheese Slices

Prep time: 15 minutes | Cook time: 10 minutes | Serves: 4

Ingredients:
4 large eggs
8 strips of bacon
4 slices cheddar or American cheese
8 slices sourdough bread
2 tablespoons butter
2 tablespoons vegetable oil

Preparation:
1. Grease the cooking surface of the griddle with cooking spray.
2. Turn on the 4 burners and turn their knobs to medium heat.
3. Let the Griddle preheat for 5 minutes.
4. Place the strips of bacon on one side. Cook until just slightly crispy.
5. Add oil on the other side of the griddle and crack eggs onto the griddle then cook for 5 minutes.
6. Butter one side of the slices of bread and place them butter side down on the griddle.
7. Place a cheese slice on each of the slices of bread and when the cheese melts.
8. Add the bacon to the sandwiches and place the other slice of bread on top.
9. Serve.

Per Serving: Calories: 699; Sodium: 1148 mg; Fiber: 1.5g; Fat: 47.7g; Carbs: 37.8g; Protein: 29.3g

Yogurt Oatmeal Pancake

Prep time: 15 minutes | Cook time: 10 minutes | Serves: 2

Ingredients:
6 egg whites
1 cup steel-cut oats
¼ teaspoon vanilla
1 cup Greek yogurt
½ teaspoon baking powder
1 teaspoon liquid stevia
¼ teaspoon cinnamon

Preparation:
1. Grease the cooking surface of the griddle with cooking spray.
2. Turn on the 4 burners and turn their knobs to medium heat.
3. Let the Griddle preheat for 5 minutes.
4. Add oats to a suitable blender and blend until a fine powder is a form.
5. Add the rest of the recipe's ingredients into the blender and blend until well combined.
6. Pour ¼ cup batter onto the preheated griddle top.
7. Cook pancake until golden brown from both sides.
8. Serve.

Per Serving: Calories: 295; Fat: 4 g; Carbs: 37 g; Sugar: 9 g; Protein: 23 g; Cholesterol: 7 mg

Simple Omelet with Cheddar Cheese

Prep time: 10 minutes | Cook time: 10 minutes | Serves: 2

Ingredients:
6 eggs
7 oz. (198 g) cheddar cheese, shredded
3 oz. (85 g) butter
½ teaspoon black pepper
½ teaspoon salt

Preparation:
1. Preheat the Griddle by turning all its knob to medium-heat setting.
2. Grease the griddle top with butter.
3. Whisk together the eggs, half of the cheese, pepper, and salt in a suitable mixing dish.
4. Pour the egg mixture onto the griddle top once the butter has melted, and heat until set.
5. Add the rest of the cheese fold and the servings.
6. Serve warm.

Per Serving: Calories: 896; Fat: 80.4 g; Sodium: 1628 mg; Carbs: 3g; Fiber: 0.3g; Sugar: 1.6g; Protein: 41.8g

Butter Almond Cauliflower Patties

Prep time: 10 minutes | Cook time: 15 minutes | Serves: 6

Ingredients:
2 eggs
1 large head cauliflower, cut into florets
1 tablespoon butter
½ teaspoon turmeric
1 tablespoon Nutrition yeast
⅔ cup almond flour
¼ teaspoon black pepper
½ teaspoon salt

Preparation:
1. In a big saucepan, place cauliflower florets.
2. Cover the cauliflower florets with enough water to cover them.
3. Allow 8-10 minutes for the water to boil.
4. Preheat the Griddle by turning all its knob to medium-heat setting.
5. Grease the griddle top with butter.
6. Drain cauliflower thoroughly and add to a food processor then blend.
7. Place cauliflower rice in a suitable mixing bowl.
8. Toss in the remaining ingredients, excluding the butter, and whisk to incorporate.
9. Form small patties from the cauliflower mixture and cook for 3-4 minutes per side on the hot griddle top.
10. Serve and enjoy.

Per Serving: Calories: 107; Fat: 6 g; Sodium: 271 mg; Carbs: 9.9g; Fiber: 4.5g; Sugar: 3.7g; Protein: 6.6g

Butter Cheese Sandwiches

Prep time: 10 minutes | Cook time: 10 minutes | Serves: 1

Ingredients:
2 bread slices
2 teaspoons butter
2 cheese slices

Preparation:
1. Preheat the Griddle by turning all its knob to medium-heat setting.
2. Grease the griddle top with cooking spray.
3. Pour the egg mixture onto the hot griddle top
4. Arrange cheese slices on top of one bread slice, then top with another slice of bread.
5. Butter both bread slices and place them on a plate.
6. Cook the sandwich on the hot griddle top until golden brown and the cheese has melted.
7. Serve and enjoy.

Per Serving: Calories: 341; Fat: 26.8 g; Sodium: 525 mg; Carbs: 9.8g; Fiber: 0.4g; Sugar: 1.1g; Protein: 15.4g

Herbed Cheese Omelet

Prep time: 15 minutes | Cook time: 5 minutes | Serves: 4

Ingredients:
4 large eggs
2 tablespoons olive oil
1 teaspoon herb de Provence
2 oz cheese
8 olives, pitted
½ teaspoon salt

Preparation:
1. Grease the cooking surface of the griddle with cooking spray.
2. Turn on the 4 burners and turn their knobs to medium heat.
3. Let the Griddle preheat for 5 minutes.
4. Add eggs, salt, olives, herb de Provence, and olive oil in a suitable bowl and whisk well.
5. Pour egg mixture on preheated griddle top and then let it cook for 3 minutes or until omelet lightly golden brown.
6. Turn omelet and then let it cook for 2 minutes more.
7. Serve.

Per Serving: Calories: 252; Fat: 23 g; Carbs: 1 g; Sugar: 0.5 g; Protein: 10 g; Cholesterol: 216 mg

Cheese Coconut Pancakes

Prep time: 15 minutes | Cook time: 5 minutes | Serves: 1

Ingredients:
2 eggs
½ teaspoon cinnamon
2 oz cream cheese
1 tablespoon coconut flour
5 drops liquid stevia

Preparation:
1. Grease the cooking surface of the griddle with cooking spray.
2. Turn on the 4 burners and turn their knobs to medium heat.
3. Let the Griddle preheat for 5 minutes.
4. Add all the recipe's ingredients into the bowl and blend until smooth.
5. Pour batter ½ batter on preheated griddle top and then let it cook until lightly golden brown from both sides.
6. Serve.

Per Serving: Calories: 385; Fat: 30 g; Carbs: 12 g; Sugar: 1 g; Protein: 17 g; Cholesterol: 390 mg

Simple Toad in a Hole

Prep time: 15 minutes | Cook time: 5 minutes | Serves: 4

Ingredients:
- 4 slices white, wheat, or sourdough bread
- 4 eggs
- 2 tablespoons butter
- Black pepper and salt, to taste

Preparation:
1. Grease the cooking surface of the griddle with butter.
2. Turn on the 4 burners and turn their knobs to medium heat.
3. Let the Griddle preheat for 5 minutes.
4. Cut a cute hole in the center of each slice of bread.
5. Place the slices of bread on the griddle and crack an egg into the holes in each slice of bread.
6. Cook until the bread begins to brown, then flip and then let it cook until the egg whites are firm.
7. Remove from the griddle and season by adding black pepper and salt before serving.
8. Serve.

Per Serving: Calories: 206; Sodium: 311 mg; Fiber: 0.8g; Fat: 10.7g; Carbs: 18.4g; Protein: 9.4g

French Toast with Maple Syrup

Prep time: 15 minutes | Cook time: 10 minutes | Serves: 4

Ingredients:
- 6 eggs, beaten
- ¼ cup "½ ½" or heavy cream
- 8 slices thick cut white or sourdough bread
- 2 tablespoons sugar
- 1 tablespoon cinnamon
- 1 teaspoon salt
- Butter
- Powdered sugar
- Maple syrup

Preparation:
1. Grease the cooking surface of the griddle with cooking oil.
2. Turn on the 4 burners and turn their knobs to medium heat.
3. Let the Griddle preheat for 5 minutes.
4. In a suitable bowl, combine the eggs, cream, sugar, cinnamon, and salt. Mix well until smooth.
5. Dip each slice of bread in the prepared mixture until well saturated with egg then place onto the griddle.
6. When the French toast has begun to brown, flip and then let it cook until the other side has browned as well.
7. Remove the French toast from the griddle, dust with powdered sugar, and garnish with warm maple syrup.
8. Serve.

Per Serving: Calories: 332; Sodium: 593 mg; Fiber: 2.4g; Fat: 10.5.g; Carbs: 44.2g; Protein: 16g

Spicy Bacon Vegetable Tortillas

Prep time: 15 minutes | Cook time: 20 minutes | Serves: 2

Ingredients:
- 4 eggs
- 4 strips bacon
- 1 large potato, peeled and cubed
- 1 red bell pepper
- ½ yellow onion
- 1 ripe avocado, sliced
- 2 tablespoons hot sauce
- 2 large flour tortillas
- Vegetable oil

Preparation:
1. Turn on the 2 burners of the Griddle and turn their knobs to medium heat.
2. Then switch the other two burners to medium-high heat.
3. Let the Griddle preheat for 5 minutes and grease it with oil.
4. Add the bacon to the medium heat and peppers and onions to the medium-high side.
5. When the bacon finishes cooking, place on paper towels and chop into small pieces.
6. Add the potatoes to the bacon; Fat: on the griddle. Cook the potatoes until softened.
7. Add the eggs to the vegetable side and then let it cook until firm.
8. Place the ingredients onto the tortillas and top with slices of avocado and a tablespoon of hot sauce.
9. Fold the tortillas. Serve.

Per Serving: Calories: 793; Sodium: 1800 mg; Fiber: 10.7g; Fat: 41.3.g; Carbs: 73.4g; Protein: 35.8g

Crispy Bacon Potato Hash

Prep time: 15 minutes | Cook time: 3 hrs | Serves: 8

Ingredients:
- 6 slices thick cut bacon
- 2 russet potatoes, cut into ½ inch chunks
- 1 yellow onion, chopped
- 1 red bell pepper, chopped
- 1 clove garlic, chopped
- 1 teaspoon salt
- ½ teaspoon black pepper
- 1 tablespoon tabasco sauce

Preparation:
1. Grease the cooking surface of the griddle with cooking spray.
2. Turn on the 4 burners and turn their knobs to medium heat.
3. Let the Griddle preheat for 5 minutes.
4. Cook the bacon on the griddle until just crispy.
5. Add the potato, onion, and bell pepper to the griddle and then let it cook until the potato has softened.
6. Use the large surface of the griddle to spread out the ingredients.
7. When the potato has softened, add the garlic, salt, and pepper.
8. Chop the cooked bacon into small pieces and add it to the griddle.
9. Stir the mixture well and add the hot sauce right before removing the hash from the griddle.
10. Serve.

Per Serving: Calories: 154, Sodium: 475 mg; Fiber: 1.8g; Fat: 10.2g; Carbs:11.3g; Protein: 4.5g

Sausage Scramble Vegetable

Prep time: 15 minutes | Cook time: 20 minutes | Serves: 4

Ingredients:
- 8 eggs, beaten
- ½ lb. sausage, sliced into thin rounds or chopped
- 1 green bell pepper, sliced
- 1 yellow onion, sliced
- 1 cup white mushrooms, sliced
- 1 teaspoon salt
- ½ teaspoon black pepper
- Vegetable oil

Preparation:
1. Turn on the 4 burners of the Griddle and turn their knobs to medium heat.
2. Let the Griddle preheat for 5 minutes.
3. Brush the griddle top with vegetable oil and add the peppers and mushrooms.
4. Cook until browned and then add the onions.
5. Season by adding black pepper and salt and then let it cook until the onions are soft.
6. Add the sausage to the griddle and mix with the vegetables. Cook until lightly browned.
7. Add the eggs and mix with the vegetables and then let it cook until eggs reach desired doneness.
8. Use a large spatula to remove the scramble from the griddle.
9. Serve.

Per Serving: Calories: 342, Sodium: 1131 mg; Fiber: 1.2g; Fat: 24.9.g; Carbs: 6.3g; Protein: 23.2g

Bacon, Egg and Cheese Sandwich

Prep time: 5 minutes | Cook time: 10 minutes | Serves: 4

Ingredients:
- 4 large eggs
- 8 strips of bacon
- 4 slices cheddar or American cheese
- 8 slices sourdough bread
- 2 tablespoons butter
- 2 tablespoons vegetable oil

Preparation:
1. Preheat the Griddle by turning all its knob to medium-heat setting.
2. Grease the griddle top with cooking spray.
3. Add bacon to the hot griddle top and cook until brown then transfer to a plate.
4. Crack egg, scramble and cook for 5 minutes then transfer to a bowl.
5. Butter one side of each slice of bread and set it on the hot griddle top with butter-side down.
6. Place a slice of cheese on four slices of bread.
7. Stack the eggs on the bread when the cheese has just begun to melt and the eggs are done.
8. Top the sandwiches with the bacon and the second slice of bread.
9. Serve right away.

Per Serving: Calories: 622; Fat: 36.4 g; Sodium: 1556 mg; Carbs: 36.8g; Fiber: 1.5g; Sugar: 2.2g; Protein: 34.9g

Chapter 1 Breakfast Recipes

Scrambled Bean with Cheese

Prep time: 5 minutes | Cook time: 10 minutes | Serves: 4

Ingredients:
- 8 eggs, beaten
- 1 pound Chorizo
- ½ yellow onion
- 1 cup cooked black beans
- ½ cup green chilies
- ½ cup jack cheese
- ¼ cup green onion, chopped
- ½ teaspoon black pepper
- 2 tablespoons vegetable oil

Preparation:
1. Preheat the Griddle by turning all its knob to medium-heat setting.
2. Grease the griddle top with cooking spray.
3. Brush the chorizo on one side and place the onions on the other side of the griddle with vegetable oil.
4. Mix well the onion, beans, chorizo, and chilies.
5. Add the cheese, eggs, and green onion to the pan and cook until the eggs are set.
6. Remove the scrambled egg from the griddle and season with black pepper.
7. Serve scrambled eggs with beans mixture.

Per Serving: Calories: 904; Fat: 61.1 g; Sodium: 1554 mg; Carbs: 38.2g; Fiber: 9.2g; Sugar: 4.3g; Protein: 50.4g

Broccoli Onion Hash with Cheddar Cheese

Prep time: 15 minutes | Cook time: 15 minutes | Serves: 12

Ingredients:
- 1 egg
- 4 oz cheddar cheese, shredded
- 3 cups broccoli rice
- ¼ teaspoon garlic powder
- ¼ teaspoon onion powder
- 3 cups cauliflower rice
- Pepper
- Salt

Preparation:
1. Grease the cooking surface of the griddle with cooking spray.
2. Turn on the 4 burners and turn their knobs to medium heat.
3. Let the Griddle preheat for 5 minutes.
4. Add broccoli rice and cauliflower rice in a microwave-safe bowl and microwave for 5 minutes.
5. Squeeze out all excess liquid of broccoli and cauliflower rice.
6. Add vegetable rice to a suitable bowl.
7. Add egg, garlic powder, onion powder, cheese, pepper, and salt and mix well to combine.
8. Make patties from mixture and place on preheated griddle top and then let it cook until lightly browned from both sides.
9. Serve.

Per Serving: Calories: 115; Fat: 7.2 g; Carbs: 6.2 g; Sugar: 2.2 g; Protein: 7.9 g; Cholesterol: 47 mg

Tomato Omelet

Prep time: 10 minutes | Cook time: 10 minutes | Serves: 1

Ingredients:
- 3 eggs
- 2 tablespoons sun-dried tomatoes, chopped
- 2 tablespoons mozzarella cheese, shredded
- 1 tablespoon fresh basil, chopped
- 2 tablespoons ricotta cheese, shredded

Preparation:
1. Whisk together the sun-dried tomatoes, eggs, and basil in a suitable mixing dish.
2. Preheat the Griddle by turning all its knob to medium-heat setting.
3. Grease the griddle top with cooking spray.
4. Pour the egg mixture onto the hot griddle top
5. Mix well the mozzarella and ricotta cheeses in a suitable mixing bowl.
6. Top the omelet with the mozzarella mixture and cook for 1-2 minutes.
7. Serve and enjoy.

Per Serving: Calories: 396; Fat: 25.8 g; Sodium: 565 mg; Carbs: 5.6g; Fiber: 0.3g; Sugar: 1.7g; Protein: 36.4g

Soft Blueberry Pancakes

Prep time: 10 minutes | Cook time: 10 minutes | Serves: 2

Ingredients:
- 1 cup flour
- ¾ cup milk
- 2 tablespoons white vinegar
- 2 tablespoons sugar
- 1 teaspoon baking powder
- ½ teaspoon baking soda
- ½ teaspoon salt
- 1 egg
- 2 tablespoons butter, melted
- 1 cup fresh blueberries
- Butter for cooking

Preparation:
1. Mix well the milk and vinegar in a suitable mixing dish. Allow 2 minutes to pass.
2. Beat together the flour, sugar, baking powder, baking soda, and salt in a suitable mixing bowl.
3. Mix well the milk, egg, blueberries, and melted butter in a suitable mixing bowl.
4. Preheat the Griddle by turning all its knob to medium-heat setting.
5. Grease the griddle top with butter.
6. Pour a ladle of the pancake batter on the hot griddle top
7. Cook for 5 minutes per side until golden brown.
8. Garnish with maple syrup and serve.

Per Serving: Calories: 199; Fat: 17.9g; Sodium: 525mg; Carbs: 1.1g; Fiber: 0.3g; Sugar: 0.6g; Protein: 9.9g

Flavored Buttermilk Pancakes

Prep time: 15 minutes | Cook time: 10 minutes | Serves: 4

Ingredients:
- 2 cups all-purpose flour
- 3 tablespoons sugar
- 1 ½ teaspoons baking powder
- 1 ½ teaspoons baking soda
- 1 ¼ teaspoons salt
- 2 ½ cups buttermilk
- 2 eggs
- 3 tablespoons unsalted butter, melted

Preparation:
1. Grease the cooking surface of the griddle with cooking spray.
2. Turn on the 4 burners and turn their knobs to medium heat.
3. Let the Griddle preheat for 5 minutes.
4. In a suitable bowl, combine the flour, sugar, baking soda, baking powder, and salt.
5. Stir in the buttermilk, eggs, and butter, and mix until combined but not totally smooth.
6. Use a ladle to pour the prepared batter onto the griddle allowing a few inches between pancakes.
7. When the surface of the pancakes is bubbly, flip and then let it cook a few additional minutes.
8. Remove the pancakes from the griddle with butter and maple syrup.
9. Serve.

Per Serving: Calories: 432; Sodium: 458 mg; Fiber: 1.7g; Fat: 12.8g; Carbs: 65.1g; Protein: 14.4g

Golden Potato Hash Browns

Prep time: 15 minutes | Cook time: 15 minutes | Serves: 4

Ingredients:
- 3 russet potatoes, peeled
- 1 tablespoon onion powder
- 1 tablespoon salt
- 1 teaspoon black pepper

Preparation:
1. Grease the cooking surface of the griddle with cooking spray.
2. Turn on the 4 burners and turn their knobs to medium heat.
3. Let the Griddle preheat for 5 minutes.
4. Grate the potatoes and place in a suitable bowl.
5. Squeeze as much water out of the potatoes as possible and return to the bowl.
6. Add the onion powder, salt, and pepper to the bowl and stir to combine.
7. Spread the potato mixture onto the griddle creating a layer about ½ inch thick.
8. Cook for approximately 8 minutes.
9. Turn the potatoes and then let it cook an additional 5 to 8 minutes or until both sides are golden brown.
10. Remove the potatoes from the griddle in sections and add to plates.
11. Sprinkle with a pinch of salt.
12. Serve.

Per Serving: Calories: 118; Sodium: 1755 mg; Fiber: 4.1g; Fat: 0.2g; Carbs: 26.8g; Protein: 2.9g

Chorizo Scramble Greens

Prep time: 15 minutes | Cook time: 10 minutes | Serves: 4

Ingredients:
8 eggs, beaten
1 lb. chorizo
½ yellow onion
1 cup cooked black beans
½ cup green chilies
½ cup jack cheese
¼ cup green onion, chopped
½ teaspoon black pepper
Vegetable oil

Preparation:
1. Grease the cooking surface of the griddle with cooking spray.
2. Turn on the 4 burners and turn their knobs to medium heat.
3. Let the Griddle preheat for 5 minutes.
4. Brush the griddle's top with vegetable oil and add the chorizo to one side and the onions to the other side.
5. When the onion has softened, combine it with the chorizo and add the beans and chilies.
6. Add the eggs, cheese, and green onion and then let it cook until eggs have reached desired firmness.
7. Remove the scramble from the griddle and season by adding black pepper before serving.
8. Serve.
Per Serving: Calories: 843; Sodium: 1554 mg; Fiber: 9.2g; Fat: 54.1g; Carbs: 38.2g; Protein: 50.7g

Basil Tomato Omelet

Prep time: 15 minutes | Cook time: 10 minutes | Serves: 1

Ingredients:
3 eggs
2 tablespoons sun-dried tomatoes, chopped
2 tablespoons mozzarella cheese, shredded
1 tablespoon fresh basil, chopped
2 tablespoons ricotta cheese, shredded

Preparation:
1. Grease the cooking surface of the griddle with cooking spray.
2. Turn on the 4 burners and turn their knobs to medium heat.
3. Let the Griddle preheat for 5 minutes.
4. In a suitable bowl, whisk together eggs, sun-dried tomatoes, and basil.
5. Pour egg mixture on preheated griddle top and then let it cook until eggs are done.
6. Mix together mozzarella cheese and ricotta.
7. Add mozzarella mixture on top of the omelet and then let it cook for 1-2 minutes.
8. Serve.
Per Serving: Calories: 441; Fat: 31 g; Carbs: 4.9 g; Sugar: 1.7 g; Protein: 36.4 g; Cholesterol: 61 mg

Fluffy Vanilla Pancakes

Prep time: 15 minutes | Cook time: 10 minutes | Serves: 5

Ingredients:
4 eggs
2 tablespoons swerve
1 tablespoon coconut oil
½ cup butter, melted
2 cups almond flour
1 teaspoon baking powder
½ teaspoon vanilla
¼ cup of water
Pinch of salt

Preparation:
1. Grease the cooking surface of the griddle with cooking spray.
2. Turn on the 4 burners and turn their knobs to medium heat.
3. Let the Griddle preheat for 5 minutes.
4. Add all the recipe's ingredients into the blender and blend until well combined.
5. Pour ⅓ cup of pancake batter on preheated griddle top and then let it cook until pancake edges are firm.
6. Flip and then let it cook for a minute.
7. Serve.
Per Serving: Calories: 495; Fat: 47 g; Carbs: 11.2 g; Sugar: 1.9 g; Protein: 14.2 g; Cholesterol: 180 mg

Scrambled Eggs with Cilantro

Prep time: 10 minutes | Cook time: 10 minutes | Serves: 2

Ingredients:
4 eggs
2 tablespoons cilantro, chopped
⅓ cup heavy cream
1 tomato, diced
3 tablespoons butter
1 Serrano chili pepper, chopped
2 tablespoons scallions, sliced
¼ teaspoon black pepper
½ teaspoon salt

Preparation:
1. Preheat the Griddle by turning all its knob to medium-heat setting.
2. Grease the griddle top with butter.
3. Add chili pepper and tomato then cook for 2 minutes.
4. Beat cilantro, eggs, black pepper, cream, and salt in a suitable mixing dish.
5. Pour over the veggies, cook and scramble for 8 minutes.
6. Serve warm.
Per Serving: Calories: 315; Fat: 28.6 g; Sodium: 1020 mg; Carbs: 3.1g; Fiber: 0.6g; Sugar: 1.7g; Protein: 11.7g

Egg Scrambled with Tomato and Chili

Prep time: 15 minutes | Cook time: 10 minutes | Serves: 2

Ingredients:
4 eggs
2 tablespoons cilantro, chopped
⅓ cup heavy cream
1 tomato, diced
3 tablespoons butter
1 serrano chili pepper, chopped
2 tablespoons scallions, sliced
¼ teaspoon black pepper
½ teaspoon salt

Preparation:
1. Turn on the 4 burners of the Griddle and turn their knobs to medium heat.
2. Let the Griddle preheat for 5 minutes.
3. Melt butter on top of the preheated griddle.
4. Add tomato and chili pepper and sauté for 2 minutes.
5. In a suitable bowl, whisk eggs with cilantro, cream, pepper, and salt.
6. Pour egg mixture over tomato and chili pepper and stir until egg is set.
7. Garnish with scallions and servings.
8. Serve.
Per Serving: Calories: 355; Fat: 33 g; Carbs: 3 g; Sugar: 1.7 g; Protein: 12 g; Cholesterol: 401 mg

Kale Omelet with Parmesan Cheese

Prep time: 15 minutes | Cook time: 15 minutes | Serves: 3

Ingredients:
4 eggs
4 cups kale, chopped
1 tablespoon Fresh sage, chopped
⅓ cup parmesan cheese, grated
½ teaspoon pepper
½ teaspoon salt

Preparation:
1. Grease the cooking surface of the griddle with cooking spray.
2. Turn on the 4 burners and turn their knobs to medium heat.
3. Let the Griddle preheat for 5 minutes.
4. Add kale on preheated griddle top and then let it cook for minutes or until wilted.
5. Beat eggs with sage, cheese, black pepper and salt in a suitable bowl.
6. Pour this egg mixture over the kale leaves and mix well.
7. Cook for almost 2 ½ minutes per side.
8. Serve.
Per Serving: Calories: 338; Fat: 12g; Sodium: 521mg; Carbs: 14g; Fiber 5.1g; Sugar: 3g; Protein: 27g

Vanilla Oatmeal Pancakes

Prep time: 10 minutes | Cook time: 10 minutes | Serves: 2

Ingredients:
- 6 egg whites
- 1 cup steel-cut oats
- ¼ teaspoon vanilla
- 1 cup Greek yogurt
- ½ teaspoon baking powder
- 1 teaspoon liquid stevia
- ¼ teaspoon cinnamon

Preparation:
1. Preheat the Griddle by turning all its knob to medium-heat setting.
2. Grease the griddle top with cooking spray.
3. Place the oats in a blender and process until a fine powder forms.
4. In a blender, mix well the other ingredients and blend until smooth.
5. Pour ¼ cup batter over the griddle's hot surface.
6. Cook pancakes for 5 minutes per side until golden brown.
7. Serve and enjoy.

Per Serving: Calories: 451; Fat: 8.4 g; Sodium: 134 mg; Carbs: 59.6g; Fiber: 8.2g; Sugar: 4.8g; Protein: 32.9g

Bacon Gruyere Omelet

Prep time: 5 minutes | Cook time: 15 minutes | Serves: 2

Ingredients:
- 6 eggs, beaten
- 6 strips bacon
- ¼ pound gruyere, shredded
- 1 teaspoon black pepper
- 1 teaspoon salt
- 1 tablespoon chives, chopped
- Vegetable oil

Preparation:
1. Preheat the Griddle by turning all its knob to medium-heat setting.
2. Grease the griddle top with cooking spray.
3. Season the beaten eggs with salt and put aside for 10 minutes.
4. Place the bacon strips on the hot griddle top and cook for 5 minutes per side until crispy then transfer to a plate lined with parchment paper.
5. Chop the bacon into small pieces once it has been drained.
6. Pour the beaten eggs into two parts on the hot griddle top.
7. Cook for 2 minutes then add cheese and bacon on top.
8. Fold the omelet in half and flip to cook for 5 minutes per side.
9. Serve warm with peppers and chives.

Per Serving: Calories: 795; Fat: 62.1 g; Sodium: 2855 mg; Carbs: 2.8 g; Fiber: 0.3 g; Sugar: 1.3 g; Protein: 58.4 g

Garlic Cauliflower and Broccoli Patties

Prep time: 10 minutes | Cook time: 15 minutes | Serves: 12

Ingredients:
- 1 egg
- 4 oz. cheddar cheese, shredded
- 3 cups broccoli rice
- ¼ teaspoon garlic powder
- ¼ teaspoon onion powder
- 3 cups cauliflower rice
- ½ teaspoon black pepper
- ½ teaspoon salt

Preparation:
1. Microwave broccoli rice and cauliflower rice for 5 minutes in a microwave-safe bowl.
2. Squeeze the broccoli and cauliflower rice to remove any extra moisture.
3. Preheat the Griddle by turning all its knob to medium-heat setting.
4. Grease the griddle top with cooking spray.
5. Place the veggie rice in a suitable mixing bowl.
6. Mix well the egg, garlic powder, onion powder, cheese, pepper, and salt in a suitable mixing bowl.
7. Form patties from the mixture and fry until lightly browned on both sides on the hot griddle top.
8. Serve and enjoy.

Per Serving: Calories: 59; Fat: 3.6 g; Sodium: 192 mg; Carbs: 3.1g; Fiber: 1.1g; Sugar: 1g; Protein: 4g

Chapter 2 Burger Recipes

Garlicky Pork Burgers

Prep time: 5 minutes | Cook time: 10 minutes | Serves: 2

Ingredients:
½ teaspoon salt
½ teaspoon black pepper
2 cloves garlic, chopped
2 hard rolls

Preparation:
1. In a food processor, pulse the meat, salt, pepper, and garlic until coarsely ground, but not much finer than chopped. (If using pre-ground beef, add it in a mixing dish with the salt, pepper, and garlic and mix gently with your hands.)
2. To prevent crushing the meat, shape it into four 1- to 112-inch thick burgers with as little manipulation as possible. (You can make this ahead of time and keep it refrigerated until you're ready to griddle it.)
3. Set the Griddle to high heat and place the burgers on it; cook for 10 minutes without flipping; the internal temperature should be 160°F.
4. Serve on a serving platter.
5. In the oven, warm the rolls.
6. Serve the patties on a slice of bread.

Per Serving: Calories: 154; Fat: 8g; Sodium: 781mg; Carbs: 18.3g; Fiber 1.6g; Sugar: 3.1g; Protein: 4.3g

Mustard Pork Tenderloin Sandwiches

Prep time: 10 minutes | Cook time: 25 minutes | Serves: 6

Ingredients:
2(¾-lb.) pork tenderloins
1 teaspoon garlic powder
1 teaspoon sea salt
1 teaspoon dry mustard
½ teaspoon coarsely ground
pepper
Olive oil, for brushing
Whole wheat hamburger buns
2 tablespoons barbecue sauce

Preparation:
1. In a small mixing bowl, combine the garlic powder, salt, pepper, and mustard.
2. Rub pork tenderloins with olive oil and seasoning mix evenly.
3. Preheat the griddle to medium-high heat and cook the steaks for 10 to 12 minutes on each side, or until a meat thermometer inserted into the thickest piece reads 155°F.
4. Remove the griddle from the heat and set aside for 10 minutes.
5. Thinly slice the hamburger buns and distribute evenly.
6. Drizzle barbecue sauce over each sandwich and serve.

Per Serving: Calories: 256; Fat: 12g; Sodium: 464mg; Carbs: 5.5g; Fiber 0.6g; Sugar: 2g; Protein: 34.6g

Lamb amd Cucumber Burger

Prep time: 5 minutes | Cook time: 5 minutes | Serves: 4

Ingredients:
1¼ pounds lean ground lamb
tablespoon ground cumin
¼ teaspoon ground cinnamon
½ teaspoon salt
½ teaspoon freshly ground black pepper
whole wheat pitas
½ medium cucumber, peeled and sliced
½ cup Simple Garlic Yogurt Sauce

Preparation:
1. Combine the lamb, cumin, cinnamon, salt, and black pepper in a medium mixing basin. Mix the seasonings into the meat with a fork, then form the mixture into four 1-inch-thick patties with your hands.
2. Set the Griddle to high heat, then place the burgers on the griddle and cook for 5 minutes without flipping.
3. Remove the burgers from the pan and keep them covered to keep them heated.
4. Place a burger in each pita, along with a few cucumber slices and a dollop of the yoghurt sauce on top.
5. Serve right away.

Per Serving: Calories: 635; Fat: 23.7g; Sodium: 616mg; Carbs: 11.1g; Fiber 1.6g; Sugar: 0.6g; Protein: 89g

Pinapple and Ham Sandwich

Prep time: 05 minutes | Cook time: 15 minutes | Serves: 2

Ingredients:
1 (10 ounce) package deli sliced ham
4 pineapple rings
4 slices Swiss cheese
8 slices of thick bread
Butter, softened, for brushing

Preparation:
1. Butter one side of all the bread slices and preheat your griddle to medium.
2. Place ¼ of the ham, a pineapple ring, and 1 slice of cheese on top of each piece of bread.
3. Place the sandwiches on the griddle and top with the last bread slice.
4. Cook until the bottom side of the bread is golden brown, then flip and cook until the other side is browned and the cheese has melted.
5. When done, serve and enjoy!

Per Serving: Calories: 271; Fat: 12.9g; Sodium: 920 mg; Carbs: 18.6g; Fiber 1.6g; Sugar: 5.4g; Protein: 21.8g

Tasty Bacon Cheese Serrano Wraps

Prep time: 05 minutes | Cook time: 15 minutes | Serves:4

Ingredients:
2package bacon, uncured and nitrate free
2 fresh Serrano peppers, halved
lengthwise and seeded
1 (8 ounce) package cream cheese
1 dozen toothpicks, soaked

Preparation:
1. Preheat the griddle to medium-high heat.
2. Cream cheese is stuffed into the halves of Serrano.
3. Bacon should be wrapped around each one. To keep it in place, use a toothpick.
4. Place on the griddle and cook for 5 to 7 minutes per side, or until bacon is crispy.
5. Transfer to a serving platter to chill before serving.

Per Serving: Calories: 252; Fat: 23.9g; Sodium: 517 mg; Carbs: 2.6g; Fiber 0.3g; Sugar: 0.4g; Protein: 7.8g

Veggie Pesto Flatbread with Mozzarella Cheese

Prep time: 35 minutes | Cook time: 15 minutes | Serves: 8

Ingredients:
8 flatbreads
2 jar pesto
For the topping:
1 cup cherry tomatoes, halved
2 small red onions, sliced thin
2 red bell pepper, sliced
2 yellow bell pepper, sliced
2 cups black olives, halved
2 cup shredded mozzarella cheese
2 small yellow squash or zucchini, sliced
2 teaspoons olive oil
½ teaspoon sea salt
½ teaspoon black pepper

Preparation:
1. Set the griddle to a low heat setting and preheat it. Spread a thin layer of pesto across each flatbread.
2. Top each flatbread with ½ cup mozzarella cheese.
3. Using a rubber spatula, combine all of the topping ingredients in a large mixing basin.
4. Place flatbreads on griddle and spread a uniform amount of topping mixture over each, spreading it to the edges.
5. Cover the flatbreads with foil and bake for 5 minutes, or until the cheese is melted.
6. Place flatbreads on a flat surface or cutting board, and cut with a pizza cutter or kitchen scissors into individual pieces.
7. Serve immediately!

Per Serving: Calories: 217; Fat: 12g; Sodium: 476mg; Carbs: 21.1g; Fiber 3.6g; Sugar: 4.4g; Protein: 7.8g

Marinated Portobello Cheese Burgers

Prep time: 05 minutes | Cook time: 10 minutes | Serves: 2

Ingredients:
- 4 Portobello mushroom caps
- 4 slices mozzarella cheese
- 4 buns, like brioche

For the marinade:
- ¼ cup balsamic vinegar
- 2 tablespoons olive oil
- 1 teaspoon dried basil
- 1 teaspoon dried oregano
- 1 teaspoon garlic powder
- ¼ teaspoon sea salt
- ¼ teaspoon black pepper

Preparation:
1. Whip together the marinade ingredients in a huge mixing bowl. Toss the mushroom caps in the sauce to coat them.
2. Set aside at room temperature for 15 minutes, rotating twice.
3. Preheat the griddle to medium-high temperature.
4. Place the mushrooms on the griddle and keep the marinade aside for basting.
5. Cook the meat for 5–8 minutes on each side, or until done.
6. Brush the marinade on the meat on a regular basis.
7. Sprinkle mozzarella cheese on top during the last 2 minutes of cooking.
8. Serve the brioche buns straight from the griddle.

Per Serving: Calories: 254; Fat: 14 g; Sodium: 496mg; Carbs: 24.6g; Fiber 1.6g; Sugar: 3.6g; Protein: 13g

Garlic Parsley Cheese Sandwiches

Prep time: 2 minutes | Cook time: 7 minutes | Serves: 1

Ingredients:
- 2 slices Italian bread, sliced thin
- 2 slices provolone cheese
- 2 tablespoons butter, softened
- Garlic powder, for dusting
- Dried parsley, for dusting
- Parmesan Cheese, shredded, for dusting

Preparation:
1. Spread butter evenly across 2 slices of bread and season with garlic and parsley on each greased side.
2. Spread a few teaspoons of Parmesan cheese over each greased side of the bread and gently press it in.
3. Preheat the griddle to medium heat and set one slice of bread on the griddle, buttered side down.
4. Top with provolone slices and a butter-side-up second slice of bread.
5. Cook for 3 minutes on one side, then flip and cook for another 3 minutes, or until bread is golden and parmesan cheese is crunchy.
6. Serve immediately with your favorite side dishes!

Per Serving: Calories: 555; Fat: 44.7 g; Sodium: 1034mg; Carbs: 14.6g; Fiber 1g; Sugar: 1.2g; Protein: 25.8g

Croque Ham Cheese Buegers

Prep time: 10 minutes | Cook time: 10 minutes | Serves: 2

Ingredients:
- 2 tablespoons butter
- 1 tablespoon flour
- ⅔ cup milk
- 2 slices thick cut bread
- 2 slices black forest ham
- 2 slices gruyere cheese
- Salt and black pepper
- 2 eggs
- Béchamel sauce, as you like

Preparation:
1. Melt one tablespoon of butter in a small skillet over medium heat, then add the flour. Add the milk after whisking until barely browned.
2. Continue to stir until the sauce thickens. Season with salt and pepper after removing from the fire.
3. Preheat the griddle to medium.
4. Butter one side of each slice of bread and spread the other with a liberal amount of béchamel sauce.
5. Top each sandwich with two slices of ham and the last slice of bread. Preheat the griddle and cook the pancakes till golden brown.
6. Place the gruyere cheese on top of the sandwiches and flip them over.
7. Crack the eggs on the other side of the griddle and cook until the whites are set.
8. Cook until the gruyere on top has melted and the other side of the sandwich is golden brown. Before serving, place a fried egg on top of each sandwich.

Per Serving: Calories: 475; Fat: 30 g; Sodium: 641 mg; Carbs: 24.6g; Fiber 3.6g; Sugar: 4.1g; Protein: 26.1g

Beef & Corn Burgers

Prep time: 20 minutes | Cook time: 30 minutes | Serves: 6

Ingredients:
- 1 large egg, lightly beaten
- 1 cup whole kernel corn, cooked
- ½ cup bread crumbs
- 2 tablespoons shallots, minced
- 1 teaspoon Worcestershire sauce
- 2 pounds ground beef
- 1 teaspoon salt
- ½ teaspoon pepper
- ½ teaspoon ground sage

Preparation:
1. Whisk together the egg, corn, bread crumbs, shallots, and Worcestershire sauce in a mixing bowl.
2. Combine the ground beef and the remaining seasonings in a separate bowl.
3. Cover a level surface with waxed paper.
4. From the meat mixture, make 12 thin burger patties.
5. Fill the centre of each of the 6 patties with the corn mixture and spread evenly to within an inch of the edge.
6. To seal the corn mixture in the middle, place a second circle of meat on top of each burger and push the edges together.
7. Over medium heat, griddle for 12-15 minutes on each side, or until thermometer reads 160°F and juices run clear.

Per Serving: Calories: 354; Fat: 11.9g; Sodium: 578 mg; Carbs: 12.4g; Fiber 1.6g; Sugar: 1.6g; Protein: 48.1g

Bulgur Beet Burgers

Prep time: 5 minutes | Cook time: 10 minutes | Serves: 6

Ingredients:
- 1 pound beets, peeled and grated (about 2 cups)
- ½ cup packed pitted dates, broken into pieces
- ½ cup almonds
- 1 teaspoon ginger powder
- ½ cup bulgur
- Salt and pepper
- ¾ cup boiling red wine or water
- 1 tablespoon Dijon or other mustard
- Cayenne or red chili flakes (optional)

Preparation:
1. In a food processor, pulse the beets, dates, almonds, and ginger powder until finely minced but not quite a paste.
2. Add the bulgur and a pinch of salt and pepper to the mixture in a large mixing bowl. Cover the bowl with a plate and stir in the boiling wine, mustard, and cayenne to taste if using.
3. Allow the bulgur to soften for 20 minutes.
4. Season with salt and pepper to taste. Refrigerate for at least 1 hour after shaping into ½ burgers and placing on a tray without touching.
5. When the griddle is heated, turn the control knob to high and set the burgers on it. Cook for 10 minutes without rotating.
6. Serve with the fixings or toppings of your choice.

Per Serving: Calories: 154; Fat: 4.5g; Sodium: 111mg; Carbs: 29.7g; Fiber 6g; Sugar: 15.6g; Protein: 4.8g

Cheese and Tomato Burgers

Prep time: 10 minutes | Cook time: 10 minutes | Serves: 4

Ingredients:
- 8 slices sourdough bread
- 4 slices provolone cheese
- 4 slices yellow American cheese
- 4 slices sharp cheddar cheese
- 4 slices tomato
- 3 tablespoons mayonnaise
- 3 tablespoons butter

Preparation:
1. Preheat the griddle to medium-high heat.
2. Spread mayo on one side of each slice of bread and butter the other.
3. Arrange the cheeses on top of the buttered side of the griddle.
4. Place the other slices of bread on top of the cheese, butter side up.
5. Cook for 10 minutes, flipping halfway through, until the other piece of bread is golden brown and the cheese has melted.
6. Take it from the griddle, slice it in half, and eat.

Per Serving: Calories: 518; Fat: 30.3g; Sodium: 976 mg; Carbs: 40.3g; Fiber 1.6g; Sugar: 3.1g; Protein: 22g

Garlic Cheese Pizza

Prep time: 05 minutes | Cook time: 18 minutes | Serves: 2

Ingredients:
8 slices French bread
3 tablespoons butter, softened
½ cup pizza sauce
¼ cup mozzarella cheese
½ cup pepperoni diced
Garlic powder, for dusting
Oregano, for dusting

Preparation:
1. Each piece of French bread should be brushed with butter on one side.
2. Place a piece of aluminum foil with the butter side down and sprinkle with garlic powder and oregano.
3. Spread pizza sauce on the opposite side of each slice of French bread.
4. Top 4 slices of bread with mozzarella cheese, pepperoni slices, and more mozzarella.
5. Place the remaining French bread slices, butter side up, on top of the pizza-topped bread to make 4 sandwiches.
6. Preheat the griddle to medium heat and set one slice of bread on the griddle, buttered side down.
7. Cook for 3 minutes on one side, then flip and cook for another 3 minutes on each side, or until bread is brown and cheese has melted.
8. Enjoy while it's still warm!

Per Serving: Calories: 305; Fat: 17 g; Sodium: 664mg; Carbs: 40.6g; Fiber 2.3g; Sugar: 2.8g; Protein: 9.8g

Mozzarella Vegetable Pizza

Prep time: 15 minutes | Cook time: 15 minutes | Serves: 6

Ingredients:
8 small fresh mushrooms, halved
1 small zucchini, cut into ¼-inch slices
1 small yellow pepper, sliced
1 small red pepper, sliced
1 small red onion, sliced
1 tablespoon white wine vinegar
1 tablespoon water
1 teaspoon olive oil, divided
½ teaspoon dried basil
¼ teaspoon sea salt
¼ teaspoon pepper
prebaked, 12-inch thin whole wheat pizza crust
1 can (8 ounces) pizza sauce
small tomatoes, chopped
2 cups shredded part-skim mozzarella cheese

Preparation:
1. Preheat the griddle on a low temperature setting. Spread a thin layer of pesto across each flatbread.
2. Top each with ½ cup mozzarella cheese.
3. Using a rubber spatula, combine all of the topping ingredients in a large mixing basin.
4. Place flatbreads on griddle and spread a uniform amount of topping mixture over each, spreading it to the edges.
5. Cover the flatbreads with foil and cook for 5 minutes, or until the cheese is melted.
6. Place flatbreads on a flat surface or cutting board, and cut with a pizza cutter or kitchen scissors into individual pieces.
7. Serve immediately!

Per Serving: Calories: 215; Fat: 17.9g; Sodium: 467 mg; Carbs: 21.6g; Fiber 3.6g; Sugar: 4.4g; Protein: 7.8g

Chapter 3 Vegetarian and Sides Recipes

Steamed Carrots in Ranch Dressing

Prep time: 15 minutes | Cook time: 20 minutes | Serves: 5

Ingredients:
12 petite carrots
1 packet dry ranch dressing/ seasoning mix
2 olive oil
Water

Preparation:
1. Grease the cooking surface of the griddle with cooking spray.
2. Turn on the 4 burners and turn their knobs to medium heat.
3. Let the Griddle preheat for 5 minutes.
4. In a suitable bowl, combine carrots, olive oil and ranch seasoning mix,.
5. Stir until well-combined and all the carrots are coated evenly with oil and seasoning.
6. Add carrots to the griddle and then let it cook for almost 3 minutes, with occasional stirring.
7. Add 3 tablespoons water to the pile of carrots to generate steam.
8. Cover carrot pile with basting cover or similar metal dish.
9. Toss carrots, add 2-3 tablespoons water, and re-cover with basting marinade to continue steaming.
10. Cook carrots for approximately 12 minutes or to desired tenderness.
11. Serve.
Per Serving: Calories: 304; Fat: 14.9g; Sodium: 304mg; Carbs: 12g; Fiber 6g; Sugar: 2g; Protein: 21g

Zucchini Squash Mix

Prep time: 15 minutes | Cook time: 10 minutes | Serves: 6

Ingredients:
2 zucchini, diced
2 squash, diced
1 large onion, diced
2-3 tomatoes on the vine, diced
5-6 garlic cloves, roughly chopped
1 can cannelloni beans, drained
Olive oil
Black pepper and salt to taste

Preparation:
1. Toss all the veggies and beans with black pepper and salt in a suitable bowl.
2. Grease the cooking surface of the griddle with cooking spray.
3. Turn on the 4 burners and turn their knobs to medium heat.
4. Let the Griddle preheat for 5 minutes.
5. Add the veggie mixture to the griddle top and then let it cook until soft.
6. Serve.
Per Serving: Calories: 381; Fat: 21g; Sodium: 561mg; Carbs: 21g; Fiber 6.1g; Sugar: 5g; Protein: 32g

Sautéed Savoury Green Beans

Prep time: 15 minutes | Cook time: 20 minutes | Serves: 6

Ingredients:
2 lbs. fresh green beans
1 tablespoon of olive oil
1 teaspoon of garlic powder
Black pepper and salt to taste

Preparation:
1. In a suitable bowl, mix all the recipe's ingredients until beans are well-coated.
2. Grease the cooking surface of the griddle with cooking spray.
3. Turn on the 4 burners and turn their knobs to medium-high heat.
4. Let the Griddle preheat for 5 minutes.
5. Spread the beans on the griddles and then let it cook for 20 minutes with stirring.
6. Serve.
7. Cook beans on griddle until they reach desired tenderness, with occasional stirring.
Per Serving: Calories: 339; Fat: 13g; Sodium: 421mg; Carbs: 16g; Fiber 4.1g; Sugar: 3.2g; Protein: 27g

Crispy Cooked Potatoes

Prep time: 15 minutes | Cook time: 25 minutes | Serves: 6

Ingredients:
6 potatoes, diced
2 tablespoons olive oil
2 teaspoons of black pepper
2 ½ teaspoons of garlic powder
2 teaspoons of dried rosemary
Salt to taste

Preparation:
1. In a suitable pot, boil sliced potatoes until fork tender.
2. Transfer potatoes from water into a suitable bowl.
3. Add olive oil, garlic powder, black pepper, rosemary, and salt.
4. Toss until potatoes are evenly coated.
5. Grease the cooking surface of the griddle with cooking spray.
6. Turn on the 4 burners and turn their knobs to medium heat.
7. Let the Griddle preheat for 5 minutes.
8. Add potatoes to griddle and then let it cook for 5-6 minutes each side or until crispy.
9. Serve.
Per Serving: Calories: 416; Fat: 11g; Sodium: 501mg; Carbs: 16g; Fiber 2.1g; Sugar: 2.2g; Protein: 28g

Parmesan Zucchini

Prep time: 15 minutes | Cook time: 15 minutes | Serves: 4

Ingredients:
3 medium zucchinis, sliced
1 tablespoon of olive oil
1 tablespoon of grated parmesan cheese
½ teaspoon of garlic powder
¼ teaspoon of black pepper

Preparation:
1. Grease the cooking surface of the griddle with cooking spray.
2. Turn on the 4 burners and turn their knobs to medium heat.
3. Let the Griddle preheat for 5 minutes.
4. Add sliced zucchini then cook for about 3 minutes, with occasional stirring.
5. Add parmesan cheese, garlic powder, and pepper and continue sautéing until zucchini is tender.
6. Serve.
Per Serving: Calories: 338; Fat: 12g; Sodium: 521mg; Carbs: 14g; Fiber 5.1g; Sugar: 3g; Protein: 27g

Fried Green Tomatoes with Parsley

Prep time: 15 minutes | Cook time: 10 minutes | Serves: 1

Ingredients:
4 green tomatoes
3 cups of Italian style bread crumbs
2 cups of flour
2 teaspoons of garlic powder
3 eggs
½ cup of milk
Black pepper and salt to taste
Parsley garnish, chopped
Lemon zest garnish
3 tablespoons of butter
2 ½ tablespoons of flour

Preparation:
1. Beat 3 eggs with ½ cup of milk, black pepper and salt in a suitable bowl.
2. Mix 2 cups flour with 2 teaspoon garlic powder in another.
3. Spread Italian seasoned bread crumbs in a plate.
4. Slice tomatoes ¼ to a ½ inch thick
5. Coat the slices in the flour mixture evenly and shaking off any excess flour.
6. Then dip and coat evenly in the egg wash , then into the breadcrumb, pressing slices into the crumbs.
7. Grease the cooking surface of the griddle with cooking spray.
8. Turn on the 4 burners and turn their knobs to medium heat.
9. Let the Griddle preheat for 5 minutes.
10. Place the coated tomato slices on the griddle top and then let it cook for 5 minutes per side.
11. Serve.
Per Serving: Calories: 304; Fat: 14.9g; Sodium: 304mg; Carbs: 12g; Fiber 6g; Sugar: 2g; Protein: 21g

Cotija Vegetable Scrable

Prep time: 15 minutes | Cook time: 10 minutes | Serves: 4

Ingredients:
- 3 cups of 4 ears corn
- ½ jalapeno, deseeded
- 3 tablespoons of mayo
- 2 tablespoon of butter
- 1 clove garlic, minced
- 2 green onions, chopped
- ½ bunch of cilantro
- 1 lime
- ¼ cup of cotija or feta cheese

Preparation:
1. Turn on the 4 burners of the griddle and turn their knobs to medium heat.
2. Let the Griddle preheat for 5 minutes.
3. Melt the butter on the griddle top and add the corn.
4. Cook for almost 5-10 minutes.
5. Mix jalapeno, mayo, green onions, garlic, lime, cilantro, and cheese together in a suitable bowl.
6. Add the charred corn and toss together until well mixed.
7. Serve warm.

Per Serving: Calories: 428; Fat: 11g; Sodium: 501mg; Carbs: 16g; Fiber 2.1g; Sugar: 2.2g; Protein: 27g

Homemade Caribbean Jerk Vegetables

Prep time: 15 minutes | Cook time: 45 minutes | Serves: 6

Ingredients:
- 1 tablespoon of onion powder
- 1 tablespoon of ground allspice
- 1 teaspoon of five-spice powder
- 1 teaspoon of ground ginger
- 1 teaspoon of ground nutmeg
- ½ teaspoon of garlic powder
- ½ teaspoon of cayenne pepper
- 1 tablespoon of dried thyme
- Black pepper and salt, to taste
- 1 zucchini, thickly sliced
- 1 yellow zucchini squash, thickly sliced
- 1 bunch of asparagus, tough ends removed
- 1 cup of sliced mushrooms
- 1 red bell pepper, sliced
- 1 orange bell pepper, sliced
- 2 tablespoons of olive oil

Preparation:
1. Grease the cooking surface of the griddle with cooking spray.
2. Turn on the 4 burners and turn their knobs to medium heat.
3. Let the Griddle preheat for 5 minutes.
4. In a suitable bowl, mix together all spices for jerk seasoning.
5. Wash, cut, and prepare vegetables as directed.
6. Spread the cut vegetables in a single layer on a large cookie sheet.
7. Drizzle with olive oil and sprinkle jerk seasoning over the vegetables, then gently toss so that the vegetables are equally coated.
8. Let vegetables sit for 10 minutes.
9. Add vegetables to griddle and then let it cook for 10-15 minutes or until desired doneness, with occasional stirring.
10. Serve.

Per Serving: Calories: 392; Fat: 31g; Sodium: 501mg; Carbs: 16g; Fiber 2.1g; Sugar: 2.2g; Protein: 28g

Rosemary Bread

Prep time: 15 minutes | Cook time: 20 minutes | Serves: 4

Ingredients:
- 2 cups of warm water
- 2 ¼ teaspoons of dry yeast
- ½ tablespoon of kosher salt
- 4 ½ cups of all-purpose flour
- 8 tablespoons of olive oil
- Salt to taste
- Black pepper to taste

Preparation:
1. Mix all the prepared dough ingredients until smooth, knead well, cover and leaver for 1 hour,
2. Punch it down and knead again then spread out the prepared dough into a flatbread.
3. Sprinkle salt over dough and let it sit for 30 minutes.
4. Grease the cooking surface of the griddle with cooking oil.
5. Turn on the 4 burners and turn their knobs to medium heat.
6. Let the Griddle preheat for 5 minutes.
7. Carefully place flat bread dough onto the griddle and press from top.
8. Cook for almost 4 minutes per side.
9. Serve.

Per Serving: Calories: 317; Fat: 32g; Sodium: 311mg; Carbs: 12g; Fiber 3.1g; Sugar: 4g; Protein: 22g

Vegetable Fried Rice

Prep time: 5 minutes | Cook time: 10 minutes | Serves: 4

Ingredients:
- ½ cup soy sauce
- ½ cup water
- ½ cup oyster sauce
- 2 tablespoons sesame oil
- 1 tablespoon sriracha
- ½ cup diced carrots
- ½ cup diced sweet onions
- 4 cloves garlic, minced
- ½ cup frozen peas
- 4 cups cooked rice, cooled
- ½ cup sliced scallions
- Cooking oil, as needed

Preparation:
1. Set aside a medium bowl containing sesame oil, soy sauce, water, oyster sauce, and sriracha.
2. Preheat the Griddle by turning all its knob to medium-heat setting.
3. Grease the griddle top with cooking oil.
4. Add the onions, carrots, and garlic when the oil begins to shimmer.
5. Cook for almost 5 minutes and add the peas to the mixture.
6. Pour some cooking oil onto the griddle's top and spread the rice out evenly in a single layer.
7. Cook for 4 minutes until the rice begins to turn golden.
8. Mix well the rice and half of the fried rice sauce, the cooked veggies and half of the scallions.
9. Stir the rice and vegetables, then spread the rice back out to a single layer on the hot griddle top.
10. Continue to pour in the fried rice sauce, toss and mix the rice until it is well coated.
11. Place the rice on a serving plate and scatter the remaining scallions on top.
12. Serve warm.

Per Serving: Calories: 826; Fat: 11.3 g; Sodium: 2078 mg; Carbs: 154.9g; Fiber: 4.5g; Sugar: 3.3g; Protein: 17g

Fried Brussels Sprouts and Dried Cranberries

Prep time: 15 minutes | Cook time: 15 minutes | Serves: 1

Ingredients:
- 2 bags brussels sprouts
- Olive oil
- 3 tablespoons of butter
- 1 onion, diced
- Black pepper and salt to taste
- 1 tablespoon of sugar
- 1 tablespoon of balsamic vinegar
- ⅓ cup of dried cranberries
- ½ cup of chicken stock

Preparation:
1. Put shredded brussels sprouts and chicken stock in a bowl, cover, and microwave for almost 3-5 minutes.
2. Turn on the 4 burners of the Griddle and turn their knobs to medium heat.
3. Let the Griddle preheat for 5 minutes.
4. Spread olive oil and butter to the preheated griddle with diced onions.
5. Toss in brussels sprouts, black pepper, salt and chicken stock to gas griddle then cook until goldne brown.
6. Stir in balsamic vinegar, sugar, dried cranberries.
7. Serve.

Per Serving: Calories: 366; Fat: 13g; Sodium: 421mg; Carbs: 16g; Fiber 4.1g; Sugar: 3.2g; Protein: 27g

Asparagus with Butter and Pepper

Prep time: 15 minutes | Cook time: 10 minutes | Serves: 4 to 6

Ingredients:
- 1½ pounds thick asparagus spears, trimmed
- 3 tablespoons butter, melted
- Salt and black pepper, to taste

Preparation:
1. Preheat the Griddle by turning all its knob to medium-heat setting.
2. Grease the griddle top with cooking spray.
3. Drizzle melted butter over asparagus and season with salt and black pepper.
4. Arrange asparagus on the hot griddle top and cook for 10 minutes.
5. Serve warm.

Per Serving: Calories: 117; Fat: 5.8 g; Sodium: 1460 mg; Carbs: 9.9g; Fiber: 3.3g; Sugar: 3.3g; Protein: 6.7g

Pita Bread

Prep time: 15 minutes | Cook time: 10 minutes | Serves: 1

Ingredients:
2 teaspoons of instant dry yeast
1 teaspoon of sugar
1 teaspoon of salt
½ cup of warm milk
½ cup of warm water
1 tablespoon of olive oil
2 ½ cups of bread flour

Preparation:
1. In a suitable bowl, combine sugar, yeast, salt, water and olive oil.
2. Stir in 2 ½ cups of flour to the liquid mixture then mix well.
3. Place the prepared dough to a lightly floured working surface and knead for 4-5 minutes.
4. Transfer to a suitable grease bowl.
5. Cover this bowl with a towel, place in a warm place, and let it rise for about 40 minutes.
6. Transfer the prepared dough to your working surface.
7. Divide the prepared dough into 8 pieces and roll into balls.
8. Drizzle a little olive oil on them and cover them with plastic wrap.
9. Let the prepared dough balls rest for 10 more minutes.
10. Grease the cooking surface of the griddle with cooking spray.
11. Turn on the 4 burners and turn their knobs to medium heat.
12. Let the Griddle preheat for 5 minutes.
13. Place a dough ball on a working surface and flatten it.
14. Roll each of them out to a circle 6" to 8" in diameter.
15. Place pitas on the griddle top and then let it cook for 1-2 minutes per side.
16. Serve.

Per Serving: Calories: 379; Fat: 13g; Sodium: 421mg; Carbs: 16g; Fiber 4.1g; Sugar: 3.2g; Protein: 27g

Bacon Brussels Topped with Blue Cheese

Prep time: 15 minutes | Cook time: 20 minutes | Serves: 8

Ingredients:
2 lbs. bag of brussel sprouts, shredded
8 slices bacon, thick cut
4 garlic cloves, grated
1 tablespoon duck; Fat:
5 oz. bag dried cherry and walnuts (salad toppers)
4 oz. blue cheese wedge
Black pepper, to taste

Preparation:
1. Grease the cooking surface of the griddle with cooking spray.
2. Turn on the 4 burners and turn their knobs to medium heat.
3. Let the Griddle preheat for 5 minutes.
4. Place bacon on the griddle and then let it cook until crispy.
5. Combine the shredded Brussel sprouts, bacon, and bacon; Fat: in a mixing bowl.
6. Toss with a tablespoon of duck; Fat: or olive oil to coat.
7. Allow bacon to finish cooking and sprouts to become soft and slightly charred by tossing every couple of minutes. Add black pepper to taste.
8. Mix in dried cherries and walnuts. Let cook 1 minute.
9. Top with crumbled blue cheese.
10. Serve.

Per Serving: Calories: 318; Fat: 15g; Sodium: 521mg; Carbs: 14g; Fiber 5.1g; Sugar: 3g; Protein: 27g

Sweet Potato Black Bean Burritos

Prep time: 15 minutes | Cook time: 10 minutes | Serves: 6

Ingredients:
2 sweet potatoes, diced
1 red bell pepper, diced
1 purple onion, diced
1 jalapeno, diced
1 ½ teaspoon of cumin
1 ½ teaspoon of chili powder
1 teaspoon of salt
¼ teaspoon of black pepper
Avocado oil
1 small bunch of cilantro
1 lime to juice
1 can of black beans, rinsed
12 tortillas
Colby and Monterey jack cheese

Preparation:
1. Grease the cooking surface of the griddle with avocado oil.
2. Turn on the 4 burners and turn their knobs to medium heat.
3. Let the Griddle preheat for 5 minutes.
4. Add all the ingredients except tortillas and then let it cook for 10 minutes.
5. Divide the filling into the burritos, roll and sear them for 2 minutes per side.
6. Serve.

Per Serving: Calories: 386; Fat: 13g; Sodium: 421mg; Carbs: 16g; Fiber 4.1g; Sugar: 3.2g; Protein: 27g

Savory Candied Sweet Potatoes

Prep time: 15 minutes | Cook time: 10 minutes | Serves: 6

Ingredients:
4 large sweet potatoes, diced small
1 lb. savory sage ground sausage
2 tablespoons oil
5 tablespoons butter, unsalted
1 cup brown sugar
Black pepper and salt, to taste
Dried parsley

Preparation:
1. Turn on the 4 burners of the Griddle and turn their knobs to medium heat.
2. Let the Griddle preheat for 5 minutes.
3. Place sweet potatoes in a large mixing bowl and dice them into small pieces.
4. Season with black pepper and salt and toss to lightly coat with oil.
5. Preheat the gas griddle to medium-low or low-medium heat.
6. Simmer the sausage and crumble on one side while the potatoes cook on the other.
7. In the centre of the sausage and potato mixture, make a well.
8. Melt the butter in the centre, then stir in the brown sugar.
9. Add a little sprinkle of parsley and then let it cook for another 1-2 minutes.
10. Serve.

Per Serving: Calories: 304; Fat: 14.9g; Sodium: 304mg; Carbs: 12g; Fiber 6g; Sugar: 2g; Protein: 21g

Rosemary Potatoes

Prep time: 15 minutes | Cook time: 20 minutes | Serves: 4

Ingredients:
1 pound red potatoes, quartered
8 large garlic cloves, smashed
3 large sprigs rosemary
2 tablespoons unsalted butter
Black pepper and salt, to taste
Olive oil

Preparation:
1. Grease the cooking surface of the griddle with cooking spray.
2. Turn on the 4 burners and turn their knobs to medium heat.
3. Let the Griddle preheat for 5 minutes.
4. Add the potatoes, a dash of black pepper and salt, and 1-2 tablespoons of olive oil to a large mixing bowl.
5. Toss to ensure that all of the ingredients are uniformly distributed.
6. Cook the potatoes on the skillet for 4-5 minutes, stirring often.
7. Reduce the heat to low on your griddle and toss in the garlic and rosemary to combine.
8. Cook for another 4-5 minutes after covering with a dome.
9. Toss all of the ingredients in the recipe together with the butter. Cook for another 4-5 minutes after covering with a dome. Serve.

Per Serving: Calories: 381; Fat: 21g; Sodium: 561mg; Carbs: 21g; Fiber 6.1g; Sugar: 5g; Protein: 32g

Green Beans Pancetta

Prep time: 15 minutes | Cook time: 20 minutes | Serves: 6

Ingredients:
4 oz diced pancetta
2 cups sliced shitake mushrooms
½ pound fresh green beans, cleaned and trimmed
2-3 cloves fresh garlic, sliced
⅓ cup dried cranberries
2 tablespoons unsalted butter
1 tablespoon lemon juice
Black pepper and salt, to taste

Preparation:
1. Grease the cooking surface of the griddle with cooking spray.
2. Turn on the 4 burners and turn their knobs to medium heat.
3. Let the Griddle preheat for 5 minutes.
4. Add and then let it cook the pancetta until crispy.
5. Remove the crisp pancetta from the heat and reserve for later.
6. Add the mushrooms and butter to the pancetta; Fat: with a bit of black pepper and salt and toss to evenly coat.
7. Cook for 3-4 minutes.
8. Add the garlic, cranberries and pancetta and toss to mix evenly. Cook for another 4-5 minutes.
9. Add a bit of water and the lemon juice. Cook for another 2 minutes to steam the beans.
10. Serve.

Per Serving: Calories: 449; Fat: 21g; Sodium: 421mg; Carbs: 16g; Fiber 4.1g; Sugar: 3.2g; Protein: 27g

Mayonnaise Corn Fritters

Prep time: 15 minutes | Cook time: 10 minutes | Serves: 1

Ingredients:
- ½ cup of all-purpose flour
- ½ cup of corn meal
- 1 teaspoon of baking powder
- Black pepper and salt to taste
- ½ cup of milk
- 1 fresh corn ear
- ¼ cup of cilantro, chopped
- ¼ cup of mayonnaise
- ¼ cup of sour cream
- 2 tablespoons of honey
- ½ teaspoon of chipotle chili powder
- ½ teaspoon of smoked paprika
- 1 lemon

Preparation:
1. Mix the mayo, sour cream, honey, chipotle powder, smoked paprika, black pepper and salt, and lemon juice in a suitable bowl.
2. In a suitable bowl mix flour, corn meal, baking powder, and milk.
3. Season by adding a pinch of Black pepper and salt.
4. Cut the kernels off of a fresh ear of corn and mix it in the prepared batter.
5. Grease the cooking surface of the griddle with cooking oil.
6. Turn on the 4 burners and turn their knobs to medium heat.
7. Let the Griddle preheat for 5 minutes.
8. Add spoonful of the prepared batter to griddle and spread them out slightly.
9. Cook each side until golden brown.
10. Serve with the sauce and chopped cilantro.

Per Serving: Calories: 327; Fat: 22g; Sodium: 421mg; Carbs: 10g; Fiber 4.1g; Sugar: 2g; Protein: 31g

Collards Greens Stew in Chicken Stock

Prep time: 15 minutes | Cook time: 30 minutes | Serves: 4

Ingredients:
- 1 pound shredded collard greens
- 8 strips thick cut bacon
- ⅓ cup chopped yellow onion
- ½ cup chicken stock
- 2 tablespoons red wine vinegar
- 2 teaspoons red pepper flake
- Black pepper and salt, to taste
- Olive oil

Preparation:
1. Grease the cooking surface of the griddle with cooking spray.
2. Turn on the 4 burners and turn their knobs to medium heat.
3. Let the Griddle preheat for 5 minutes.
4. Add the bacon to the griddle top.
5. Cook for 5-6 minutes, or until well cooked and crisp.
6. Drain on a few pieces of paper towel after removing from the griddle.
7. Cook the onion for 4-5 minutes on the skillet, stirring frequently.
8. Toss in the collard greens with a touch of salt and a huge pinch of pepper to combine.
9. Cook, tossing frequently, for 4-5 minutes.
10. Cover with a dome and 12 cup chicken stock. Cook for a total of 3-4 minutes.
11. Combine the remaining chicken stock, red wine vinegar, and red pepper flake in a large mixing bowl.
12. Toss to ensure that all of the ingredients are uniformly distributed. Cover and then let it cook for a further 4-5 minutes before serving.
13. Serve.

Per Serving: Calories: 317; Fat: 32g; Sodium: 311mg; Carbs: 12g; Fiber 3.1g; Sugar: 4g; Protein: 22g

Ginger Coleslaw Egg Rolls

Prep time: 8 minutes | Cook time: 10 minutes | Serves: 8

Ingredients:
- 8 egg roll wrappers
- 4 cups bagged coleslaw mix
- 2 tablespoons ginger paste
- 2 tablespoons soy sauce
- 2 tablespoons sesame oil
- 1 tablespoon garlic powder
- 1 teaspoon ground ginger
- Cooking oil, as needed

Preparation:
1. In a suitable mixing bowl, mix well all of the remaining ingredients, except the wrappers.
2. Cook the vegetable mixture for 6 to 8 minutes.
3. Place the wrapper on a dry work surface.
4. Cover the bottom third of the wrapper with approximately ¼ cup of the vegetable mixture.
5. Fill a small bowl with water to dip your fingers in.
6. Fold the moistened sides of the wrapper toward the vegetables, pinching them together.
7. Roll the wrapper over the veggies toward the top of the wrapper.
8. Repeat with the remaining ingredients, placing the egg roll seam-side down on a dry tray.
9. Preheat the Griddle by turning all its knob to medium-heat setting.
10. Grease the griddle top with cooking spray.
11. Place the egg rolls on the hot griddle top and cook for 4 minutes per side.
12. Serve and enjoy!

Per Serving: Calories: 249; Fat: 5.7 g; Sodium: 574 mg; Carbs: 23.9g; Fiber: 0.9g; Sugar: 1.9g; Protein: 3.6g

Delicous Pepper Butternut Squash

Prep time: 6 minutes | Cook time: 10 minutes | Serves: 4 to 6

Ingredients:
- 1 small butternut squash (2 pounds), peeled, seeded, and sliced
- Salt and black pepper, to taste
- 3 tablespoons olive oil

Preparation:
1. Add squash slice to a pot filled with boiling water and cook for 3 minutes then drain.
2. Preheat the Griddle by turning all its knob to medium-heat setting.
3. Grease the griddle top with cooking oil.
4. Place squash slices on the hot griddle top and cook 5 minutes per side while seasoning with black pepper and salt.
5. Serve warm.

Per Serving: Calories: 81; Fat: 7.1 g; Sodium: 2 mg; Carbs: 5.5g; Fiber: 0.9g; Sugar: 1g; Protein: 0.5g

Sautéed Zucchini and Carrots

Prep time: 05 minutes | Cook time: 05 minutes | Serves: 2

Ingredients:
- 2 zucchinis, sliced
- 1-teaspoon garlic powder
- 1-teaspoon dried parsley
- 1-teaspoon dried thyme
- 3 carrots, sliced
- 2-tablespoon olive oil
- ½-teaspoon dried oregano
- Pepper
- Salt

Preparation:
1. Toss the zucchini, carrots, and additional ingredients together in a mixing bowl.
2. Preheat the griddle to medium-high.
3. Coat the top of the griddle with cooking spray.
4. Cook for 8-10 minutes on a heated griddle top with the zucchini and carrot combination.
5. Serve and have fun.

Per Serving: Calories: 98; Fat: 7.2g; Sodium: 81mg; Carbs: 8.6g; Fiber 2.6g; Sugar: 4.1g; Protein: 1.8g

Cranberry Jalapeño Stuffed Sausage

Prep time: 15 minutes | Cook time: 10 minutes | Serves: 11

Ingredients:
- 16 oz. breakfast sausage
- 1 cup of diced red onion
- ½ cup of diced jalapeno
- 1 cup of dried cranberries
- 1 large loaf bakery fresh French bread, cubed
- 1 cup of chicken stock
- Black pepper and salt to taste

Preparation:
1. Grease the cooking surface of the griddle with cooking spray.
2. Turn on the 4 burners and turn their knobs to medium heat.
3. Let the Griddle preheat for 5 minutes.
4. Cook sausage on the griddle top, breaking it apart with spatulas as it cooks.
5. Add onion and jalapeno when sausage is getting close to done.
6. Allow the onion and jalapeno to cook in the sausage grease, mixing frequently.
7. Cook for a few minutes, until soft.
8. Add cranberries and mix, allowing to cook in sausage grease.
9. Stir in bread and mix together with other ingredients.
10. Add chicken stock and quickly mix ingredients allow stock to soak into all the bread.
11. Allow bread to slightly toast on some edges while mixing, adding black pepper and salt to taste.
12. Serve.

Per Serving: Calories: 346; Fat: 13g; Sodium: 421mg; Carbs: 16g; Fiber 4.1g; Sugar: 3.2g; Protein: 27g

Maple Glazed Green Beans Fried Bacon and Onion

Prep time: 15 minutes | **Cook time:** 10 minutes | **Serves:** 8

Ingredients:
2 (12 oz.) bags of frozen green beans
12 oz. package of bacon
1 cup of diced onion
Pure maple syrup
Black pepper and salt to taste

Preparation:
1. Grease the cooking surface of the griddle with cooking spray.
2. Turn on the 4 burners and turn their knobs to medium heat.
3. Let the Griddle preheat for 5 minutes.
4. Slice bacon into small strips and add to the griddle top then cook until crispy.
5. To the other side of the griddle add beans, adding black pepper and salt to taste
6. When the bacon is nearly done, add the onions and sauté them in the bacon grease.
7. After 2 minutes, combine all of the ingredients in the recipe, allowing the bacon grease to flavour everything.
8. Serve.

Per Serving: Calories: 392; Fat: 31g; Sodium: 501mg; Carbs: 16g; Fiber 2.1g; Sugar: 2.2g; Protein: 28g

Basil Veggie Salad with Cheese

Prep time: 15 minutes | **Cook time:** 10 minutes | **Serves:** 5

Ingredients:
2 small zucchinis, cut lengthwise
1 corn on the cob, sliced
1 sweet bell pepper, seeded
Olive oil
Salt and pepper to taste
1 onion, sliced
2 large tomatoes, chopped
4-tablespoon grated Parmesan cheese
2-tablespoon balsamic vinegar
½ cup torn basil leaves

Preparation:
1. Preheat the griddle to medium heat and heat the oil.
2. After brushing zucchini, corn, and bell pepper with olive oil, season to taste with salt and pepper.
3. Place the zucchini, corn, and bell pepper on the griddle and grill for 3 -4 minutes on each on the side. Eliminate the corn kernels from the ear of corn.
4. To properly distribute the seasonings, toss all of the ingredients in a basin.
5. When done, serve and enjoy.

Per Serving: Calories: 146; Fat: 8g; Sodium: 219mg; Carbs: 11.6g; Fiber 2.6g; Sugar: 6g; Protein: 9.3g

Herded Broccoli Rice

Prep time: 7 minutes | **Cook time:** 16 minutes | **Serves:** 4 to 6

Ingredients:
6 large tomatillos, peeled and rinsed
Oil, for coating
1 white onion, chopped
2 cups cilantro, leaves
1 tablespoon roasted garlic
2 teaspoons salt
1½ cups water
2 cups white rice
1 bunch scallions, bases trimmed
1 head broccoli, cut in half
1 cup basil leaves, chopped
1 cup parsley leaves, chopped

Preparation:
1. Preheat the Griddle by turning all its knob to medium-heat setting.
2. Grease the griddle top with cooking oil.
3. Toss the tomatillos with oil to coat them and cook over for about 5 minutes on the hot griddle top.
4. Blend the onion, tomatillos, garlic, 1 cup cilantro, salt, and water in a blender until smooth.
5. Transfer this mixture to a pan and place on the hot griddle top.
6. Add the rice and cook, for 3 minutes, or until toasted and slightly transparent.
7. Toss in the tomatillo puree and mix well.
8. Cook for 10 to 12 minutes, or until liquid has been absorbed.
9. Cook for another 5 minutes, covered.
10. Remove from the griddle with the cover on and set aside to steam until ready to serve.
11. Toss the scallions and broccoli in enough oil to coat and cook over medium heat until charred.
12. Add broccoli and rest of the ingredients to the rice.
13. Serve warm.

Per Serving: Calories: 281; Fat: 3.3 g; Sodium: 802 mg; Carbs: 56.5g; Fiber: 3.2g; Sugar: 1.7g; Protein: 6.3g

Spicy Onion Patties

Prep time: 15 minutes | **Cook time:** 10 minutes | **Serves:** 1

Ingredients:
1 cup of all-purpose flour
2 teaspoons of sugar
2 teaspoons of baking powder
½ teaspoon of salt
½ teaspoon of black pepper
½ teaspoon of garlic powder
2 tablespoons of cornmeal
2 ½ cups of chopped onion
1 cup of milk
Vegetable oil
Hot sauce

Preparation:
1. Grease the cooking surface of the griddle with cooking oil.
2. Turn on the 4 burners and turn their knobs to medium heat.
3. Let the Griddle preheat for 5 minutes.
4. Mix dry ingredients together, add the onions and mix so the onions get coated well.
5. Mix in milk and hot sauce.
6. Add extra flour and cornmeal if you want a thicker patty.
7. Begin dropping spoonful's, about ¼ cup of onion batter in the oil.
8. Cook until golden brown, and flip. Adjust heat if needed.
9. Serve.

Per Serving: Calories: 392; Fat: 32g; Sodium: 354mg; Carbs: 14g; Fiber 1.2g; Sugar: 5g; Protein: 31g

Radish Bell Pepper

Prep time: 8 minutes | **Cook time:** 13 minutes | **Serves:** 3 to 4

Ingredients:
1 bunch radishes, cleaned and grated
½ cup diced red bell pepper
2 cloves garlic, minced
½ cup cooked black beans, drained
1 teaspoon garlic powder
1 teaspoon onion powder
Sour cream, to serve
Coconut oil or other cooking oil, as needed
Salt and black pepper, to taste

Preparation:
1. Preheat the Griddle by turning all its knob to medium-heat setting.
2. Grease the griddle top with cooking oil.
3. Add the chopped red pepper and minced garlic to the hot griddle then cook for 2 minutes.
4. Transfer the mixture to a suitable bowl.
5. Stir in black beans, shredded radishes, garlic powder, and onion powder, salt and black pepper, and form a 12-inch thick cake.
6. Cook the cakes on the griddle for 5 minutes per side.
7. Top with a dollop of sour cream.

Per Serving: Calories: 116; Fat: 2.3 g; Sodium: 15 mg; Carbs: 18.9g; Fiber: 4.5g; Sugar: 2.2g; Protein: 6g

Garlic Eggplant

Prep time: 13 minutes | **Cook time:** 15 minutes | **Serves:** 6 to 8

Ingredients:
6 tablespoons olive oil
5 garlic cloves, minced
⅛ teaspoon red pepper flakes
½ cup plain whole-milk yogurt
3 tablespoons minced fresh mint
1 teaspoon grated lemon zest plus
2 teaspoons juice
1 teaspoon ground cumin
Salt and black pepper, to taste
2 pounds eggplant, sliced into ¼-inch-thick rounds

Preparation:
1. In a microwave-safe bowl, heat the garlic, oil, and pepper flakes for 2 minutes then strain.
2. Mix yoghurt, 1 tablespoon garlic oil, lemon zest and juice, mint, cumin, and ¼ teaspoon salt in a bowl. Season eggplant with remaining garlic oil, salt and black pepper.
3. Preheat the Griddle by turning all its knob to medium-heat setting.
4. Grease the griddle top with cooking spray.
5. Pour the egg mixture onto the hot griddle top
6. Half of the eggplant should be placed on the hot griddle top. Cook for 5 minutes per side.
7. Repeat with the remaining eggplant on a dish.
8. Drizzle with yoghurt sauce and top with garlic mixture.
9. Serve.

Per Serving: Calories: 134; Fat: 11 g; Sodium: 14 mg; Carbs: 8.7g; Fiber: 4.2g; Sugar: 4.5g; Protein: 2.2 g

Chapter 3 Vegetarian and Sides Recipes

Parsley Parmesan Ravioli with Sauce

Prep time: 5 minutes | Cook time: 8 minutes | Serves: 4

Ingredients:
- 12 frozen cheese ravioli
- ½ cup all-purpose flour
- 1 egg beaten with 2 tablespoons water
- 1 cup Italian-flavored bread crumbs
- ¼ cup freshly grated Parmesan cheese
- 1 tablespoon minced fresh parsley
- Cooking oil, as needed
- Marinara sauce, for dipping

Preparation:
1. In three separate plates, spread the flour, egg mixture, and bread crumbs.
2. Preheat the Griddle by turning all its knob to medium-heat setting.
3. Grease the griddle top with cooking oil.
4. Dredge the ravioli in flour, then egg wash, and finally Italian bread crumbs.
5. Mix the Parmesan cheese and parsley in a bowl.
6. Place the ravioli on the hot griddle for 4 minutes per side.
7. Sprinkle with the parsley-cheese mixture.
8. Serve with marinara sauce.

Per Serving: Calories: 685; Fat: 18.3 g; Sodium: 865 mg; Carbs:99.3g; Fiber: 6.5g; Sugar: 7.9g; Protein: 27.6g

Sweet Yogurt Flatbread

Prep time: 5 minutes | Cook time: 10 minutes | Serves: 8

Ingredients:
- 1 cup warm water
- 1 teaspoon sugar
- 1 tablespoon instant dry yeast
- 3 cups all-purpose flour
- ½ cup plain yogurt
- 1 tablespoon olive oil
- 1 teaspoon salt
- Cooking oil, as needed

Preparation:
1. Mix well the warm water, sugar, and yeast in a suitable mixing bowl.
2. Allow 10 minutes for the yeast to activate.
3. Stir until everything is smooth then allow the dough to sit and rise for 1 hour, covered.
4. On a floured surface, roll out the dough.
5. Make eight balls out of the dough. Roll out each into a 14 to 18 inch thick round.
6. Preheat the Griddle by turning all its knob to medium-heat setting.
7. Grease the griddle top with cooking spray.
8. Cook the dough circles on the hot griddle top for 2 minutes per side.
9. Serve warm.

Per Serving: Calories: 213; Fat: 4.1 g; Sodium: 303 mg; Carbs: 37.9g; Fiber: 1.5g; Sugar: 1.9g; Protein: 6.6g

Cinnamon Seed Eggplant

Prep time: 25 minutes | Cook time: 40 minutes | Serves: 6

Ingredients:
For the Mole:
- ¼ cup coriander seeds
- 4 cloves
- 1 cinnamon stick
- 1 cup unsalted peanuts
- ½ cup raw pumpkin seeds (pepitas)
- ½ cup raw sunflower seeds
- 5 chipotle chiles, seeded
- 4 guajillo chiles, seeded
- 3 Passilla chiles, seeded
- 2 ancho chiles, seeded
- 2 oz. dark chocolate

Others
- 1 teaspoon dried oregano
- 1 head roasted garlic; cloves removed
- 1 white or red onion, quartered
- 3 ripe plantains, unpeeled
- ½ ripe pineapple, cored
- ¾ cup apple juice
- ¼ cup apple cider vinegar
- ½ cup honey
- Salt, for seasoning
- 3 large globe eggplants
- Oil, for coating

Preparation:
1. Toast the mole ingredients in a skillet for 1-2 minutes then transfer to a bowl.
2. Preheat the Griddle by turning all its knob to medium-heat setting.
3. Grease the griddle top with cooking spray.
4. Sear onions, pineapple and plantains on the hot griddle top for 3-4 minutes per side.
5. Add mole, honey, apple juice, vinegar and seasoning to the fruits and cook for 15 minutes on low heat.
6. Cut the eggplants in half, brush with oil and cook for 3 minutes per side.
7. Serve the eggplants with the mole mixture.
8. Enjoy.

Per Serving: Calories: 605; Fat: 25.3 g; Sodium: 57 mg; Carbs: 91.5g; Fiber: 16.9g; Sugar: 58g; Protein: 15.7g

Thyme Lemon Cabbage

Prep time: 7 minutes | Cook time: 10 minutes | Serves: 4

Ingredients:
- Salt and black pepper, to taste
- 1 cup vinaigrette
- 1 (2-pound) head green cabbage, cut into wedges
- 1 tablespoon minced fresh thyme
- 2 teaspoons minced shallot
- 2 teaspoons honey
- 1 teaspoon Dijon mustard
- ½ teaspoon grated lemon zest
- 2 tablespoons juice
- 6 tablespoons olive oil

Preparation:
1. Season cabbage wedges evenly with 1 teaspoon salt and set aside for 45 minutes.
2. In a suitable mixing bowl, mix well the shallot, thyme, honey, lemon zest and juice, mustard, and ¼ teaspoon black pepper.
3. Whisk in the oil slowly until it is all incorporated.
4. Preheat the Griddle by turning all its knob to medium-heat setting.
5. Grease the griddle top with cooking oil.
6. Brush half of the vinaigrette on one cut side of the cabbage wedges.
7. Place cabbage on a hot griddle top, and cook for 7 minutes
8. Brush the tops of the wedges with the remaining vinaigrette; flip and cook for 7 minutes.
9. Serve and enjoy.

Per Serving: Calories: 81; Fat: 7.1 g; Sodium: 2 mg; Carbs: 5.5g; Fiber: 0.9g; Sugar: 1g; Protein: 0.5g

Celery Onion Corn Bread

Prep time: 15 minutes | Cook time: 30 minutes | Serves: 8

Ingredients:
- 16 oz. dry corn bread mix
- 2 tablespoons of butter
- 3 stocks of celery, chopped
- 1 onion, diced
- 2 cups of chicken stock
- 2 tablespoons of dried sage
- Black pepper and salt to taste

Preparation:
1. Grease the cooking surface of the griddle with cooking spray.
2. Turn on the 4 burners and turn their knobs to medium heat.
3. Let the Griddle preheat for 5 minutes.
4. Make the cornbread as per the instructions on the box.
5. When the cornbread is done, let it cool.
6. Put the butter on the gas griddle.
7. Add the chopped onions and celery and then let it cook until they start to get soft.
8. Add all the cornbread and use a metal spatula to roughly chop it up.
9. Add the chicken stock about ½ cup at a time to let the corn bread absorb it.
10. Add the sage and black pepper and salt to taste.
11. Continue to cook the stuffing until it starts to brown.
12. Serve.

Per Serving: Calories: 354; Fat: 7.9g; Sodium: 704mg; Carbs: 6g; Fiber 3.6g; Sugar: 6g; Protein: 18g

Savoury Plantains

Prep time: 14 minutes | Cook time: 10 minutes | Serves: 4

Ingredients:
- 2 large ripe plantains, peeled and sliced
- 2 tablespoons vegetable oil
- Salt, to taste

Preparation:
1. Preheat the Griddle by turning all its knob to medium-heat setting.
2. Grease the griddle top with cooking spray.
3. Place plantains in a suitable mixing bowl.
4. Season with oil and salt, and then sear on griddle top for 4 minutes per side.
5. Serve.

Per Serving: Calories: 169; Fat: 7.1 g; Sodium: 42 mg; Carbs: 28.5g; Fiber: 2.1g; Sugar: 13.4g; Protein: 1.2g

Cabbage Bacon Pancake

Prep time: 8 minutes | Cook time: 15 minutes | Serves: 2 to 4

Ingredients:
- 2 cups shredded cabbage
- ¼ cup 1 tablespoon minced green onion
- 2 cups Buttermilk Pancake batter
- 4 strips sliced bacon
- ½ cup barbecue sauce
- ¼ cup hoisin sauce
- ½ cup mayonnaise
- 1 teaspoon mirin
- Black sesame seeds, for garnish

Preparation:
1. Stir the shredded cabbage and green onions into the pancake batter in a suitable mixing bowl.
2. Preheat the Griddle by turning all its knob to medium-heat setting.
3. Grease the griddle top with cooking spray.
4. Cook the bacon in two batches on the hot griddle top for 5 minutes per side.
5. Divide the bacon into parts and top them with 1 cup of the cabbage mixture.
6. Allow the pancake to cook for almost 5 minutes.
7. Flip the pancake and cook for 3 minutes.
8. Mix well the barbecue sauce and hoisin in a small bowl.
9. Stir the mayonnaise and mirin in a separate bowl.
10. Remove the pancakes from the griddle and coat them with a thin layer of hoisin barbecue sauce.
11. Fill a squeeze bottle with the mayonnaise mixture and add mayonnaise to garnish cabbage cakes. Finish with a sprinkling of black sesame seeds and the remaining green onion.
12. Serve warm.

Per Serving: Calories: 539; Fat: 17.5 g; Sodium: 1875 mg; Carbs: 79.2g; Fiber: 4.5g; Sugar: 26.9g; Protein: 15.6g

Arugula and Mushroom Burgers

Prep time: 15 minutes | Cook time: 30 minutes | Serves: 4

Ingredients:
- 4 (4- to 5-inch) Portobello mushroom caps, stems and gills removed
- 1 large red onion, sliced
- 3 tablespoons 1 teaspoon olive oil
- Salt and black pepper, to taste
- 2 garlic cloves, minced
- 2 teaspoons minced fresh thyme
- 2 oz. goat cheese, crumbled
- 4 hamburger buns
- 1 cup baby arugula
- ¼ teaspoon balsamic vinegar
- 1 tomato, cored and sliced thin

Preparation:
1. Lightly score the top of each mushroom cap in a crosshatch pattern with the tip of a sharp knife. Season onion rounds with salt, black pepper and 1 tablespoon oil.
2. In a bowl, whisk together garlic, 2 tablespoons oil, salt, thyme, and 1/4 teaspoon black pepper.
3. Preheat the Griddle by turning all its knob to medium-heat setting.
4. Grease the griddle top with cooking spray.
5. Add onion and mushroom on the hot griddle top and cook until soft.
6. Split the hamburger buns and cook for about 5 minutes.
7. In a suitable mixing bowl, toss the arugula with 1 teaspoon oil, salt and black pepper to taste.
8. Divide vinegar, mushroom caps, arugula, tomato, and onion in the buns.
9. Serve.

Per Serving: Calories: 281; Fat: 15.5 g; Sodium: 262 mg; Carbs: 27.5g; Fiber: 2.2g; Sugar: 5g; Protein: 8.5g

Grilled Bok Choy

Prep time: 15 minutes | Cook time: 6 minutes | Serves: 6

Ingredients:
- ½ cup miso paste
- ½ cup tamari
- 1-tablespoon brown sugar
- 2-teaspoon sesame oil
- 2-teaspoon grated garlic
- 2-teaspoon grated ginger
- 1-teaspoon togarishi seasoning
- 6 baby bok choy, halved

Preparation:
1. Preheat the griddle on medium-high heat and heat the oil.
2. Combine miso, tamari, brown sugar, sesame oil, garlic, ginger, and togarashi seasoning in a mixing bowl.
3. Using salt and pepper, season the bok choy. Cook for 3 minutes on each side on the griddle pan, or until the bok choy is wilted.
4. When done, serve and enjoy.

Per Serving: Calories: 94; Fat: 3.1g; Sodium: 2204mg; Carbs: 11.1g; Fiber: 2.6g; Sugar: 4.2g; Protein: 6.4g

Paprika Cheese Ears Corn

Prep time: 8 minutes | Cook time: 20 minutes | Serves: 2

Ingredients:
- 2 ears corn, shucked
- ½ cup cream cheese, softened
- 1 tablespoon smoked paprika
- ½ cup diced seeded jalapeno
- 6 strips thin-cut bacon

Preparation:
1. Spread cream cheese on the corn.
2. Using a pastry brush, coat each ear of corn in paprika and place it on the cream cheese.
3. Roll the corn through the chopped jalapenos on a chopping board.
4. Wrap a strip of bacon around the corn.
5. Wrap the bacon slices around the ear of corn until it is covered.
6. Preheat the Griddle by turning all its knob to medium-heat setting.
7. Grease the griddle top with cooking spray.
8. Place the bacon-wrapped corn directly on the hot griddle top and cook for 3 minutes per side.
9. Serve warm.

Per Serving: Calories: 398; Fat: 27 g; Sodium: 416mg; Carbs: 34.9g; Fiber: 6.5g; Sugar: 6.9g; Protein: 11.6g

Lemon Mushrooms

Prep time: 8 minutes | Cook time: 13 minutes | Serves: 4 to 6

Ingredients:
- ½ cup olive oil
- 3 tablespoons lemon juice
- 6 garlic cloves, minced
- ¼ teaspoon salt
- 4 Portobello mushrooms (6 inches in diameter), stemmed

Preparation:
1. Mix well the lemon juice, oil, garlic, and salt in a ziplock bag.
2. Toss in the mushrooms, seal the bag, shake well and marinate for 30 minutes.
3. Preheat the Griddle by turning all its knob to medium-heat setting.
4. Grease the griddle top with cooking spray.
5. Pour the egg mixture onto the hot griddle top
6. Cut four 12-inch squares of aluminum foil sheet.
7. Remove the mushrooms from the marinade and lay them, on a foil square.
8. Seal the edges of the foil around each mushroom.
9. Place foil packets on griddle top, sealed side up, and cook for 12 minutes.
10. Unwrap mushrooms with tongs and set on griddle for 60 seconds.
11. Serve.

Per Serving: Calories: 164; Fat: 16.9 g; Sodium: 99 mg; Carbs: 3.2g; Fiber: 0.8g; Sugar: 0.2g; Protein: 2.3g

Steamed Bell Peppers with Vinaigrette

Prep time: 20 minutes | Cook time: 35 minutes | Serves: 4

Ingredients:
- ¼ cup olive oil
- 3 garlic cloves, peeled and smashed
- Salt and black pepper, to taste
- 6 red bell peppers
- 1 tablespoon sherry vinegar

Preparation:
1. Mix well the garlic, oil, ¼ teaspoon black pepper and ½ teaspoon salt.
2. Cut the stems of peppers, remove the cores and seeds.
3. Place the peppers in a bowl and toss them with oil.
4. Wrap aluminum foil around the bowl securely.
5. Preheat the Griddle by turning all its knob to medium-heat setting.
6. Grease the griddle top with cooking spray.
7. Pour the egg mixture onto the hot griddle top
8. Place the peppers on the hot griddle top and cook, for 15 minutes.
9. In a suitable dish, mix well the garlic, vinegar and juices.
10. Remove the peppers from the griddle and place them in a separate bowl, carefully covered with foil. Allow 5 minutes for the peppers to steam.
11. Scrape the charred skin off each pepper with a spoon.
12. Quarter the peppers lengthwise and toss with the vinaigrette in a suitable mixing bowl.
13. Serve with a pinch of salt and black pepper to taste.

Per Serving: Calories: 170; Fat: 13.1 g; Sodium: 6 mg; Carbs: 14.8 g; Fiber: 2.5g; Sugar: 9g; Protein: 1.9g

Chapter 3 Vegetarian and Sides Recipes | 25

Onion and Tomato Sandwich

Prep time: 10 minutes | **Cook time:** 5 minutes | **Serves:** 1

Ingredients:
- 2 bread slices
- 1 onion sliced
- 1 tomato, sliced
- 1-tablespoon butter
- 4 fresh basil leaves
- ½ cup mozzarella cheese, shredded

Preparation:
1. Spread butter on one side of each bread slice.1 slice of bread, topped with tomato, onion, basil, and cheese
2. Cover with the last slice of bread.
3. Preheat the griddle to medium-high heat.
4. Coat the top of the griddle with cooking spray.
5. Place the sandwich on a hot griddle top and cook for 5 minutes, or until both sides are softly golden brown.
6. Serve and have fun.

Per Serving: Calories: 208; Fat: 14.9g; Sodium: 292mg; Carbs: 14.1g; Fiber 1.6g; Sugar: 3.4g; Protein: 6.1g

Healthy Basil Wine Zucchini and Eggplant Salad

Prep time: 14 minutes | **Cook time:** 15 minutes | **Serves:** 4 to 6

Ingredients:
- 3 tablespoons white wine vinegar
- 3 garlic cloves, minced
- 1½ teaspoons Dijon mustard
- Salt and black pepper, to taste
- 6 tablespoons olive oil
- 3 (8-oz. / 227-g) zucchini, halved lengthwise
- 1 red onion, sliced into ½-inch-thick rounds
- 1 red bell pepper, stemmed, seeded, and halved lengthwise
- 1 pound eggplant, sliced into ½-inch-thick rounds
- 3 tablespoons chopped fresh basil
- 1 tablespoon minced fresh parsley

Preparation:
1. In a suitable mixing bowl, mix well the garlic, vinegar, ½ teaspoon salt, mustard, and ½ teaspoon black pepper.
2. Whisk in the oil slowly until. Set aside 2 teaspoons of salad dressing.
3. Toss the onion, zucchini, and bell pepper with the remaining dressing.
4. Preheat the Griddle by turning all its knob to medium-heat setting.
5. Grease the griddle top with cooking oil.
6. Sear eggplant and all the veggies on the hot griddle top for 5-6 minutes per side
7. Toss veggies with leftover dressing, black pepper, salt, basil, and parsley in 1-inch pieces.
8. Serve.

Per Serving: Calories: 178; Fat: 14.6 g; Sodium: 67 mg; Carbs: 12.4g; Fiber: 4.8 g; Sugar: 6.1g; Protein: 2.9 g

Basil Tomato and Zucchini Ratatouille

Prep time: 16 minutes | **Cook time:** 37 minutes | **Serves:** 6 to 8

Ingredients:
- 1 red onion, sliced
- 2 pounds eggplant, sliced
- 1½ pounds zucchini, sliced
- 2 bell peppers, halved, half cut into thirds
- 1 pound tomatoes, cored and halved
- ¼ cup olive oil
- Salt and black pepper, to taste
- 3 tablespoons sherry vinegar
- ¼ cup fresh basil, chopped
- 1 tablespoon fresh thyme, minced
- 1 garlic clove, minced to paste

Preparation:
1. Toss the eggplant, onion, bell peppers, zucchini, and tomatoes with oil, salt and black pepper on a baking sheet.
2. In a suitable mixing bowl, combine ¼ cup oil, basil, vinegar, thyme, and garlic.
3. Preheat the Griddle by turning all its knob to medium-heat setting.
4. Grease the griddle top with cooking oil.
5. Cook onions for 12 minutes, eggplant and squash for 10 minutes, peppers for 9 minutes, and tomatoes for 5 minutes on a griddle.
6. Allow the veggies to cool then chop.
7. Serve warm.

Per Serving: Calories: 161; Fat: 7.3 g; Sodium: 39 mg; Carbs: 24g; Fiber: 9g; Sugar: 12.4g; Protein: 5.9g

Garlic Tofu with Cilantro

Prep time: 13 minutes | **Cook time:** 25 minutes | **Serves:** 4 to 6

Ingredients:
Glaze
- ⅓ cup soy sauce
- ⅓ cup water
- ⅓ cup sugar
- ¼ cup mirin
- 1 tablespoon fresh ginger, grated
- 2 garlic cloves, minced
- 2 teaspoons cornstarch
- 1 teaspoon Asian chili-garlic sauce

Tofu
- 28 oz. firm tofu, sliced
- 2 tablespoons vegetable oil
- Salt and black pepper, to taste
- ¼ cup fresh cilantro, minced

Preparation:
1. Preheat the Griddle by turning all its knob to low-heat setting.
2. Grease the griddle top with cooking oil.
3. Mix water, soy sauce, mirin, sugar, garlic, ginger, cornstarch, and chili-garlic sauce on griddle top.
4. Cook this mixture for 10 minutes on low heat with stirring.
5. Season tofu with oil, black pepper and salt.
6. Place the tofu on the hot griddle top and cook for 5 minutes per side.
7. Serve and enjoy.

Per Serving: Calories: 187; Fat: 10.9 g; Sodium: 2512 mg; Carbs: 12g; Fiber: 1.7 g; Sugar: 4.9g; Protein: 13.7g

Carrot Coleslaw

Prep time: 9 minutes | **Cook time:** 15 minutes | **Serves:** 4

Ingredients:
- ½ (1-pound) head green cabbage, cut into wedges
- 2 tablespoons olive oil
- Salt and black pepper, to taste
- ¼ cup mayonnaise
- 1 shallot, minced
- 4 teaspoons cider vinegar
- 1 carrot, peeled and shredded
- 2 tablespoons minced fresh cilantro

Preparation:
1. Preheat the Griddle by turning all its knob to medium-heat setting.
2. Grease the griddle top with cooking oil.
3. Season the cabbage wedges with salt and black pepper after brushing them with oil.
4. Arrange the cabbage on the hot griddle top. Cook, for 12 minutes until browned.
5. Place cabbage on a plate and cover with aluminum foil to keep it warm.
6. In a suitable mixing bowl, mix shallot, mayonnaise, and vinegar.
7. Remove the core from the cabbage and slice it into thin strips.
8. Mix well the carrot, cabbage, salt, black pepper and cilantro with the mayonnaise.
9. Serve and enjoy.

Per Serving: Calories: 149; Fat: 12 g; Sodium: 132 mg; Carbs: 10.5g; Fiber: 2.6g; Sugar: 4.6g; Protein: 1.5g

Garlic Potato Cubes with Corn and Black Beans

Prep time: 8 minutes | **Cook time:** 20 minutes | **Serves:** 4

Ingredients:
- 3 baked russet potatoes, cut to 1-inch cubes
- ½ cup cooked broccoli florets
- ½ cup cooked diced onion
- 3 cloves garlic, minced
- 1 tablespoon garlic salt
- 1 tablespoon smoked paprika
- 1 teaspoon black pepper
- ½ cup corn
- ½ cup cooked black beans
- ½ cup diced ham
- ½ cup crumbled cooked sausage
- ½ cup diced bacon
- Cooking oil, as needed

Preparation:
1. Preheat the Griddle by turning all its knob to medium-heat setting.
2. Grease the griddle top with cooking spray.
3. Spread the diced potatoes on the griddle top in a single layer and cook for 5 minutes per side.
4. Add the broccoli, onion, and garlic then cook for 5 minutes per side.
5. Stir in smoked paprika, garlic salt, and pepper then cook for almost 12 minutes.
6. Serve warm.

Per Serving: Calories: 399; Fat: 13 g; Sodium: 626 mg; Carbs: 52.9g; Fiber: 8.8g; Sugar: 3.9g; Protein: 19.6g

Delectable Egg Fried Rice with Green Onion

Prep time: 10 minutes | Cook time: 15 minutes | Serves: 2

Ingredients:
2 cups rice, cooked
1 large eggs
1-tablespoon green onion, sliced
1-tablespoon olive oil
½-teaspoon salt

Preparation:
1. In a bowl, whisk together the eggs and leave aside.
2. Heat the griddle to a high temperature.
3. Spray the top of the griddle with cooking spray.
4. Place prepared rice on a heated griddle top and fry until the grains separate.
5. Push the rice to one side of the griddle's surface. Pour a beaten egg into the griddle with some oil.
6. Season with salt and quickly combine the egg with the rice, cooking until the rice grains are completely covered by the egg.
7. Stir in the green onion and cook for 2 minutes.
8. Finally, serve and enjoy.

Per Serving: Calories: 774; Fat: 10.9g; Sodium: 626mg; Carbs: 146g; Fiber 2.6g; Sugar: 0.6g; Protein: 16.8g

Oregano Vegetable Frittata

Prep time: 10 minutes | Cook time: 15 minutes | Serves: 4

Ingredients:
6 large eggs
2 large egg whites
2-tablespoon 2% reduced-; Fat: milk
2 cups packaged vegetables
2-teaspoon oregano
½-teaspoon salt
¼-teaspoon black pepper
¼-teaspoon crushed red pepper
1-ounce Parmesan cheese
2 Yukon Gold potatoes, peeled and diced

Preparation:
1. Preheat the griddle to medium heat the heat the oil.
2. Combine the eggs and egg whites in a mixing dish. Whisk until the mixture is foamy. Mix in the milk and mixing well.
3. Season with oregano, salt, pepper, and crushed red pepper after adding the vegetables.
4. Line the bottom of the griddle pan with potatoes and a steel ring.
5. Pour the egg mixture into the pan and sprinkle with parmesan cheese.
6. Cook for 10 minutes after covering with foil.
7. When done, serve and enjoy.

Per Serving: Calories: 212; Fat: 9.4g; Sodium: 536mg; Carbs: 17.6g; Fiber 1.6g; Sugar: 1.6g; Protein: 15.8g

Garlic Lemon Zucchini Slices with Parsley

Prep time: 15 minutes | Cook time: 05 minutes | Serves: 4

Ingredients:
2 zucchinis, cut into ½-inch-thick slices
1-teaspoon Italian seasoning
2 garlic cloves, minced
¼ cup butter, melted
1 ½-tablespoon fresh parsley, chopped
1-tablespoon fresh lemon juice
Pepper
Salt

Preparation:
1. In a small bowl, combine melted butter, lemon juice, Italian seasoning, garlic, pepper, and salt.
2. Brush the melted butter mixture over the zucchini slices.
3. Preheat the griddle to medium-high.
4. Cook zucchini slices for 2 minutes per side on the griddle top.
5. Place the zucchini slices on a serving platter and top with parsley.
6. Serve and have fun.

Per Serving: Calories: 84; Fat: 8.1g; Sodium: 90mg; Carbs: 2.6g; Fiber 0.6g; Sugar: 1.6g; Protein: 1g

Grilled Bell Pepper and Zucchini

Prep time: 15 minutes | Cook time: 6 minutes | Serves: 4

Ingredients:
1 yellow bell pepper, seeded and sliced
1 red bell pepper, seeded and sliced
1 green bell pepper, seeded and sliced
2 zucchinis, sliced
1 red onion, chopped
½ cup feta cheese
2-tablespoon balsamic vinegar
2-tablespoon olive oil
Salt and pepper to taste

Preparation:
1. Preheat the griddle to medium-high heat and heat the oil.
2. Cook the vegetables for 3 minutes on each side on the griddle pan.
3. Place the cooked veggies in a mixing dish with the other ingredients.
4. Toss to evenly distribute the seasoning throughout the ingredients.
5. Serve.

Per Serving: Calories: 166; Fat: 11.9g; Sodium: 223mg; Carbs: 13.6g; Fiber 2.6g; Sugar: 8.6g; Protein: 5.1g

Basil Tomatoes with Cheese

Prep time: 15 minutes | Cook time: 6 minutes | Serves: 2

Ingredients:
1 cup shredded mozzarella cheese
½ cup shredded basil
4 Roma tomatoes, halved and pitted

Preparation:
1. Preheat the griddle to medium heat and heat the oil.
2. In a mixing dish, combine the mozzarella cheese and basil.
3. Using the parmesan cheese mixture, stuff the tomatoes.
4. Cook the stuffed tomatoes for 6 minutes on the griddle.

Per Serving: Calories: 84; Fat: 3g; Sodium: 97 mg; Carbs: 10.2g; Fiber 3.1g; Sugar: 6.5g; Protein: 6.8g

Sesame Pineapple Fried Rice

Prep time: 05 minutes | Cook time: 15 minutes | Serves: 2

Ingredients:
3 cups cooked brown rice
½ cup frozen corn
2 carrots, peeled and grated
1 onion, diced
2 garlic cloves, minced
2-tablespoon olive oil
½-teaspoon ginger powder
1-tablespoon sesame oil
3-tablespoon soy sauce
¼ cup green onion, sliced
½ cup ham, diced
2 cups pineapple, diced
½ cup frozen peas

Preparation:
1. Whisk together soy sauce, ginger powder, sesame oil and olive oil in a small bowl and set aside.
2. Heat the griddle to a high temperature.
3. Pour oil on top of the hot griddle.
4. For 3-4 minutes, stir-fry the onion and garlic. Stir in the corn, carrots, and peas continually for 3-4 minutes.
5. Stir in the cooked rice, green onions, peas, ham, pineapple, and soy sauce mixture for 2- minutes while constantly stirring.
6. Finally, serve and enjoy.

Per Serving: Calories: 741; Fat: 16.1g; Sodium: 944mg; Carbs: 134.1g; Fiber 9.6g; Sugar: 12.6g; Protein: 18.1g

Vinegar Coleslaw with Mayo Dressing

Prep time: 15 minutes | Cook time: 30 minutes | Serves: 4

Ingredients:
For the coleslaw:
1 head shredded green cabbage
1 cup shredded carrots
For the dressing
⅛ cup white wine vinegar
1-tablespoon celery seed
1-½ cups mayonnaise
2 thinly sliced scallions
1 head shredded purple cabbage
1-teaspoon sugar
Salt and pepper, to taste

Preparation:
1. Preheat the griddle to low heat.
2. Cook the vegetables for around 25 minutes on the grill.
3. When done, place it in the refrigerator to chill after cooling under the room temperature.
4. To make the dressing:
5. In a small mixing basin, combine all of the ingredients.
6. Place the cabbage and carrot in a large mixing dish.
7. Drizzle the dressing over it and whisk to thoroughly cover it.
8. Serve in a serving dish with scallions on top.
9. Remove from the griddle and serve.

Per Serving: Calories: 344; Fat: 10.9g; Sodium: 504mg; Carbs: 39.6g; Fiber 10g; Sugar: 17.6g; Protein: 5.8g

Chapter 3 Vegetarian and Sides Recipes | 27

Grilled Thyme Zucchini

Prep time: 15 minutes | Cook time: 15 minutes | Serves: 6

Ingredients:
4 midsized zucchinis
2 springs thyme with the leaves pulled out
1-tablespoon sherry vinegar
2-tablespoon Olive oil
Salt and pepper as per your taste

Preparation:
1. Remove the zucchini ends and slice them off. Now cut each one in half, and then each half into thirds.
2. Place all of the leftover ingredients in a medium zip lock bag, followed by the spears.
3. Toss everything in a bowl and toss it around to coat the zucchini.
4. Preheat the Griddle to medium-high heat.
5. Place the spears immediately on the grill grate after removing them from the bag. Make sure the side you're working with is facing down.
6. Cook for 3 to 4 minutes per side, or until the zucchini is soft.
7. Remove from the griddle and garnish with additional thyme leaves if desired.
8. Serve and savor.
Per Serving: Calories: 64; Fat: 4.9g; Sodium: 14mg; Carbs: 4.6g; Fiber 1.6g; Sugar: 2.6g; Protein: 1.8g

Garlicky Tomatoes

Prep time: 15 minutes | Cook time: 05 minutes | Serves: 3

Ingredients:
1 cup Roma tomatoes, halved
1 clove garlic, minced
A drizzle olive oil
3-tablespoon olive oil

Preparation:
1. Preheat the griddle on medium heat and then heat the oil.
2. Toss the remaining ingredients together in a bowl to coat them.
3. Cook for 5 minutes on the preheated griddle with the tomatoes.
4. When cooked, serve and enjoy.
Per Serving: Calories: 132; Fat: 14.1 g; Sodium: 4mg; Carbs: 2.6g; Fiber 0.6g; Sugar: 1.6g; Protein: 0.8g

Garlic Thyme Mushrooms

Prep time: 15 minutes | Cook time: 10 minutes | Serves: 2

Ingredients:
10 oz. mushrooms, sliced
¼ cup olive oil
1-tablespoon garlic, minced
¼-teaspoon dried thyme
Pepper
Salt

Preparation:
1. Heat the griddle to high temperature.
2. Pour 2 tablespoons of oil onto the hot griddle surface.
3. Add the mushrooms, garlic, dried thyme, pepper, and salt to the griddle and cook until the mushrooms are soft.
4. Finish with a drizzle of the remaining oil and serve.
Per Serving: Calories: 254; Fat: 27.9g; Sodium: 74mg; Carbs: 6.2g; Fiber 1.6g; Sugar: 2.6g; Protein: 4.8g

Gold Potato Hobo Packs

Prep time: 16 minutes | Cook time: 30 minutes | Serves: 4

Ingredients:
2 pounds Yukon Gold potatoes, unpeeled
1 tablespoon olive oil
2 garlic cloves, peeled and chopped
1 teaspoon minced fresh thyme
1 teaspoon salt
½ teaspoon black pepper

Preparation:
1. Halve each potato lengthwise, then cut each half into eight wedges.
2. Microwave potatoes in large bowl, covered, for 7 minutes. Drain thoroughly.
3. Toss the potatoes in a bowl with the oil, garlic, thyme, salt, and pepper.
4. Cut four sheets of heavy-duty aluminum foil into 14 by 10-inch rectangles.
5. Spread one-quarter of the potato mixture over half of the foil, fold foil and crimp edges tightly to seal.
6. Preheat the Griddle by turning all its knob to medium-heat setting.
7. Grease the griddle top with cooking spray.
8. Place hobo packs on the hot griddle top and cook, for 10 minutes.
9. Serve.
Per Serving: Calories: 98; Fat: 3.7 g; Sodium: 591 mg; Carbs: 16g; Fiber: 1.4 g; Sugar: 0.6g; Protein: 1.9g

Rosemary Red Potatoes

Prep time: 18 minutes | Cook time: 20 minutes | Serves: 4

Ingredients:
¼ cup olive oil
9 garlic cloves, minced
1 teaspoon chopped fresh rosemary
Salt and black pepper, to taste
2 pounds small red potatoes, halved
2 tablespoons chopped fresh chives

Preparation:
1. Preheat the Griddle by turning all its knob to medium-heat setting.
2. Grease the griddle top with cooking spray.
3. Pour the egg mixture onto the hot griddle top
4. On a griddle, heat the oil, garlic, rosemary, and ½ teaspoon salt until they sizzle, about 3 minutes.
5. Reduce heat to medium-low and simmer for another 3 minutes, or until garlic is light blond. Pour the mixture into a small bowl through a fine-mesh strainer, pressing on the particles.
6. In a suitable mixing bowl, combine 1 tablespoon solids and 1 tablespoon oil and put aside. Discard the leftover particles, but keep the oil.
7. Arrange skewered potatoes in a single layer on a large platter, poking each potato with a skewer several times. Season with salt and 1 tablespoon of strained oil. Microwave for 8 minutes, or until potatoes are slightly resistant when punctured with a paring knife, flipping halfway through.
8. Place potatoes on a griddle that has been coated with 1 tablespoon of strained oil. Season with salt and black pepper to taste after brushing with the remaining 1 tablespoon strained oil.
9. Pour the oil onto the griddle and preheat to medium-high heat.
10. Cook the potatoes on the hot griddle top for 3 to 5 minutes, flipping halfway through. Reduce the heat to medium-low on the hot griddle top. Cover and cook for another 5 to 8 minutes, or until a paring knife easily slides in and out of the potatoes.
11. Remove the potatoes from the skewers and place them in a suitable mixing dish with the garlic-oil mixture that was set aside. Toss in the chives, season to taste with salt and black pepper, and toss until evenly covered.
12. Serve and enjoy.
Per Serving: Calories: 278; Fat: 13 g; Sodium: 15 mg; Carbs: 38.5g; Fiber: 4.2g; Sugar: 2.4g; Protein: 4.8g

Cheese Buffalo Turds

Prep time: 15 minutes | Cook time: 20 minutes | Serves: 10

Ingredients:
8 ounces cream cheese
10 medium jalapeno peppers
¾ cup of cheddar cheese
Monterey jack blend and shredded
1 teaspoon of smoked paprika
1 teaspoon of garlic powder
½ teaspoon of red pepper flakes
20 little smokies sausages
10 bacon strips, sliced and halved

Preparation:
1. Wash the jalapenos, then slice them up along the length.
2. Get a spoon or a paring knife if you prefer, and use that to take out the seeds and the veins.
3. Place the scooped-out jalapenos on a griddling veggies tray and put it all aside.
4. Mix the shredded cheese, cream cheese, paprika, cayenne pepper, garlic powder, and red pepper flakes in a suitable bowl.
5. Take jalapenos then stuff them with the cream cheese mixture.
6. Get little smokies sausage, and then put it right onto each of the cheese-stuffed jalapenos.
7. Grab some of the sliced and halved bacon strips and wrap them around each of the stuffed jalapenos.
8. Use toothpicks to keep the bacon nicely secured to the sausage.
9. Grease the cooking surface of the griddle with cooking spray.
10. Turn on the 4 burners and turn their knobs to medium heat.
11. Let the Griddle preheat for 5 minutes.
12. Put your jalapeno peppers on the griddle top and then let it cook for 20 minutes while flipping after every 5 minutes.
13. Serve.
Per Serving: Calories: 327; Fat: 22g; Sodium: 421mg; Carbs: 10g; Fiber 4.1g; Sugar: 2g; Protein: 31g

Grilled Dijon Artichokes

Prep time: 15 minutes | Cook time: 30 minutes | Serves: 6

Ingredients:
- 6 whole artichokes
- ½-gallon water
- 3-tablespoon sea salt
- Sea salt to taste
- Olive oil
- ¼ cup raw honey
- ¼ cup boiling water
- 3 Tbsp. Dijon mustard

Preparation:
1. Top to bottom, cut the artichokes in half lengthwise.
2. Combine 3-tablespoon sea salt and 3-tablespoon water in a mixing bowl. Before cooking, soak the artichokes in the brine for 30 minutes to several hours.
3. Preheat the griddle to medium heat.
4. Remove the artichokes from the brine and season with the remaining sea salt and a drizzle of olive oil on the cut side.
5. Grill for 15 minutes on each side, starting with the cut side down.
6. Reduce the heat to low and place the artichokes cut-side down on the grill while you prepare the honey, boiling water, and Dijon.
7. Brush the Dijon mixture over the cut side of the artichokes until it is completely absorbed.
8. Serve alongside a ; Protein: like salmon, beef, pork, or chicken, or as a vegetarian option with rice or potatoes.

Per Serving: Calories: 98; Fat: 2.6g; Sodium: 3704mg; Carbs: 18.6g; Fiber 1.3g; Sugar: 12.6g; Protein: 2.8g

Green Beans with Sesame Seed

Prep time: 15 minutes | Cook time: 10 minutes | Serves: 6

Ingredients:
- 1 ½ pounds green beans, trimmed
- 1 ½-tablespoon rice vinegar
- 3-tablespoon soy sauce
- 1 ½-tablespoon sesame oil
- 2-tablespoon sesame seeds, toasted
- 1 ½-tablespoon brown sugar
- ¼-teaspoon black pepper

Preparation:
1. Green beans should be cooked for 3 minutes in boiling water and then drained properly.
2. Drain the green beans and return them to the cold ice water. Green beans should be patted dry.
3. Preheat the griddle to medium-high.
4. Oil the top of the heated griddle.
5. Stir in the green beans for 2 minutes.
6. Stir in the soy sauce, brown sugar, vinegar, and pepper for another 2 minutes.
7. Toss in the sesame seeds and coat thoroughly.
8. Serve and enjoy.

Per Serving: Calories: 98; Fat: 5g; Sodium: 459mg; Carbs: 11.6g; Fiber 4.6g; Sugar: 3.6g; Protein: 3.1g

Salty Sweet Potatoes

Prep time: 05 minutes | Cook time: 15 minutes | Serves: 2

Ingredients:
- 2 Sweet Potatoes
- Olive Oil
- Sea Salt to Taste

Preparation:
1. Cut the sweet potatoes lengthwise in half.
2. Season the sweet potato generously with sea salt after brushing it with olive oil.
3. Preheat the Griddle to high heat and cook the sweet potatoes for 5–7 minutes, cut-side down.
4. Turn the sweet potatoes over and continue to cook over medium heat until they are tender.
5. Before serving, let the potatoes rest for a few minutes.

Per Serving: Calories: 207; Fat: 7.9g; Sodium: 704mg; Carbs: 6g; Fiber 3.6g; Sugar: 6g; Protein: 18g

Garlic Cabbage in Soy Sauce

Prep time: 15 minutes | Cook time: 05 minutes | Serves: 8

Ingredients:
- 2 cabbage heads,
- 4 green onions, sliced
- 2-tablespoon ginger, minced
- 4 garlic cloves, minced
- 2-tablespoon soy sauce
- 1-tablespoon vinegar
- 8 dried chilies
- 4-tablespoon olive oil
- 1-teaspoon salt

Preparation:
1. Preheat the griddle to medium-high heat.
2. Oil the top of the heated griddle.
3. Sauté for 2-3 minutes with the ginger, garlic, and green onion.
4. Sauté for 30 seconds after adding the dried chilies.
5. Stir in the cabbage, vinegar, soy sauce, and salt for 1-2 minutes over high heat, or until the cabbage has wilted.
6. Cook the remaining half of ingredients with the same steps.
7. Serve and have fun.

Per Serving: Calories: 118; Fat: 7.3g; Sodium: 551mg; Carbs: 16g; Fiber 5g; Sugar: 6.2g; Protein: 2.8g

Garlic Cauliflower in BBQ Sauce

Prep time: 15 minutes | Cook time: 6 minutes | Serves: 3

Ingredients:
- 1 medium cauliflower head, cut into florets then blanched
- 1-teaspoon garlic powder
- ½-teaspoon salt
- Ground pepper for taste
- ½ cup BBQ sauce

Preparation:
1. Preheat the griddle to medium heat and heat the oil.
2. Toss all of the ingredients together in a basin to coat the cauliflower in the sauce.
3. Grill the cauliflower for 3 minutes on each side on the griddle.
4. When done, serve and enjoy.

Per Serving: Calories: 354; Fat: 7.9g; Sodium: 704mg; Carbs: 6g; Fiber 3.6g; Sugar: 6g; Protein: 18g

Lemon Pepper Vegetables

Prep time: 05 minutes | Cook time: 15 minutes | Serves: 8

Ingredients:
- 4 zucchinis, sliced
- 2 eggplants, sliced
- 6 Roma tomatoes, sliced
- 24 mini peppers
- 16-ounce Brussels sprouts
- 4 lemons, juiced
- ½ cup olive oil
- 1-teaspoon sumac
- Salt and pepper

Preparation:
1. Preheat the griddle to medium heat and heat the oil.
2. Toss the first five ingredients together in a basin to coat the veggies in spice.
3. For each side, grill for 3 to 5 minutes.
4. Meanwhile, combine the lemon juice, olive oil, sumac, salt, and pepper in a mixing bowl.
5. Serve and enjoy.

Per Serving: Calories: 277; Fat: 13.9g; Sodium: 31mg; Carbs: 36g; Fiber 12.6g; Sugar: 18.6g; Protein: 8.4g

Paprika Lemon Eggplant

Prep time: 5 minutes | Cook time: 10 minutes | Serves: 2

Ingredients:
- ½ large eggplant, cut into ½-inch slices
- ½-tablespoon salt
- 2-tablespoon olive oil
- 2 ounces' feta cheese, crumbled
- ½-teaspoon sweet paprika
- ½-teaspoon Freshly ground black pepper
- ½ lemon, cut in half

Preparation:
1. Getting the ingredients ready.
2. Sprinkle half of the salt over the eggplant slices on a rimmed baking sheet. Toss the pieces in the remaining salt and turn them over. Allow 15 minutes for the bitterness of the eggplant to dissipate.
3. Place the slices on paper towels to absorb any excess moisture.
4. Preheat your Griddle to medium-high.
5. Allow the griddle to heat until the oil is glistening but not smoking.
6. Spray the eggplant parts with olive oil on equally sides. Grill the slices for 6 minutes, or until golden brown and grill marks form.
7. On a serving platter, combine the eggplant, feta, paprika, pepper, and a squeeze of lemon juice.
8. Serve warm or at room temperature.

Per Serving: Calories: 200; Fat: 17.9g; Sodium: 2004mg; Carbs: 9.6g; Fiber 4.6g; Sugar: 5g; Protein: 5.8g

Paprika Potatoes

Prep time: 10 minutes | Cook time: 45 minutes | Serves: 2

Ingredients:
4 Yellow Potatoes
½-teaspoon Olive Oil
Sea Salt and Black Pepper to
Taste
½-teaspoon Paprika

Preparation:
1. Peel the potatoes and cut them in half lengthwise into a big bag or dish.
2. Drizzle the potatoes with olive oil and toss or shake them to coat them.
3. Season to taste with salt, pepper, and paprika, and whisk or shake until thoroughly blended.
4. Spray the Griddle with oil and preheat it to medium heat.
5. Place the potatoes on the grill, sliced-side down, for several minutes, or until grill marks appear and the cut side feels soft.
6. Cook until the potatoes are totally cooked, then flip them.
7. Turn off the heat and serve.
Per Serving: Calories: 354; Fat: 7.9g; Sodium: 704mg; Carbs: 6g; Fiber 3.6g; Sugar: 6g; Protein: 18g

Lemon Wilted Spinach

Prep time: 15 minutes | Cook time: 1 minutes | Serves: 4

Ingredients:
8 ounces' fresh baby spinach
1-tablespoon olive oil
¼-teaspoon garlic powder
¼-teaspoon salt
1 lemon, halved

Preparation:
1. Getting the ingredients ready.
2. Toss the spinach with the olive oil, garlic powder, and salt in a medium mixing bowl.
3. Preheat your Griddle to medium-high heat.
4. Allow the griddle to heat until the oil is glistening but not smoking.
5. Grill for 30 seconds after spreading the spinach in an even layer across the grill.
6. The leaves should wilt but still have some firmness.
7. Transfer to a serving bowl and garnish with a squeeze of lemon juice.
8. Serve right away.
Per Serving: Calories: 44; Fat: 3.9g; Sodium: 192mg; Carbs: 3.6g; Fiber 1.6g; Sugar: 0.6g; Protein: 1.8g

Simple Cooked Ears Corn

Prep time: 6 minutes | Cook time: 13 minutes | Serves: 4 to 6

Ingredients:
8 ears corn, husks and silk removed
2 tablespoons vegetable oil
Salt and black pepper, to taste

Preparation:
1. Preheat the Griddle by turning all its knob to medium-heat setting.
2. Grease the griddle top with cooking oil.
3. Pour the egg mixture onto the hot griddle top
4. Season corn with oil, black pepper and salt.
5. Place corn on the hot griddle top and cook for 9 minutes until lightly golden on all sides.
6. Cover and cook for 3 minutes.
7. Serve the corn.
Per Serving: Calories: 216; Fat: 6.9 g; Sodium: 31 mg; Carbs: 38.5g; Fiber: 5.6g; Sugar: 6.7g; Protein: 6.7g

Grilled Squash

Prep time: 15 minutes | Cook time: 10 minutes | Serves: 12

Ingredients:
1 Summer Squash
2-tablespoon Olive Oil
Sea Salt and pepper, to Taste

Preparation:
1. Cut the squash lengthwise in half. Season the squash with salt and pepper after brushing it with olive oil.
2. Preheat the Griddle to medium heat and place the squash cut-side down on the grill.
3. Cook for 5 minutes on each side, or until tender.
4. Turn off the heat and serve.
Per Serving: Calories: 44; Fat: 4.7g; Sodium: 40mg; Carbs: 0.6g; Fiber 0.6g; Sugar: 0.6g; Protein: 0.8g

Cheese Cauliflower Cakes

Prep time: 10 minutes | Cook time: 25 minutes | Serves: 6

Ingredients:
2 eggs
½ cup breadcrumbs
1 cauliflower head, cut into florets
¼-teaspoon cayenne
½ cup cheddar cheese, shredded
¼ cup onion, chopped
Pepper
Salt

Preparation:
1. Boil cauliflower florets for 15 minutes or until tender in a pot of boiling water.
2. Place the cauliflower florets in a mixing basin after thoroughly draining them. Cauliflower florets should be mashed.
3. Toss in the other ingredients and stir until fully blended.
4. Heat the griddle to a high temperature.
5. Spray the top of the griddle with cooking spray.
6. Form patties from the mixture and fry for 4-5 minutes on each side on a hot griddle top.
7. Finally, serve and enjoy.
Per Serving: Calories: 104; Fat: 5.1 g; Sodium: 186mg; Carbs: 9.6g; Fiber 1.6g; Sugar: 2g; Protein: 6.8g

Chapter 4 Snack, Dessert and Appetizer Recipes

Honey Nectarines Topped with Blackberries

Prep time: 15 minutes | Cook time: 3 minutes | Serves: 2

Ingredients:
2 tablespoons honey
2 large ripe nectarines, quartered
½ teaspoon ground cinnamon
1 pint blackberries, blueberries, raspberries
¼ cup mascarpone

Preparation:
1. Spoon the honey into a small shallow baking dish.
2. Dip the nectarine sections into the honey and then sprinkle the flesh side with the cinnamon.
3. Grease the cooking surface of the griddle with cooking spray.
4. Turn on the 4 burners and turn their knobs to medium heat.
5. Let the Griddle preheat for 5 minutes.
6. Griddle the nectarines, flesh side down, for about 3 minutes, until the flesh is crisp, hot, and browned.
7. Serve the nectarines in shallow bowls, topped with the berries and a spoonful of mascarpone.
8. Serve.

Per Serving: Calories: 338; Fat: 12g; Sodium: 521mg; Carbs: 14g; Fiber 5.1g; Sugar: 3g; Protein: 27g

Gorgonzola Pear Bowls with Craisins

Prep time: 15 minutes | Cook time: 8 minutes | Serves: 3

Ingredients:
3 pears, ripe but firm
2 cups baby arugula
½ cup crumbled gorgonzola cheese
¼ cup honey
¼ cup craisins
¼ cup candied walnuts
1 tablespoon olive oil
1½ teaspoon ground cinnamon

Preparation:
1. Grease the cooking surface of the griddle with cooking oil.
2. Turn on the 4 burners and turn their knobs to medium heat.
3. Let the Griddle preheat for 5 minutes.
4. Cut each pear in ½, remove the core, and dig suitable bowl in each pear with a melon baller.
5. Coat each pear ½ with a light drizzle of olive oil.
6. Place pears cut side down over the heat.
7. Fill each pear bowl with a heaping portion of gorgonzola cheese.
8. Remove from griddle and plate each pear ½ on a bed of baby arugula.
9. Drizzle with honey, dust with cinnamon, and garnish with craisins and candied walnuts.
10. Serve.

Per Serving: Calories: 428; Fat: 11g; Sodium: 501mg; Carbs: 16g; Fiber 2.1g; Sugar: 2.2g; Protein: 27g

Garlic Cauliflower Skewers

Prep time: 15 minutes | Cook time: 15 minutes | Serves: 6

Ingredients:
1 large cauliflower head, cut into florets
1 onion, cut into wedges
1 yellow bell pepper, cut into squares
1 fresh lemon juice
3 teaspoon curry powder
¼ cup olive oil
½ teaspoon garlic powder
½ teaspoon ground ginger
½ teaspoon salt

Preparation:
1. Grease the cooking surface of the griddle with cooking spray.
2. Turn on the 4 burners and turn their knobs to medium heat.
3. Let the Griddle preheat for 5 minutes.
4. In a suitable bowl, whisk together oil, lemon juice, garlic powder, ginger, curry powder, and salt.
5. Toss in cauliflower florets and mix until well coated.
6. Thread cauliflower florets, onion, and bell pepper onto the skewers.
7. Place skewers onto the preheated griddle top and then let it cook for 6-7 minutes on each side.
8. Serve.

Per Serving: Calories: 381; Fat: 21g; Sodium: 561mg; Carbs: 21g; Fiber 6.1g; Sugar: 5g; Protein: 32g

S'mores Toast

Prep time: 15 minutes | Cook time: 15 minutes | Serves: 4

Ingredients:
½ cup sugar
1 tablespoon cinnamon
4 slices bread
¼ cup margarine
15 baby marshmallows
1 (4.4-oz.) Chocolate bar

Preparation:
1. Grease the cooking surface of the griddle with cooking spray.
2. Turn on the 4 burners and turn their knobs to medium heat.
3. Let the Griddle preheat for 5 minutes.
4. Combine sugar and cinnamon in a suitable bowl.
5. Spread margarine over one side of each slice of bread. Sprinkle with cinnamon and sugar mixture.
6. Arrange 2 slices of bread onto the griddle, margarine side down.
7. Cover each slice with marshmallows and ½ of the chocolate bar.
8. Top with remaining 2 slices of bread. Use griddle press to cook on both sides, 3 minutes per side.
9. Serve.

Per Serving: Calories: 377; Fat: 15g; Sodium: 521mg; Carbs: 14g; Fiber 5.1g; Sugar: 3g; Protein: 27g

Honey Walnut Figs

Prep time: 15 minutes | Cook time: 10 minutes | Serves: 4

Ingredients:
8 ripe figs, stemmed
2 tablespoons walnut oil
8 walnut halves, toasted
¼ cup honey

Preparation:
1. Brush the figs with the walnut oil, then cut an x in the stem ends. Push 1 walnut ½ into each fig.
2. Grease the cooking surface of the griddle with cooking oil.
3. Turn on the 4 burners and turn their knobs to medium heat.
4. Let the Griddle preheat for 5 minutes.
5. Put the figs on the griddle grate, stem side up, and then let it cook until the fruit softens, 5 to 10 minutes.
6. Transfer to a platter, drizzle with the honey, and serve.
7. Serve.

Per Serving: Calories: 304; Fat: 14.9g; Sodium: 304mg; Carbs: 12g; Fiber 6g; Sugar: 2g; Protein: 21g

Cocoa Vanilla Pies

Prep time: 15 minutes | Cook time: 15 minutes | Serves: 8

Ingredients:
⅓ cup cocoa powder
1½ cup flour
1 teaspoon baking soda
½ teaspoon salt
¾ cup buttermilk
¾ cup butter
¾ cup brown sugar
1 egg
½ teaspoon vanilla extract
Marshmallow cream filling

Preparation:
1. Grease the cooking surface of the griddle with cooking spray.
2. Turn on the 4 burners and turn their knobs to medium heat.
3. Let the Griddle preheat for 5 minutes.
4. In a suitable bowl, sift the cocoa powder, flour, baking soda, and salt.
5. In an electric mixer, cream the buttermilk, butter, and brown sugar together.
6. Stir in the egg and vanilla. Slowly add the flour mixture to the creamed ingredients. Blend.
7. Arrange 8 ¼ cup scoops of cake mix onto the griddle pan.
8. Bake 12-15 minutes or until done. Repeat step 6 to make second batch of cake halves.
9. In the mixer, cream the butter and confectioners' sugar together until creamy.
10. Add the marshmallow and vanilla. Place the marshmallow cream in a piping bag and fill the whoopie pies.
11. Serve.

Per Serving: Calories: 318; Fat: 15g; Sodium: 521mg; Carbs: 14g; Fiber 5.1g; Sugar: 3g; Protein: 27g

Colada Tacos

Prep time: 15 minutes | Cook time: 15 minutes | Serves: 4

Ingredients:
½ ripe pineapple, peeled, cored, and cubed
¼ cup dark rum
¼ cup coconut milk
4 tablespoons (½ stick) butter, softened
4 7-inch flour tortillas
1 tablespoon sugar, or as needed
lime wedges for serving
½ cup shredded coconut, toasted

Preparation:
1. Grease the cooking surface of the griddle with cooking spray.
2. Turn on the 4 burners and turn their knobs to medium heat.
3. Let the Griddle preheat for 5 minutes.
4. Put the pineapple, rum, and coconut milk in a suitable bowl and toss to combine.
5. Let the fruit macerate for at least 20 minutes, or up to several hours in the refrigerator.
6. Spread the butter on both sides of the tortillas, then sprinkle with the sugar.
7. Thread the pineapple cubes onto 4 skewers, letting excess marinade drip back in the bowl.
8. Put the skewers on the griddle and then let it cook until the pineapple is caramelized, 5 to 8 minutes per side.
9. Transfer the skewers to a platter. Put the tortillas on the griddle, and then let it cook, for 1 to 2 minutes per side.
10. Put a skewer on top of each tortilla, squeeze with some lime and sprinkle with toasted coconut.
11. Serve.
Per Serving: Calories: 392; Fat: 31g; Sodium: 501mg; Carbs: 16g; Fiber 2.1g; Sugar: 2.2g; Protein: 28g

French Fruit Stuffed Toast

Prep time: 15 minutes | Cook time: 15 minutes | Serves: 2

Ingredients:
2 French bread loaves, cut into
Custard
¼ cup milk
1 egg
juice of ½ blood orange
3 strawberries, stemmed and
Filling
¼ cup mascarpone
zest of 1 blood orange
1 teaspoon Real maple syrup
1-inch slices
hulled
1 pinch of ground cloves
¼ teaspoon Vanilla
1 pinch of sea salt
Sliced strawberries
Powdered sugar

Preparation:
1. Grease the cooking surface of the griddle with cooking spray.
2. Turn on the 4 burners and turn their knobs to medium heat.
3. Let the Griddle preheat for 5 minutes.
4. Mix the custard ingredients together in a suitable blender, and set aside in a suitable bowl.
5. Stir the mascarpone, blood orange zest, and maple syrup together in a suitable bowl.
6. Add the mascarpone mixture and the sliced strawberries between 2 slices of French bread.
7. Dip the outsides of the sandwich in the custard and drip the remaining custard off.
8. Cook for 5–6 minutes on the griddle until the custard is lightly golden brown and the bread is golden.
9. Dust with powdered sugar and serve.
10. Serve.
Per Serving: Calories: 304; Fat: 14.9g; Sodium: 304mg; Carbs: 12g; Fiber 6g; Sugar: 2g; Protein: 21g

Sugared Peaches with Ginger Ice Cream

Prep time: 15 minutes | Cook time: 25 minutes | Serves: 4

Ingredients:
1 pint vanilla ice cream
¼ cup chopped candied ginger
4 ripe peaches
4 tablespoons butter, melted
¼ cup demerara sugar
Fresh mint sprigs for garnish

Preparation:
1. Mix the ice cream and ginger in a suitable bowl and mash together with a spoon.
2. Put it back in the ice cream container and freeze at least a couple hours.
3. Grease the cooking surface of the griddle with cooking spray.
4. Turn on the 4 burners and turn their knobs to medium heat.
5. Let the Griddle preheat for 5 minutes.
6. Cut the peaches in ½ through the stem end and remove the pits.
7. Brush with the melted butter. Put the sugar on a plate and dredge the cut side of each peach in it.
8. Put the peaches on the griddle, cut side up, and then let it cook until they soften, 10 to 15 minutes.
9. Turn them cut side down and then let it cook until the sugar caramelizes to a golden brown, 2 to 5 minutes.
10. Transfer to a platter. To serve, put the warm peaches on plates or in dessert bowls, cut side up.
11. Divide the ice cream between them, or pass the ice cream at the table. Garnish with the mint.
12. Serve.
Per Serving: Calories: 326; Fat: 13g; Sodium: 421mg; Carbs: 16g; Fiber 4.1g; Sugar: 3.2g; Protein: 27g

Mayonnaise Bacon Patties

Prep time: 10 minutes | Cook time: 15 minutes | Serves 2

Ingredients:
1 pound (454 g) ground beef (80% lean)
½ teaspoon of garlic salt
½ teaspoon salt
½ teaspoon of garlic
½ teaspoon onion
½ teaspoon black pepper
6 bacon slices, cut in half
½ cup mayonnaise
2 teaspoons of creamy wasabi (optional)
6 (1 ounce / 28-g) sliced sharp cheddar cheese, cut in half (optional)
sliced red onion
½ cup sliced kosher dill pickles
12 mini breads sliced horizontally
ketchup

Preparation:
1. In a medium mixing bowl, combine the ground beef, garlic salt, seasoned salt, garlic powder, onion powder, and black hupe pepper.
2. Divide the beef mixture into 12 equal portions and form into small thin round patties (about 2 ounces each).
3. Cook the bacon for 5-8 minutes over medium heat, until it is crispy. Remove from the equation.
4. In a small bowl, combine the mayonnaise and horseradish, if using, to make the sauce.
5. Preheat the griddle to 350 degrees Fahrenheit. The temperature of the griddle should be around 400 degrees Fahrenheit.
6. For the greatest non-stick results, apply a cooking spray on the griddle cooking surface. Griddle the putty for 3-4 minutes on each side, or until it reaches 160°F inside.
7. If desired, put a slice of sharp cheddar cheese on each patty while it is still on the griddle or after it has been removed.
8. In the lower half of each roll, spread a tiny amount of mayonnaise mixture, a slice of red onion, and a hamburger pate. Ketchup, pickled slices, and bacon.
9. Enjoy.
Per Serving: Calories: 1138; Fat: 80.3g; Sodium: 2074mg; Carbs: 16g; Fiber 0.6g; Sugar: 5.8g; Protein: 81.8g

Banana and Strawberry Pizza

Prep time: 15 minutes | Cook time: 8 minutes | Serves: 8

Ingredients:
1 (8-oz.) Thin crust pizza dough
¼ cup caramel sauce
2 bananas, sliced and
8 strawberries, halved and
2 tablespoons Chocolate sauce

Preparation:
1. Grease the cooking surface of the griddle with cooking spray.
2. Turn on the 4 burners and turn their knobs to medium heat.
3. Let the Griddle preheat for 5 minutes.
4. Arrange pizza dough to fit onto the griddle pan. Cook on both sides to desired doneness.
5. Spread caramel sauce over the pizza. Layer with bananas and strawberries.
6. Spry with chocolate and raspberry sauces. Top with peanuts.
7. Add 2 tablespoons Raspberry sauce ¼ cup peanuts, chopped on each slice.
8. Sprinkling toasted coconut or crumbled graham crackers will add extra flavor and crunch!
9. Serve.
Per Serving: Calories: 317; Fat: 32g; Sodium: 311mg; Carbs: 12g; Fiber 3.1g; Sugar: 4g; Protein: 22g

Doughnut with Vanilla Ice Cream

Prep time: 15 minutes | Cook time: 10 minutes | Serves: 4

Ingredients:
- 4 apple cider doughnuts, sliced in ½
- 2 pears, halved, cored and sliced
- 4 cups vanilla ice cream
- ½ cup chocolate sauce whipped cream, for serving

Preparation:
1. Grease the cooking surface of the griddle with cooking spray.
2. Turn on the 4 burners and turn their knobs to medium heat.
3. Let the Griddle preheat for 5 minutes.
4. Arrange doughnut and pears halves on the griddle pan.
5. Cook to desired doneness. Place the ice cream in a small baking pan and cover with plastic wrap.
6. Press flat, about 2 inches thick, then place the pan into the freezer.
7. Cut frozen ice cream into 8 discs the same size as the prepared doughnuts.
8. Place 1 doughnut ½ on each dish. Layer with sliced pears and ice cream.
9. Top with a second doughnut ½. Repeat to make it a triple decker.
10. Spry with chocolate sauce and whipped cream before serving.
11. Serve.

Per Serving: Calories: 412; Fat: 14.9g; Sodium: 554mg; Carbs: 7g; Fiber 2.2g; Sugar: 8g; Protein: 26g

Golden Banana Coconut Fritters

Prep time: 15 minutes | Cook time: 8 minutes | Serves: 16

Ingredients:
- 2 bananas, mashed
- ⅓ cup flour
- ½ teaspoon Cinnamon
- 2 eggs
- ½ cup shredded coconut

Preparation:
1. Grease the cooking surface of the griddle with cooking spray.
2. Turn on the 4 burners and turn their knobs to medium heat.
3. Let the Griddle preheat for 5 minutes.
4. Combine all the recipe's ingredients except oil in a suitable bowl.
5. Drop heaping tablespoons of fritter batter onto the pan.
6. Cook until golden on each side before serving.
7. Serve.

Per Serving: Calories: 376; Fat: 13g; Sodium: 421mg; Carbs: 16g; Fiber 4.1g; Sugar: 3.2g; Protein: 27g

Vanilla Peanut Butter Sundae

Prep time: 15 minutes | Cook time: 10 minutes | Serves: 4

Ingredients:
- 4 bananas, peeled and sliced into medallions
- 4 large scoops vanilla ice cream
- ½ cup creamy peanut butter
- Salted caramel peanut butter sundae

Preparation:
1. Grease the cooking surface of the griddle with cooking spray.
2. Turn on the 4 burners and turn their knobs to medium heat.
3. Let the Griddle preheat for 5 minutes.
4. Sprinkle the bananas with cinnamon and cayenne pepper.
5. Griddle bananas on the griddle for 5 minutes per side. Scoop ice cream into a serving bowl.
6. Top with bananas, then peanut butter, caramel sauce, and chopped peanuts.
7. Sprinkle lightly with pink sea salt before serving.
8. Serve.

Per Serving: Calories: 317; Fat: 32g; Sodium: 311mg; Carbs: 12g; Fiber 3.1g; Sugar: 4g; Protein: 22g

Raspberry Cobbler

Prep time: 15 minutes | Cook time: 20 minutes | Serves: 2

Ingredients:
- 2 cans (21-ounces) pie filling, **Vanilla ice cream**
- 1 (8-ounces) package of cake mix
- ½ cup olive oil
- raspberry flavor
- 1-¼ cups water

Preparation:
1. Grease the cooking surface of the griddle with cooking spray.
2. Turn on the 4 burners and turn their knobs to medium heat.
3. Let the Griddle preheat for 5 minutes.
4. Mix your cake mix with olive oil and water in a suitable bowl until smooth.
5. Place a foil packet on the working surface along with pie filling.
6. Spread your cake mix on top of the pie filling.
7. Cover your foil packet and seal it then place on the griddle.
8. Serve.

Per Serving: Calories: 397; Fat: 21g; Sodium: 711mg; Carbs: 8g; Fiber 3.1g; Sugar: 4g; Protein: 22g

Griddle-Baked Stuffed Apple

Prep time: 15 minutes | Cook time: 15 minutes | Serves: 1

Ingredients:
- 1 apple
- 1 tablespoon butter, softened
- 1 tablespoon brown sugar
- ⅛ teaspoon ground cinnamon, or more to taste

Preparation:
1. Grease the cooking surface of the griddle with cooking spray.
2. Turn on the 4 burners and turn their knobs to medium heat.
3. Let the Griddle preheat for 5 minutes.
4. Mash the butter, brown sugar, and cinnamon with the back of a fork.
5. Stuff the mixture into the cavity of the apple.
6. Put the apple on the griddle, and then let it cook for 8 to 10 minutes.
7. Transfer to plate and let cool a few minutes before serving.
8. Serve.

Per Serving: Calories: 421; Fat: 11g; Sodium: 361mg; Carbs: 11g; Fiber 3.1g; Sugar: 2g; Protein: 26g

Chocolate Marshmallows Toast

Prep time: 15 minutes | Cook time: 12 minutes | Serves: 2

Ingredients:
- ½ cup sugar
- 1 tablespoon Cinnamon
- 4 slices bread
- ¼ cup margarine
- 15 baby marshmallows
- 1 (4.4-oz.) Chocolate bar

Preparation:
1. Grease the cooking surface of the griddle with cooking spray.
2. Turn on the 4 burners and turn their knobs to medium heat.
3. Let the Griddle preheat for 5 minutes.
4. Combine sugar and cinnamon in a suitable bowl.
5. Spread margarine over one side of each slice of bread. Sprinkle with cinnamon and sugar mixture.
6. Arrange 2 slices of bread onto the griddle pan, margarine side down.
7. Cover each slice with marshmallows and ½ of the chocolate bar. Top with remaining 2 slices of bread.
8. Use griddle press to cook on both sides, 3 minutes per side.
9. Serve.

Per Serving: Calories: 304; Fat: 14.9g; Sodium: 304mg; Carbs: 12g; Fiber 6g; Sugar: 2g; Protein: 21g

Cinnamon Apple Pie

Prep time: 15 minutes | Cook time: 10 minutes | Serves: 4

Ingredients:
- 8 slices white bread
- 4 tablespoons Butter, softened
- 2 granny smith apples, cored, and sliced
- ¼ cup brown sugar
- 1 teaspoon Cinnamon
- ½ cup cream cheese, softened

Preparation:
1. Grease the cooking surface of the griddle with cooking spray.
2. Turn on the 4 burners and turn their knobs to medium heat.
3. Let the Griddle preheat for 5 minutes.
4. Brush the bread on one side with butter.
5. In a suitable bowl, combine the apples, brown sugar, and cinnamon. Mix.
6. Spread cream cheese thinly on the unbuttered side of the bread.
7. Assemble the paninis with the apple mixture and second slice of bread.
8. Griddle on each side at medium heat until golden.
9. Cut paninis in ½ before serving with vanilla ice cream. 2 cups vanilla ice cream.
10. Serve.

Per Serving: Calories: 395; Fat: 15g; Sodium: 521mg; Carbs: 14g; Fiber 5.1g; Sugar: 3g; Protein: 27g

Sweet Apple Bowls

Prep time: 15 minutes | Cook time: 10 minutes | Serves: 4

Ingredients:
simple syrup
1 cup sugar
1 cup water
1 cinnamon stick
2 apples, large

Preparation:
1. Grease the cooking surface of the griddle with cooking spray.
2. Turn on the 4 burners and turn their knobs to medium heat.
3. Let the Griddle preheat for 5 minutes.
4. In a saucepan, bring the sugar, water, and cinnamon stick to a boil. Set aside.
5. Cut the apples in ½ and core with a melon baller. Add to the hot simple syrup.
6. Arrange apples on the griddle pan, cut side down, cook for 3 minutes.
7. Turnover and continue cooking until tender. Baste with simple syrup.
8. Top the apples with ice cream, caramel sauce, and chopped pecans.
9. Serve.
Per Serving: Calories: 395; Fat: 21g; Sodium: 451mg; Carbs: 17g; Fiber 4.1g; Sugar: 1.2g; Protein: 24g

Fruits Pound Cake

Prep time: 15 minutes | Cook time: 10 minutes | Serves: 6

Ingredients:
6 slices pound cake
3 peaches, sliced and pitted
3 bananas, peeled and sliced
24 strawberries, large
½ cup simple syrup
Suitable raspberry sauce and whipped cream
Mint leaves, for grarnishing

Preparation:
1. Grease the cooking surface of the griddle with cooking spray.
2. Turn on the 4 burners and turn their knobs to medium heat.
3. Let the Griddle preheat for 5 minutes.
4. Arrange the pound cake, bananas, peaches, and strawberries on the griddle.
5. Cook on both sides to desired doneness. Toss the fruit with simple syrup.
6. Set aside. Plate the pound cake with fruit. Top with raspberry sauce and whipped cream.
7. Garnish with mint leaves immediately before serving.
8. Serve.
Per Serving: Calories: 338; Fat: 12g; Sodium: 521mg; Carbs: 14g; Fiber 5.1g; Sugar: 3g; Protein: 27g

Honey Peaches Apricots

Prep time: 5 minutes | Cook time: 10 minutes | Serves: 4

Ingredients:
2 plums, peaches apricots
3 tablespoons sugar, turbinate
¼ cup of Honey
Gelato, as desired

Preparation:
1. Preheat the Griddle by turning all its knob to medium-heat setting.
2. Grease the griddle top with cooking spray.
3. Halve each fruit and remove the pits. Add some sugar on the top.
4. Cook on the hot griddle top for 5 minutes per side.
5. Top each serving with a dollop of gelato.
6. Serve and enjoy.
Per Serving: Calories: 148; Fat: 0.3 g; Sodium: 3 mg; Carbs: 38.9g; Fiber: 0.5g; Sugar: 33.9g; Protein: 0.6g

Chocolate Marshmallows Dip

Prep time: 10 minutes | Cook time: 25 minutes | Serves: 8

Ingredients:
12 oz. semisweet chocolate chips
¼ cup milk
2 tablespoons melted salted butter
16 oz. marshmallows
Apple wedges
Graham crackers

Preparation:
1. Preheat the Griddle by turning all its knob to medium-heat setting.
2. Grease the griddle top with cooking spray.
3. Pour the milk and melted butter into a cast iron and place it on the hot griddle top.
4. Mix everything together for a minute.
5. Once it's heated through, sprinkle the chocolate chips on top in a single layer.
6. Place the marshmallows on top of the chocolate, standing them on end and coating it.
7. Cover and cook for 7 minutes to smoke.
8. Serve with graham crackers and apple wedges.
Per Serving: Calories: 416; Fat: 8.3 g; Sodium: 208 mg; Carbs: 22.9g; Fiber: 0.5g; Sugar: 19g; Protein: 60.6g

Lime Pineapple with Maple Walnut Ice Cream

Prep time: 5 minutes | Cook time: 5 minutes | Serves: 8

Ingredients:
1 (16-oz.) can pineapple rings
¼ cup maple syrup
Juice of 1 lime
¼ teaspoon ground cinnamon
Butter, clarified butter, or coconut
oil
1 pint maple walnut ice cream, to serve
Chocolate sauce, to serve

Preparation:
1. Preheat the Griddle by turning all its knob to medium-heat setting.
2. Grease the griddle top with cooking butter and oil.
3. Mix well the lime juice, maple syrup, and cinnamon in a small bowl and leave aside.
4. Cook the pineapple for 3 to 4 minutes in the oil, flipping regularly.
5. When the pineapple has turned a golden hue, brush both sides of the rings with maple-lime syrup. Remove for 45 seconds per side per side.
6. Drizzle with chocolate sauce and a small scoop of maple walnut ice cream.
7. Serve and enjoy!
Per Serving: Calories: 416; Fat: 8.3 g; Sodium: 208 mg; Carbs: 22.9g; Fiber: 0.5g; Sugar: 19g; Protein: 60.6g

Cinnamon Pumpkin Seeds

Prep time: 15 minutes | Cook time: 30 minutes | Serves: 8

Ingredients:
2 tablespoons of sugar
Seeds from a pumpkin
1 teaspoon of cinnamon
2 tablespoons of melted butter

Preparation:
1. Grease the cooking surface of the griddle with cooking spray.
2. Turn on the 4 burners and turn their knobs to medium heat.
3. Let the Griddle preheat for 5 minutes.
4. Toss the seeds in the melted butter after cleaning them.
5. Combine the sugar and cinnamon in a mixing bowl.
6. Spread them out on a baking sheet and smoke them for 25 minutes on the griddle.
7. Serve.
Per Serving: Calories: 395; Fat: 21g; Sodium: 451mg; Carbs: 17g; Fiber 4.1g; Sugar: 1.2g; Protein: 24g

Caramel Bananas

Prep time: 15 minutes | Cook time: 15 minutes | Serves: 4

Ingredients:
⅓ cup pecans, chopped
½ cup sweetened condensed milk
4 slightly green bananas
½ cup brown sugar
2 tablespoons corn syrup
½ cup butter

Preparation:
1. In a heavy saucepan, bring the corn syrup, butter, milk, and brown sugar to a boil.
2. Simmer the mixture over low heat for 5 minutes. Stir the mixture constantly.
3. Preheat the Griddle by turning all its knob to medium-heat setting.
4. Grease the griddle top with cooking spray.
5. Place the bananas on the hot griddle top with their peels on and cook for 5 minutes.
6. Cook for another 5 minutes on the other side.
7. Arrange on a dish for serving. Remove the ends of the bananas and split the peel in half.
8. Remove the skin from the bananas and top with caramel.
9. Garnish with pecans, serve and enjoy.
Per Serving: Calories: 551; Fat: 29.3 g; Sodium: 74 mg; Carbs: 73.9g; Fiber: 3.5g; Sugar: 55.9g; Protein: 5g

34 | Chapter 4 Snack, Dessert and Appetizer Recipes

Peanut Butter Chips with Banana

Prep time: 15 minutes | **Cook time:** 15 minutes | **Serves:** 4

Ingredients:
- 4 ripe bananas
- 1 cup peanut butter baking chips
- 1 cup mini marshmallows
- ¼ cup brown sugar

Preparation:
1. Leaving banana in peel, slice down the length of the banana, but don't cut it in ½.
2. Pry apart the bananas and evenly distribute brown sugar inside each banana.
3. On top of the brown sugar, evenly distribute the peanut butter chips.
4. Add peanut butter chips, place the mini marshmallows.
5. Grease the cooking surface of the griddle with cooking spray.
6. Turn on the 4 burners and turn their knobs to medium heat.
7. Let the Griddle preheat for 5 minutes.
8. Place bananas in griddle, and then let it cook for 10 minutes
9. Serve.

Per Serving: Calories: 412; Fat: 14.9g; Sodium: 554mg; Carbs: 7g; Fiber 2.2g; Sugar: 8g; Protein: 26g

Honey Peaches with Vanilla Ice Cream

Prep time: 15 minutes | **Cook time:** 10 minutes | **Serves:** 4

Ingredients:
- 2 fresh peaches
- 1 tablespoon fresh honey
- Cinnamon to taste
- plain yogurt or ice cream for topping

Preparation:
1. Grease the cooking surface of the griddle with cooking spray.
2. Turn on the 4 burners and turn their knobs to medium heat.
3. Let the Griddle preheat for 5 minutes.
4. Slice the peaches lengthwise top to bottom and remove the pits.
5. Drizzle honey on the cut side of the peach and sprinkle with cinnamon.
6. Set the peaches sliced-side up and griddle peaches for a couple minutes cut side down.
7. Then flip and brush with coconut oil honey and cinnamon
8. Griddle for several minutes until the skin is starting to brown and pull back.
9. Serve with vanilla ice cream.

Per Serving: Calories: 379; Fat: 13g; Sodium: 421mg; Carbs: 16g; Fiber 4.1g; Sugar: 3.2g; Protein: 27g

Crispy Seasoned Eggplant Bites

Prep time: 15 minutes | **Cook time:** 10 minutes | **Serves:** 4

Ingredients:
- 1 eggplant, cut into 1-inch pieces
- 2 tablespoons olive oil
- ½ teaspoon Italian seasoning
- 1 teaspoon paprika
- ½ teaspoon red pepper
- 1 teaspoon garlic powder

Preparation:
1. Grease the cooking surface of the griddle with cooking spray.
2. Turn on the 4 burners and turn their knobs to medium heat.
3. Let the Griddle preheat for 5 minutes.
4. Add all the recipe's ingredients into the suitable bowl and toss well.
5. Transfer eggplant mixture onto the preheated griddle top and then let it cook until eggplant pieces are crispy.
6. Serve.

Per Serving: Calories: 395; Fat: 21g; Sodium: 451mg; Carbs: 17g; Fiber 4.1g; Sugar: 1.2g; Protein: 24g

Sweet and Sour Watermelon

Prep time: 15 minutes | **Cook time:** 8 minutes | **Serves:** 4

Ingredients:
- 2 (1½-inch-thick) watermelon slices, halved
- 1 pinch salt
- ¼ cup honey
- Lime wedges for serving

Preparation:
1. Lightly salt the watermelon on both sides, then brush both sides with the honey.
2. Grease the cooking surface of the griddle with cooking spray.
3. Turn on the 4 burners and turn their knobs to medium heat.
4. Let the Griddle preheat for 4 minutes.
5. Place the watermelon on the griddle top and garnish with lime wedges.
6. Serve.

Per Serving: Calories: 421; Fat: 11g; Sodium: 361mg; Carbs: 11g; Fiber 3.1g; Sugar: 2g; Protein: 26g

Vanilla Pineapple Sundae

Prep time: 15 minutes | **Cook time:** 15 minutes | **Serves:** 2

Ingredients:
- ¼ pineapple, peeled and sliced
- 2 cups vanilla ice cream
- ¼ cup whipped cream

Preparation:
1. Grease the cooking surface of the griddle with cooking spray.
2. Turn on the 4 burners and turn their knobs to medium heat.
3. Let the Griddle preheat for 5 minutes.
4. Place the pineapple on the griddle top and then let it cook for 4 minutes per side.
5. Top each slice with a scoop of ice-cream and whipped cream.
6. Serve.

Per Serving: Calories: 327; Fat: 22g; Sodium: 421mg; Carbs: 10g; Fiber 4.1g; Sugar: 2g; Protein: 31g

Chocolate Bacon Pecan Pie

Prep time: 1 hour 45 minutes | **Cook time:** 45 minutes | **Serves:** 8

Ingredients:
- 4 eggs
- 1 cup pecans, chopped
- 1 tablespoon of vanilla
- ½ cup semi chocolate chips
- ½ cup dark corn syrup
- ½ cup light corn syrup
- ¾ cup bacon, crumbled
- ¼ cup bourbon
- ¼ cup of butter
- ½ cup white sugar
- 1 tablespoon cornstarch
- 1 package refrigerated pie dough
- 16 oz. heavy cream
- ¾ cup white sugar
- ¼ cup bacon
- 1 tablespoon vanilla

Preparation:
1. In a suitable mixing dish, Mix ½ cup darker sugar, 4 tablespoons spread, and ½ cup white sugar.
2. In a separate dish, whisk together 4 eggs and 1 tablespoon cornstarch; add to blender.
3. In a suitable mixing bowl, mix ½ cup dull corn syrup, ¼ cup whiskey, ½ cup light corn syrup, 1 cup sliced walnuts, 1 cup bacon, and 1 tablespoon vanilla.
4. Pour pie batter into a 9-inch pie pan. Flour mixture in a delicate manner.
5. Evenly distribute ½ cup chocolate into the pie dish.
6. Pour the mixture into the pie plate.
7. Preheat the Griddle by turning all its knob to medium-heat setting.
8. Grease the griddle top with butter.
9. Place on the griddle top for 40 minutes.
10. Allow to cool before topping with bacon whipped cream.
11. Serve.

Per Serving: Calories: 416; Fat: 8.3 g; Sodium: 208 mg; Carbs: 22.9g; Fiber: 0.5g; Sugar: 19g; Protein: 60.6g

Creamy Berries Cake

Prep time: 10 minutes | **Cook time:** 20 minutes | **Serves:** 6

Ingredients:
- 2 pounds cake
- 3 cups of whipped cream
- ¼ cup melted butter
- 1 cup of blueberries
- 1 cup of raspberries
- 1 cup sliced strawberries

Preparation:
1. Preheat the Griddle by turning all its knob to medium-heat setting.
2. Grease the griddle top with cooking spray.
3. Cut the cake loaf into 10 slices (34 inch). Butter both sides of the bread.
4. Cook for 7 minutes per side on a griddle.
5. Place the cake first, then the berries, and finally the cream.
6. Serve.

Per Serving: Calories: 839; Fat: 48.3 g; Sodium: 598 mg; Carbs: 98g; Fiber: 2.5g; Sugar: 4.9g; Protein: 7.6g

Griddle-Cooked Potatoes and Carrots

Prep time: 15 minutes | Cook time: 15 minutes | Serves: 2

Ingredients:
- ½ lb. potatoes, cubed
- ½ onion, diced
- ½ teaspoon Italian seasoning
- ¼ teaspoon garlic powder
- ½ lb. carrots, peeled and diced into chunks
- 1 tablespoon olive oil
- Black pepper, to taste
- salt, to taste

Preparation:
1. Grease the cooking surface of the griddle with cooking spray.
2. Turn on the 4 burners and turn their knobs to medium heat.
3. Let the Griddle preheat for 5 minutes.
4. In a suitable bowl, toss carrots, potatoes, garlic powder, Italian seasoning, oil, onion, pepper, and salt.
5. Transfer carrot potato mixture on preheated griddle top and then let it cook until tender.
6. Serve.

Per Serving: Calories: 395; Fat: 15g; Sodium: 521mg; Carbs: 14g; Fiber: 5.1g; Sugar: 3g; Protein: 27g

Sausage and Cheese Balls

Prep time: 20 minutes | Cook time: 40 minutes | Serves: 4

Ingredients:
- 1 pound hot breakfast sausage
- 2 cups Bisquick baking mix
- 8 oz. cream cheese
- 8 oz. sharp cheddar cheese
- ¼ cup Fresno peppers
- 1 tablespoon dried parsley
- 1 teaspoon killer hogs ap rub
- ½ teaspoon onion powder

Preparation:
1. In a suitable mixing bowl, mix well the baking mix, sausage, cream cheddar, and crumbled cheddar.
2. Using a small scoop, portion the mixture into chomp-sized balls.
3. Preheat the Griddle by turning all its knob to medium-heat setting.
4. Grease the griddle top with cooking spray.
5. Arrange the wiener and cheddar balls on the griddle top and cook for 14 minutes per side.
6. Serve.

Per Serving: Calories: 1196; Fat: 98.3 g; Sodium: 2208 mg; Carbs: 42.9g; Fiber: 1.5g; Sugar: 9.3g; Protein: 45.6g

Sweet Chocolate Bread

Prep time: 10 minutes | Cook time: 1 hour | Serves: 8

Ingredients:
- 1½ quart full-; Fat: butter pecan ice cream
- 1 teaspoon salt
- 2 cups semisweet chocolate chips
- 1 cup sugar
- 1 stick melted butter
- Butter, for greasing
- 4 cups self-rising flour

Preparation:
1. With an electric mixer set to medium, mix well the salt, sugar, flour, and ice cream for two minutes. While the mixer is still running, add the chocolate chips and beat until well combined.
2. Using cooking spray, coat a Bundt pan or tube pan.
3. Pour the batter into the pan that has been prepared.
4. Preheat the Griddle by turning all its knob to medium-heat setting.
5. Grease the griddle top with cooking spray.
6. Place the cake on the hot griddle top, cover it, and cook for 60 minutes.
7. Serve.

Per Serving: Calories: 506; Fat: 48.3 g; Sodium: 608 mg; Carbs: 158.9g; Fiber: 6.5g; Sugar: 83.9g; Protein: 12.6g

Vanilla Butter Blackberry Pie

Prep time: 15 minutes | Cook time: 40 minutes | Serves: 8

Ingredients:
- Butter, for greasing
- ½ cup all-purpose flour
- ½ cup milk
- 2 pints blackberries
- 2 cup sugar, divided
- 1 box refrigerated piecrusts
- 1 stick melted butter
- 1 stick of butter
- Vanilla ice cream

Preparation:
1. Preheat the Griddle by turning all its knob to medium-heat setting.
2. Grease the griddle top with butter.
3. Unroll a piecrust and place it in the griddle's bottom and up the sides.
4. Poke holes in the crust with a fork.
5. Place the griddle on the grill and cook for 5 minutes.
6. Combine 1-½ cup sugar, flour, and melted butter in a suitable mixing bowl.
7. Toss in the blackberries and combine everything.
8. Transfer the berry mixture to the griddle. After that, the milk should be poured on top.
9. Half of the diced butter goes on top.
10. Serve and enjoy.

Per Serving: Calories: 276; Fat: 2.1 g; Sodium: 18 mg; Carbs: 65.9g; Fiber: 4.5g; Sugar: 59g; Protein: 2.6g

Pineapple and Strawberry Sundae

Prep time: 15 minutes | Cook time: 10 minutes | Serves: 2

Ingredients:
Strawberry sauce
- 8 oz. Strawberries
- 2 teaspoon sugar

Pineapple sauce
- 8 oz. Pineapple rounds
- ¼ cup light brown sugar
- Sundae basics

Preparation:
1. Grease the cooking surface of the griddle with cooking spray.
2. Turn on the 4 burners and turn their knobs to medium heat.
3. Let the Griddle preheat for 5 minutes.
4. Sear strawberries, pineapple, and banana halves to desired doneness. Set aside.
5. Combine the strawberries and sugar in a small saucepan.
6. Cook until the sugar has melted and the strawberries have been thoroughly mixed.
7. Pineapple sauce: mix the pineapples and light brown sugar in a separate saucepan.
8. Cook until the sugar has melted and the pineapples have been thoroughly mixed.
9. Bananas should be used to line a dish. 3 scoops vanilla and/or chocolate ice cream, as well as fruit sauces
10. Peanuts should be sprinkled on top. Before serving, top with chocolate sauce and whipped cream.
11. Serve.

Per Serving: Calories: 421; Fat: 11g; Sodium: 361mg; Carbs: 11g; Fiber: 3.1g; Sugar: 2g; Protein: 26g

Vanilla Chocolate Bread Pudding

Prep time: 20 minutes | Cook time: 1hour | Serves: 12

Ingredients:
- 1 loaf French bread
- 4 cups heavy cream
- 3 large eggs
- 2 cups white sugar
- 1 package white chocolate

Bourbon white chocolate sauce
- 1 package white chocolate morsels
- 1 cup heavy cream
- morsels
- ¼ cup melted butter
- 2 teaspoons vanilla
- 1 teaspoon ground nutmeg
- 1 teaspoon salt
- 2 tablespoons melted butter
- 2 tablespoons bourbon
- ½ teaspoon salt

Preparation:
1. Tear French bread into small pieces and place in a large mixing dish.
2. Douse the bread in four cups of heavy cream for 30 minutes.
3. In a medium mixing bowl, whisk the sugar, eggs, butter, vanilla extract, salt and nutmeg
4. Preheat the Griddle by turning all its knob to medium-heat setting.
5. Grease the griddle top with cooking spray.
6. Pour the egg mixture over the splattered French bread and combine until smooth.
7. Pour the mixture into a well-buttered 9-by-13-inch dish and place it on the hot griddle top.
8. Cook for 60 second.
9. Melt the margarine in a suitable saucepot over medium heat.
10. Cook for three to four minutes.
11. Add a lot of cream and boil until thick.
12. Remove from the heat and gradually add white chocolate pieces, and mix.
13. Serve over bread pudding, seasoning with a pinch of salt.

Per Serving: Calories: 351; Fat: 20.3 g; Sodium: 298 mg; Carbs: 40.9g; Fiber: 0.5g; Sugar: 35.5g; Protein:3.6g

Mozzarella Broccoli Fritters

Prep time: 15 minutes | Cook time: 12 minutes | Serves: 4

Ingredients:
- 2 eggs, lightly beaten
- 3 cups broccoli florets, steam and chopped
- 2 garlic cloves, minced
- 2 cups mozzarella cheese, shredded
- ¼ cup breadcrumbs
- Black pepper, to taste
- Salt, to taste

Preparation:
1. Grease the cooking surface of the griddle with cooking spray.
2. Turn on the 4 burners and turn their knobs to medium heat.
3. Let the Griddle preheat for 5 minutes.
4. Add all the recipe's ingredients into the suitable bowl and mix until well combined.
5. Make patties from broccoli mixture and place on preheated griddle top and then let it cook until golden brown from both sides.
6. Serve.

Per Serving: Calories: 449; Fat: 21g; Sodium: 421mg; Carbs: 16g; Fiber 4.1g; Sugar: 3.2g; Protein: 27g

Brioche Apricots with Ice Cream

Prep time: 15 minutes | Cook time: 10 minutes | Serves: 4

Ingredients:
- 2 cups vanilla ice cream
- 2 tablespoons honey
- 4 slices brioches, diced
- 2 tablespoons sugar
- 2 tablespoons butter
- 8 ripe apricots

Preparation:
1. Mix the halved apricots with sugar and butter.
2. Grease the cooking surface of the griddle with cooking spray.
3. Turn on the 4 burners and turn their knobs to medium heat.
4. Let the Griddle preheat for 5 minutes.
5. Put the brioche slices onto the griddle for 1 minute per side.
6. Griddle your apricots in the griddle for 1 minute per side.
7. Top your brioche slices with honey, apricot slices, and a scoop of vanilla ice cream.
8. Serve.

Per Serving: Calories: 376; Fat: 13g; Sodium: 421mg; Carbs: 16g; Fiber 4.1g; Sugar: 3.2g; Protein: 27g

Sweet Apple Cobbler

Prep time: 1 hour 30 minutes | Cook time: 50 minutes | Serves: 8

Ingredients:
- 8 Granny Smith apples
- 1 cup sugar
- 1 stick melted butter
- 1 teaspoon cinnamon
- Pinch salt
- ½ cup brown sugar
- 2 eggs
- 2 teaspoons baking powder
- 2 cup plain flour
- 1½ cup sugar

Preparation:
1. Peel and quarter the apples and set them in a suitable mixing dish.
2. Mix well the cinnamon and one cup of sugar in a suitable mixing bowl.
3. Stir thoroughly to coat, then set aside for one hour.
4. Preheat the Griddle by turning all its knob to low-heat setting.
5. Grease the griddle top with cooking spray.
6. Mix well the salt, baking powder, eggs, brown sugar, sugar, and flour in a suitable mixing bowl.
7. Mix until crumbs form.
8. Arrange apples on the griddle. Drizzle the melted butter on top of the crumble mixture and cook for 50 minutes.
9. Serve.

Per Serving: Calories: 477; Fat: 13.3 g; Sodium: 128 mg; Carbs: 89.5g; Fiber: 6.5g; Sugar: 59.2g; Protein: 5.4g

Cauliflower and Zucchini Fritters

Prep time: 15 minutes | Cook time: 8 minutes | Serves: 4

Ingredients:
- 2 medium zucchini, grated and squeezed
- 1 tablespoon olive oil
- ¼ cup coconut flour
- 3 cups cauliflower rice
- ½ teaspoon sea salt

Preparation:
1. Grease the cooking surface of the griddle with cooking spray.
2. Turn on the 4 burners and turn their knobs to medium heat.
3. Let the Griddle preheat for 5 minutes.
4. Add all the recipe's ingredients except oil into the bowl and mix until well combined.
5. Make small patties from the mixture and place onto the griddle top and then let it cook for 3-4 minutes on each side.
6. Serve.

Per Serving: Calories: 428; Fat: 11g; Sodium: 501mg; Carbs: 16g; Fiber 2.1g; Sugar: 2.2g; Protein: 27g

Rosemary Cauliflower Bites

Prep time: 15 minutes | Cook time: 10 minutes | Serves: 4

Ingredients:
- 1 lb. cauliflower florets
- 1 teaspoon ground coriander
- ½ teaspoon dried rosemary
- 1 ½ teaspoon garlic powder
- 1 tablespoon olive oil
- 1 teaspoon sesame seeds
- Black pepper, to taste
- salt, to taste

Preparation:
1. Add cauliflower florets and the rest of the recipe's ingredients into the bowl and toss well.
2. Grease the cooking surface of the griddle with cooking spray.
3. Turn on the 4 burners and turn their knobs to medium heat.
4. Let the Griddle preheat for 5 minutes.
5. Cook cauliflower florets on the griddle until tender.
6. Serve.

Per Serving: Calories: 376; Fat: 13g; Sodium: 421mg; Carbs: 16g; Fiber 4.1g; Sugar: 3.2g; Protein: 27g

Sweet Cinnamon Peaches

Prep time: 15 minutes | Cook time: 5 minutes | Serves: 4

Ingredients:
- 4 ripe peaches, halved and pitted
- ¼ cup salted butter
- 1 teaspoon granulated sugar
- ¼ teaspoon cinnamon

Preparation:
1. Grease the cooking surface of the griddle with cooking spray.
2. Turn on the 4 burners and turn their knobs to medium heat.
3. Let the Griddle preheat for 5 minutes.
4. Mix your sugar, butter and cinnamon in a suitable bowl until smooth.
5. Once your griddle is preheated, place the peaches on the griddle.
6. Griddle it for 1 minute per side.
7. Serve the peaches with cinnamon butter on top and enjoy!

Per Serving: Calories: 326; Fat: 13g; Sodium: 421mg; Carbs: 16g; Fiber 4.1g; Sugar: 3.2g; Protein: 27g

Pain Perdu Strawberries

Prep time: 15 minutes | Cook time: 12 minutes | Serves: 4

Ingredients:
- 3 cups sliced hulled strawberries
- 3 tablespoons sugar
- 1 tablespoon balsamic vinegar
- 2 eggs
- ½ cup milk
- 1 teaspoon vanilla extract
- 1 pinch salt
- 4 slices bread
- Black pepper, to taste

Preparation:
1. Grease the cooking surface of the griddle with cooking spray.
2. Turn on the 4 burners and turn their knobs to medium heat.
3. Let the Griddle preheat for 5 minutes.
4. Put the strawberries in a suitable bowl, sprinkle with 1 to 2 tablespoons of the sugar and toss gently to coat.
5. Add the vinegar and toss again. Let macerate at room temperature.
6. Beat the eggs lightly in a large shallow bowl, then beat in the milk, the remaining 1 tablespoon sugar, vanilla, and salt.
7. Give each slice of bread a quick dip in the egg wash on both sides, put on a large plate, and immediately take out them to the griddle.
8. Put the bread on the griddle and then let it cook until the bread develops griddle marks, 2 to 3 minutes per side.
9. Transfer to a clean platter. To serve, top each toast with a spoonful of the balsamic strawberries.
10. Let diners add black pepper to their strawberries.
11. Serve.

Per Serving: Calories: 397; Fat: 21g; Sodium: 711mg; Carbs: 8g; Fiber 3.1g; Sugar: 4g; Protein: 22g

Creamy Vanilla Fruit Skewers

Prep time: 15 minutes | Cook time: 15 minutes | Serves: 6

Ingredients:
8 strawberries, large
2 peaches, sliced thick
1 pear, sliced thick
1 cup pineapple, cubed
1 banana, sliced thick

Preparation:
1. Grease the cooking surface of the griddle with cooking spray.
2. Turn on the 4 burners and turn their knobs to medium heat.
3. Let the Griddle preheat for 5 minutes.
4. Thread all the fruits on the skewers and then let it cook for 5 minutes per side on the griddle.
5. In a sauce pot, bring the heavy cream to a boil.
6. Add the chocolate chips and remove from heat.
7. Mix until creamy, then add vanilla.
8. Serve fruit with chocolate dipping sauce.
Per Serving: Calories: 412; Fat: 14.9g; Sodium: 554mg; Carbs: 7g; Fiber: 2.2g; Sugar: 8g; Protein: 26g

Tasty Mushrooms with Herbs

Prep time: 15 minutes | Cook time: 10 minutes | Serves: 4

Ingredients:
1 lb. mushroom caps
1 tablespoon basil, minced
1 garlic clove, minced
½ tablespoons vinegar
½ teaspoon ground coriander
1 teaspoon rosemary, chopped
Black pepper, to taste
salt, to taste

Preparation:
1. Grease the cooking surface of the griddle with cooking spray.
2. Turn on the 4 burners and turn their knobs to medium heat.
3. Let the Griddle preheat for 5 minutes.
4. Add all the recipe's ingredients into the bowl and toss well.
5. Spread mushroom mixture onto the preheated griddle top and then let it cook until mushroom is tender.
6. Serve.
Per Serving: Calories: 397; Fat: 21g; Sodium: 711mg; Carbs: 8g; Fiber: 3.1g; Sugar: 4g; Protein: 22g

Golden Zucchini Patties

Prep time: 15 minutes | Cook time: 30 minutes | Serves: 6

Ingredients:
1 cup zucchini, shredded and squeeze out all liquid
½ tablespoons Dijon mustard
1 egg, lightly beaten
¼ teaspoon red pepper flakes
¼ cup parmesan cheese, grated
½ tablespoons mayonnaise
½ cup breadcrumbs
2 tablespoons onion, minced
Black pepper, to taste
Salt, to taste

Preparation:
1. Grease the cooking surface of the griddle with cooking spray.
2. Turn on the 4 burners and turn their knobs to medium heat.
3. Let the Griddle preheat for 5 minutes.
4. Add all the recipe's ingredients into the bowl and mix until well combined.
5. Make small patties from the zucchini mixture.
6. Place on preheated griddle top and then let it cook until golden brown from both sides.
7. Serve.
Per Serving: Calories: 317; Fat: 32g; Sodium: 311mg; Carbs: 12g; Fiber: 3.1g; Sugar: 4g; Protein: 22g

Butter Pumpkin Seeds with Cinnamon

Prep time: 15 minutes | Cook time: 30 minutes | Serves: 8

Ingredients:
2 tablespoons sugar
Seeds from a pumpkin
1 teaspoon cinnamon
2 tablespoons melted butter

Preparation:
1. Preheat the Griddle by turning all its knob to medium-heat setting.
2. Grease the griddle top with butter.
3. Toss the seeds in the melted butter after cleaning them.
4. Mix well the sugar and cinnamon in a suitable mixing bowl.
5. Place them on the griddle top and cook for 25 minutes.
6. Serve.
Per Serving: Calories: 56; Fat: 4.3 g; Sodium: 21 mg; Carbs: 2.9g; Fiber: 0.3g; Sugar: 3.9g; Protein: 0.6g

Sweet Pear Crisp

Prep time: 15 minutes | Cook time: 15 minutes | Serves: 4

Ingredients:
2 pears, cored and sliced
Crisp topping
¼ cup brown sugar
¼ cup flour
3 tablespoons butter

Preparation:
1. Combine brown sugar, flour, butter, walnuts, and cinnamon in a suitable bowl.
2. Grease the cooking surface of the griddle with cooking spray.
3. Turn on the 4 burners and turn their knobs to medium heat.
4. Let the Griddle preheat for 5 minutes.
5. Place the pears on the griddle and then let it cook for 2 minutes per side.
6. Spread the pear to a casserole dish and drizzle flour mixture on top.
7. Bake the crisp for 4 minutes in the oven at 450 degrees F.
8. Serve.
Per Serving: Calories: 449; Fat: 21g; Sodium: 421mg; Carbs: 16g; Fiber: 4.1g; Sugar: 3.2g; Protein: 27g

Coconut Chocolate Brownies

Prep time: 15 minutes | Cook time: 35 minutes | Serves: 6

Ingredients:
4 eggs
1 cup cane sugar
¾ cup of coconut oil
4 oz. chocolate, chopped
½ teaspoon of sea salt
¼ cup cocoa powder, unsweetened
½ cup flour
4 oz. chocolate chips
1 teaspoon of vanilla

Preparation:
1. Preheat the Griddle by turning all its knob to medium-heat setting.
2. Grease the griddle top with cooking spray.
3. Pour the egg mixture onto the hot griddle top
4. Grease a 9x9 baking pan and line it with parchment paper.
5. Mix well the salt, cocoa powder, and flour in a suitable mixing dish. Set aside after stirring.
6. Melt the coconut oil and chopped chocolate in the microwave or in a double boiler.
7. Mix well the vanilla, eggs, and sugar in a suitable mixing bowl.
8. To mix well the ingredients, whisk them together.
9. Mix in the chocolate chunks with the flour. Fill a pan halfway with the mixture.
10. Set the pan on the hot griddle top to cook for 30 minutes.
11. Allow them to cool completely before cutting.
12. Serve the brownies cut into squares.
Per Serving: Calories: 426; Fat: 36.3 g; Sodium: 248 mg; Carbs: 22.1g; Fiber: 2g; Sugar: 10.9g; Protein: 6.6g

Vanilla Chocolate Chip Cookies

Prep time: 30 minutes | Cook time: 20 minutes | Serves: 6

Ingredients:
8 slices bacon, cooked and crumbled
2½ teaspoons apple cider vinegar
1 teaspoon vanilla
2 cup semisweet chocolate chips
2 room temp eggs
1½ teaspoons baking soda
1 cup granulated sugar
½ teaspoon salt
2 ¾ cup all-purpose flour
1 cup light brown sugar
1½ stick softened butter

Preparation:
1. Stir well the salt, baking soda, and flour in a suitable mixing bowl
2. Mix well the sugar and butter in a suitable mixing bowl.
3. Beat well the eggs, vinegar, and vanilla extract in a suitable mixing bowl.
4. Gradually add the flour mixture, bacon, and chocolate chips.
5. Preheat the Griddle by turning all its knob to medium-heat setting.
6. Grease the griddle top with cooking spray.
7. Drop a teaspoon of cookie batter onto the griddle top and cook for 12 minutes.
8. Serve.
Per Serving: Calories: 876; Fat: 27.3 g; Sodium: 1608 mg; Carbs: 149.9g; Fiber: 5.5g; Sugar: 94.9g; Protein: 10.6g

Jalapeno Corn Cakes

Prep time: 10 minutes | Cook time: 10 minutes | Serves 10

Ingredients:
- 4 eggs
- 2 cups corn
- ½ teaspoon pepper
- ½ cup cornmeal
- ½ cup flour
- ½ cup cheddar cheese, shredded
- ⅔ cup green onions, sliced
- 1 jalapeno, chopped
- ½ teaspoon kosher salt

Preparation:
1. Place the corn in a food processor and pulse until it is coarsely chopped.
2. In a mixing bowl, combine the corn and the remaining ingredients and stir until well blended.
3. Heat the griddle to a high temperature.
4. Spray the top of the griddle with cooking spray.
5. Form patties from the mixture and fry on a heated griddle top until golden brown on both sides.
6. Serve and have fun.

Per Serving: Calories: 120; Fat: 4.3g; Sodium: 184mg; Carbs: 16.3g; Fiber 1.6g; Sugar: 1.8g; Protein: 5.8g

Thyme Mushroom Skewers

Prep time: 8 minutes | Cook time: 10 minutes | Serves 4

Ingredients:
- 2 pounds (907 g) sliced ¼-inch thick mushrooms
- ½ teaspoon chopped thyme
- 3 chopped garlic cloves
- 1 tablespoon soy sauce
- 2 tablespoons balsamic vinegar
- Pepper and salt to taste

Preparation:
1. Combine the mushrooms and remaining ingredients in a mixing dish, cover, and chill for 30 minutes.
2. Skewer the marinated mushrooms on skewers.
3. Preheat the griddle over a medium-high heat.
4. Cook the mushroom skewers for 2-3 minutes per side on a hot griddle.
5. When done, serve and enjoy.

Per Serving: Calories: 37; Fat: 0.3g; Sodium: 160mg; Carbs: 5.6g; Fiber 1.6g; Sugar: 2.8g; Protein: 6g

Maple-Glazed Bananas with Vanilla Ice Cream

Prep time: 15 minutes | Cook time: 10 minutes | Serves: 4

Ingredients:
- 4 bananas
- 3 tablespoons maple syrup
- 8 tablespoons dark brown sugar
- 1 pinch ground cinnamon
- 6 tablespoons hot fudge sauce
- 6 tablespoons cinnamon caramel sauce
- vanilla ice cream, for serving

Preparation:
1. Grease the cooking surface of the griddle with cooking spray.
2. Turn on the 4 burners and turn their knobs to medium heat.
3. Let the Griddle preheat for 5 minutes.
4. Place the bananas on a work surface and cut each in ½ lengthwise.
5. Brush the cut sides with the maple syrup and sprinkle brown sugar over them.
6. Lightly dust the cut sides of the bananas with cinnamon.
7. Arrange the bananas, cut side up, on the preheated griddle, cook for 3 to 5 minutes until the cut side is caramelized.
8. Transfer the banana halves still in their skins to a platter or plates.
9. Place a scoop of vanilla ice cream alongside.
10. Drizzle hot fudge sauce on top.
11. Serve.

Per Serving: Calories: 346; Fat: 13g; Sodium: 421mg; Carbs: 16g; Fiber 4.1g; Sugar: 3.2g; Protein: 27g

Brioche Toast with Maple Syrup

Prep time: 15 minutes | Cook time: 15 minutes | Serves: 6

Ingredients:
- 10 eggs
- ¾ cup half and half
- 2 teaspoon cinnamon powder
- 1 teaspoon almond extract
- ¼ cup maple syrup, to serve
- 1 loaf brioche bread, sliced

Preparation:
1. Whisk the eggs, half and half, cinnamon, and almond extract in a suitable bowl.
2. Soak bread in the egg batter for 5 minutes.
3. Grease the cooking surface of the griddle with butter.
4. Turn on the 4 burners and turn their knobs to medium heat.
5. Let the Griddle preheat for 5 minutes.
6. Place the bread on the griddle top and then let it cook for 5 minutes per side.
7. Drizzle maple syrup on top.
8. Serve.

Per Serving: Calories: 318; Fat: 15g; Sodium: 521mg; Carbs: 14g; Fiber 5.1g; Sugar: 3g; Protein: 27g

Honey-Glazed Pineapple Slices

Prep time: 15 minutes | Cook time: 12 minutes | Serves: 5

Ingredients:
- 1 small ripe pineapple, peeled and sliced
- ¼ cup honey
- ¼ cup fresh lime juice
- 1 tablespoon light brown sugar
- 2 tablespoons chopped fresh mint leaves

Preparation:
1. Mix honey, and lime juice in a suitable bowl and brush over the pineapple slices.
2. Grease the cooking surface of the griddle with cooking spray.
3. Turn on the 4 burners and turn their knobs to medium heat.
4. Let the Griddle preheat for 5 minutes.
5. Place the pineapple on the griddle top and then let it cook for 3 minutes per side.
6. Drizzle mint and sugar on top.
7. Serve.

Per Serving: Calories: 428; Fat: 11g; Sodium: 501mg; Carbs: 16g; Fiber 2.1g; Sugar: 2.2g; Protein: 27g

Herbed Potatoes

Prep time: 15 minutes | Cook time: 12 minutes | Serves: 2

Ingredients:
- ½ lb. baby potatoes, wash and cut in ½
- ¼ teaspoon garlic powder
- ½ tablespoons olive oil
- ¼ teaspoon dill
- ¼ teaspoon chives
- ¼ teaspoon parsley
- ¼ teaspoon paprika
- ¼ teaspoon onion powder
- Salt, to taste

Preparation:
1. Grease the cooking surface of the griddle with cooking spray.
2. Turn on the 4 burners and turn their knobs to medium heat.
3. Let the Griddle preheat for 5 minutes.
4. Add all the recipe's ingredients into the mixing bowl and toss well.
5. Spread potatoes on preheated griddle top and then let it cook until tender.
6. Serve.

Per Serving: Calories: 354; Fat: 7.9g; Sodium: 704mg; Carbs: 6g; Fiber 3.6g; Sugar: 6g; Protein: 18g

Oregano Spinach Turkey Burgers

Prep time: 08 minutes | Cook time: 08 minutes | Serves 4

Ingredients:
- 1 pound (454 g). ground turkey
- 1 tablespoon breadcrumbs
- ¼ teaspoon. crushed red pepper
- 1 teaspoon. parsley
- 1 teaspoon. oregano
- 1 teaspoon. garlic powder
- ⅓ cup sun-dried tomatoes
- ½ cup crumbled feta cheese
- ½ cup chopped baby spinach
- ½ teaspoon pepper
- ½ teaspoon sea salt

Preparation:
1. In a mixing basin, add all of the ingredients and stir until well blended.
2. Form the ingredients into four equal-sized patties.
3. Heat the griddle to a high temperature.
4. Cook patties for 3-5 minutes on each side on a hot griddle, or until internal temperature reaches 165°F (74°C).
5. When cooked, serve and enjoy.

Per Serving: Calories: 70; Fat: 1.3g; Sodium: 10mg; Carbs: 7.6g; Fiber 1.1g; Sugar: 1.2g; Protein: 6.8g

Walnut Chocolate Chip Cookies

Prep time: 30 minutes | Cook time: 30 minutes | Serves: 8

Ingredients:
1½ cup chopped walnuts
1 teaspoon vanilla
2 cup chocolate chips
1 teaspoon baking soda
2½ cup plain flour
½ teaspoon salt
1½ stick softened butter
2 eggs
1 cup brown sugar
½ cup sugar

Preparation:
1. Preheat the Griddle by turning all its knob to medium-heat setting.
2. Grease the griddle top with cooking spray.
3. Mix well the salt, baking soda, and flour in a suitable mixing bowl.
4. Whisk the brown sugar, sugar, and butter in a suitable mixing bowl.
5. Mix in the vanilla and eggs until everything is well combined.
6. Continue to beat while gradually adding the flour.
7. Add the chocolate chips and walnuts after all of the flour has been mixed.
8. Fold the egg whites into the batter with a spoon.
9. Cover the griddle with aluminum foil.
10. Drop a spoonful of dough onto aluminum foil and cook for 17 minutes.
11. Serve.
Per Serving: Calories: 1416; Fat: 68.3 g; Sodium: 368 mg; Carbs: 189.9g; Fiber: 11.5g; Sugar: 53.9g; Protein: 42.6g

Mayo Potato Skewers

Prep time: 12 minutes | Cook time: 25 minutes | Serves 8

Ingredients:
2 pounds (907 g) quartered potatoes
1 teaspoon garlic powder
2 teaspoons crushed dried
rosemary
4 tablespoons dry white wine
½ cup mayonnaise
½ cup water

Preparation:
1. Combine potatoes and water in a microwave-safe bowl and heat for 15 minutes, or until potatoes are cooked.
2. Drain potatoes thoroughly and set aside to cool. Combine mayonnaise, garlic powder, rosemary, and wine in a large mixing basin.
3. Toss in the potatoes to coat. Refrigerate for 1 hour after covering the bowl.
4. Oil the grates and preheat the griddle to high heat. Take away the potatoes from the marinade and skewer them.
5. Cook for 6-8 minutes on a hot griddle with covered potato skewers. Halfway through, turn the skewers.
6. When cooked, serve and enjoy.
Per Serving: Calories: 98; Fat: 5g; Sodium: 114mg; Carbs: 11.6g; Fiber 0.6g; Sugar: 1.8g; Protein: 1.8g

Lemon Strawberry Shortcake

Prep time: 15 minutes | Cook time: 10 minutes | Serves: 6

Ingredients:
1 angel food cake, sliced into wedges
½ stick butter
1 lb. Strawberries, cut in ½
zest of 1 lemon juice of ½ lemon
1 strawberry shortcake

Preparation:
1. Grease the cooking surface of the griddle with cooking spray.
2. Turn on the 4 burners and turn their knobs to medium heat.
3. Let the Griddle preheat for 5 minutes.
4. Brush the cake wedges with butter.
5. Cook the strawberries and cake wedges on the griddle for 2 minutes per side.
6. Let cool before tossing with lemon zest, lemon juice, and 1 tablespoon sugar.
7. Whip the cream with ¼ cup confectioners' sugar and vanilla.
8. Top cake wedges with strawberries and whipped cream immediately before serving.
9. Serve.
Per Serving: Calories: 354; Fat: 7.9g; Sodium: 704mg; Carbs: 6g; Fiber 3.6g; Sugar: 6g; Protein: 18g

Cheese Pepperoni Chicken Sandwich

Prep time: 10 minutes | Cook time: 5 minutes | Serves 2

Ingredients:
4 bread slices
1 chicken breast, cooked and sliced
1 tablespoon butter
4 mozzarella cheese slices
2 tablespoons olives, sliced
2 tablespoons pizza sauce
8 pepperoni slices

Preparation:
1. Each slice of bread should be brushed with butter on one side.
2. Spread pizza sauce over 2 slices of bread and top with chicken, pepperoni slices, olives, and cheese.
3. Add the remaining bread slices on top.
4. Heat the griddle to a high temperature. Spray the top of the griddle with cooking spray.
5. Place the sandwiches on a hot griddle top and cook for 5 minutes, or until both sides are softly golden brown.
6. Serve and have fun.
Per Serving: Calories: 443; Fat: 28.3g; Sodium: 1024mg; Carbs: 13.6g; Fiber 1g; Sugar: 1.8g; Protein: 33.8g

Peanut Butter Pancake

Prep time: 15 minutes | Cook time: 5 minutes | Serves: 4

Ingredients:
Pancakes
2 eggs
1 ½ cups whole milk
½ cup smooth peanut butter
1 ¼ cups pancake mix
Peanut butter cream
½ cup smooth peanut butter
1 (8-oz.) Container whipped topping
¼ cup grape jelly

Preparation:
1. Grease the cooking surface of the griddle with cooking spray.
2. Turn on the 4 burners and turn their knobs to medium heat.
3. Let the Griddle preheat for 5 minutes.
4. Make pancake batter: beat together the egg and milk.
5. Add the peanut butter and beat until smooth. Mix in the pancake mix.
6. Peanut butter cream: beat together the peanut butter and whipped topping.
7. Grape syrup: combine the jelly and syrup. Microwave until melted, about 20 seconds.
8. Mix to combine. Ladle a ½ cup of the pancake batter onto the pan.
9. Cook until golden brown, about 2 minutes per side. Continue until all batter is used up.
10. Stack the pancakes, spreading a smear of the peanut butter cream between each pancake.
11. Spry with the grape syrup before serving. ½ cup maple syrup.
12. Serve.
Per Serving: Calories: 327; Fat: 22g; Sodium: 421mg; Carbs: 10g; Fiber 4.1g; Sugar: 2g; Protein: 31g

Rum-Soaked Pineapple with Vanilla Ice Cream

Prep time: 15 minutes | Cook time: 8 minutes | Serves: 6

Ingredients:
½ cup packed brown sugar
½ cup rum
1 teaspoon ground cinnamon
1 pineapple, cored and sliced
Cooking spray
Vanilla ice cream

Preparation:
1. Grease the cooking surface of the griddle with cooking spray.
2. Turn on the 4 burners and turn their knobs to medium heat.
3. Let the Griddle preheat for 5 minutes.
4. Mix the rum with brown sugar and cinnamon in a suitable mixing bowl.
5. Pour this mixture over your pineapple rings and mix well.
6. Let the pineapple rings soak for about 15 minutes and flip the rings after 7 minutes.
7. Place the pineapple on the griddle for 4 minutes per side.
8. Serve your pineapple rings with a scoop of ice cream on top.
Per Serving: Calories: 412; Fat: 14.9g; Sodium: 554mg; Carbs: 7g; Fiber 2.2g; Sugar: 8g; Protein: 26g

Star Fruit Skewers with Orange-Clove Syrup

Prep time: 15 minutes | Cook time: 16 minutes | Serves: 4

Ingredients:
- ½ cup sugar
- zest of 1 large orange
- 1 tablespoon whole cloves
- 1 small pineapple
- 3 star fruit

Preparation:
1. Grease the cooking surface of the griddle with cooking spray.
2. Turn on the 4 burners and turn their knobs to medium heat.
3. Let the Griddle preheat for 5 minutes.
4. Put the sugar, orange zest, cloves, and ½ cup water in a small saucepan over medium heat.
5. Bring to a boil, reduce the heat, and gently bubble for 5 to 10 minutes.
6. Remove from the heat and let sit for at least 30 minutes.
7. Trim, peel, and core the pineapple, then cut it into 2-inch chunks.
8. Cut the star fruit into ½-inch-thick slices. Skewer the fruit; using 2 skewers makes them easier to turn.
9. Skewer the star fruit through the points of the star on 2 sides. Brush lightly with the orange-clove syrup.
10. Put the skewers on the griddle, and then let it cook, until the pineapple chunks brown in spots, 6 to 8 minutes per side; Brush the fruit several times with the syrup while it griddles.
11. Serve.

Per Serving: Calories: 421; Fat: 11g; Sodium: 361mg; Carbs: 11g; Fiber 3.1g; Sugar: 2g; Protein: 26g

Sweet Potato Pancakes

Prep time: 15 minutes | Cook time: 10 minutes | Serves: 2

Ingredients:
- ¾ cup sweet potato, cooked and pureed
- 2 eggs
- 1 cup buttermilk
- 3 tablespoons Butter, melted, for batter

Preparation:
1. Grease the cooking surface of the griddle with butter.
2. Turn on the 4 burners and turn their knobs to medium heat.
3. Let the Griddle preheat for 5 minutes.
4. Mix the wet ingredients together and set aside. In a suitable bowl, mix all the dry recipe's ingredients together.
5. Combine the wet ingredients and dry ingredients.
6. Pour the prepared batter on the griddle into pancakes.
7. Serve with walnut or pecan syrup and bananas.

Per Serving: Calories: 392; Fat: 32g; Sodium: 354mg; Carbs: 14g; Fiber 1.2g; Sugar: 5g; Protein: 31g

Buttermilk Biscuits

Prep time: 15 minutes | Cook time: 20 minutes | Serves: 14

Ingredients:
- 2½ cups all-purpose flour
- 2¼ teaspoons instant yeast
- 1 teaspoon baking powder
- 1 teaspoon baking soda
- 1 teaspoon salt
- 8 tablespoons butter, melted
- 1 cup buttermilk

Preparation:
1. Grease the cooking surface of the griddle with cooking spray.
2. Turn on the 4 burners and turn their knobs to medium heat.
3. Let the Griddle preheat for 5 minutes.
4. Whisk the flour, yeast, baking powder and soda, and salt together in a suitable bowl.
5. Stir the melted butter into the buttermilk, then add to the flour and stir it in.
6. With your hands, gather the prepared dough into a ball and transfer to a lightly floured work surface.
7. Knead the prepared dough until smooth, 1 to 2 minutes, then pat it down to a ½- to ¾-inch thickness.
8. Cut the biscuits using a 2½-inch cutter. Pat the scraps together, flatten again, and cut more biscuits.
9. Coat the insides of 2 ½-inch cast-iron skillets with softened butter.
10. Put the biscuits in the pans, not touching. Cover with plastic wrap and let rise until doubled, 1 to 1½ hours.
11. Put the biscuits on the griddle, and let it cook for 5 to 7 minutes per side.
12. Serve.

Per Serving: Calories: 392; Fat: 31g; Sodium: 501mg; Carbs: 16g; Fiber 2.1g; Sugar: 2.2g; Protein: 28g

Chili Pineapple Slices

Prep time: 9 minutes | Cook time: 15 minutes | Serves: 2

Ingredients:
- 4 pineapple slices
- 1 tablespoon butter, melted
- ¼ teaspoon chili powder
- ¼ teaspoon salt

Preparation:
1. Preheat the griddle to high heat.
2. Drizzle butter, chili powder, and salt over pineapple slices.
3. Cook pineapple slices for 5-6 minutes on each side on a hot griddle top.
4. Serve and have fun.

Per Serving: Calories: 108; Fat: 3.3g; Sodium: 174mg; Carbs: 21.7g; Fiber 2.6g; Sugar: 18.8g; Protein: 0.8g

Sweet Potato Fries

Prep time: 08 minutes | Cook time: 15 minutes | Serves: 4

Ingredients:
- 2 pounds (907 g) peeled and cut into ½-inch wedges sweet potatoes
- 2 tablespoons olive oil
- pepper and salt to taste

Preparation:
1. Preheat the griddle to a medium-high temperature.
2. Toss sweet potatoes with oil, pepper, and salt in a large mixing bowl.
3. Cook sweet potato wedges for 6 minutes on a heated griddle over medium heat. Flip and cook for another 6-8 minutes.
4. When done, serve and enjoy.

Per Serving: Calories: 125; Fat: 7g; Sodium: 24mg; Carbs: 16.5g; Fiber 1.6g; Sugar: 3.8g; Protein: 1g

Banana Chocolate Peanut Chips

Prep time: 15 minutes | Cook time: 5 minutes | Serves: 4

Ingredients:
- 1 tablespoon butter, softened
- 2 tablespoons chopped peanut brittle
- 2 tablespoons chopped dark chocolate
- 1 ripe banana

Preparation:
1. In a good bowl, mash together the butter, peanut brittle, and chocolate.
2. Slit one side of the banana from top to bottom, through the top but not the bottom peel.
3. Pull the banana open to the point where the filling can be pushed into the slit.
4. Grease the cooking surface of the griddle with cooking oil.
5. Turn on the 4 burners and turn their knobs to medium heat.
6. Let the Griddle preheat for 5 minutes.
7. Put the banana on the griddle grate slit side up, and then let it cook until the peel turns black, about 5 minutes.
8. Transfer to a plate.
9. Serve.

Per Serving: Calories: 397; Fat: 21g; Sodium: 711mg; Carbs: 8g; Fiber 3.1g; Sugar: 4g; Protein: 22g

Taco-Seasoned Chicken Drumsticks

Prep time: 10 minutes | Cook time: 30 minutes | Serves: 8

Ingredients:
- 2 pounds (907 g) chicken legs
- 2 tablespoons taco seasoning
- 2 tablespoons olive oil

Preparation:
1. Preheat the griddle to medium-high heat and heat the oil.
2. Drizzle some oil on the chicken legs and season them with taco seasoning.
3. Cook for 30 minutes on a hot griddle with chicken legs.
4. After every 10 minutes, turn the chicken legs.
5. When done, serve and enjoy.

Per Serving: Calories: 250; Fat: 11.3g; Sodium: 204mg; Carbs: 1g; Fiber 0g; Sugar: 0.3g; Protein: 32.8g

Rosemary Cheese Tomatoes

Prep time: 8 minutes | Cook time: 21 minutes | Serves 6

Ingredients:
- 9 halved tomatoes
- 1 cup grated parmesan cheese
- 1 teaspoon ground black pepper
- ½ teaspoon onion powder
- ¼ tablespoon dried rosemary
- 2 tablespoons olive oil
- 5 minced garlic cloves
- 1 teaspoon kosher salt

Preparation:
1. Oil the grates of a griddle and heat it to medium-low heat.
2. Cook for 5-7 minutes on the griddle, cut side down, tomatoes halves.
3. In a medium-sized pan, heat the olive oil. Cook for 3-5 minutes with the garlic, rosemary, black pepper, onion powder, and salt.
4. Turn off the heat and set the pan aside.
5. Brush each tomato half with the olive oil garlic mixture and sprinkle with grated parmesan cheese before serving. Close the griddle and continue to cook for another 7-10 minutes, or until the cheese has melted.
6. Remove the tomatoes from the grill as soon as possible.
7. Serve and enjoy.

Per Serving: Calories: 86; Fat: 6g; Sodium: 434mg; Carbs: 6.9g; Fiber 2g; Sugar: 3.8g; Protein: 3.8g

Chicken Burger Patties

Prep time: 8 minutes | Cook time: 15 minutes | Serves 6

Ingredients:
- 1 pound (454 g) ground chicken
- 1 teaspoon chili powder
- 1 teaspoon cayenne powder
- 1 tablespoon honey
- ¼ cup almond flour
- ¼ teaspoon pepper
- 2 teaspoons dried parsley
- 1 teaspoon paprika
- ¼ teaspoon salt

Preparation:
1. In a large mixing basin, combine all of the ingredients and stir until well blended.
2. Preheat the griddle to a high heat.
3. Spray the top of the griddle with cooking spray.
4. Form patties from the mixture and cook for 4-6 minutes on each side on a hot griddle.
5. Serve and have fun.

Per Serving: Calories:185; Fat: 8.3g; Sodium: 174mg; Carbs: 2.6g; Fiber 0.6g; Sugar: 3.8g; Protein: 23.8g

Mint Five-Spice Oranges

Prep time: 15 minutes | Cook time: 15 minutes | Serves: 4

Ingredients:
- ¼ cup sugar
- ½ teaspoon five-spice powder
- 2 large oranges
- ¼ cup chopped fresh mint

Preparation:
1. Grease the cooking surface of the griddle with cooking spray.
2. Turn on the 4 burners and turn their knobs to medium heat.
3. Let the Griddle preheat for 5 minutes.
4. Stir the sugar and five-spice powder together on a small plate.
5. Cut a sliver off the top and bottom of each orange.
6. Remove any seeds. Press the cut side of each ½ into the sugar.
7. Put the orange halves on the griddle, sugared side up, and then let it cook for 6 or 8 minutes.
8. Turn them over and then let it cook just until the cut sides brown, 2 to 3 minutes.
9. Transfer to individual serving plates, sprinkle with the mint.
10. Serve.

Per Serving: Calories: 397; Fat: 21g; Sodium: 711mg; Carbs: 8g; Fiber 3.1g; Sugar: 4g; Protein: 22g

Seared Fruits with Berries

Prep time: 15 minutes | Cook time: 10 minutes | Serves: 6

Ingredients:
- 2 halved apricot
- 1 halved nectarine
- 2 halved peaches
- ¼ cup of blueberries
- ½ cup of raspberries
- 2 tablespoons of honey
- 1 orange, the peel
- 2 cups of cream
- ½ cup of balsamic vinegar

Preparation:
1. Preheat the Griddle by turning all its knob to medium-heat setting.
2. Grease the griddle top with cooking spray.
3. Sear the peaches, nectarines, and apricots on the hot griddle top for 4 minutes per side.
4. Add 2 tablespoons honey, 2 tablespoons vinegar, 2 tablespoons orange peel to a saucepan.
5. Cook on a stove until the sauce has thickened to a medium consistency.
6. In the meantime, whisk together honey and cream in a suitable mixing dish.
7. Whip until the mixture achieves a soft consistency.
8. Arrange the fruits on a platter for serving.
9. Lastly, top with berries. Drizzle the balsamic reduction over the top.
10. Enjoy with a dollop of sour cream!

Per Serving: Calories: 116; Fat: 4.3 g; Sodium: 28 mg; Carbs: 32.9g; Fiber: 2.5g; Sugar: 29g; Protein: 1.6g

Delectable Turkey Burger

Prep time: 15 minutes | Cook time: 14 minutes | Serves: 6

Ingredients:
- 1 lb. ground turkey
- 1 egg, lightly beaten
- 1 cup Monterey jack cheese, grated
- 1 cup carrot, grated
- 1 cup cauliflower, grated
- 2 garlic cloves, minced
- ½ cup onion, minced
- ¾ cup breadcrumbs
- Black pepper, to taste
- salt, to taste

Preparation:
1. Grease the cooking surface of the griddle with cooking spray.
2. Turn on the 4 burners and turn their knobs to medium heat.
3. Let the Griddle preheat for 5 minutes.
4. Add all the recipe's ingredients into the mixing bowl and mix until well combined.
5. Make small patties from mixture and place on preheated griddle top and then let it cook until golden brown from both sides.
6. Serve.

Per Serving: Calories: 304; Fat: 14.9g; Sodium: 304mg; Carbs: 12g; Fiber 6g; Sugar: 2g; Protein: 21g

Peach Apple Pie

Prep time: 15 minutes | Cook time: 40 minutes | Serves: 6

Ingredients:
- ¼ cup of sugar
- 4 apples, sliced
- 1 tablespoon of cornstarch
- 1 teaspoon cinnamon, ground
- 1 pie crust, refrigerated
- ½ cup of peach preServes

Preparation:
1. Mix well the cornstarch, cinnamon, sugar, and apples in a suitable mixing bowl.
2. Line a pie pan with the piecrust. Place the apples on top of the preServes. Slightly fold the crust.
3. Preheat the Griddle by turning all its knob to medium-heat setting.
4. Grease the griddle top with cooking spray.
5. Place the pan on the hot griddle top and cook for 40 minutes.
6. Serve and have fun!

Per Serving: Calories: 386; Fat: 10.3 g; Sodium: 238 mg; Carbs: 72.9g; Fiber: 4.5g; Sugar: 59g; Protein: 2.6g

Chapter 5 Fish and Seafood Recipes

Fried Fish with Cilantro Mixture

Prep time: 5 minutes | Cook time: 15 minutes | Serves: 4

Ingredients:
4 cups oil
4 garlic cloves, minced
1 white onion, quartered
1 jalapeño chile, stemmed, halved
1 (3- pounds) whole fish, scaled and gutted
Salt, for seasoning
1 bunch cilantro leaves
Juice of 2 limes

Preparation:
1. Preheat the Griddle by turning all its knob to medium-heat setting.
2. Grease the griddle top with cooking oil.
3. Add the garlic, onion, and jalapeno and cook for 3 minutes then transfer to a plate.
4. Make cuts on top of the fish and season them with black pepper, salt and oil.
5. Place the fish on the hot griddle top and cook for 5 minutes per side.
6. Blend cilantro, lime juice, garlic, onion, and jalapeno in a food processor until smooth.
7. Serve the fish with the sauce.
Per Serving: Calories: 219; Fat: 14.8 g; Sodium: 78 mg; Carbs: 3.7 g; Fiber: 0.7g; Sugar: 1.3g; Protein: 17g

Seasoned Rainbow Trout

Prep time: 7 minutes | Cook time: 15 minutes | Serves: 4

Ingredients:
Cumin and Burnt Citrus Vinaigrette
1½ tablespoons cumin seeds
3 oranges, juiced
3 lemons, juiced
1½ cups oil
3 tablespoons honey
¼ cup vinegar
½ shallot, grated
1½ teaspoons salt
½ teaspoon Mexican oregano
Fish
4 (12 oz.) whole rainbow trout
Oil and salt, for coating

Preparation:
1. Roast the cumin on a skillet over medium heat for about 2 minutes.
2. In a spice grinder or blender, grind until extremely fine and set aside.
3. Mix all the vinaigrette ingredients in a bowl.
4. Add fish fillets, rub well and marinate for 30 minutes.
5. Preheat the Griddle by turning all its knob to medium-heat setting.
6. Grease the griddle top with cooking oil.
7. Place the fish on the hot griddle top and cook for 5 minutes per side.
8. Serve warm.
Per Serving: Calories: 449; Fat: 26.1 g; Sodium: 3255 mg; Carbs: 37.5g; Fiber: 5.4g; Sugar: 27.4g; Protein: 19.2g

Gremolata Swordfish Skewers

Prep time: 15 minutes | Cook time: 15 minutes | Serves: 4

Ingredients:
1 ½ lb. skinless swordfish fillet
2 teaspoons of lemon zest
3 tablespoons of lemon juice
½ cup of chopped parsley
2 teaspoons of garlic, minced
¾ teaspoon sea salt
¼ teaspoon black pepper
2 tablespoons of olive oil
½ teaspoon of red pepper flakes
3 lemons, cut into slices

Preparation:
1. Grease the cooking surface of the griddle with cooking spray.
2. Turn on the 4 burners and turn their knobs to medium heat.
3. Let the Griddle preheat for 5 minutes.
4. Combine lemon zest, parsley, garlic, ¼ teaspoon of salt, and pepper in a suitable bowl with a fork.
5. Mix swordfish pieces with reserved lemon juice, olive oil, red pepper flakes, and remaining salt.
6. Thread swordfish and lemon slices, alternating each, onto the metal skewers.
7. Sear skewers for 5 minutes per side on the griddle top.
8. Place skewers on a serving platter and sprinkle with gremolata.
9. Drizzle with olive oil and serve.
Per Serving: Calories: 449; Fat: 21g; Sodium: 421mg; Carbs: 16g; Fiber 4.1g; Sugar: 3.2g; Protein: 27g

Cod Fish Fillets

Prep time: 15 minutes | Cook time: 15 minutes | Serves: 4

Ingredients:
2 cod fillets, cut in ½
1 lemon, juiced
2 tablespoons of butter, melted
¼ teaspoon black pepper
½ teaspoon of lemon black pepper, to taste
1 tablespoon of Cajun seasoning
¼ teaspoon of salt

Preparation:
1. Grease the cooking surface of the griddle with cooking spray.
2. Turn on the 4 burners and turn their knobs to medium-high heat.
3. Let the Griddle preheat for 5 minutes.
4. Add fish fillets and the rest of the recipe's ingredients into the mixing bowl and mix well.
5. Place fish fillets on a preheated griddle top and then let it cook for 4-5 minutes on each side.
6. Serve.
Per Serving: Calories: 366; Fat: 13g; Sodium: 421mg; Carbs: 16g; Fiber 4.1g; Sugar: 3.2g; Protein: 27g

Tasty Ceviche

Prep time: 20 minutes | Cook time: 22 minutes | Serves: 4

Ingredients:
Marinade:
1 cucumber
1 cup lime juice
1 jalapeño chile, stemmed
½ cup basil leaves
1 teaspoon salt
Pickled Onions:
8 spring onions, white and green parts
Oil, for coating
1 teaspoon salt
1 teaspoon sugar
Vinegar, for pickling
Cucumber:
1 cucumber
Oil and salt, for coating
1½ pounds boneless snapper or any other whitefish
Salt, for seasoning
½ cup basil leaves, chopped
1 celery stalk, sliced

Preparation:
1. Blend lime juice, cucumber, basil, jalapeno, and salt in a blender and puree until smooth.
2. Push the mixture through a cheesecloth over a large bowl then discard solids.
3. Preheat the Griddle by turning all its knob to High-heat setting.
4. Grease the griddle top with cooking oil.
5. Toss the greens with the oil and salt and cook for 1 minute over high heat, then chop.
6. Slice the white onions and mix with sugar, 1 teaspoon salt, and vinegar in a suitable mixing bowl.
7. Season the fish with salt and marinade thoroughly.
8. Sear the fish on the hot griddle top for 5 minutes per side.
9. In a suitable mixing bowl, mix well the onion greens, drained pickled onions, basil, cucumber, and celery.
10. Serve.
Per Serving: Calories: 283; Fat: 6.6g; Sodium: 693mg; Carbs: 8.5g; Fiber: 1.4g; Sugar: 3.4g; Protein: 45.2g

Simple Garlic Haddock

Prep time: 15 minutes | Cook time: 15 minutes | Serves: 4

Ingredients:
4 haddock fish fillets
2 tablespoons of garlic, minced
2 tablespoons of olive oil
Salt, to taste

Preparation:
1. Grease the cooking surface of the griddle with cooking spray.
2. Turn on the 4 burners and turn their knobs to medium-high heat.
3. Let the Griddle preheat for 5 minutes.
4. Brush fish fillets with oil and season by adding garlic and salt.
5. Place fish fillets on a preheated griddle top and then let it cook for 4-5 minutes on each side.
6. Serve.
Per Serving: Calories: 412; Fat: 14.9g; Sodium: 554mg; Carbs: 7g; Fiber 2.2g; Sugar: 8g; Protein: 26g

Lemon Oysters with Spiced Tequila Butter

Prep time: 15 minutes | Cook time: 10 minutes | Serves: 6

Ingredients:
3 dozen medium oysters, scrubbed and shucked
Butter
¼ teaspoon of crushed red black pepper, to taste
7 tablespoons of unsalted butter
¼ teaspoon of chili oil
Flakey sea salt, for serving
1 teaspoon of dried oregano
2 tablespoons lemon juice
2 tablespoons of tequila Blanco

Preparation:
1. Grease the cooking surface of the griddle with cooking spray.
2. Turn on the 4 burners and turn their knobs to medium heat.
3. Let the Griddle preheat for 5 minutes.
4. Combine butter ingredients in a suitable mixing bowl until well incorporated and set aside.
5. Cook the oysters for about 1 to 2 minutes on the griddle top.
6. Sprinkle the oysters with salt flakes.
7. Warm the butter in a microwave for 30 seconds, and spoon the warm tequila butter over the oysters and serve.
8. Serve.

Per Serving: Calories: 342; Fat: 12g; Sodium: 354mg; Carbs: 24g; Fiber 1.2g; Sugar: 5g; Protein: 28g

Cajun White Fish Fillets

Prep time: 15 minutes | Cook time: 15 minutes | Serves: 4

Ingredients:
4 white fish fillets
1 tablespoon of olive oil
¼ teaspoon of onion powder
½ teaspoon of ground cumin
½ teaspoon of cayenne
½ teaspoon of oregano
1 teaspoon of paprika
½ teaspoon black pepper
½ teaspoon of salt

Preparation:
1. Grease the cooking surface of the griddle with cooking spray.
2. Turn on the 4 burners and turn their knobs to medium-high heat.
3. Let the Griddle preheat for 5 minutes.
4. In a suitable bowl, onion powder, cumin, cayenne, oregano, paprika, pepper, and salt.
5. Brush fish fillets with oil and rub with spice mixture.
6. Place fish fillets on a preheated griddle top and then let it cook for 4 minutes on each side.
7. Serve.

Per Serving: Calories: 339; Fat: 13g; Sodium: 421mg; Carbs: 16g; Fiber 4.1g; Sugar: 3.2g; Protein: 27g

Flavorful Tilapia

Prep time: 15 minutes | Cook time: 15 minutes | Serves: 4

Ingredients:
4 tilapia fillets
1 teaspoon of garlic powder
2 teaspoons of paprika
3 tablespoons of olive oil
½ teaspoon of black pepper
1 teaspoon of salt

Preparation:
1. Grease the cooking surface of the griddle with cooking spray.
2. Turn on the 4 burners and turn their knobs to medium-high heat.
3. Let the Griddle preheat for 5 minutes.
4. Brush fish fillets with oil and season by adding garlic powder, paprika, pepper, and salt.
5. Place fish fillets on a preheated griddle top and then let it cook for 4 minutes on each side.
6. Serve.

Per Serving: Calories: 421; Fat: 11g; Sodium: 361mg; Carbs: 11g; Fiber 3.1g; Sugar: 2g; Protein: 26g

Dijon Lump Crab Cakes

Prep time: 15 minutes | Cook time: 15 minutes | Serves: 4

Ingredients:
1 lb. of lump crab meat
½ cup of panko breadcrumbs
⅓ cup of mayonnaise
1 egg, beaten
2 tablespoons of Dijon mustard
2 teaspoons of Worcestershire sauce
½ teaspoon of paprika
½ teaspoon of salt
¼ teaspoon black pepper
3 tablespoons of vegetable oil

Preparation:
1. Grease the cooking surface of the griddle with cooking spray.
2. Turn on the 4 burners and turn their knobs to medium heat.
3. Let the Griddle preheat for 5 minutes.
4. In a suitable bowl, combine the crab, breadcrumbs, mayo, egg, mustard Worcestershire sauce, paprika, black pepper and salt.
5. Form the crab mixture into 4 large balls and flatten them slightly.
6. Add the oil to the griddle and then let it cook the crab cakes for approximately 5 minutes per side or until browned and crispy.
7. Serve.

Per Serving: Calories: 378; Fat: 15g; Sodium: 521mg; Carbs: 14g; Fiber 5.1g; Sugar: 3g; Protein: 27g

Halibut Fillets with Spinach

Prep time: 15 minutes | Cook time: 15 minutes | Serves: 4

Ingredients:
4 (6 ounces) halibut fillets
⅓ cup of olive oil
4 cups of baby spinach
¼ cup of lemon juice
2 ounces of pitted black olives
halved
2 tablespoons of flat-leaf parsley, chopped
2 teaspoons of fresh dill, chopped
Lemon wedges, to serve

Preparation:
1. Grease the cooking surface of the griddle with cooking spray.
2. Turn on the 4 burners and turn their knobs to medium heat.
3. Let the Griddle preheat for 5 minutes.
4. Toss spinach with lemon juice in a suitable mixing bowl and set aside.
5. Brush fish with olive oil and then let it cook for 3-4 minutes per side, or until cooked through.
6. Remove from heat, cover with foil and let rest for 5 minutes.
7. Add remaining oil and then let it cook spinach for 2 minutes, or until just wilted. Remove from heat.
8. Toss with olives and herbs, then transfer to serving plates with fish, and serve with lemon wedges.
9. Serve.

Per Serving: Calories: 449; Fat: 11g; Sodium: 501mg; Carbs: 16g; Fiber 2.1g; Sugar: 2.2g; Protein: 27g

Simple Grouper

Prep time: 8 minutes | Cook time: 10 minutes | Serves: 2

Ingredients:
1 (3-pounds) whole grouper, scaled and gutted
Oil and salt, for coating

Preparation:
1. Preheat the Griddle by turning all its knob to medium-heat setting.
2. Grease the griddle top with cooking spray.
3. Season the whole grouper with salt and oil.
4. Sear the fish for 5 minutes per side on the hot griddle top.
5. Serve warm.

Per Serving: Calories: 100; Fat: 1 g; Sodium: 45 mg; Carbs: 0g; Fiber: 0 g; Sugar: 0g; Protein: 21g

Spicy Cod Fillets

Prep time: 15 minutes | Cook time: 15 minutes | Serves: 4

Ingredients:
4 cod fillets
½ teaspoon of garlic, minced
½ teaspoon of ground coriander
½ teaspoon of ground cumin
2 teaspoons of chili powder
2 teaspoons of lime juice
3 tablespoons of olive oil

Preparation:
1. Grease the cooking surface of the griddle with cooking spray.
2. Turn on the 4 burners and turn their knobs to medium-high heat.
3. Let the Griddle preheat for 5 minutes.
4. Add fish fillets and the rest of the recipe's ingredients into the bowl and mix well.
5. Place fish fillets on a preheated griddle top and then let it cook for 4-5 minutes on each side or until cooked through.
6. Serve.

Per Serving: Calories: 376; Fat: 13g; Sodium: 421mg; Carbs: 16g; Fiber 4.1g; Sugar: 3.2g; Protein: 27g

Delicious Bacon-Wrapped Scallops

Prep time: 15 minutes | Cook time: 10 minutes | Serves: 4

Ingredients:
- 12 large sea scallops, side muscle removed
- 8 slices of bacon
- 1 tablespoon of vegetable oil
- 12 toothpicks

Preparation:
1. Grease the cooking surface of the griddle with cooking spray.
2. Turn on the 4 burners and turn their knobs to medium heat.
3. Let the Griddle preheat for 5 minutes.
4. Add bacon to the griddle top and then let it cook until crispy.
5. Transfer the cooked bacon to a plate, lined with paper towel.
6. Cut the bacon in half and wrap each scallop with one bacon half.
7. Secure the bacon with a toothpick and sear for 2 minutes per side on the griddle.
8. Serve.

Per Serving: Calories: 421; Fat: 11g; Sodium: 361mg; Carbs: 11g; Fiber 3.1g; Sugar: 2g; Protein: 26g

Savoury Red Snapper Fillets

Prep time: 15 minutes | Cook time: 15 minutes | Serves: 2

Ingredients:
- 2 red snapper fish fillets
- 1 tablespoon of olive oil
- 1 teaspoon of chili powder
- ½ teaspoon black pepper
- ½ teaspoon of garlic powder
- ½ teaspoon of onion powder
- 1 tablespoon of paprika
- ½ teaspoon of salt

Preparation:
1. Grease the cooking surface of the griddle with cooking spray.
2. Turn on the 4 burners and turn their knobs to medium-high heat.
3. Let the Griddle preheat for 5 minutes.
4. In a suitable bowl, mix chili powder, pepper, garlic powder, onion powder, paprika, and salt.
5. Brush fish fillets with oil and rub with spice mixture.
6. Place fish fillets on a preheated griddle top and then let it cook for 3-4 minutes on each side.
7. Serve.

Per Serving: Calories: 338; Fat: 12g; Sodium: 521mg; Carbs: 14g; Fiber 5.1g; Sugar: 3g; Protein: 27g

Quick-Cooking Shrimp

Prep time: 15 minutes | Cook time: 10 minutes | Serves: 4

Ingredients:
- 1 ½ lbs. of shrimp, peeled and deveined
- 1 tablespoon of soy sauce
- 2 tablespoons of butter
- 2 tablespoons of olive oil
- Black pepper, to taste
- Salt, to taste

Preparation:
1. Grease the cooking surface of the griddle with cooking spray.
2. Turn on the 4 burners and turn their knobs to medium-high heat.
3. Let the Griddle preheat for 5 minutes.
4. Toss shrimp with oil, pepper, and salt.
5. Place shrimp on preheated griddle top and then let it cook for 3 minutes.
6. Add butter and soy sauce and then let it cook shrimp for 2 minutes.
7. Serve.

Per Serving: Calories: 354; Fat: 7.9g; Sodium: 704mg; Carbs: 6g; Fiber 3.6g; Sugar: 6g; Protein: 18g

Tasty Herb-Seasoned Fish

Prep time: 15 minutes | Cook time: 10 minutes | Serves: 2

Ingredients:
- A ½ lb. of cod fillets
- 1 egg, beaten
- ½ teaspoon of dried basil
- 2 tablespoons of breadcrumbs
- ¼ cup of Bisquick mix
- ⅛ teaspoon of salt

Preparation:
1. Grease the cooking surface of the griddle with cooking spray.
2. Turn on the 4 burners and turn their knobs to medium-high heat.
3. Let the Griddle preheat for 5 minutes.
4. In a shallow dish, add the egg.
5. In a separate shallow dish, mix breadcrumbs, Bisquick mix, basil, and salt.
6. Dip fish fillets with egg, then coat with breadcrumb mixture.
7. Place fish fillets on a preheated griddle top and then let it cook for 8-10 minutes.
8. Serve.

Per Serving: Calories: 326; Fat: 13g; Sodium: 421mg; Carbs: 16g; Fiber 4.1g; Sugar: 3.2g; Protein: 27g

Spicy Amberjack Fillets

Prep time: 15 minutes | Cook time: 2 hours | Serves: 4

Ingredients:
- 1½ pounds boneless amberjack fillets
- 1½ cups oil
- 1 teaspoon salt
- 4 guajillo chiles, toasted, stemmed, and seeded

Preparation:
1. Use oil and salt to coat the amberjack.
2. Preheat the Griddle by turning all its knob to medium-heat setting.
3. Grease the griddle top with cooking spray.
4. Place the fillets on the hot griddle top and cook for 5 minutes per side.
5. In a blender, mix well the 1½ cup oil, chiles, and 1 teaspoon salt and blend until smooth.
6. Strain the liquid and pour it over the fish to completely cover it.
7. Serve immediately or keep refrigerated, covered.

Per Serving: Calories: 469; Fat: 34.1 g; Sodium: 1242 mg; Carbs: 23.5g; Fiber: 0.6g; Sugar: 0g; Protein: 19.2g

Spicy Squid in Sauce

Prep time: 15 minutes | Cook time: 10 minutes | Serves: 4

Ingredients:
- 1 ½ lbs. of squid, prepared

Marinade
- 2 cloves of garlic, minced
- ½ teaspoon of ginger, minced
- 3 tablespoons of gochujang
- 3 tablespoons of corn syrup
- 1 teaspoon of yellow mustard
- 1 teaspoon of soy sauce
- 2 teaspoons of sesame oil
- 1 teaspoon of sesame seeds
- 2 green onions, chopped

Preparation:
1. Grease the cooking surface of the griddle with cooking spray.
2. Turn on the 4 burners and turn their knobs to medium heat.
3. Let the Griddle preheat for 5 minutes.
4. Add the squid and tentacles to the griddle and then let it cook for 1 minute until the bottom looks firm and opaque.
5. Turn them over and then let it cook for another minute; straigh10 out the body with tongs if it curls.
6. Baste with sauce on top of the squid and then let it cook for 2 additional minutes.
7. Flip and baste the other side, cook 1 minute until the sauce evaporates and the squid turns red and shiny.
8. Serve.

Per Serving: Calories: 449; Fat: 11g; Sodium: 501mg; Carbs: 16g; Fiber 2.1g; Sugar: 2.2g; Protein: 27g

Garlicky Tuna Steaks

Prep time: 6 minutes | Cook time: 14 minutes | Serves: 4

Ingredients:
Rub:
- 2 tablespoons salt
- 2 teaspoons cayenne pepper
- 2 teaspoons sweet paprika
- 1 teaspoon ground white pepper
- 1 teaspoon celery salt
- 1 tablespoon peeled and grated fresh ginger
- 1 large garlic clove, grated
- 2 tablespoons oil
- 1 tablespoon honey
- 2 (12-oz.) tuna steaks, about 1½ inches thick
- Oil, for drizzling
- Lemon wedges, for serving

Preparation:
1. In a suitable mixing bowl, mix the cayenne, salt, white pepper, paprika, ginger, celery salt, garlic, oil, and honey.
2. Coat the tuna with the wet rub, rub well, then chill for 60 minutes uncovered.
3. Preheat the Griddle by turning all its knob to medium-heat setting.
4. Grease the griddle top with cooking oil.
5. Place the tuna steaks on the hot griddle top and cook for 3-5 minutes per side.
6. Slice and serve.

Per Serving: Calories: 274; Fat: 9.5 g; Sodium: 3542 mg; Carbs: 6.3g; Fiber: 0.9g; Sugar: 4.6g; Protein: 40.5g

Sweet Potato Snapper Apple Ceviche

Prep time: 15 minutes | Cook time: 10 minutes | Serves: 4

Ingredients:
1 small fennel bulb, with fronds attached
1 teaspoon salt
1 tablespoon sugar
Vinegar, for pickling
¼ cup oil
¼ cup honey
1 large sweet potato, sliced lengthwise into ¾-inch slices
5 limes
2 oranges
2 mandarins
1 grapefruit
1½ pounds boneless snapper or any other whitefish
½ small red onion, sliced paper thin
2 plum tomatoes, diced
½ Granny Smith apple, peeled, cored, and cut into matchstick-size batons
¼ cup chopped cilantro leaves

Preparation:
1. Toss the salt, fennel, sugar, and vinegar in a bowl to coat the fennel.
2. In a suitable mixing bowl, mix well the oil and honey.
3. Toss in the sweet potato in the oil-honey mixture to coat it completely then drain.
4. Preheat the Griddle by turning all its knob to medium-heat setting.
5. Grease the griddle top with cooking oil.
6. Season the sweet potatoes with salt and sear for about 5 minutes per side until caramelized.
7. Transfer to a bowl with tongs, then cover securely with plastic wrap
8. Set aside 2 limes and half the rest of the fruit.
9. Brush the cut sides with the remaining oil–honey mixture and cook over medium heat, for almost 2 minutes.
10. Mix fish with salt and citrus juice thoroughly.
11. Mix well the drained pickled fennel, sweet potato, tomato, onion, cilantro, apple, and 2 teaspoons fennel fronds in a suitable mixing bowl.
12. Serve.

Per Serving: Calories: 597; Fat: 17.1 g; Sodium: 723 mg; Carbs: 66.5g; Fiber: 9.3g; Sugar: 45g; Protein: 48.6g

Pineapple and Shrimp Skewers

Prep time: 15 minutes | Cook time: 12 minutes | Serves: 4

Ingredients:
1 ½ pounds of uncooked jumbo shrimp, peeled and deveined
½ cup of light coconut milk
1 tablespoon of cilantro, chopped
4 teaspoons of tabasco original red sauce
2 teaspoons of soy sauce
¼ cup orange juice
¼ cup lime juice
¾ pound of pineapple, cut into 1-inch chunks
Olive oil for cooking

Preparation:
1. Grease the cooking surface of the griddle with cooking spray.
2. Turn on the 4 burners and turn their knobs to medium heat.
3. Let the Griddle preheat for 5 minutes.
4. Combine the coconut milk, cilantro, tabasco sauce, soy sauce, orange juice, lime juice.
5. Add the shrimp and toss to coat.
6. Cover and place in the refrigerator to marinate for 1 hour.
7. Thread shrimp and pineapple onto metal skewers, alternating.
8. Cook 5-6 minutes, flipping once, until shrimp turn opaque pink.
9. Serve.

Per Serving: Calories: 327; Fat: 22g; Sodium: 421mg; Carbs: 10g; Fiber 4.1g; Sugar: 2g; Protein: 31g

Chipotle Salmon Fillets

Prep time: 15 minutes | Cook time: 20 minutes | Serves: 4

Ingredients:
4 salmon fillets
1 and ¼ teaspoon of chipotle powder
½ tablespoons of ground cumin
1 tablespoon of brown sugar
1 teaspoon of salt

Preparation:
1. Grease the cooking surface of the griddle with cooking spray.
2. Turn on the 4 burners and turn their knobs to medium-high heat.
3. Let the Griddle preheat for 5 minutes.
4. In a suitable bowl, mix chipotle powder, cumin, brown sugar, and salt and sprinkle over salmon fillets.
5. Place salmon fillets on a preheated griddle top and then let it cook for 10-15 minutes or until cooked.
6. Serve.

Per Serving: Calories: 376; Fat: 13g; Sodium: 421mg; Carbs: 16g; Fiber 4.1g; Sugar: 3.2g; Protein: 27g

Lobster Tails

Prep time: 15 minutes | Cook time: 12 minutes | Serves: 4

Ingredients:
4 lobster tails (cut in ½ lengthwise)
3 tablespoons of olive oil
For the lime basil butter
1 stick of unsalted butter softened
½ bunch basil, roughly chopped
1 lime, zested and juiced
Lime wedges (to serve)
Sea salt, to taste
2 cloves of garlic, minced
¼ teaspoon of red pepper flakes

Preparation:
1. Grease the cooking surface of the griddle with cooking spray.
2. Turn on the 4 burners and turn their knobs to medium heat.
3. Let the Griddle preheat for 5 minutes.
4. Add the butter ingredients to a suitable mixing bowl and combine; set aside until ready to use.
5. Drizzle the lobster tail halves with olive oil and season by adding black pepper and salt.
6. Place the lobster tails, flesh-side down, on the griddle.
7. Allow to cook until opaque, about 3 minutes, flip and then let it cook another 3 minutes.
8. Add a dollop of the lime basil butter during the last minute of cooking.
9. Serve.

Per Serving: Calories: 338; Fat: 12g; Sodium: 521mg; Carbs: 14g; Fiber 5.1g; Sugar: 3g; Protein: 27g

Honey-Lime Tilapia

Prep time: 15 minutes | Cook time: 20 minutes | Serves: 4

Ingredients:
4 fillets tilapia
2 tablespoons of honey
4 limes, sliced
2 ears corn, shucked
2 tablespoons of fresh cilantro
leaves
¼ cup of olive oil
Kosher salt, to taste
Black pepper, to taste

Preparation:
1. Grease the cooking surface of the griddle with cooking spray.
2. Turn on the 4 burners and turn their knobs to medium heat.
3. Let the Griddle preheat for 5 minutes.
4. Cut 4 squares of foil about 12" long.
5. Top each piece of foil with tilapia fillets.
6. Brush the fillets with honey and top with corn, lime, and cilantro.
7. Pour some olive oil and season by adding pepper and sea salt.
8. Cook until tilapia is cooked through and corn tender, about 15 minutes.
9. Serve.

Per Serving: Calories: 326; Fat: 13g; Sodium: 421mg; Carbs: 16g; Fiber 4.1g; Sugar: 3.2g; Protein: 27g

Spicy Shrimp

Prep time: 15 minutes | Cook time: 10 minutes | Serves: 4

Ingredients:
1 lb. of shrimp, peeled and deveined
1 tablespoon of lemon juice
4 teaspoons of Worcestershire sauce
2 teaspoons of old bay seasoning
2 teaspoons of chili powder
1 teaspoon of garlic, minced
3 tablespoons of olive oil
Black pepper, to taste
Salt, to taste

Preparation:
1. Grease the cooking surface of the griddle with cooking spray.
2. Turn on the 4 burners and turn their knobs to medium-high heat.
3. Let the Griddle preheat for 5 minutes.
4. Add shrimp and the rest of the recipe's ingredients into the mixing bowl and mix well.
5. Cover and place in the refrigerator for 2 hours.
6. Place shrimp on preheated griddle top and then let it cook for 3-5 minutes or until cooked.
7. Serve.

Per Serving: Calories: 350; Fat: 13g; Sodium: 421mg; Carbs: 16g; Fiber 4.1g; Sugar: 3.2g; Protein: 27g

Garlic Shrimp with Lime Juice

Prep time: 15 minutes | Cook time: 5 minutes | Serves 4

Ingredients:
12 Large Raw Shrimp, Peeled and Mud Vein Removed	1-teaspoon Garlic Salt to Taste
Olive Oil	2 Fresh Lime Juice

Preparation:
1. Preheat the griddle to high heat.
2. Place the shrimp on the skewers in the same direction through the centre.
3. Brush with extra virgin olive oil and season with garlic salt.
4. Cook for 2 minutes on each side on the grill, or until the part closest to the heat has turned pink and white.
5. Drizzle the lime juice over the steaks and grill for a few seconds on each side.
6. Remove from the heat and serve right away.

Per Serving: Calories: 50; Fat: 3.8g; Sodium: 40mg; Carbs: 0.6g; Fiber 0g; Sugar: 0g; Protein: 3.8g

Delectable Crab Legs

Prep time: 15 minutes | Cook time: 15 minutes | Serves: 4

Ingredients:
4 lbs. of king crab legs, cooked	2 tablespoons of chili oil

Preparation:
1. Grease the cooking surface of the griddle with cooking spray.
2. Turn on the 4 burners and turn their knobs to medium heat.
3. Let the Griddle preheat for 5 minutes.
4. Place crab legs on griddle after brushing both sides with chile oil. Make a foil tent.
5. Cook for 4 to 5 minutes on each side, flipping once.
6. Transfer to plates and top with a dollop of melted butter.
7. Serve.

Per Serving: Calories: 392; Fat: 31g; Sodium: 501mg; Carbs: 16g; Fiber 2.1g; Sugar: 2.2g; Protein: 28g

Palatable Cod Patties

Prep time: 15 minutes | Cook time: 12 minutes | Serves: 4

Ingredients:
1 egg	1 lb. of cod fillets, cubed
1 tablespoon of parsley, chopped	2 potatoes, cooked, peel and mash
1 tablespoon of onion, grated	Black pepper, to taste
1 tablespoon of butter	Salt, to taste

Preparation:
1. Grease the cooking surface of the griddle with cooking spray.
2. Turn on the 4 burners and turn their knobs to medium heat.
3. Let the Griddle preheat for 5 minutes.
4. Add all the recipe's ingredients into the mixing bowl and mix until well combined.
5. Make patties from mixture and place on preheated griddle top and then let it cook until golden brown from both sides.
6. Serve.

Per Serving: Calories: 392; Fat: 31g; Sodium: 501mg; Carbs: 16g; Fiber 2.1g; Sugar: 2.2g; Protein: 28g

Delicious Crab Cakes

Prep time: 15 minutes | Cook time: 20 minutes | Serves: 6

Ingredients:
1 egg	1 teaspoon of lemon juice
1 lb. of crab meat	1 teaspoon of old bay seasoning
1 tablespoon of parsley, chopped	2 teaspoons of Dijon mustard
1 cup of breadcrumbs	⅓ cup of mayonnaise

Preparation:
1. Grease the cooking surface of the griddle with cooking spray.
2. Turn on the 4 burners and turn their knobs to medium heat.
3. Let the Griddle preheat for 5 minutes.
4. Add all the recipe's ingredients into the mixing bowl and mix until well combined.
5. Make 6 patties from the mixture and place them on a preheated griddle top, and then let it cook for 6 minutes on each side.
6. Serve.

Per Serving: Calories: 317; Fat: 32g; Sodium: 311mg; Carbs: 12g; Fiber 3.1g; Sugar: 4g; Protein: 22g

Salmon Patties

Prep time: 15 minutes | Cook time: 15 minutes | Serves: 6

Ingredients:
2 eggs	1 small bell pepper, chopped
15 oz can of salmon, bones removed	½ cup of breadcrumbs
2 tablespoons of green onion, chopped	⅓ cup of parmesan cheese, shredded
2 tablespoons of mayonnaise	Black pepper, to taste
	Salt, to taste

Preparation:
1. Grease the cooking surface of the griddle with cooking spray.
2. Turn on the 4 burners and turn their knobs to medium heat.
3. Let the Griddle preheat for 5 minutes.
4. Add all the recipe's ingredients into the mixing bowl and mix until well combined.
5. Make patties from mixture and place on preheated griddle top and then let it cook for 5 minutes on each side.
6. Serve.

Per Serving: Calories: 395; Fat: 21g; Sodium: 451mg; Carbs: 17g; Fiber 4.1g; Sugar: 1.2g; Protein: 24g

Lobster Tails with basil Butter

Prep time: 5 minutes | Cook time: 6 minutes | Serves: 4

Ingredients:
4 lobster tails, cut in half lengthwise	Lime wedges, to serve
3 tablespoons olive oil	Sea salt and black pepper, to taste

For the Lime Basil Butter:
1 stick butter, softened	2 cloves garlic, minced
½ bunch basil, roughly chopped	¼ teaspoon red pepper flakes
1 lime, zested and juiced	

Preparation:
1. In a suitable mixing dish, mix well the basil butter ingredients.
2. Preheat the Griddle by turning all its knob to medium-heat setting.
3. Drizzle olive oil over the lobster tail halves and season with salt and black pepper.
4. Place the lobster tails on the hot griddle top.
5. Cook for 3 minutes or until opaque, then flip and cook for another 3 minutes.
6. In the last minute of cooking, add a dollop of lime basil butter.
7. Serve with the lime wedges.

Per Serving: Calories: 376; Fat: 34.2 g; Sodium: 635 mg; Carbs: 2.4g; Fiber: 0.5g; Sugar: 0.3g; Protein: 16.2g

Snapper with Mango Salad

Prep time: 15 minutes | Cook time: 25 minutes | Serves: 4

Ingredients:
2 red snappers, cleaned	⅓ cup of tandoori spice
Sea salt, to taste	Lime wedges, for serving

Salsa
1 ripe but firm mango, peeled and chopped	1 bunch cilantro, chopped
1 small red onion, sliced	3 tablespoons of fresh lime juice

Preparation:
1. Grease the cooking surface of the griddle with cooking spray.
2. Turn on the 4 burners and turn their knobs to medium heat.
3. Let the Griddle preheat for 5 minutes.
4. Toss lime juice, onion, mango, cilantro, and salt in a suitable mixing bowl; drizzle olive oil and toss to coat.
5. Place snapper on a cutting board and pat dry with paper towels. Cut slashes diagonal crosswise along the body on both sides, with a sharp knife, all the way down to the bones.
6. Season fish inside and out with salt. Coat fish with tandoori spice.
7. Cook fish on the griddle top for 10 minutes, until skin is puffed and charred.
8. Flip the fish until the other side is charred and skin is puffed for about 8 to 12 minutes.
9. Put it on a plate. Top with mango salad and lime wedges.
10. Serve.

Per Serving: Calories: 395; Fat: 15g; Sodium: 521mg; Carbs: 14g; Fiber 5.1g; Sugar: 3g; Protein: 27g

Pop-Open Clams with Horseradish Sauce

Prep time: 15 minutes | **Cook time:** 10 minutes | **Serves:** 4

Ingredients:
- 2 dozen littleneck clams, scrubbed
- 4 tablespoons of unsalted butter softened
- 2 tablespoons of horseradish, drained
- 1 tablespoon of hot sauce, like tabasco
- ¼ teaspoon of lemon zest, grated
- 1 tablespoon of fresh lemon juice
- ¼ teaspoon of smoked paprika
- Sea salt, to taste

Preparation:
1. Grease the cooking surface of the griddle with cooking spray.
2. Turn on the 4 burners and turn their knobs to medium heat.
3. Let the Griddle preheat for 5 minutes.
4. Blend the butter with horseradish, hot sauce, lemon zest, lemon juice, paprika, and a pinch of salt.
5. Arrange the clams over 450 degrees F and griddle until they pop open, about 25 seconds.
6. Carefully turn the clams over using tongs so the meat side is down.
7. Griddle for about 20 seconds longer until the clam juices start to simmer.
8. Transfer the clams to a serving bowl.
9. Top each with about ½ a teaspoon of the sauce and serve

Per Serving: Calories: 366; Fat: 13g; Sodium: 421mg; Carbs: 16g; Fiber 4.1g; Sugar: 3.2g; Protein: 27g

Mayo Mussels with Italian Bread

Prep time: 15 minutes | **Cook time:** 05 minutes | **Serves** 4

Ingredients:
- ¾ cup mayonnaise
- 1 tablespoon minced garlic, or more to taste
- 2 (4-ounce) slice pancetta, chopped
- Salt and pepper
- 4 pounds' mussels
- 8 thick slices Italian bread
- ¼ cup good-quality olive oil

Preparation:
1. Getting the ingredients ready.
2. In a small bowl, combine the mayonnaise and garlic. In a cold small skillet, place the pancetta and cook, stirring periodically, until most of the; Fat: has rendered and the pork is brown and crisp, about 5 minutes.
3. Drain on paper towels, then add 1 teaspoon of the rendered; Fat: from the pan to the mayonnaise. Taste and season with extra garlic and salt if desired. Refrigerate until ready to use, covered. (Make the aioli ahead of time and keep it refrigerated in an airtight container.)
4. Rinse the mussels thoroughly and remove any beards. Any that are broken or don't close when tapped should be discarded.
5. Brush the bread pieces on both sides with the oil.
6. Preheat the Griddle to high temperature. Grease the griddle.
7. Place the bread on the grill and toast it for 1 to 2 minutes per side, flipping once, until it has grill marks and some charring. Take away the steaks from the grill and save them warm.
8. Place the mussels on the griddle in a single layer, spreading them out as much as possible. 3 minutes in the oven with tongs, transfer the open mussels to a large bowl.
9. If any have not opened, leave them on the grill for another 2 minutes, checking often and removing any that have opened until all of the mussels have been removed from the grill.
10. Dollop the aioli over the tops of the mussels and turn them over with a large spoon to coat them. Serve the mussels over (or alongside) the bread, sprinkled with their juices.

Per Serving: Calories: 773; Fat: 37.3g; Sodium: 2074mg; Carbs: 36g; Fiber 0.6g; Sugar: 3.8g; Protein: 66.8g

Seasoning Salmon Fillets

Prep time: 15 minutes | **Cook time:** 10 minutes | **Serves** 5

Ingredients:
- 1 ¼ lbs. salmon fillets
- 2 tbsps. blackened seasoning
- 2 tbsps. butter

Preparation:
1. Blacken the seasoning on the salmon fillets.
2. Preheat the griddle to medium-high heat.
3. Melt the butter on the griddle's surface.
4. Cook the salmon fillets for 4-5 minutes on a hot griddle top.
5. On the other side, cook for another 4-5 minutes.
6. Serve and have fun.

Per Serving: Calories: 191; Fat: 11.3g; Sodium: 83mg; Carbs: 0g; Fiber 0g; Sugar: 0g; Protein: 22.1g

Quick Halibut

Prep time: 15 minutes | **Cook time:** 15 minutes | **Serves:** 2

Ingredients:
- 2 halibut fish fillets
- 2 teaspoons of olive oil
- 1 teaspoon of dried thyme
- ½ teaspoon of onion powder
- ¾ teaspoon of garlic powder
- 1 tablespoon of paprika
- ¼ teaspoon of salt

Preparation:
1. Grease the cooking surface of the griddle with cooking spray.
2. Turn on the 4 burners and turn their knobs to medium-high heat.
3. Let the Griddle preheat for 5 minutes.
4. In a suitable bowl, mix paprika, garlic powder, onion powder, thyme, and salt.
5. Brush fish fillets with oil and rub with spice mixture.
6. Place fish fillets on a preheated griddle top and then let it cook for 3-5 minutes on each side.
7. Serve.

Per Serving: Calories: 397; Fat: 21g; Sodium: 711mg; Carbs: 8g; Fiber 3.1g; Sugar: 4g; Protein: 22g

Golden Zucchini Tuna Patties

Prep time: 15 minutes | **Cook time:** 10 minutes | **Serves:** 6

Ingredients:
- 13 oz can of tuna, drained and flaked
- ⅓ cup of parsley, chopped
- 2 teaspoons of lemon juice
- 2 egg whites
- 2 eggs, lightly beaten
- 2 cups of shredded zucchini, squeezed
- ¾ cup of breadcrumbs
- 1 cup of onion, chopped
- Black pepper, to taste
- Salt, to taste

Preparation:
1. Grease the cooking surface of the griddle with cooking spray.
2. Turn on the 4 burners and turn their knobs to medium heat.
3. Let the Griddle preheat for 5 minutes.
4. Add all the recipe's ingredients into the mixing bowl and mix until well combined.
5. Make patties from mixture and place on preheated griddle top and then let it cook until golden brown from both sides.
6. Serve.

Per Serving: Calories: 449; Fat: 21g; Sodium: 421mg; Carbs: 16g; Fiber 2.1g; Sugar: 2.2g; Protein: 27g

Scallops with Lemony Salsa Verde

Prep time: 15 minutes | **Cook time:** 5 minutes | **Serves:** 2

Ingredients:
- 1 tablespoon of olive oil
- 12 large sea scallops, side muscle removed
- Sea salt for seasoning

Lemony salsa Verde
- ½ lemon, with peel, seeded and chopped
- Five tomatillos, peeled and pulsed in a suitable blender
- 1 small shallot, chopped
- 1 garlic clove, chopped
- ¼ cup of olive oil
- ¾ cup of chopped fresh parsley
- ½ cup of chopped fresh cilantro
- ¼ cup of chopped fresh chives
- ¼ teaspoon of sea salt, to taste
- ¼ teaspoon black pepper

Preparation:
1. Grease the cooking surface of the griddle with cooking spray.
2. Turn on the 4 burners and turn their knobs to medium heat.
3. Let the Griddle preheat for 5 minutes.
4. Toss lemony salsa ingredients in a suitable mixing bowl and set aside.
5. Toss scallops with 1 tablespoon of olive oil on a baking sheet and season by adding salt.
6. Add scallops to the griddle, turning once after 45 seconds to 1 minute.
7. Cook an additional 1 minute before removing from the griddle.
8. Serve scallops topped with lemony salsa Verde.

Per Serving: Calories: 342; Fat: 12g; Sodium: 354mg; Carbs: 24g; Fiber 1.2g; Sugar: 5g; Protein: 28g

Lobster Salad with Vinaigrette

Prep time: 4 minutes | Cook time: 15 minutes | Serves: 4

Ingredients:
4 ears of corn, shucked
4 spring onions, chopped
Oil, for coating
Salt, for seasoning
4 large lobster tails meat (8 oz.)
1 serrano chile, stemmed and
sliced into rounds
3 celery stalks, sliced
½ cup basil leaves, chopped
¼ cup dill, chopped
¼ cup mint leaves, chopped
½ cup celery leaves, chopped

Citrus–Brown Butter Vinaigrette
2 oranges, juiced
2 limes, juiced
Oil and honey, for coating
½ cup 1 stick butter

Preparation:
1. Preheat the Griddle by turning all its knob to medium-heat setting.
2. Grease the griddle top with cooking spray.
3. Pour the egg mixture onto the hot griddle top
4. Mix the corn and spring onions with the oil and salt.
5. Cook over medium heat for about 4 minutes then transfer to a plate.
6. Season the lobster flesh with salt and oil and cook for 2 minutes per side on the hot griddle top.
7. Transfer the lobster meat to a bowl.
8. Remove the kernels and add to the lobster.
9. Stir in rest of the ingredients to the lobster.
10. Cut the oranges and limes in half, mix with the oil and honey.
11. Cook for 3 minutes or until charred, then transfer to a plate.
12. Meanwhile, in a suitable saucepan, melt the butter until it turns a light brown color.
13. Remove the pan from the heat and add the lemon juice.
14. Whisk, then season with more honey and salt.
15. Serve the lobster salad with a generous amount of vinaigrette.

Per Serving: Calories: 512; Fat: 7.1 g; Sodium: 42 mg; Carbs: 28.5g; Fiber: 2.1g; Sugar: 13.4g; Protein: 1.2g

Easy Scallops

Prep time: 15 minutes | Cook time: 4 minutes | Serves: 4

Ingredients:
1 lb. of scallops
1 tablespoon of olive oil
2 tablespoons of butter, melted
Black pepper, to taste
Salt, to taste

Preparation:
1. Grease the cooking surface of the griddle with cooking spray.
2. Turn on the 4 burners and turn their knobs to medium-high heat.
3. Let the Griddle preheat for 5 minutes.
4. Add scallops, butter, oil, pepper, and salt into the bowl and toss well.
5. Place scallops on a preheated griddle top and then let it cooks for 2 minutes on each side.
6. Serve.

Per Serving: Calories: 421; Fat: 11g; Sodium: 361mg; Carbs: 11g; Fiber 3.1g; Sugar: 2g; Protein: 26g

Fennel Clam and Shrimp Bouillabaisse

Prep time: 5 minutes | Cook time: 10 minutes | Serves: 4

Ingredients:
Bouillabaisse:
1 large tomato
½ small fennel bulb, with fronds attached
¼ cup oil
½ white onion, minced
4 garlic cloves, sliced
2-inch piece fresh ginger, peeled and sliced
2 tablespoons tarragon leaves, chopped
6 basil leaves, chopped
4 cups fish stock
Salt and black pepper, for seasoning
½ pound small hard-shell clams, scrubbed and rinsed of all sand
½ pound large shrimp
1½ pounds boneless whitefish fillets

Tarragon–Garlic Toasts
6 tablespoons oil
3 tablespoons minced garlic
Generous pinch of salt
¼ cup minced tarragon leaves
8 (½-inch-thick) slices French bread

Preparation:
1. Preheat the Griddle by turning all its knob to medium-heat setting.
2. Grease the griddle top with cooking oil.
3. Place the tomato on the hot griddle top and cook it until it is blackened. Set aside
4. Add the onion, garlic, ginger, and minced fennel to griddle and cook for about 5 minutes then transfer the tomatoes and mash lightly.
5. Add 2 tablespoons of the fennel fronds, basil, fish stock, the tarragon, and salt and black pepper.
6. Place the clams on the hot griddle top, cover, and cook until the shells open.
7. Place the shrimp and fish directly on the hot griddle top and cook for 2-3 mintues per side.
8. Cook until the garlic begins to turn golden brown, then add the garlic and salt.
9. Toast the bread slices over medium heat until golden brown.
10. Brush the slices thickly with oil. With the bouillabaisse, serve right away.

Per Serving: Calories: 379; Fat: 20.9 g; Sodium: 1598 mg; Carbs: 10g; Fiber: 2.2g; Sugar: 2.1g; Protein: 37g

Yummy Jumbo Shrimp

Prep time: 15 minutes | Cook time: 8 minutes | Serves: 6

Ingredients:
1 ½ pounds of uncooked jumbo shrimp, peeled and deveined
For the marinade
2 tablespoons of fresh parsley
1 bay leaf, dried
1 teaspoon of chili powder
1 teaspoon of garlic powder
¼ teaspoon of cayenne pepper, to taste
¼ cup of olive oil
¼ teaspoon of salt
⅛ teaspoon black pepper

Preparation:
1. Grease the cooking surface of the griddle with cooking spray.
2. Turn on the 4 burners and turn their knobs to medium heat.
3. Let the Griddle preheat for 5 minutes.
4. Add marinade ingredients to a food processor and process until smooth.
5. Transfer marinade to a large mixing bowl.
6. Fold in shrimp and toss to coat; refrigerate, covered, 30 minutes.
7. Thread shrimp onto metal skewers.
8. Cook 5-6 minutes on griddle top, flipping once, until shrimp turn opaque pink.
9. Serve.

Per Serving: Calories: 379; Fat: 13g; Sodium: 421mg; Carbs: 16g; Fiber 4.1g; Sugar: 3.2g; Protein: 27g

Lemon Pepper Scallops

Prep time: 15 minutes | Cook time: 12 minutes | Serves: 4

Ingredients:
20 scallops
1 ½ tablespoons of lemon pepper seasoning
4 tablespoons of olive oil
1 teaspoon of salt

Preparation:
1. Grease the cooking surface of the griddle with cooking spray.
2. Turn on the 4 burners and turn their knobs to medium-high heat.
3. Let the Griddle preheat for 5 minutes.
4. Add scallops and the rest of the recipe's ingredients into the mixing bowl and mix well and place in the refrigerator for 30 minutes.
5. Place scallops on a preheated griddle top and then let it cooks for 2-3 minutes on each side.
6. Serve.

Per Serving: Calories: 395; Fat: 15g; Sodium: 521mg; Carbs: 14g; Fiber 5.1g; Sugar: 3g; Protein: 27g

Chili Crab Legs

Prep time: 5 minutes | Cook time: 5 minutes | Serves: 4

Ingredients:
4 pounds king crab legs
2 tablespoons chili oil

Preparation:
1. Preheat the Griddle by turning all its knob to medium-heat setting.
2. Grease the griddle top with cooking spray.
3. Brush the crab legs on both sides with chili oil and set them on the hot griddle top.
4. Cook them for 5 minutes per side.
5. Arrange on plates and serve with a dollop of drawn butter.

Per Serving: Calories: 487; Fat: 15 g; Sodium: 4856 mg; Carbs: 0g; Fiber: 0g; Sugar: 0g; Protein: 85.4g

Lemon Spinach Halibut

Prep time: 10 minutes | Cook time: 10 minutes | Serves: 4

Ingredients:
- 4 (6-oz.) halibut fillets
- ⅓ cup olive oil
- 4 cups baby spinach
- ¼ cup lemon juice
- 2 oz. pitted black olives, halved
- 2 tablespoons flat leaf parsley, chopped
- 2 teaspoons fresh dill, chopped
- Lemon wedges, to serve

Preparation:
1. In a suitable mixing bowl, toss the spinach with the lemon juice and leave aside.
2. Preheat the Griddle by turning all its knob to medium-heat setting.
3. Grease the griddle top with cooking spray.
4. Pour the egg mixture onto the hot griddle top
5. Brush each side of the salmon with olive oil and cook on the hot griddle for 3-4 minutes per side
6. Add the remaining oil and spinach then cook for 3 minutes.
7. Toss in olives and remaining herbs, then serve with lemon wedges and the fish.

Per Serving: Calories: 362; Fat: 22.6 g; Sodium: 242 mg; Carbs: 2.9g; Fiber: 1.4g; Sugar: 0.5g; Protein: 37.4g

Mustard Crab Panko Cakes

Prep time: 10 minutes | Cook time: 10 minutes | Serves: 4

Ingredients:
- 1 pound lump crab meat
- ½ cup panko bread crumbs
- ⅓ cup mayonnaise
- 1 egg, beaten
- 2 tablespoons Dijon mustard
- 2 teaspoons Worcestershire sauce
- ½ teaspoon paprika
- ½ teaspoon salt
- ¼ teaspoon black pepper
- 3 tablespoons vegetable oil

Preparation:
1. Mix well the bread crumbs, crab, egg, mayonnaise, paprika, mustard Worcestershire sauce, salt, and pepper in a suitable mixing bowl.
2. Roll the crab mixture into four large balls and slightly flatten them.
3. Preheat the Griddle by turning all its knob to medium-heat setting.
4. Grease the griddle top with cooking oil.
5. Fry the crab cakes for 5 minutes per side until golden brown and crispy.
6. Serve right away.

Per Serving: Calories: 273; Fat: 24 g; Sodium: 1181 mg; Carbs: 12.8g; Fiber: 1g; Sugar: 1.4g; Protein: 20g

Butter Salmon Fillets with Broccolini

Prep time: 10 minutes | Cook time: 20 minutes | Serves: 2

Ingredients:
- 2 (6-oz.) salmon fillets, skin removed
- 2 tablespoons butter, unsalted
- 2 basil leaves, minced
- 1 garlic clove, minced
- 6 oz. (170 g) broccolini
- 2 teaspoons olive oil
- Sea salt, to taste

Preparation:
1. In a suitable mixing bowl, mix well the butter, basil, and garlic. Form into a ball and store in the fridge.
2. Season the salmon fillets with salt and put aside.
3. Toss broccolini with a teaspoon of salt and a drizzle of olive oil in a suitable mixing dish to coat, then set aside.
4. Preheat the Griddle by turning all its knob to medium-heat setting.
5. Grease the griddle top with cooking oil.
6. Pour the egg mixture onto the hot griddle top
7. Cook the salmon on the hot griddle top for 12 minutes per side then transfer to a plate.
8. Add the broccolini to the griddle, and cook for almost 6 minutes.
9. Serve salmon with a serving of broccolini and a slice of basil butter.
10. Enjoy.

Per Serving: Calories: 445; Fat: 28.2 g; Sodium: 322 mg; Carbs: 6.2g; Fiber: 2.2g; Sugar: 1.4g; Protein: 43.7g

Tomato Crab-stuffed Trout

Prep time: 05 minutes | Cook time: 10 minutes | Serves: 8

Ingredients:
- 24 ounces' crabmeat, picked over for shells and cartilage
- 2 cups chopped seeded fresh tomato,
- Grated zest of 1 lemon
- 2-tablespoon good-quality olive oil, plus more for brushing the fish
- 4 scallions, trimmed and chopped
- Salt and pepper
- 20-ounce rainbow trout, cleaned and butterflied
- Lemon wedges for serving

Preparation:
1. Getting the ingredients ready.
2. In a medium mixing bowl, combine the crab, tomato, and lemon zest. In a small skillet over medium heat, combine the oil and scallions; cook, turning occasionally, until softened, 2 to 3 minutes. Season with salt and pepper, stir gently with the crab, and taste and adjust the seasoning.
3. Using paper towels, pat the trout dry. On both sides, brush with oil and season with salt and pepper. Fill the cavities of the trout with the crab mixture that has been divided between them. Pull the two edges together and, if necessary, push the filling in to prevent it from pouring out.
4. Preheat the Griddle to high heat.
5. Allow the griddle to heat up after oiling it. Cook the trout with the open side of the fish facing you for 8 to 10 minutes, or until the skin browns and the fish easily releases.
6. Turn the fish carefully, then lower them back to the grates with a second spatula. Close the lid and cook for 4 to 5 minutes, or until the stuffing is hot and a skewer or thin knife inserted in the thickest point of a fish easily pierces it all the way through.
7. Place the trout on a serving plate and garnish with lemon wedges.

Per Serving: Calories: 200; Fat: 4g; Sodium: 976mg; Carbs: 29.9g; Fiber 1.9g; Sugar: 5.8g; Protein: 11.8g

Pepper Shrimp with Parsley

Prep time: 15 minutes | Cook time: 8 minutes | Serves: 6

Ingredients:
- 1½ pounds uncooked jumbo shrimp, peeled and deveined

For the Marinade:
- 2 tablespoons fresh parsley
- 1 bay leaf, dried
- 1 teaspoon chili powder
- 1 teaspoon garlic powder
- ¼ teaspoon cayenne pepper
- ¼ cup olive oil
- ¼ teaspoon salt
- ⅛ teaspoon black pepper

Preparation:
1. In a food processor, mix well all marinade ingredients and pulse until smooth.
2. Pour the marinade into a big mixing bowl.
3. Toss in the shrimp and toss to coat; chill for 30 minutes, covered.
4. Preheat the Griddle by turning all its knob to medium-heat setting.
5. Grease the griddle top with cooking spray.
6. Pour the egg mixture onto the hot griddle top
7. Skewer the shrimp on metal skewers.
8. Cook, flipping once, for 5 to 6 minutes, or until shrimp are opaque pink.
9. Serve right away.

Per Serving: Calories: 373; Fat: 8.5 g; Sodium: 4928 mg; Carbs: 0.8g; Fiber: 0.3g; Sugar: 7.6g; Protein: 74.5g

Lime Corn Tilapia

Prep time: 10 minutes | Cook time: 10 minutes | Serves: 4

Ingredients:
- 4 fillets tilapia
- 2 tablespoons honey
- 4 limes, sliced
- 2 ears corn, shucked
- 2 tablespoons fresh cilantro leaves
- ¼ cup olive oil
- Kosher salt, to taste
- Freshly ground black pepper, to taste

Preparation:
1. Cut 4 foil squares about 12" long.
2. Place a piece of tilapia on top of each piece of foil.
3. Preheat the Griddle by turning all its knob to medium-heat setting.
4. Grease the griddle top with cooking spray.
5. Pour the egg mixture onto the hot griddle top
6. Drizzle olive oil, salt, black pepper, honey, lime, corn, and cilantro over the tilapia.
7. Cook for 15 minutes on the hot griddle top.
8. Serve.

Per Serving: Calories: 319; Fat: 14.7 g; Sodium: 92 mg; Carbs: 30.3g; Fiber: 4g; Sugar: 12.3g; Protein: 24g

Shrimp and Pineapple Skewers

Prep time: 20 minutes | Cook time: 5 minutes | Serves: 4

Ingredients:
1½ pounds uncooked jumbo shrimp, peeled and deveined
½ cup light coconut milk
1 tablespoon cilantro, chopped
4 teaspoons Tabasco Red Sauce
2 teaspoons soy sauce
¼ cup orange juice
¼ cup lime juice
¾ pound pineapple, cut into 1 inch chunks
Olive oil, for grilling

Preparation:
1. Whisk together the coconut milk, cilantro, orange juice, Tabasco sauce, soy sauce, and lime juice in a suitable mixing bowl.
2. Toss in the shrimp to coat them.
3. Cover and marinate for 1 hour in the refrigerator.
4. Alternate threading shrimp and pineapple onto metal skewers.
5. Heat the griddle to medium heat and brush it with the oil.
6. Preheat the Griddle by turning all its knob to medium-heat setting.
7. Grease the griddle top with cooking spray.
8. Pour the egg mixture onto the hot griddle top
9. Cook, flipping once, for 5 to 6 minutes, or until shrimp are opaque pink.
10. Serve right away.

Per Serving: Calories: 596; Fat: 10.8 g; Sodium: 7429 mg; Carbs: 14.9g; Fiber: 1.9g; Sugar: 21.9g; Protein: 112.2g

Boneless Salmon Fillets

Prep time: 05 minutes | Cook time: 15 minutes | Serves 2

Ingredients:
2 Boneless Salmon Fillets, Scaled
½ tablespoon Olive Oil
Sea Salt and Pepper to Taste

Preparation:
1. Preheat the griddle to high heat.
2. Season the fillets with sea salt and black pepper after drizzling them with olive oil.
3. Cook for 3 minutes on each side on the Griddle.
4. Reduce the heat to medium and continue grilling for several minutes, or until the fillet is uniformly colored and white begins to show on top.
5. Take it off the fire and set it aside to cool for a few minutes before serving.

Per Serving: Calories: 265; Fat: 14.3g; Sodium: 78mg; Carbs: 0g; Fiber 0g; Sugar: 0g; Protein: 34.8g

Lemon Scallops

Prep time: 15 minutes | Cook time: 05 minutes | Serves2

Ingredients:
1 lb. frozen bay scallops, thawed, rinsed & pat dry
1-teaspoon garlic, minced
2-tablespoon olive oil
1-teaspoon parsley, chopped
1-teaspoon lemon juice
Pepper
Salt

Preparation:
1. Heat the griddle to high temperature.
2. Brush the griddle surface with oil.
3. Cook for another 30 seconds after adding the garlic.
4. Add the scallops, lemon juice, pepper, and salt to the pan and cook until the scallops become opaque.
5. Serve with a parsley garnish.

Per Serving: Calories: 450; Fat: 28.3g; Sodium: 74mg; Carbs: 2.6g; Fiber 0.6g; Sugar: 1.8g; Protein: 23.8g

Paprika Shrimp

Prep time: 15 minutes | Cook time: 05 minutes | Serves 4

Ingredients:
1-pound shrimp, deveined
1-teaspoon Italian seasoning
1-teaspoon paprika
1 ½ tsp garlic, minced
1 stick butter
1 fresh lemon juice
¼-teaspoon pepper
½-teaspoon salt

Preparation:
1. Preheat the griddle to medium-high heat.
2. On a heated griddle, melt the butter.
3. After adding the garlic, cook for another 30 seconds.
4. Combine the shrimp, paprika, Italian seasoning, pepper, and salt in a mixing bowl.
5. Cook the shrimp for 2-3 minutes per side in the pan.
6. Pour lemon juice over the prawns.
7. Serve after a quick stir.

Per Serving: Calories: 347; Fat: 25.3g; Sodium: 734mg; Carbs: 2.6g; Fiber 0.6g; Sugar: 0.8g; Protein: 26.8g

Shrimps with Cherry Tomatoes Asparagus Salad

Prep time: 15 minutes | Cook time: 5 minutes | Serves 5

Ingredients:
½ pint cherry tomatoes
3 tablespoons olive oil
½ teaspoon salt
1-pound medium to thin asparagus, woody stems snapped off and discarded
1 pound shelled and deveined medium shrimp
¼ teaspoon freshly ground black pepper
¼ teaspoon dried thyme
Grated zest and juice of ½ lemon

Preparation:
1. Getting the ingredients ready.
2. Place the cherry tomatoes in a medium bowl, quartered. 1 tablespoon olive oil and a quarter teaspoon of salt Set aside after gently tossing.
3. 1 tablespoon olive oil, poured over the asparagus spears in a medium bowl, rubbed gently to coat them.
Set the control knob to the highest setting.
4. Allow to heat the griddle until the oil is shimmering but not smoking. For around 5 minutes, grill the asparagus.
5. The thicker ones will retain some crunch, while the thinner ones will be tender.
6. Keep the griddle on high and transfer to a chopping board. Cut the spears into 1-inch pieces once they've cooled enough to handle. Toss in with the cherry tomatoes.
7. Clean the shrimp by rinsing them and patting them dry with paper towels.
8. Toss them in a medium mixing dish with the remaining tablespoon of olive oil to coat. Grill for 3 minutes, or until the shrimp are opaque and firm to the touch.
9. Toss the tomatoes and asparagus with the prawns. Toss in the remaining 14 teaspoon salt, the pepper, the thyme, and the lemon juice and zest.
10. Refrigerate and serve chilled, or serve warm or at room temperature.

Per Serving: Calories: 187; Fat: 10; Sodium: 456mg; Carbs: 2.6g; Fiber 0.6g; Sugar: 1g; Protein: 21

Grilled Teriyaki-glazed Coho Salmon Fillets

Prep time: 05 minutes | Cook time: 20minutes | Serves 2

Ingredients:
1–2 coho salmon filets
Sauce
1 cup water
¼ cup brown sugar
¼ cup soy sauce
1-tablespoon honey
1½-tablespoon finely minced ginger root (about 1-inch piece)
2 cloves garlic, finely minced
½-teaspoon white pepper
Thickener
2-tablespoon cornstarch
¼ cup cold water

Preparation:
1. Getting the ingredients ready.
2. Combine the sauce ingredients in a medium saucepan over medium heat and bring to a low boil.
3. When the sauce has reached a low boil, combine cornstarch and water in a separate basin with a fork until fully combined. Slowly whisk in the cornstarch mixture until the sauce thickens.
4. Add one chunk of pecan wood to your grill's hot coals.
5. Brush the salmon fillets with the sauce.
6. Preheat the Griddle to high temperature. Cook for 15 minutes on a griddle that has been oiled.
7. Cook for an additional 10 minutes after applying another coat of sauce to the fish.
8. Remove from the grill, garnish with parsley, and serve immediately.

Per Serving: Calories: 710; Fat: 38.3g; Sodium: 1074mg; Carbs: 26g; Fiber 1.6g; Sugar: 2.8g; Protein: 63.8g

Paprika Salmon with Parsley

Prep time: 15 minutes | Cook time: 05 minutes | Serves 2

Ingredients:

½ cup fresh cilantro leave
½ cup fresh flat-leaf parsley leaves
2 cloves garlic, coarsely chopped
½ teaspoon sweet paprika
½ teaspoon coarse salt
½ teaspoon freshly ground black pepper
½ teaspoon ground coriander
½ teaspoon ground cumin
½ teaspoon hot red pepper flakes
3 tablespoons fresh lemon juice
½ cup extra-virgin olive oil
4 pieces salmon fillet or salmon steaks

Preparation:
1. Getting the ingredients ready.
2. In a food processor, pulse the cilantro, parsley, garlic, paprika, salt, black pepper, coriander, cumin, and hot pepper flakes until finely chopped.
3. Process until a coarse purée develops, adding the lemon juice as needed. Put the olive oil in a thin stream while the motor is in a row.
4. Season with additional salt, hot pepper flakes, and/or lemon juice as needed; the charmoula should be well-seasoned.
5. If you're using salmon fillets, feel them for bones with your fingertips. Remove any you find with needle-nose pliers or tweezers (you will not need to do this with salmon steaks).
6. Using paper towels, wipe the fish dry after rinsing it under cold running water. Fill a nonreactive baking dish just large enough to hold the salmon in one layer with a third of the charmoula.
7. On top, arrange the salmon chunks. Half of the remaining charmoula should be spooned over the fish, and the remainder should be set aside.
8. Allow the salmon to marinade in the refrigerator for 2 to 4 hours, covered (the longer it marinates, the richer the flavor will be).
9. Drain the fish and discard the marinade when ready to cook.
10. Preheat the Griddle to high temperature.
11. When the griddle is heated, set the fish on it. After 3 to 5 minutes of grilling, the salmon should be browned and cooked thoroughly. Press the fish with your finger to see whether it's done; it should break into clear flakes.
12. Place the salmon on a dish or individual plates. Recombine the remaining charmoula and spoon it on top of the salmon.

Per Serving: Calories: 459; Fat: 36.3g; Sodium: 83mg; Carbs: 1.2g; Fiber 0.6g; Sugar: 0.3g; Protein: 34.8g

Pine Nuts Shrimp

Prep time: 15 minutes | Cook time: 6 minutes | Serves 4

Ingredients:

1 lb. shrimp, peeled and deveined
2-tablespoon parmesan cheese, grated
1-tablespoon fresh lemon juice
1-tablespoon pine nuts, toasted
1 garlic clove
½ cup basil
1-tablespoon olive oil
Pepper
Salt

Preparation:
1. In a blender, combine basil, lemon juice, cheese, pine nuts, garlic, pepper, and salt until smooth.
2. In a mixing dish, combine the shrimp and basil paste.
3. Refrigerate the shrimp bowl for 20 minutes.
4. Preheat the griddle to high heat.
5. Coat the top of the griddle with cooking spray.
6. Place skewers on the hot griddle top and thread marinated shrimp onto them.
7. Cook for 3 minutes on each side or until shrimp are fully cooked.
8. Serve and have fun.

Per Serving: Calories: 710; Fat: 38.3g; Sodium: 1074mg; Carbs: 26g; Fiber 1.6g; Sugar: 2.8g; Protein: 63.8g

Basil Salmon Fillets with Broccolini

Prep time: 2 minutes | Cook time: 12 minutes | Serves 4

Ingredients:

2 (6 ounce) salmon fillets, skin removed
2 tablespoons butter, unsalted
2 basil leaves, minced
1 garlic clove, minced
6 ounces broccolini
2 teaspoons olive oil
Sea salt, to taste

Preparation:
1. Combine the butter, basil, and garlic in a blender and blend until smooth. Form into a ball and store in the fridge until ready to use.
2. Heat the griddle to medium-high heat.
3. Season the salmon fillets on both sides with salt and put aside.
4. In a mixing dish, combine the broccolini, a pinch of salt, and the olive oil; toss to coat and set aside.
5. Brush the griddle with olive oil and cook the salmon for 12 minutes, skin side down. Cook for another 4 minutes after turning the salmon. Remove the griddle from the heat and set aside to cool while the broccolini cooks.
6. Add the broccolini to the griddle and cook, stirring regularly, for about 6 minutes, or until slightly browned.
7. Serve with a serving of broccolini and a slice of basil butter on top of each salmon fillet.

Per Serving: Calories: 398, Sodium: 303 mg, Dietary Fiber: 2.2g, Fat: 26.7g, Carbs: 6.2g ; Protein: 35.6g

Paprika Crab Cakes

Prep time: 10 minutes | Cook time: 25 minutes | Serves 2

Ingredients:

1 lb. lump crab meat
½ cup panko breadcrumbs
⅓ cup mayonnaise
1 egg, beaten
1 tablespoons Dijon mustard
1 teaspoons Worcestershire sauce
½ teaspoon paprika
½ teaspoon salt
¼ teaspoon black pepper
3 tablespoons vegetable oil

Preparation:
1. Preheat the griddle over medium heat.
2. Combine the crab, breadcrumbs, mayonnaise, egg, mustard Worcestershire sauce, paprika, salt, and pepper in a large mixing bowl. To blend, whisk everything together thoroughly.
3. Form the crab mixture into four large balls and slightly flatten them.
4. Cook the crab cakes for approximately 5 minutes per side on the griddle, or until golden and crispy.
5. Serve right away.

Per Serving: Calories: 308; Fat: 27.3g; Sodium: 1274mg; Carbs: 16g; Fiber 1.4g; Sugar: 2.2g; Protein: 19.8g

Lemon Seafood Salad

Prep time: 20 minutes | Cook time: 35 minutes | Serves 5

Ingredients:

1-pound firm white fish fillets
8-ounce sea scallops,
8-ounce large shrimp, peeled
½ cup good-quality olive oil
Salt and pepper
1 tablespoon white wine vinegar
1 tablespoon capers, drained and chopped
1 small shallot, minced
1 cup fresh parsley leaves, chopped
Lemon wedges, for serving

Preparation:
1. Getting the ingredients ready.
2. Dry the fish, scallops, and shrimp using paper towels before brushing them with 14 cup olive oil and seasoning them with salt and pepper.
3. In a small bowl, whisk together the remaining ¼ cup oil, vinegar, capers, and shallot. Flavor with salt and pepper if preferred.
4. Preheat the Griddle to high temperature. Allow to heat the griddle until the oil is shimmering but not smoking. Cook for 10 minutes, until the scallops are golden brown in places. On the exterior, you want a good sear, but the middle of the scallop should still be slightly translucent. Into a large serving basin, transfer the mixture.
5. Place the shrimp on the griddle and cook for 10 minutes, flipping once, until opaque all the way through. Transfer to a mixing basin.
6. Place the fish on the grill (skin side down if it has skin) and cook for 6 to 7 minutes, or until the bottoms brown and release easily.
7. Turn the fillets carefully with a second spatula to prevent them from splitting apart. Cook for 2 to 4 minutes, depending on thickness, until a skewer or sharp knife inserted at the thickest point of a fillet easily pierces it all the way through. Transfer to a mixing basin.
8. Drizzle the vinaigrette over the top of the fish and parsley. Toss the salad gently together, breaking the fish into bite-size pieces as you do so.
9. Enjoy!

Per Serving: Calories: 510; Fat: 34.3g; Sodium: 300mg; Carbs: 3.1g; Fiber 0.1g; Sugar: 0.1g; Protein: 48g

Corn Tilapia Fillets

Prep time: 14 minutes | Cook time: 20 minutes | Serves 2

Ingredients:
- 4 fillets tilapia
- 2 tablespoons honey
- 4 limes, thinly sliced
- 2 ears corn, shucked
- 2 tablespoon fresh cilantro leaves
- ¼ cup olive oil
- Kosher salt
- Freshly ground black pepper

Preparation:
1. Preheat the griddle to high temperature.
2. Cut 4 foil squares about 12" long.
3. Place a piece of tilapia on top of each piece of foil.
4. Tilapia should be brushed with honey and topped with lime, corn, and cilantro.
5. Flavor with sea salt and pepper and drizzle with olive oil.
6. Cook for about 15 minutes, or until the tilapia is cooked through and the corn is soft.

Per Serving: Calories: 319; Fat: 14.3g; Sodium: 92mg; Carbs: 30.6g; Fiber 4g; Sugar: 12.8g; Protein: 24g

Stir-Fried Shrimp and Veggie

Prep time: 15 minutes | Cook time: 10 minutes | Serves 1

Ingredients:
- ½ lb. shrimp, peeled and deveined
- 1 tbsp. garlic, minced
- ⅓ cup olives
- 1 cup mushrooms, sliced
- 2 tbsp. olive oil
- 1 cup tomatoes, diced
- 1 small onion, chopped
- Pepper
- Salt

Preparation:
1. Preheat the griddle to medium-high heat. Pour in the oil.
2. Sauté the onion, mushrooms, and garlic until the onion softens.
3. Stir in the shrimp and tomatoes until the shrimp is fully cooked.
4. Stir in the olives thoroughly.
5. Remove the pan from the heat and leave it to cool for 5 minutes. Season with salt and pepper.
6. Serve and have fun.

Per Serving: Calories: 265; Fat: 11.3g; Sodium: 558mg; Carbs: 126g; Fiber 3g; Sugar: 4.8g; Protein: 28g

Swordfish Skewers

Prep time: 20 minutes | Cook time: 10 minutes | Serves: 4

Ingredients:
- 1 (½-pound) skinless swordfish fillet
- 2 teaspoons lemon zest
- 3 tablespoons lemon juice
- ½ cup chopped parsley
- 2 teaspoons garlic, minced
- ¾ teaspoon sea salt
- ¼ teaspoon black pepper
- 2 tablespoons olive oil, plus extra for serving
- ½ teaspoon red pepper flakes
- 3 lemons, cut into slices

Preparation:
1. Blend parsley, lemon zest, ¼ teaspoon salt, garlic, and pepper black in a small bowl.
2. Mix well the swordfish pieces with the reserved lemon juice, red pepper flakes, olive oil, and the remaining salt in a suitable mixing bowl.
3. Thread swordfish and lemon slices onto metal skewers alternately.
4. Preheat the Griddle by turning all its knob to medium-heat setting.
5. Grease the griddle top with cooking spray.
6. Pour the egg mixture onto the hot griddle top
7. Grill skewers for 4 minutes per side.
8. Arrange the skewers on a plate and top with gremolata.
9. Finish with a drizzle of olive oil and serve.

Per Serving: Calories: 157; Fat: 10.1 g; Sodium: 423 mg; Carbs: 1.6g; Fiber: 0.5g; Sugar: 0.4g; Protein: 14.9g

Mayo Salmon Patties

Prep time: 10 minutes | Cook time: 10 minutes | Serves 2

Ingredients:
- 6 oz. can salmon, drained, remove bones, and pat dry
- 2-tablespoon mayonnaise
- ½ cup almond flour
- ¼-teaspoon thyme
- 1 egg, lightly beaten
- 2-tablespoon olive oil
- Pepper
- Salt

Preparation:
1. In a large mixing bowl, combine the salmon, thyme, egg, mayonnaise, almond flour, pepper, and salt.
2. Preheat the griddle to high heat.
3. Oil the griddle's surface.
4. Make tiny patties with the salmon mixture and fry for 5-6 minutes on a hot griddle.
5. Cook for 3-4 minutes longer on the new side.
6. Serve and have fun.

Per Serving: Calories: 435; Fat: 32.3g; Sodium: 208mg; Carbs: 8g; Fiber 3.1g; Sugar: 1.8g; Protein: 30.8g

Basil Halibut Fillets

Prep time: 04 minutes | Cook time: 10 minutes | Serves 4

Ingredients:
- 24 oz halibut fillets
- 2 garlic cloves, crushed
- 2-tablespoon olive oil
- 2-teaspoon capers, drained
- 3-tablespoon fresh basil, sliced
- 2-½-tablespoon fresh lemon juice

Preparation:
1. Combine the garlic, olive oil, and lemon juice in a small mixing bowl. 2-tablespoon basil, stirred in.
2. Flavor the garlic mixture with salt and pepper.
3. Brush fish fillets with garlic mixture after seasoning with pepper and salt.
4. Preheat the griddle to high heat.
5. Cook the fish fillets for 4 minutes on each side on a hot griddle.
6. Serve the fish fillets with the remaining garlic mixture and basil on the side.
7. Serve and have fun.

Per Serving: Calories: 1205; Fat: 31.3g; Sodium: 574mg; Carbs: 0.6g; Fiber 0.2g; Sugar: 0.2 g; Protein: 213.8g

Quick Shrimp

Prep time: 15 minutes | Cook time: 10 minutes | Serves 4

Ingredients:
- 1-½ lbs. shrimp,
- 1 tbsp. garlic, minced
- ¼ cup butter
- ¼ cup fresh parsley, chopped
- ¼ cup fresh lemon juice
- Pepper
- Salt

Preparation:
1. Preheat the griddle to medium-high heat.
2. Melt the butter on the griddle's surface.
3. Sauté for 30 seconds after adding the garlic.
4. Cook for 4-5 minutes, or until shrimp turns pink, seasoning with pepper and salt.
5. Cook for 2 minutes after adding the lemon juice and parsley.
6. Serve and have fun.

Per Serving: Calories: 312; Fat: 18.3g; Sodium: 389mg; Carbs: 3.6g; Fiber 0.6g; Sugar: 0.8g; Protein: 39.8g

Lemon Butter Shrimp

Prep time: 10 minutes | Cook time: 20 minutes | Serves 4

Ingredients:
- 1-½ lbs. shrimp, peeled and deveined
- 3 garlic cloves, minced
- 1 small onion, minced
- ½ cup butter
- 1-½ tbsps. fresh parsley, chopped
- 1 tbsp. fresh lemon juice
- ½ tsp red pepper flakes
- Pepper
- Salt

Preparation:
1. Preheat the griddle to medium-high heat.
2. Melt the butter on the griddle's surface.
3. For 2 minutes, whisk in the garlic, onion, red chili flakes, pepper, and salt.
4. Season the shrimp with salt and pepper before threading them onto skewers.
5. Brush the butter mixture over the shrimp skewers.
6. Place shrimp skewers on griddle top and cook for 3-4 minutes, or until shrimp turns pink.
7. Place the shrimp on a serving platter.
8. Drizzle lemon juice over the shrimp and sprinkle parsley on top.
9. Serve and have fun.

Per Serving: Calories: 410; Fat: 26; Sodium: 620mg; Carbs: 5.2g; Fiber 0.6g; Sugar: 0.8g; Protein: 39.8g

Halibut Dill with Herbs and Olives

Prep time: 20 minutes | Cook time: 10 minutes | Serves 4

Ingredients:
4 (6 ounce) halibut fillets
⅓ cup olive oil
4 cups baby spinach
¼ cup lemon juice
2 ounces pitted black olives, halved
2 tablespoons flat leaf parsley, chopped
2 teaspoons fresh dill, chopped
Lemon wedges, to serve

Preparation:
1. Preheat the griddle over medium heat.
2. In a mixing basin, toss the spinach with the lemon juice and leave aside.
3. Brush each side of the salmon with olive oil and cook for 3-4 minutes, or until cooked through.
4. When cooked, leave it aside for 5 minutes.
5. Add the remaining oil and heat for 2 minutes, or until the spinach is barely wilted. Remove from the heat.
6. Toss with olives and herbs, then serve with lemon wedges on serving dishes with the fish.

Per Serving: Calories: 491; Fat: 25.3g; Sodium: 308mg; Carbs: 2.6g; Fiber 1.4g; Sugar: 0.8g; Protein: 61.8g

Cheese Halibut with Parsley

Prep time: 10 minutes | Cook time: 10 minutes | Serves 4

Ingredients:
4 Halibut Fillets, Cut About 1 Inch Thick
1 tablespoon Olive oil
Sea Salt and Pepper
4 Fresh Grated Parmesan Cheese
1 tablespoon Fresh Chopped Parsley
1 tablespoon Fresh Lemon Juice

Preparation:
1. Season the halibut fillets with salt and pepper after brushing them with olive oil.
2. Preheat the griddle to high heat.
3. Spray the barbecue with spray oil and place the halibut on the grill right away.
4. 2 minutes per side on the grill
5. Reduce the heat to medium and cook for 2 minutes per side.
6. Sprinkle the parmesan over the halibut and cook for another minute before removing it from the heat.
7. Before serving, sprinkle the fillets with parsley and lemon juice and set aside for 5 minutes.

Per Serving: Calories: 710; Fat: 38.3g; Sodium: 1074mg; Carbs: 26g; Fiber 1.6g; Sugar: 2.8g; Protein: 63.8g

Grilled Soy Salmon

Prep time: 10 minutes | Cook time: 15 minutes | Serves 2

Ingredients:
2 Salmon Fillets
½-teaspoon Lemon Pepper
½-teaspoon Garlic Powder
Salt and Pepper
⅓ Cup Soy Sauce
⅓ Cup sugar
1 tablespoon Olive Oil

Preparation:
1. Get the ingredients ready. Lemon pepper, garlic powder, and salt are used to season salmon fillets.
2. Combine the olive oil, soy sauce, and sugar in a small basin with a third cup of water.
3. Place the salmon in a bowl and cover it with the sauce. Allow to marinate for at least an hour in the refrigerator, covered with cling film.
4. Set the Griddle to the highest heat.
5. Allow the griddle to heat until the oil is shimmering but not smoking, then place the salmon on the griddle and cook for 5 minutes per side or until the fish is cooked. With lemon slices on the side.
6. When cooked, serve and enjoy.

Per Serving: Calories: 447; Fat: 18g; Sodium: 2474mg; Carbs: 37.4g; Fiber 0.6g; Sugar: 34.8g; Protein: 37.8g

Grilled Jumbo Shrimp

Prep time: 15 minutes | Cook time: 8 minutes | Serves 6

Ingredients:
1-½ pounds uncooked shrimp, peeled and deveined

For the marinade:
2 tablespoons fresh parsley
1 bay leaf, dried
1 teaspoon chili powder
1 teaspoon garlic powder
¼ teaspoon cayenne pepper
¼ cup olive oil
¼ teaspoon salt
⅛ teaspoon pepper

Preparation:
1. Add marinade ingredients to a food processor and process until smooth.
2. In a large mixing bowl, pour the marinade.
3. Refrigerate, covered, for 30 minutes after adding the shrimp and tossing to coat.
4. Using metal skewers, thread shrimp onto them.
5. Preheat the griddle over medium-high heat.
6. Cook, flipping once, for 5-6 minutes, or until shrimp are opaque pink.
7. Serve right away.

Per Serving: Calories: 130; Fat: 8.3g; Sodium: 980mg; Carbs: 0.6g; Fiber 0.6g; Sugar: 1.8g; Protein: 13.8g

Salmon Fillets with Broccolini

Prep time: 15 minutes | Cook time: 25 minutes | Serves: 2

Ingredients:
2 (6 ounces) salmon fillets, skin removed
2 tablespoons of butter, unsalted
2 minced basil leaves
1 garlic clove, minced
6 ounces of broccolini
2 teaspoons of olive oil
Sea salt, to taste

Preparation:
1. Grease the cooking surface of the griddle with cooking spray.
2. Turn on the 4 burners and turn their knobs to medium heat.
3. Let the Griddle preheat for 5 minutes.
4. Combine the butter, basil, and garlic in a blender and blend until smooth. Refrigerate after forming into a ball.
5. Season the fish on all sides with salt and set it aside.
6. In a large mixing bowl, combine the broccolini, a pinch of salt, and the olive oil; toss to coat and set aside. Brush the griddle with olive oil and then let it cook the salmon for 12 minutes, skin side down. Cook for another 4 minutes after turning the salmon. Remove the griddle from the heat and set aside to cool while the broccolini cooks.
7. Toss the broccolini to the griddle, with occasional stirring, until slightly charred, about 6 minutes.
8. Top each salmon fillet with basil butter.
9. Serve with broccolini on the side.

Per Serving: Calories: 327; Fat: 22g; Sodium: 421mg; Carbs: 10g; Fiber 4.1g; Sugar: 2g; Protein: 31g

Octopus with Lemon and Oregano

Prep time: 14 minutes | Cook time: 10 minutes | Serves 4

Ingredients:
3 lemons
3 pounds cleaned octopus, thawed if frozen
6 cloves garlic, peeled
4 sprigs fresh oregano
2 bay leaves
Salt and pepper
3 tablespoons good-quality olive oil
Minced fresh oregano for garnish

Preparation:
1. Getting the ingredients ready.
2. Cut one of the lemons in half. In a large saucepan with enough water to cover by a couple of inches, combine the octopus, garlic, oregano sprigs, bay leaves, a heavy pinch of salt, and lemon halves.
3. Bring to a boil, then reduce to a low heat so the liquid bubbles gently but steadily, and cook, turning occasionally with tongs, for 30 to 90 minutes, or until the octopus is cooked. (Use the tip of a sharp knife to test; it should easily go in.)
4. Drain and toss out the seasonings. (The octopus can be covered and refrigerated for up to 24 hours.)
5. 1 of the remaining lemons' juice should be squeezed and whisked with the oil, salt, and pepper to taste. Toss the octopus with the oil mixture after cutting it into generous serving pieces.
6. Preheat the Griddle to high temperature. Grease the griddle.
7. Place the octopus on the grill and cook for 4 to 5 minutes per side, or until heated through and blackened. The remaining lemon should be cut into wedges.
8. Serve the octopus on a dish with the lemon wedges and a sprinkling of chopped oregano.

Per Serving: Calories: 673; Fat: 17.3g; Sodium: 1574mg; Carbs: 21.6g; Fiber 2g; Sugar: 1.8g; Protein: 102.8g

Sour and Sweet Shrimp

Prep time: 9 minutes | Cook time: 43 minutes | Serves: 4

Ingredients:
Rub:
- 1 tablespoon coriander seeds
- 1 tablespoon whole allspice berries
- ½ tablespoon cumin seeds
- 1 teaspoon black peppercorns
- 1 teaspoon ground cloves
- 1 teaspoon sweet paprika
- 1 teaspoon cayenne pepper
- Zest of 2 limes
- 1 tablespoon salt
- 16 jumbo shrimp, peeled and deveined
- Honey, as needed
- 4 limes, halved, for serving

Preparation:
1. Roast the allspice, coriander, cumin, and peppercorns in a suitable skillet for 3 minutes.
2. In a spice grinder, grind the paprika, cloves, lime zest, cayenne, roasted spices and salt to a fine powder.
3. Preheat the Griddle by turning all its knob to medium-heat setting.
4. Grease the griddle top with cooking oil.
5. Liberally coat the shrimp with the spice mixture, lime juice and honey.
6. Sear the skewers for 3 minutes per side.
7. Serve warm.

Per Serving: Calories: 183; Fat: 0.4 g; Sodium: 4347 mg; Carbs: 5.6g; Fiber: 0.6g; Sugar: 8.4g; Protein: 40.2g

Spice Popcorn Shrimp

Prep time: 15 minutes | Cook time: 5 minutes | Serves 5

Ingredients:
Spicerub
- 2 teaspoons garlic powder
- 2 teaspoons sweet paprika
- 1 teaspoon onion powder
- 1 teaspoon dried oregano
- 1 teaspoon cayenne pepper
- 1 teaspoon salt

Shrimp
- 1½ pounds shelled and deveined small shrimp
- 1 teaspoon freshly ground black pepper
- 1 teaspoon sugar
- In a large plastic bag, combine the spices and shake to blend them.
- 1 lemon, cut into wedges

Preparation:
1. Getting the ingredients ready.
2. Toss the shrimp with the spice rub in a plastic bag and shake to coat.
3. Set the Griddle to high heat.
4. Allow to heat the griddle until the oil is shimmering but not smoking.
5. Grill the shrimp for 1 minute on each side, or until opaque and firm to the touch.
6. Immediately serve the shrimp in a bowl with lemon wedges on top (and with plenty of napkins).

Per Serving: Calories: 201; Fat: 2.8g; Sodium: 849mg; Carbs: 6.3g; Fiber 1.1g; Sugar: 1.8g; Protein: 36.8g

Rosemary Skinless Salmon

Prep time: 15 minutes | Cook time: 10 minutes | Serves 4

Ingredients:
- 4 rosemary branches
- 4 pieces' skinless salmon fillet (each about 2 inches wide, 3 to 4 inches long, ¾ to 1 inch thick, and 6 ounces)
- 2 tablespoons extra-virgin olive oil
- Coarse salt
- freshly ground black pepper
- 2 cloves garlic, minced
- 1 teaspoon finely grated lemon zest
- Lemon wedges, for serving

Preparation:
1. Getting the ingredients ready.
2. Remove the leaves from the bottom 4 inches of each rosemary branch (take them off with your thumb and forefinger) and finely chop them; you'll season the salmon with the chopped rosemary.
3. Feel the salmon fillets with your fingertips for any bones. Using needle-nose pliers or tweezers, remove any you locate. Using paper towels, wipe the fish dry after rinsing it under cold running water.
4. Using the bare part of a rosemary branch, skewer each salmon fillet through the centre of a short side.
5. Brush both sides of the fish with olive oil and place on a big dish. Seasoning the fish fine on both sides with salt and pepper.
6. In a small mixing dish, combine the chopped rosemary, garlic, and lemon zest.
7. Sprinkle the rosemary mixture on both sides of the salmon, patting it in with your fingertips. Allow the fish to come to room temperature while the grill is heating up.
8. Preheat the Griddle to high temperature. Allow the griddle to heat up after oiling it.
9. Place the fish on a hot grill to cook. After 3 to 5 minutes of cooking, it will be done.
10. Press the fish with your finger to see whether it's done; it should break into clear flakes.
11. Serve the salmon on a platter or individual plates with lemon wedges on the side.

Per Serving: Calories: 268; Fat: 18.3g; Sodium: 66mg; Carbs: 2.6g; Fiber 0.6g; Sugar: 0.8g; Protein: 23.8g

Pepper Swordfish

Prep time: 12 minutes | Cook time: 20 minutes | Serves 4

Ingredients:
- 4 Swordfish Fillets, Cut About 1.5 Inches Thick
- Olive Oil
- Sea Salt and Pepper To Taste

Preparation:
1. Preheat the griddle to high heat.
2. Season the fillets with sea salt and black pepper after drizzling them with olive oil.
3. Cook for 3 minutes on each side on the grill.
4. Reduce the heat to medium and continue grilling for 5 minutes per side, or until the swordfish's sides are uniformly colored.
5. Allow 5 minutes for the fish to rest before serving.

Per Serving: Calories: 194; Fat: 9g; Sodium: 122mg; Carbs: 0g; Fiber 0g; Sugar: 0g; Protein: 28g

Mexican Shrimp

Prep time: 15 minutes | Cook time: 15 minutes | Serves 4

Ingredients:
- 1 lb. shrimp, cleaned
- 3-tablespoon fresh parsley, chopped
- 1-tablespoon garlic, minced
- ¼ onion, sliced
- ¼-teaspoon paprika
- ¼-teaspoon ground cumin
- 2 fresh lime juice
- 2-teaspoon olive oil
- ¼ cup butter
- Pepper
- Salt

Preparation:
1. Paprika, cumin, pepper, and salt are used to season the shrimp.
2. Preheat the griddle to high heat.
3. Top the griddle with oil and butter.
4. Sauté for 5 minutes with the onion and garlic.
5. Cook for 5-8 minutes, or until shrimp is done.
6. Toss in the parsley and lime juice.
7. Serve with a good stir.

Per Serving: Calories: 310; Fat: 20.3g; Sodium: 400mg; Carbs: 5.2g; Fiber 0.6g; Sugar: 0.8g; Protein: 26.8g

Lemon Pepper Salmon

Prep time: 05 minutes | Cook time: 10 minutes | Serves 4

Ingredients:
- 12 oz. salmon, cut into two pieces
- 1-teaspoon Greek seasoning
- 1-tablespoon olive oil
- ½-teaspoon lemon zest
- 1 garlic clove, minced
- Pepper
- Salt

Preparation:
1. Combine olive oil, lemon zest, garlic, pepper, salt, and Greek seasoning in a large mixing bowl.
2. Set aside for 15 minutes after adding the salmon to a bowl and coating it well with the marinade.
3. Preheat the griddle to high heat.
4. Cook for 2-3 minutes on a hot griddle top with marinated fish.
5. Cook for another 2-3 minutes on the other side of the fish.
6. Serve and have fun.

Per Serving: Calories: 291; Fat: 17.3g; Sodium: 232mg; Carbs: 1.4g; Fiber 0.1g; Sugar: 0.1g; Protein: 33.8g

Spiced Snapper with Mango Salsa and Lime Wedges

Prep time: 10 minutes | Cook time: 25 minutes | Serves: 4

Ingredients:
2 red snappers, cleaned
Sea salt, to taste
⅓ cup tandoori spice
For the Salsa:
1 ripe but firm mango, peeled and chopped
1 small red onion, sliced
Olive oil, plus more for grill
Olive oil, for drizzling
Lime wedges, for serving
1 bunch cilantro, chopped
3 tablespoons fresh lime juice

Preparation:
1. In a suitable mixing bowl, combine onion, mango, lime juice, cilantro, oil and a pinch of salt.
2. Make slashes on top of the fish fillet and season with spices, oil and salt.
3. Preheat the Griddle by turning all its knob to medium-heat setting.
4. Grease the griddle top with cooking oil.
5. Cook the fish for 5 minutes per side on the hot griddle top.
6. Garnish with mango salad and lime wedges.
7. Serve.
Per Serving: Calories: 210; Fat: 5.4 g; Sodium: 110 mg; Carbs: 18.5g; Fiber: 2.4g; Sugar: 13.1g; Protein: 23.5g

Salmon Zucchini Patties

Prep time: 15 minutes | Cook time: 10 minutes | Serves: 6

Ingredients:
2 eggs
1 ½ lbs. salmon, cooked
2 cups zucchini, shredded
2-tablespoon onion, minced
¼ cup fresh cilantro, chopped
¼ cup olive oil
¾ cup almond flour
3-tablespoon fresh lime juice
2-tablespoon jalapeno, minced
2 tsp salt

Preparation:
1. In a food processor, blend the salmon, lime juice, cilantro, zucchini, jalapenos, onion, eggs, and salt until well incorporated.
2. In a shallow plate, place the almond flour.
3. Preheat the griddle to high heat. Grease the griddle.
4. Form ¼ cup of the salmon mixture into patties, coat with almond flour, and fry for 5 minutes on each side on a hot griddle.
5. Serve and have fun.
Per Serving: Calories: 337; Fat: 24g; Sodium: 850mg; Carbs: 6.7g; Fiber 2.2g; Sugar: 1.8g; Protein: 27.8g

Oregano Shrimp Skewers

Prep time: 15 minutes | Cook time: 7 minutes | Serves: 6

Ingredients:
1-½ lbs. shrimp,
1-tablespoon dried oregano
2-teaspoon garlic paste
2 lemon juice
¼ cup olive oil
1-teaspoon paprika
Pepper
Salt

Preparation:
1. Add all ingredients into the mixing bowl and mix well and place in the refrigerator for 1 hour.
2. Remove marinated shrimp from refrigerator and thread onto the skewers.
3. Preheat the griddle to high heat.
4. Place skewers onto the griddle top and cook for 5-7 minutes.
5. Serve and enjoy.
Per Serving: Calories: 215; Fat:10.3g; Sodium: 307mg; Carbs: 2.6g; Fiber 0.6g; Sugar: 0.8g; Protein: 26g

Coconut-Rum Shrimp and Pineapple Skewers

Prep time: 15 minutes | Cook time: 10 minutes | Serves: 6

Ingredients:
½ cup coconut milk
¼ cup dark or spiced rum
¼ cup fresh lime juice
1 teaspoon ras el hanout
Salt and pepper
2 cloves garlic, chopped
2 pounds large or jumbo shrimp, peeled (and deveined if you like)
1 ripe pineapple, peeled, cored, and cut into 1½-inch cubes
Lime wedges for serving

Preparation:
1. Preparing the Ingredients
2. Stir the coconut milk, rum, lime juice, ras el hanout, and garlic together in a large bowl. Toss in the shrimp and toss well to coat.
3. Allow to marinate at room temperature while preparing the grill, or cover and chill for up to 1 hour.
4. Soak bamboo or wooden skewers in water for 30 minutes before using.
5. Alternate the shrimp and pineapple cubes on skewers. Discard any remaining marinade.
6. Turn control knob to the high position. Oil the griddle and allow it to heat. Put the skewers on the griddle and cook until the shrimp are opaque all the way through and the pineapple browns in spots 10 minutes.
7. Transfer the skewers to a platter and serve with lime wedges.
Per Serving: Calories: 140; Fat: 3.8g; Sodium: 881mg; Carbs: 6.2g; Fiber 1.2g; Sugar: 5g; Protein: 14.2g

Lemon Butter Tilapia

Prep time: 15 minutes | Cook time: 10 minutes | Serves 6

Ingredients:
2 lbs. tilapia fillets
1-teaspoon garlic powder
½ fresh lemon juice
1-tablespoon butter, melted
Pepper
Salt

Preparation:
1. Combine lemon juice, garlic powder, and butter in a small microwave-safe bowl and heat for 10 seconds.
2. Brush the lemon mixture on both sides of the fish fillet. Flavor the fillet with salt and pepper.
3. Preheat the griddle to high heat.
4. Coat the top of the griddle with cooking spray.
5. Cook the fillets for 4 minutes on each side on a hot griddle.
6. Serve and have fun.
Per Serving: Calories: 173; Fat: 3g; Sodium: 114mg; Carbs: 0.6g; Fiber: 0.6g; Sugar: 0.8g; Protein: 33.8g

Pineapple Chunks and Shrimp with Sauce

Prep time: 6 minutes | Cook time: 10 minutes | Serves: 4 to 6

Ingredients:
Fermented Pineapple–Peanut Sauce
1 cup roasted unsalted peanuts
10 dried chiles de árbol, seeded
1 cup oil
2 tablespoons honey
1 tablespoon salt
1 ripe pineapple, cored, and cut into small chunks
2 pounds unpeeled jumbo shrimp
Oil and salt, for coating

Preparation:
1. Blend the chilies, peanuts, honey, oil, and salt until smooth in a blender.
2. Preheat the Griddle by turning all its knob to medium-heat setting.
3. Grease the griddle top with cooking spray.
4. Dip the shrimp in the sauce and sear for 2-3 minutes on per side on the hot griddle top.
5. Serve with remaining sauce and pineapple chunks.
Per Serving: Calories: 720; Fat: 50.1 g; Sodium: 2142 mg; Carbs: 44.5g; Fiber: 8.2g; Sugar: 33g; Protein: 25.2g

Lemon Trout

Prep time: 15 minutes | Cook time: 15 minutes | Serves: 2

Ingredients:
2 trout fillets
2 teaspoons of lemon juice
2 tablespoons of lemon pepper seasoning

Preparation:
1. Grease the cooking surface of the griddle with cooking spray.
2. Turn on the 4 burners and turn their knobs to medium heat.
3. Let the Griddle preheat for 5 minutes.
4. Season fish fillets with lemon pepper seasoning.
5. Place fish fillets on a preheated griddle top and then let it cook for 5-10 minutes.
6. Drizzle with lemon juice and serve.
Per Serving: Calories: 379; Fat: 13g; Sodium: 421mg; Carbs: 16g; Fiber 4.1g; Sugar: 3.2g; Protein: 27g

Bacon Scallops

Prep time: 15 minutes | Cook time: 5 minutes | Serves 4

Ingredients:
12 large sea scallops, side muscle removed
8 slices of bacon
1 tablespoon vegetable oil
12 toothpicks

Preparation:
1. Cook the bacon on a medium griddle until the; Fat: has rendered but the bacon is still pliable. Place the bacon on paper towels after removing it from the grill.
2. Raise the heat on the griddle to medium heat.
3. Wrap a half slice of bacon around each scallop and skewer with a toothpick to secure it in place.
4. Cook the scallops for 90 seconds per side on the griddle.
5. On all sides, they should be lightly browned.
6. Remove the griddle from the heat and serve right away.

Per Serving: Calories: 315; Fat: 20g; Sodium: 1024mg; Carbs: 2.6g; Fiber 0g; Sugar: 0g; Protein: 29.8g

Whitefish with Garlic Mayonnaise

Prep time: 5 minutes | Cook time: 10 minutes | Serves: 4

Ingredients:
Roasted Garlic Mayo:
3 egg yolks
1 tablespoon lemon or lime juice
1¾ cups oil
2 tablespoons roasted garlic
2 teaspoons salt

For the Beer-Battered Fish:
4 tablespoon cooking oil
1½ cups all-purpose flour
1 teaspoon ancho chili powder
1 teaspoon salt
½ teaspoon baking soda
1 (12-oz.) can dark beer
2 pounds boneless whitefish fillets

Preparation:
1. Preheat the Griddle by turning all its knob to medium-heat setting.
2. Grease the griddle top with cooking oil.
3. Blend the egg yolks with lemon juice then drip in the oil slowly and continue blending for 5 minutes.
4. In a suitable mixing bowl, mix well the salt, chili powder, flour, and baking soda.
5. While mixing, slowly pour in the beer and whisk until smooth.
6. Season the fish fillets with salt and black pepper, then dredge them in plain flour.
7. Dip the fish in the beer batter then fry in the oil for 5 minutes per side.
8. Serve with a dollop of garlic mayonnaise.

Per Serving: Calories: 343; Fat: 13.1 g; Sodium: 1333 mg; Carbs: 5.7g; Fiber: 0.1g; Sugar: 0.2g; Protein: 43.6g

Cheese Pistachio Shrimp

Prep time: 13 minutes | Cook time: 10 minutes | Serves 4

Ingredients:
1-½ lb. Uncooked shrimp, peeled and deveined
2 tablespoons lemon juice
¼ cup Parmesan cheese, shredded
¼ teaspoon of sea salt
⅛ teaspoon black ground pepper
½ cup olive oil
½ cup parsley, fresh minced
1 garlic clove, peeled
⅓ cup pistachios, shelled
¼ teaspoon grated lemon zest
¾ cup arugula, fresh

Preparation:
1. To make the dressing, in a blender, combine the olive oil, lemon zest, garlic clove, pistachios, parsley, arugula, and lemon juice. Blend until completely smooth.
2. Mix in the Parmesan cheese, salt, and pepper until everything is well combined.
3. Toss in your shrimp and marinate for 30 minutes in the fridge.
4. Using skewers, thread your shrimp.
5. Preheat your Griddle to a medium heat.
6. After the grill has been prepared, place your skewers on it.
7. Grill for 6 minutes, with rotating every 2 minutes. Skewers are cooked in batches.
8. Serve and have fun!

Per Serving: Calories: 390; Fat: 30g; Sodium: 443mg; Carbs: 4.2g; Fiber 0.6g; Sugar: 0.8g; Protein: 27.8g

Blackened Cod

Prep time: 15 minutes | Cook time: 15 minutes | Serves: 4

Ingredients:
4 cod fillets
2 teaspoons of taco seasoning
1 teaspoon black pepper
1 teaspoon of garlic powder
2 teaspoons of cumin powder
2 teaspoons of chili powder

Preparation:
1. Grease the cooking surface of the griddle with cooking spray.
2. Turn on the 4 burners and turn their knobs to medium-high heat.
3. Let the Griddle preheat for 5 minutes.
4. Mix taco seasoning, pepper, garlic powder, cumin powder, and chili powder and rub all over fish fillets.
5. Place fish fillets on a preheated griddle top and then let it cook for 4-5 minutes on each side.
6. Serve.

Per Serving: Calories: 397; Fat: 21g; Sodium: 711mg; Carbs: 8g; Fiber 3.1g; Sugar: 4g; Protein: 22g

Dijon-ginger Glazed Salmon

Prep time: 8 minutes | Cook time: 15 minutes | Serves 6

Ingredients:
1 (2-pound) skin-on salmon fillet
1 tablespoon good-quality vegetable oil
Salt and pepper
¼ cup maple syrup
1 tablespoon Dijon mustard
1 tablespoon minced fresh ginger

Preparation:
1. Getting the ingredients ready.
2. Remove any pin bones that remain from the salmon. Using a sharp knife, score the skin in a crosshatch pattern.
3. Using paper towels, pat the fish dry and place it on a large baking pan.
4. Brush the skin side with oil, season both sides with salt and pepper, then turn it skin side down.
5. In a small mixing dish, combine the maple syrup, mustard, and ginger. Apply the glaze on the top.
6. Preheat the Griddle to high heat; place the salmon skin side down on the griddle and cook, without turning, for 10 minutes, or until the thickest section is as opaque as you like; nick with a sharp knife and glance inside to check a couple of times.
7. Place the salmon on a cutting board and chop it into 4 or 6 pieces before serving.
8. Enjoy!

Per Serving: Calories: 110; Fat: 18.3g; Sodium: 74mg; Carbs: 2.6g; Fiber 1.6g; Sugar: 2.8g; Protein: 3.8g

Ginger Salmon

Prep time: 15 minutes | Cook time: 10 minutes | Serves 5

Ingredients:
1 teaspoon onion, finely chopped
¼ teaspoon sea salt
1 teaspoon ginger root, fresh minced
1 tablespoon rice vinegar
1 garlic clove, minced
teaspoons sugar
⅛ cup lime juice
1 cucumber, peeled and chopped
⅙ cup cilantro, fresh chopped
¼ teaspoon coriander, ground
¼ teaspoon ground pepper

Salmon:
5 (6-ounces) salmon fillets
¼ teaspoon of sea salt
¼ teaspoon freshly ground black pepper
⅙ cup ginger root, minced
½ tablespoon olive oil
½ tablespoon lime juice

Preparation:
1. Begin by combining the first 11 ingredients until smooth in a blender.
2. Olive oil, lime juice, ginger, salt, and pepper are used to season the salmon fillets.
3. Preheat your Griddle to medium heat.
4. Place 2 salmon fillets on the grill when it has been warmed.
5. 4 minutes per side on the grill
6. Cook the remaining fillets in the same manner.
7. Enjoy the salmon fillets with the prepared sauce!

Per Serving: Calories: 253; Fat: 12g; Sodium: 174mg; Carbs: 3.6g; Fiber 0.6g; Sugar: 1.8g; Protein: 33.8g

Chapter 5 Fish and Seafood Recipes

Chapter 6 Poultry Recipes

Olive BBQ Chicken

Prep time: 05 minutes | Cook time: 1 hour 30 minutes | Serves: 4-6

Ingredients:
3 Pounds chicken, cut into pieces
Salt, to taste
1-teaspoon Olive oil
½ cup barbecue sauce

Preparation:
1. Preheat the Griddle by turning all its knob to medium-heat setting.
2. Grease the griddle top with cooking spray.
3. Season the chicken well with salt and olive oil.
4. On the hot griddle top, sear the chicken skin side down for 5-minutes per side.
5. Reduce the heat to medium-low, cover with foil, and cook for 30 minutes.
6. Flip the chicken and baste it with the barbecue sauce.
7. Baste with extra barbecue sauce then serve warm.

Per Serving: Calories: 380; Fat: 7.7g; Sodium: 403 mg; Carbs: 7.6g; Fiber: 0.1g; Sugar: 5.4g; Protein: 65.7g

Stuffed Chicken Breast

Prep time: 15 minutes | Cook time: 20 minutes | Serves: 4

Ingredients:
2-½-pound Boneless chicken breasts
2-tablespoon olive oil
2-tablespoon taco seasoning
½ red, yellow, and green pepper, very sliced
½ Small red onion, very sliced
½ cup Mexican shredded cheese
Guacamole, for serving
Sour cream, for serving
Salsa, for serving

Preparation:
1. Make small horizontal incisions across the chicken breasts.
2. Coat the chicken in olive oil and taco seasoning evenly.
3. Preheat the Griddle by turning all its knob to medium-heat setting.
4. Grease the griddle top with cooking spray.
5. Fill each cut with a mixture of bell peppers and red onions, then set the breasts on the hot griddle top.
6. Allow 15 minutes for the chicken to cook.
7. Top the chicken with cheese, cover with foil and cook for 5 minutes.
8. Remove from the griddle and serve with sour cream, guacamole, and salsa on the side.
9. Serve with.

Per Serving: Calories: 540; Fat: 26.8 g; Sodium: 309 mg; Carbs: 2.6g; Fiber: 0.4g; Sugar: 1.2g; Protein: 69.9g

Marinated Chicken Breast with Salsa Verde

Prep time: 4 hours 35 minutes | Cook time: 15 minutes | Serves: 6

Ingredients:
3-pound Boneless chicken breasts
1-tablespoon olive oil
1-teaspoon sea salt
For the salsa Verde marinade:
½-teaspoon garlic, minced
1 small onion, chopped
6 Tomatillos, husked, rinsed and chopped
1 medium jalapeño pepper, cut in
1-teaspoon chili powder
1-teaspoon ground cumin
1-teaspoon garlic powder
half, seeded
¼ cup fresh cilantro, chopped
½-teaspoon sugar or sugar substitute

Preparation:
1. In a food processor, mix well all of the ingredients for the salsa Verde marinade and pulse until smooth.
2. In a suitable mixing bowl, mix well the sea salt, chili powder, cumin, and garlic powder. Place chicken breasts in a glass baking dish and season with olive oil and seasoning mix.
3. Cover each chicken breast with a tbsp. of salsa Verde marinade, reserving the rest for serving.
4. Refrigerate for 4 hours after covering the dish with plastic wrap.
5. Preheat the Griddle by turning all its knob to medium-heat setting.
6. Grease the griddle top with cooking spray.
7. Cook 7 minutes per side on the hot griddle top
8. Serve with more salsa Verde on the side and enjoy!

Per Serving: Calories: 710; Fat: 29.5 g; Sodium: 770 mg; Carbs: 6.6g; Fiber: 1.8g; Sugar: 1.6g; Protein: 99.5g

Chili Lime Chicken with Sesame Seed

Prep time: 35 minutes | Cook time: 15 minutes | Serves: 4

Ingredients:
½ cup sweet chili sauce
¼ cup soy sauce
1-teaspoon mirin
½-teaspoon orange juice
1-teaspoon orange marmalade
1-tablespoon lime juice
1 tbsp. brown sugar
1 clove garlic, minced
4-pound Boneless chicken breasts
Sesame seeds, for garnish

Preparation:
1. In a suitable mixing bowl, combine soy sauce, brown sugar, sweet chili sauce, orange marmalade, mirin, lime and orange juice, and minced garlic.
2. Reserve ¼ cup of this orange sauce.
3. Add the chicken to the remaining sauce, mix well to coat and set aside for 30 minutes to marinate.
4. Preheat the Griddle by turning all its knob to medium-heat setting.
5. Grease the griddle top with cooking spray.
6. Place the chicken on the hot griddle top and cook for 7 minutes per side.
7. Garnish with sesame seeds and serve.

Per Serving: Calories: 950; Fat: 33.7 g; Sodium: 1541 mg; Carbs: 18.4g; Fiber: 0.2g; Sugar: 16g; Protein: 132.2g

Seared Spicy Boneless Chicken Thighs

Prep time: 8-24 hours | Cook time: 20 minutes | Serves: 4

Ingredients:
2-pound boneless chicken thighs
For the marinade:
¼ cup fresh lime juice
2-teaspoon lime zest
¼ cup honey
2 tablespoons olive oil
½-tablespoon balsamic vinegar
½-teaspoon sea salt
½-teaspoon black pepper
½ Garlic cloves, minced
¼-teaspoon onion powder

Preparation:
1. In a suitable mixing bowl, whisk all marinade ingredients; keep 2 tablespoons of the marinade for basting.
2. Mix the chicken with marinade in a sealable plastic bag, shake and refrigerate overnight.
3. Preheat the Griddle by turning all its knob to medium-heat setting.
4. Grease the griddle top with cooking oil.
5. Cook the marinated chicken for 8 minutes per side while basting on the hot griddle top.
6. Serve and enjoy!

Per Serving: Calories: 559; Fat: 23.8 g; Sodium: 430 mg; Carbs: 18.3g; Fiber: 0.3g; Sugar: 17.6g; Protein: 65.8g

Chili Chicken Wings

Prep time: 35 minutes | Cook time: 25 minutes | Serves: 6

Ingredients:
2-pound chicken wings
Marinade:
½ cup Greek yogurt, plain
½-tablespoon mild yellow curry powder
1-tablespoon olive oil
½-teaspoon sea salt
½-teaspoon black pepper
1-teaspoon red chili flakes

Preparation:
1. In a suitable mixing bowl, mix marinade ingredients until blended.
2. Toss the wings in the bowl to coat them well.
3. Refrigerate for marination for 30 minutes after covering bowl with plastic wrap.
4. Preheat the Griddle by turning all its knob to medium-heat setting.
5. Grease the griddle top with cooking spray.
6. Place the wings on the hot griddle top, flipping every 5 minutes, cook for 20 minutes.
7. Serve warm.

Per Serving: Calories: 322; Fat: 14 g; Sodium: 679 mg; Carbs: 1.1g; Fiber: 0.2g; Sugar: 0.7g; Protein: 45.5g

Oregano Boneless Chicken

Prep time: 1–24 hours | **Cook time:** 15 minutes | **Serves:** 4-6

Ingredients:
2-pound chicken thighs or breasts (boneless, skinless)
For the marinade:
¼ cup olive oil
2 chipotle peppers in adobo sauce, plus 1-teaspoon adobo sauce from the can
1-tablespoon garlic, minced
1 shallot, chopped
1 ½ tablespoons cumin
1-tablespoon cilantro, super-chopped or dried
2-teaspoon chili powder
1-teaspoon dried oregano
½-teaspoon salt
2 Fresh limes, garnish
1 Cilantro, garnish

Preparation:
1. Pulse the marinade ingredients into a paste in a food processor or blender.
2. Place the chicken in a sealable plastic bag with the marinade and massage well to coat.
3. Refrigerate for 24 hours prior to cooking.
4. Preheat the Griddle by turning all its knob to medium-heat setting.
5. Grease the griddle top with cooking spray.
6. Cook for 7 minutes on one side, then flip and cook for another 7 minutes.
7. Reduce the heat to low and simmer until the chicken reaches an internal temperature of 165°F.
8. To serve, top with fresh lime juice and cilantro.

Per Serving: Calories: 384; Fat: 20.5g; Sodium: 449 mg; Carbs: 5.1g; Fiber: 2.1g; Sugar: 0.7g; Protein: 45g

Chicken Thighs Cooked in Root Beer

Prep time: 8 hours 10 minutes | **Cook time:** 20 minutes | **Serves:** 2-4

Ingredients:
1-pound boneless chicken thighs
(12 oz.) can root beer
1 teaspoon olive oil
For the rub:
½-tablespoon garlic powder
¾-tablespoon sea salt
½-tablespoon white pepper
1-teaspoon smoked paprika
½-teaspoon garlic powder
1-teaspoon dried thyme
⅛-teaspoon cayenne pepper

Preparation:
1. In a suitable mixing bowl, mix well all of the rub ingredients; set aside half in an airtight container until ready to use.
2. Drizzle olive oil over chicken thighs and coat each with the spice rub.
3. Arrange the chicken in a baking dish that measures 13 by 9 inches.
4. Cover with two root beer cans.
5. Preheat the Griddle by turning all its knob to medium-heat setting.
6. Grease the griddle top with cooking oil.
7. In a small dish, gently fold the remaining rub and half of the third can of root beer.
8. Cook the chicken for 7 minutes per side, basting with the root beer rub mixture.
9. Serve.

Per Serving: Calories: 297; Fat: 18.4 g; Sodium: 1151 mg; Carbs: 11.6g; Fiber: 0.6g; Sugar: 10.9g; Protein: 20.5g

Gochujang Chicken Wings

Prep time: 30 minutes | **Cook time:** 30 minutes | **Serves:** 6

Ingredients:
2 pounds' chicken wings (flats and drumettes attached or separated)
Marinade:
½-tablespoon olive oil
1-teaspoon sea salt, plus more
½-teaspoon black pepper
½ cup gochujang, Korean hot pepper paste
1 scallion, sliced, for garnish

Preparation:
1. In a suitable mixing bowl, mix well all of the marinade ingredients until thoroughly blended.
2. Toss the wings in the bowl to coat well.
3. Refrigerate for marination for 30 minutes after covering with plastic wrap.
4. Preheat the Griddle by turning all its knob to medium-heat setting.
5. Grease the griddle top with cooking spray.
6. Place the wings on the hot griddle top, flipping every 5 minutes, cook for 20 minutes.
7. Serve warm.

Per Serving: Calories: 556; Fat: 37.8 g; Sodium: 1792 mg; Carbs: 16.5g; Fiber: 0.5g; Sugar: 0g; Protein: 29.8g

Glazed Chicken Wings

Prep time: 15 minutes | **Cook time:** 30 minutes | **Serves:** 4

Ingredients:
1 (12 oz.) Jar peach preserves
1 cup sweet red chili sauce
1-teaspoon lime juice
1 tbsp. fresh cilantro, minced
1 (2-½-pound) bag chicken wing sections
Non-stick cooking spray

Preparation:
1. In a suitable mixing bowl, mix the preserves, lime juice, red chili sauce, and cilantro.
2. Divide this mixture in half and set aside one half for serving.
3. Preheat the Griddle by turning all its knob to medium-heat setting.
4. Grease the griddle top with cooking spray.
5. Cook wings on the hot griddle top for 25 minutes, flipping every 5 minutes.
6. Toss them with ½ of the glaze and cook for 3 minutes more on high heat.
7. Serve with left over glaze.

Per Serving: Calories: 914; Fat: 49.5 g; Sodium: 1398 mg; Carbs: 67.7g; Fiber: 1.1g; Sugar: 38.2g; Protein: 45.3g

Garlic Chicken Breast on Tortillas

Prep time: 1 hour 05 minutes | **Cook time:** 10 minutes | **Serves:** 4-6

Ingredients:
½-pound Boneless chicken breasts, sliced thin
Chicken marinade:
1 serrano pepper, minced
1-teaspoon garlic, minced
1 lime, juiced
1-teaspoon ground cumin
⅓ cup olive oil
Sea salt, to taste
Black pepper, to taste
Avocado crema:
1 cup sour cream
2-teaspoon lime juice
1-teaspoon lime zest
1 serrano pepper, diced and seeded
1 clove garlic, minced
1 large Hass avocado
Garnish:
½ cup queso fresco, crumbled
2-teaspoon cilantro, chopped
1 lime sliced into wedges
10 corn tortillas

Preparation:
1. In a sealable plastic bag, mix well all of the chicken marinade ingredients.
2. Toss in the chicken and toss well to coat.
3. Refrigerate for 1 hour to marinate.
4. In a food processor, blend all of the avocado crema ingredients and pulse until smooth.
5. Preheat the Griddle by turning all its knob to medium-heat setting.
6. Grease the griddle top with cooking spray.
7. Cook the chicken on the hot griddle top for 5 minutes per side
8. Top chicken with a dollop of queso fresco, cilantro, avocado crema, and lime wedges.
9. Serve warm on tortillas.

Per Serving: Calories: 328; Fat: 28.7 g; Sodium: 95 mg; Carbs: 7.4g; Fiber: 2.8g; Sugar: 0.7g; Protein: 13g

Chicken Fritters with Dill

Prep time: 20 minutes | **Cook time:** 10 minutes | **Serves:** 4

Ingredients:
1-pound ground chicken
1-teaspoon onion powder
1-teaspoon garlic powder
½ cup parmesan cheese, shredded
1-tablespoon dill, chopped
½ cup breadcrumbs
Pepper
Salt

Preparation:
1. In a suitable mixing bowl, mix well all of the ingredients and stir until well blended.
2. Preheat the Griddle by turning all its knob to medium-heat setting.
3. Grease the griddle top with cooking spray.
4. Shape the chicken mixture into patties and set them on the hot griddle top, cook for 5 minutes per side.
5. Serve and enjoy.

Per Serving: Calories: 286; Fat: 9.8 g; Sodium: 270 mg; Carbs: 11.9g; Fiber: 0.9g; Sugar: 1.2g; Protein: 36.2g

Zucchini Basil Crusted Chicken

Prep time: 20 minutes | **Cook time:** 5 minutes | **Serves:** 4

Ingredients:
Salt and black pepper for taste
1 pound boneless chicken meat, cut into bite-sized pieces
1 red bell pepper, washed and diced
8-oz. mushrooms, cleaned and sliced
2 cups zucchini or other summer squash (washed, stemmed, and sliced)
3 garlic cloves (minced or pressed)
8-oz. fresh basil (chopped)

Preparation:
1. Preheat the Griddle by turning all its knob to medium-heat setting.
2. Grease the griddle top with cooking spray.
3. Season and rub the chicken to taste with salt and black pepper.
4. Place the chicken on the hot griddle top and brown on both sides.
5. Add the other ingredients and simmer for another 3 minutes.
6. Serve.

Per Serving: Calories: 263; Fat: 9.1 g; Sodium: 110 mg; Carbs: 8.3g; Fiber: 2.6g; Sugar: 3.6g; Protein: 37.5g

Garlic Chicken Thighs and Vegetable Skewers

Prep time: 1 hour 20 minutes | **Cook time:** 10 minutes | **Serves:** 4

Ingredients:
10 boneless chicken thighs, diced
1 red onion, wedged
For the marinade:
⅓ cup toasted pine nuts
1 ½ cups roasted red peppers, sliced
Hot cherry peppers, seeded, or to taste
1 red pepper, stemmed, seeded, diced
1 cup packed fresh basil leaves
2 garlic cloves, peeled
¼ cup grated Parmesan cheese
1-tablespoon paprika
Olive oil, as needed

Preparation:
1. In a food processor, blend the toasted pine nuts, hot cherry peppers, roasted red peppers, garlic, basil, Parmesan, and paprika until smooth
2. Stir in the olive oil and mix until the pesto gets a thin consistency.
3. Spoon half of the pesto into a big sealable plastic bag and set rest aside for serving.
4. Place the chicken thigh chunks in the pesto bag, shut it, and rub the chicken to coat it.
5. Set aside for 1 hour in the refrigerator for marination.
6. Using metal skewers, thread the pesto chicken cubes, red onion, and red pepper, alternately.
7. Brush the chicken with the pesto that was set aside.
8. Preheat the Griddle by turning all its knob to medium-heat setting.
9. Grease the griddle top with cooking spray.
10. Cook the pesto skewers for about 5 minutes per side.
11. Serve.

Per Serving: Calories: 855; Fat: 39.2 g; Sodium: 498 mg; Carbs: 13g; Fiber: 3.1g; Sugar: 6.7g; Protein: 109.8g

Hawaiian Chicken Kabob

Prep time: 1 hour 10 minutes | **Cook time:** 15 minutes | **Serves:** 4-6

Ingredients:
½-pound boneless chicken breast, diced
2 cups pineapple, diced
3 green peppers, diced
For the marinade:
⅓ cup tomato paste
⅓ cup brown sugar, packed
⅓ cup soy sauce
¼ cup pineapple juice
2-tablespoon olive oil
1 ½-teaspoon mirin
1 red onion, diced
2-teaspoon olive oil, to coat veggies
½-teaspoon garlic cloves, minced
1-teaspoon ginger, minced
½-teaspoon sesame oil
1 pinch sea salt
1 pinch ground black pepper
10 wooden skewers

Preparation:
1. In a suitable mixing bowl, whisk the marinade ingredients until smooth.
2. Half a cup of the marinade should be kept in the refrigerator.
3. Place the chicken in a sealable plastic bag with the remaining marinade, seal and refrigerate for 1 hour.
4. Toss the red onion, bell pepper, and pineapple in a suitable mixing bowl with 2 tablespoons olive oil.
5. Preheat the Griddle by turning all its knob to medium-heat setting.
6. Grease the griddle top with cooking spray.
7. Thread the skewers with bell pepper, red onion, pineapple, and chicken alternately.
8. Place the skewers on the hot griddle top and cook for 5 minutes per side.
9. Brush the chicken with the marinade once cooked halfway through.
10. Serve.

Per Serving: Calories: 206; Fat: 6.4 g; Sodium: 911 mg; Carbs: 28.9g; Fiber: 3.6g; Sugar: 20.4g; Protein: 11g

Seasoned Chicken Breast Stuffed with Cheese

Prep time: 10 minutes | **Cook time:** 20 minutes | **Serves:** 4

Ingredients:
¾-pound Boneless chicken breasts
8 mini sweet peppers, sliced thin and seeded
2 slices pepper jack cheese, cut in half
2 slices Colby jack cheese, cut in half
1-tablespoon Creole seasoning, like Emeril's
1-teaspoon black pepper
1-teaspoon garlic powder
1-teaspoon onion powder
1-teaspoon olive oil, separated
Toothpicks

Preparation:
1. In a suitable mixing bowl, combine garlic powder, pepper, creole seasoning, and onion powder.
2. Cut a slit down the side of each chicken breast, taking care not to cut all the way through.
3. Drizzle 1 tsp olive oil over each breast.
4. Evenly coat each chicken breast with the spice mix.
5. Stuff each chicken piece with 1 half pepper jack cheese slice, 1 half Colby cheese slice, and a handful of pepper pieces into each chicken breast.
6. Use 4 or 5 toothpicks to close the chicken.
7. Preheat the Griddle by turning all its knob to medium-heat setting.
8. Grease the griddle top with cooking spray.
9. Cook the chicken rolls for 8 minutes per side.
10. Serve.

Per Serving: Calories: 363; Fat: 17.1 g; Sodium: 1065 mg; Carbs: 19.8g; Fiber: 3.4g; Sugar: 12.9g; Protein: 33.7g

Marinated Chicken Thighs

Prep time: 30 minutes | **Cook time:** 15 minutes | **Serves:** 4

Ingredients:
2-pound boneless chicken thighs
1-teaspoon olive oil
½-teaspoon sea salt
For the Marinade:
1-tablespoon honey
1-tablespoon balsamic vinegar
¼-teaspoon black pepper
½-teaspoon paprika
¾-teaspoon onion powder
2-tablespoon tomato paste
½-teaspoon garlic, minced

Preparation:
1. In a sealable plastic bag, mix the chicken, salt, olive oil, paprika, black pepper, and onion powder.
2. Seal and set aside the chicken to coat it in spices and oil.
3. Mix the tomato paste, balsamic vinegar, garlic, and honey in a suitable mixing bowl.
4. Split the marinade in two. Combine one half with the chicken in the bag and keep the other half in the refrigerator in a covered container.
5. Close the bag and shake the chicken in it to coat it. Refrigerate for 30 to 4 hours.
6. Preheat the Griddle by turning all its knob to medium-heat setting.
7. Grease the griddle top with cooking spray.
8. Cook the marinated chicken for 7 minutes per side on the hot griddle top, or until juices flow clear and a meat thermometer reads 165°F.
9. Brush the remaining marinade on top of the chicken thighs during the last minute of cooking.
10. Serve right away.

Per Serving: Calories: 467; Fat: 18.1 g; Sodium: 438 mg; Carbs: 6.6g; Fiber: 0.5g; Sugar: 5.5g; Protein: 66.1g

California Seared Chicken Breast

Prep time: 35 minutes | Cook time: 20 minutes | Serves: 4

Ingredients:
- 2-pound Boneless chicken breasts
- ¾ cup balsamic vinegar
- 1-tablespoon olive oil
- ½-tablespoon honey
- 1-teaspoon oregano
- 1-teaspoon basil
- 1-teaspoon garlic powder

For garnish:
- Sea salt
- ½-teaspoon Black pepper, fresh ground
- 1 cup Slices fresh mozzarella cheese
- 4 slices avocado
- 4 slices beefsteak tomato
- Balsamic glaze, for drizzling

Preparation:
1. In a suitable mixing bowl, whisk honey, balsamic vinegar, oregano, olive oil, basil, and garlic powder.
2. Toss in the chicken and cover, and marinate in the refrigerator for almost 30 minutes.
3. Preheat the Griddle by turning all its knob to medium-heat setting.
4. Grease the griddle top with cooking spray.
5. Sear the chicken for 7 minutes per side on the hot griddle top.
6. Top each chicken breast with avocado, mozzarella, and tomato, then cover with foil and cook for 2 minutes.
7. Drizzle with balsamic glaze and drizzle sea salt and black pepper.
8. Serve warm.

Per Serving: Calories: 936; Fat: 60.8 g; Sodium: 391 mg; Carbs: 26g; Fiber: 14.9g; Sugar: 6.6g; Protein: 7.2g

Seasoned Chicken Wings with Buffalo Sauce

Prep time: 10 minutes | Cook time: 25 minutes | Serves: 8

Ingredients:
- 1-tablespoon sea salt
- 1-teaspoon ground black pepper
- ½-teaspoon garlic powder
- 4-pound chicken wings
- 2-tablespoon butter
- ⅓ cup buffalo sauce, like Moore's
- 1-tablespoon apple cider vinegar
- 1-tablespoon honey

Preparation:
1. In a suitable mixing bowl, combine salt, garlic powder and pepper,.
2. Season the wings by tossing them in the spice mixture.
3. Preheat the Griddle by turning all its knob to medium-heat setting.
4. Grease the griddle top with cooking spray.
5. Place the wings on the hot griddle top and cook for almost 20 minutes, flipping every 5 minutes.
6. In a suitable saucepan over low heat, melt the butter and stir in the vinegar, buffalo sauce, and honey.
7. Toss the wings in a suitable mixing bowl with the prepared sauce.
8. Return the wings to the griddle and cook for 1 to 2 minutes per side on high heat.
9. Serve warm with remaining sauce.

Per Serving: Calories: 467; Fat: 19.8 g; Sodium: 958 mg; Carbs: 2.6g; Fiber: 0.1g; Sugar: 2.2g; Protein: 65.7g

Herb Roasted Turkey in Chicken Broth

Prep time: 15 minutes | Cook time: 3 hrs. 35 minutes | Serves: 12

Ingredients:
- Fourteen pounds of turkey, cleaned
- 2 tablespoons of chopped mixed herbs
- ¼ teaspoon of ground black pepper, to taste
- 3 tablespoons of butter, unsalted, melted
- 2 cups of chicken broth

Preparation:
1. Grease the cooking surface of the griddle with cooking spray.
2. Turn on the 4 burners and turn their knobs to medium heat.
3. Let the Griddle preheat for 5 minutes.
4. Remove the giblets from the turkey, wash it inside and out, then wipe it dry with paper towels before placing it on a roasting pan and tucking the turkey wings with butcher's thread.
5. Meanwhile, make herb butter by placing melted butter in a suitable bowl, adding black pepper and mixed herbs, and whisking until frothy.
6. Using the handle of a wooden spoon, place some of the prepared herb butter beneath the skin of the turkey and massage the skin to evenly spread the butter.
7. Then massage melted butter all over the outside of the turkey, season with pork and poultry rub, and pour the liquid into the roasting pan.
8. When the griddle is hot, remove the cover, lay the roasting pan with the turkey on the griddle grate, close the griddle, and smoke for 3 hours and 30 minutes, or until the internal temperature reaches 165 degrees F and the top is golden brown.
9. When the turkey is done, take it to a cutting board and let it rest for 30 minutes before carving it into slices and serving it.
10. Serve.

Per Serving: Calories: 376; Fat: 13g; Sodium: 421mg; Carbs: 16g; Fiber 4.1g; Sugar: 3.2g; Protein: 27g

Sriracha Chicken Thighs

Prep time: 05 minutes | Cook time: 20 minutes | Serves: 6

Ingredients:
- 3-pound boneless chicken thighs
- 3-tablespoon butter, unsalted
- 1-tablespoon fresh ginger, minced
- 3 Garlic cloves, minced
- ¼-teaspoon smoked paprika
- ¼-teaspoon chili powder
- ¼-tablespoon honey
- 1-tablespoon Sriracha
- 1-tablespoon lime juice

Preparation:
1. In a suitable saucepan over medium-low heat, melt butter; add ginger and garlic.
2. Stir and cook for about 2 minutes.
3. Mix the ground cloves, smoked paprika, honey, Sriracha, and lime juice in a suitable mixing bowl.
4. Stir to mix, then reduce to a low heat and cook for almost 5 minutes.
5. Season both sides of the chicken with salt and black pepper.
6. Brush the glaze on both sides of the chicken during the last 5 minutes of griddling.
7. Preheat the Griddle by turning all its knob to medium-heat setting.
8. Grease the griddle top with cooking spray.
9. Cook the chicken for 5 minutes per side on the hot griddle.
10. Serve.

Per Serving: Calories: 546; Fat: 40 g; Sodium: 231 mg; Carbs: 3.1g; Fiber: 0.2g; Sugar: 0.9g; Protein: 40.4g

Zucchini Turkey Patties

Prep time: 20 minutes | Cook time: 10 minutes | Serves: 5

Ingredients:
- 1-pound ground turkey
- ¼ cup breadcrumbs
- 6 oz. zucchini, grated and squeezed out all liquid
- 1-tablespoon onion, grated
- 1 garlic clove, grated
- Pepper
- Salt

Preparation:
1. In a suitable mixing bowl, mix well the ground turkey and the remaining ingredients.
2. Preheat the Griddle by turning all its knob to medium-heat setting.
3. Grease the griddle top with cooking spray.
4. Shape the mixture into patties and set them on the hot griddle top.
5. Cook the patties for 5 minutes per side until golden brown.
6. Serve and enjoy.

Per Serving: Calories: 206; Fat: 10.3 g; Sodium: 171mg; Carbs: 5.4g; Fiber: 0.7g; Sugar: 1g; Protein: 26g

Avocados Chicken Fajitas with Corn Tortillas

Prep time: 20 minutes | Cook time: 15 minutes | Serves: 4

Ingredients:
- 4 boneless chicken breasts, sliced
- 1 small red onion, sliced
- 2 red bell peppers, sliced
- ½ cup spicy ranch salad dressing, divided
- ½-teaspoon dried oregano
- 8 corn tortillas
- 2 cups torn butter lettuce
- 4 avocados, peeled and chopped

Preparation:
1. In a suitable mixing dish, mix well the onion, chicken, and pepper.
2. Drizzle 1 tbsp. salad dressing and oregano on top then mix well.
3. Preheat the Griddle by turning all its knob to medium-heat setting.
4. Grease the griddle top with cooking spray.
5. Add the chicken to the hot griddle top and cook for 14 minutes, until tender.
6. Toss the chicken and veggies with the remaining salad dressing in a bowl.
7. Divide the chicken mixture, lettuce, and avocados in the tortillas and serve warm.

Per Serving: Calories: 669; Fat: 43.4 g; Sodium: 156 mg; Carbs: 36.2g; Fiber: 14.9g; Sugar: 4.3g; Protein: 38.4g

Garlic Chicken Breast with Kale Caesar Salad

Prep time: 10 minutes | **Cook time:** 15 minutes | **Serves:** 1

Ingredients:
- 1-pound Chicken breast
- 1-teaspoon garlic powder
- ½-teaspoon black pepper
- ½-teaspoon sea salt
- 2 Kale leaves, chopped
- Shaved parmesan, for serving

For the dressing:
- 1-tablespoon mayonnaise
- ½-tablespoon Dijon mustard
- ½-teaspoon garlic powder
- ½-teaspoon Worcestershire sauce
- ¼ lemon, juice of (or ½ a small lime)
- ¼-teaspoon anchovy paste
- Pinch sea salt
- Pinch black pepper

Preparation:
1. In a suitable mixing bowl, mix well black pepper, garlic powder, and sea salt.
2. Season and rub the chicken well with the spice mixture.
3. Preheat the Griddle by turning all its knob to medium-heat setting.
4. Grease the griddle top with cooking oil.
5. Sear the chicken on the hot griddle top for 7 minutes per side.
6. Mix well all of the dressing ingredients in a suitable mixing bowl.
7. Place the kale on a plate and drizzle with the dressing, tossing to mix.
8. Arrange the chicken on top of the salad in a diagonal cut.
9. Serve with shaved parmesan on top.

Per Serving: Calories: 667; Fat: 18.4 g; Sodium: 1526 mg; Carbs: 22.5g; Fiber: 3.2g; Sugar: 2.9g; Protein: 101.2g

Tasty Oregano Chicken Bites

Prep time: 20 minutes | **Cook time:** 10 minutes | **Serves:** 2

Ingredients:
- 1-pound chicken breasts, skinless, boneless, and cut into cubes
- 2-tablespoon fresh lemon juice
- 1-tablespoon fresh oregano, chopped
- 2-tablespoon olive oil
- ⅛-teaspoon cayenne pepper

Preparation:
1. Place the chicken breasts in a suitable mixing bowl.
2. Mix well the remaining ingredients and pour over the chicken.
3. Refrigerate the chicken for 1 hour before cooking.
4. Thread the marinated chicken cubes.
5. Preheat the Griddle by turning all its knob to medium-heat setting.
6. Grease the griddle top with cooking spray.
7. Cook the skewers on the hot griddle top until the chicken is cooked.
8. Serve and enjoy.

Per Serving: Calories: 562; Fat: 31.2 g; Sodium: 198 mg; Carbs: 1.9g; Fiber: 1.1g; Sugar: 0.9g; Protein: 66g

Chicken Drumsticks with Sauce

Prep time: 20 minutes | **Cook time:** 40 minutes | **Serves:** 6

Ingredients:
- ¼ cup minced garlic
- ¼ cup tomato paste
- ¾ cup minced onion
- ¾ cup sugar
- 1 cup soy sauce
- 1 cup water
- 1 cup white vinegar
- 6 chicken drumsticks
- Salt and black pepper to taste

Preparation:
1. In a Ziploc bag, mix well all of the ingredients.
2. Marinate for at least 2 hours in the refrigerator.
3. Preheat the Griddle by turning all its knob to medium-heat setting.
4. Grease the griddle top with cooking spray.
5. Sear the chicken for 40 minutes on the hot griddle top, flip every 10 minutes.
6. In the meantime, boil the leftover marinade in a suitable skillet over medium heat until it thickens.
7. Brush the glaze over the chicken and serve.

Per Serving: Calories: 226; Fat: 2.8 g; Sodium: 2448 mg; Carbs: 33.9g; Fiber: 1.2g; Sugar: 27.9g; Protein: 16.2g

Jalapeno Chicken Thighs

Prep time: 20 minutes | **Cook time:** 20 minutes | **Serves:** 4

Ingredients:
- 1-½-pound chicken thighs and boneless.
- 1-teaspoon garlic, crushed.
- 1 jalapeno pepper, minced.
- 3-tablespoon fresh lime juice
- 3-tablespoon honey
- 3-tablespoon olive oil
- 1-teaspoon kosher salt

Preparation:
1. Mix well the chicken and the rest of the ingredients in a zip-lock bag.
2. Refrigerate overnight after sealing the bag.
3. Preheat the Griddle by turning all its knob to medium-heat setting.
4. Grease the griddle top with cooking spray.
5. Cook the marinated chicken on the hot griddle top for 8-10 minutes per side.
6. Serve.

Per Serving: Calories: 291; Fat: 15.2 g; Sodium: 544 mg; Carbs: 13g; Fiber: 0.9g; Sugar: 10.9g; Protein: 26.5g

Coconut Chicken with Almond Butter Sauce

Prep time: 20 minutes | **Cook time:** 15 minutes | **Serves:** 4

Ingredients:
- 1-pound boneless chicken thighs, cut into thin strips
- Olive oil, for brushing

For the marinade:
- ½ cup canned light coconut milk
- ½ lime, juiced
- 1-tablespoon honey
- 2-teaspoon soy sauce
- 1 ½-teaspoon fish sauce
- ½-teaspoon red chili flakes
- 2-teaspoon ginger, grated
- 1 clove of garlic, grated
- ½-teaspoon curry powder
- ¼-teaspoon ground coriander

For the almond butter sauce:
- ¼ cup almond butter
- ¼ cup water
- 2-tablespoon canned, light coconut milk
- 1-tablespoon honey
- ½ lime, juiced
- 1-teaspoon fish sauce
- 1-teaspoon freshly grated ginger
- ½-teaspoon low Sodium: soy sauce
- ½-teaspoon Sriracha

Preparation:
1. In a medium mixing bowl, whisk together all of the marinade ingredients.
2. Toss the chicken in the mixing bowl to coat it.
3. Refrigerate for 2 hours or overnight, covered.
4. Preheat the Griddle by turning all its knob to medium-heat setting.
5. Grease the griddle top with cooking spray.
6. Using metal skewers, thread the chicken strips.
7. Cook the chicken skewers for 4 minutes per side on the prepared griddle
8. In a suitable saucepan, mix well all of the ingredients for the almond butter sauce.
9. Bring the sauce to a boil over medium heat, then reduce to low heat and cook for 2 minutes.
10. Enjoy the warm chicken satay with the almond butter sauce.

Per Serving: Calories: 236; Fat: 13.2 g; Sodium: 502 mg; Carbs: 6.3g; Fiber: 0.9g; Sugar: 4.4g; Protein: 23.2g

Marinated Chicken with Veggie and Brown Rice Bowls

Prep time: 8 hours 10 minutes | **Cook time:** 20 minutes | **Serves:** 4

Ingredients:
- 2 Bag brown rice

For the skewers:
- 2-pound Boneless skinless chicken breasts, cubed
- 1 red onion, quartered
- 1 red pepper, cut into cube slices
- 1 green pepper, cut into cube slices
- ½ pineapple, cut into cubes

For the marinade:
- ¼ cup light soy sauce
- ¼ cup sesame oil
- 1-tablespoon ginger, fresh grated
- 1 garlic clove, crushed
- ½ lime, juiced

Preparation:
1. In a suitable mixing bowl, mix well the marinade ingredients.
2. Toss the chicken with the marinade in a resealable plastic bag, seal, and toss to coat well.
3. Preheat the Griddle by turning all its knob to medium-heat setting.
4. Grease the griddle top with cooking spray.
5. Thread the chicken and cubed vegetables alternately onto 8 metal skewers.
6. Sear the prepared skewers on hot griddle top for 8 minutes per side.
7. Serve warm.

Per Serving: Calories: 941; Fat: 33.3 g; Sodium: 496 mg; Carbs: 83.4g; Fiber: 5.4g; Sugar: 6.2g; Protein: 74.1g

Chicken Breasts Fried Rice with Veggies

Prep time: 10 minutes | Cook time: 20 minutes | Serves: 4

Ingredients:
- 2 boneless chicken breasts, cut into small pieces
- 4 Cups long grain rice, cooked and allowed to air dry
- ⅓ cup soy sauce
- 1 Yellow onion, chopped
- 3 Cloves garlic, chopped
- ½ Cups petite peas
- 2 Carrots sliced into thin rounds
- ½ cup corn kernels
- ¼ cup vegetable oil
- ½-tablespoon butter

Preparation:
1. Preheat the Griddle by turning all its knob to medium-heat setting.
2. Grease the griddle top with cooking oil.
3. Add the carrot, onion, peas, and corn to the griddle top.
4. Cook for a few minutes, until the edges are browned.
5. Toss in the chicken and cook until it is lightly browned.
6. Mix well the rice, soy sauce, garlic, and butter in a suitable mixing bowl.
7. Stir in rice and cook until vegetables have softened.
8. Serve!

Per Serving: Calories: 1009; Fat: 21.8 g; Sodium: 1321 mg; Carbs: 161.9g; Fiber: 5.3g; Sugar: 4.9g; Protein: 36.9g

Bacon Chicken Breast with Chipotle

Prep time: 20 minutes | Cook time: 10 minutes | Serves: 1

Ingredients:
- 2 slices sourdough bread
- ¼ cup caesar salad dressing
- 1 cooked chicken breast, diced
- ½ cup shredded cheddar cheese
- 1-tablespoon bacon bits
- 1-½-teaspoon chipotle chili powder, or to taste
- 2-tablespoon softened butter

Preparation:
1. On one side of two pieces of bread, spread the salad dressing.
2. Then add a layer of chicken, bacon, cheese, and chipotle chili powder on top.
3. Place the last slice of bread on top, dressing side down.
4. Brush the top and bottom of the sandwich with butter.
5. Preheat the Griddle by turning all its knob to medium-heat setting.
6. Sear the sandwiches on the hot griddle top for 5 minutes per side.
7. Serve warm.

Per Serving: Calories: 880; Fat: 50.8 g; Sodium: 1707 mg; Carbs: 52.9g; Fiber: 2.4g; Sugar: 5.9g; Protein: 53.2g

Spicy Chicken with Blue cheese

Prep time: 20 minutes | Cook time: 25 minutes | Serves: 4

Ingredients:
- 2 cups shredded cooked chicken
- 1 large sweet onion, sliced
- 8 slices seedless rye
- 8 slices Swiss cheese
- ¼ cup blue cheese dressing
- 1 cup mayonnaise
- 1 cup buffalo hot sauce
- 2-tablespoon Butter
- Blue cheese dressing

Preparation:
1. In a suitable skillet over medium heat, melt the butter.
2. Stir in onion and saute for almost 20 minutes.
3. Toss the chicken with the buffalo sauce and mayonnaise in a suitable mixing bowl.
4. On a piece of bread, set a slice of cheese, onions, the chicken, and another slice of cheese, followed by another piece of bread.
5. Repeat with the rest of the sandwiches in the same manner.
6. Brush the top and bottom of the sandwich with butter.
7. Preheat the Griddle by turning all its knob to medium-heat setting.
8. Grease the griddle top with cooking spray.
9. Cook the sandwiches on the hot griddle top for 4 minutes per side.
10. Serve with blue cheese dressing.

Per Serving: Calories: 806; Fat: 45.8 g; Sodium: 1846 mg; Carbs: 62.2g; Fiber: 2.9g; Sugar: 18.2g; Protein: 35.7g

Garlic Turkey Patties

Prep time: 20 minutes | Cook time: 15 minutes | Serves: 2

Ingredients:
- 8 oz. ground turkey breast
- 2-teaspoon fresh oregano, chopped
- 2 garlic cloves, minced
- ½-teaspoon red pepper, crushed
- ¼-teaspoon salt

Preparation:
1. Preheat the Griddle by turning all its knob to medium-heat setting.
2. Grease the griddle top with cooking spray.
3. In a suitable mixing bowl, mix well the ground turkey and the additional ingredients.
4. Form the mixture into two patties and set them on the hot griddle top, cooking for 5 minutes per side.
5. Serve and enjoy.

Per Serving: Calories: 233; Fat: 8.7 g; Sodium: 364 mg; Carbs: 4.9g; Fiber: 1.1g; Sugar: 1.9g; Protein: 33.2g

Stir Fry Chicken Breast and Broccoli

Prep time: 20 minutes | Cook time: 15 minutes | Serves: 4

Ingredients:
- 1-pound chicken breast, skinless, boneless, and cut into chunks
- 1-tablespoon soy sauce
- 1-tablespoon ginger, minced
- ½-teaspoon garlic powder
- 1-tablespoon olive oil
- ½ onion, sliced
- 2 cups broccoli florets
- 2-teaspoon hot sauce
- 2-teaspoon vinegar
- 1-teaspoon sesame oil
- Black pepper, to taste
- Salt, to taste

Preparation:
1. Toss all of the ingredients together in a large mixing dish.
2. Preheat the Griddle by turning all its knob to medium-heat setting.
3. Grease the griddle top with cooking spray.
4. Place the chicken and broccoli mixture on the hot griddle top.
5. Cook until the broccoli is soft and the chicken is done.
6. Serve and enjoy.

Per Serving: Calories: 199; Fat: 7.8 g; Sodium: 402 mg; Carbs: 5.9g; Fiber: 1.7g; Sugar: 1.9g; Protein: 25.9g

Chicken Zucchini Pepper Stir Fry

Prep time: 20 minutes | Cook time: 10 minutes | Serves: 2

Ingredients:
- 6 oz. chicken breast, boneless and cut into cubes
- ¼ onion, sliced
- ½ bell pepper, chopped
- ½ zucchini, chopped
- 1-tablespoon olive oil
- ¼-teaspoon dried thyme
- ½-teaspoon garlic powder
- 1-teaspoon dried oregano

Preparation:
1. Toss all of the ingredients together in a large mixing dish.
2. Preheat the Griddle by turning all its knob to medium-heat setting.
3. Grease the griddle top with cooking spray.
4. Place the chicken mixture on the hot griddle top and sear for 5 minutes per side.
5. Serve and enjoy.

Per Serving: Calories: 186; Fat: 9.8 g; Sodium: 50mg; Carbs: 6.2g; Fiber: 1.7g; Sugar: 3.1g; Protein: 19.2g

Rosemary Honey Chicken Tenders

Prep time: 10 minutes | Cook time: 10 minutes | Serves: 4

Ingredients:
- 1 ½-pound chicken tenders
- 1-teaspoon dried oregano
- 1-teaspoon dried rosemary
- 2-tablespoon Herb de province
- 2-tablespoon lemon juice
- 2-tablespoon olive oil
- 4-tablespoon honey
- 1 shallot, minced
- ⅓ cup Dijon mustard
- Pepper
- Salt

Preparation:
1. In a zip-lock bag, mix well the chicken and the remaining ingredients.
2. Refrigerate overnight after sealing the bag and shaking it well.
3. Preheat the Griddle by turning all its knob to medium-heat setting.
4. Grease the griddle top with cooking spray.
5. Cook the marinated chicken tenders for 5 minutes per side on the hot griddle top.
6. Serve and enjoy.

Per Serving: Calories: 467; Fat: 20.6 g; Sodium: 424 mg; Carbs: 19.4g; Fiber: 1.1g; Sugar: 17.6g; Protein: 50.4g

Flavorful Cornish Hen

Prep time: 15 minutes | Cook time: 60 minutes | Serves: 2

Ingredients:
- 1 Cornish hen
- 1 cup of cold water
- 16 oz of apple juice
- ⅛ cup of brown sugar
- 1 cinnamon stick
- 1 cup of hot water
- ¼ cup of kosher salt

Preparation:
1. Grease the cooking surface of the griddle with cooking spray.
2. Turn on the 4 burners and turn their knobs to medium-high heat.
3. Let the Griddle preheat for 5 minutes.
4. Mix cinnamon, hot water, cold water, apple juice, brown sugar, and salt into the suitable pot.
5. Add hen in the brine and place in the refrigerator for 4 hours.
6. Remove hens from brine and place on preheated griddle top and smoke for 60 minutes or until internal temperature reaches 160 degrees°F.
7. Slice and serve.
8. Serve.

Per Serving: Calories: 397; Fat: 21g; Sodium: 711mg; Carbs: 8g; Fiber 3.1g; Sugar: 4g; Protein: 22g

Turkey Burger Patties

Prep time: 10 minutes | Cook time: 10 minutes | Serves: 4

Ingredients:
- 1-pound ground turkey
- 1-tablespoon garlic powder
- 1 ½-tablespoon dried parsley
- 3 oz. onion, diced
- Pepper
- Salt

Preparation:
1. In a suitable mixing bowl, mix well all of the ingredients and stir until well blended.
2. Preheat the Griddle by turning all its knob to medium-heat setting.
3. Grease the griddle top with cooking spray.
4. Form the mixture into patties and cook for 5 minutes per side on the hot griddle top.
5. Serve and enjoy.

Per Serving: Calories: 237; Fat: 12.8 g; Sodium: 162 mg; Carbs: 3.9g; Fiber: 0.9g; Sugar: 1.9g; Protein: 31.7g

Dijon Mustard Chicken Wings

Prep time: 20 minutes | Cook time: 20 minutes | Serves: 6

Ingredients:
- 3-pound chicken wings
- 1-½-teaspoon garlic, minced
- 1-tablespoon fresh thyme leaves, chopped
- 1-tablespoon fresh parsley, chopped
- 2-teaspoon lemon zest, grated
- 3-tablespoon soy sauce
- 1-tablespoon dijon mustard
- 3-tablespoon brown sugar
- ½ cup olive oil
- ¾-teaspoon black pepper
- 1-teaspoon salt

Preparation:
1. Place the chicken wings in a zip-lock bag.
2. Mix well the other ingredients in a medium bowl and pour over the chicken wings.
3. Refrigerate for 8 hours after sealing the Ziplock bag.
4. Preheat the Griddle by turning all its knob to medium-heat setting.
5. Grease the griddle top with cooking spray.
6. Pour the egg mixture onto the hot griddle top
7. Cook the chicken wings for 10 minutes per side on the hot griddle top.
8. Serve.

Per Serving: Calories: 722; Fat: 40.8 g; Sodium: 1229 mg; Carbs: 7.2g; Fiber: 0.9g; Sugar: 5.9g; Protein: 79.2g

Roasted BBQ Hen

Prep time: 15 minutes | Cook time: 1 hr. 30 minutes | Serves: 8

Ingredients:
- 1 Cornish hen
- 2 tablespoons of BBQ rub

Preparation:
1. Grease the cooking surface of the griddle with cooking spray.
2. Turn on the 4 burners and turn their knobs to medium-high heat.
3. Let the Griddle preheat for 5 minutes.
4. Coat hens with bbq rub and place on preheated griddle top.
5. And smoke for 1 ½ hours or until the internal temperature of hens reach 165°F.
6. Serve.

Per Serving: Calories: 395; Fat: 15g; Sodium: 521mg; Carbs: 14g; Fiber 5.1g; Sugar: 3g; Protein: 27g

Tasty Balsamic Chicken

Prep time: 20 minutes | Cook time: 6 minutes | Serves: 4

Ingredients:
- ½ cup balsamic vinegar
- 2-tablespoon olive oil
- 2 rosemary sprigs, chopped
- 2 pounds boneless chicken breasts, pounded to ½-inch thickness

Preparation:
1. In a suitable baking dish, mix well the balsamic vinegar, olive oil, and rosemary.
2. Add chicken breasts and rub with the sauce.
3. Refrigerate for at least 30 minutes after covering with plastic wrap.
4. Preheat the Griddle by turning all its knob to medium-heat setting.
5. Grease the griddle top with cooking spray.
6. Place the chicken breasts on the hot griddle top and cook for 6 minutes per side.
7. Serve warm.

Per Serving: Calories: 499; Fat: 23.8 g; Sodium: 197 mg; Carbs: 0.9g; Fiber: 0.3g; Sugar: 0.1g; Protein: 65.6g

Sizzling Chicken Breasts with Tortillas

Prep time: 05 minutes | Cook time: 25 minutes | Serves: 4-6

Ingredients:
- 2-pound Boneless chicken breast halves, sliced
- ¼ cup Yellow onion, sliced
- 1 Large green bell pepper, sliced
- 1 large red bell pepper, sliced
- 1-teaspoon ground cumin
- 1-teaspoon garlic powder
- 1-teaspoon onion powder
- 1-tablespoon lime juice
- 1-tablespoon olive oil
- ½-teaspoon black pepper
- 1-teaspoon salt
- 1-tablespoon vegetable oil
- 10 flour tortillas

Preparation:
1. Toss chicken with garlic, cumin, salt, lime juice, onion, pepper, and olive oil in a zip-lock bag then marinated for 39 minutes.
2. Preheat the Griddle by turning all its knob to medium-heat setting.
3. Grease the griddle top with cooking spray.
4. Cook until the onion and bell pepper on the griddle top until softened.
5. Add the marinated chicken on the other side of the griddle until cook until lightly browned.
6. Mix with the onion and pepper and cook until the internal temperature of the chicken reaches 165°F.
7. Serve on warm tortillas.

Per Serving: Calories: 370; Fat: 10.5 g; Sodium: 503 mg; Carbs: 21.4g; Fiber: 3.1g; Sugar: 1.9g; Protein: 46.6g

Honey Cornish Hen

Prep time: 15 minutes | Cook time: 60 minutes | Serves: 2

Ingredients:
- 1 Cornish hen
- 2 garlic cloves, minced
- ⅛ cup of honey
- ¼ cup of soy sauce
- ¾ cup of warm water
- 1 tablespoon of cornstarch
- ¼ cup of brown sugar

Preparation:
1. Mix together soy sauce, warm water, brown sugar, garlic, cornstarch, and honey.
2. Place Cornish hen in baking dish and season by adding pepper and salt.
3. Pour marinade over hen and place in the refrigerator for 10 hours.
4. Grease the cooking surface of the griddle with cooking spray.
5. Turn on the 4 burners and turn their knobs to medium-high heat.
6. Let the Griddle preheat for 5 minutes.
7. Place marinated hen on preheated griddle top. Cover and smoke for 60 minutes or until internal temperature reaches 165°F.
8. Serve.

Per Serving: Calories: 338; Fat: 12g; Sodium: 521mg; Carbs: 14g; Fiber 5.1g; Sugar: 3g; Protein: 27g

Spicy Chicken Breasts

Prep time: 20 minutes | Cook time: 15 minutes | Serves: 4

Ingredients:
- 4 chicken breasts and boneless.
- 1-tablespoon Red pepper flakes
- 1-tablespoon Chili powder
- 6-tablespoon Brown sugar
- 6-tablespoon BBQ sauce
- 1 cup Pineapple juice

Preparation:
1. Place the chicken breasts in a zip-lock bag.
2. Add pineapple juice, BBQ sauce, chili powder, brown sugar, and red pepper flakes.
3. Seal, shake well and place the Ziploc bag in the refrigerator overnight.
4. Preheat the Griddle by turning all its knob to medium-heat setting.
5. Grease the griddle top with cooking spray.
6. Cook the marinated chicken breasts for 12-15 minutes.
7. Serve.

Per Serving: Calories: 407; Fat: 11.5 g; Sodium: 412 mg; Carbs: 31.9g; Fiber: 1.3g; Sugar: 25.9g; Protein: 42.2g

Curried Chicken Kebabs

Prep time: 20 minutes | Cook time: 15 minutes | Serves: 4

Ingredients:
- 1 ½-pound chicken breasts, boneless and cut into 1-inch pieces
- ½ cup soy sauce
- 1-tablespoon olive oil
- 1-tablespoon curry powder
- 1-tablespoon brown sugar
- 2-tablespoon peanut butter

Preparation:
1. Place the chicken in a big zip-lock bag and seal it.
2. Mix well olive oil, soy sauce, brown sugar, curry powder, and peanut butter in a suitable mixing dish and pour over chicken.
3. Seal the bag and shake it well then refrigerate overnight.
4. Thread marinated chicken onto the skewers.
5. Preheat the Griddle by turning all its knob to medium-heat setting.
6. Grease the griddle top with cooking spray.
7. Cook the prepared for 12-15 minutes on the hot griddle top, flipping every 5 minutes.
8. Serve and enjoy.

Per Serving: Calories: 346; Fat: 16.8 g; Sodium: 1585 mg; Carbs: 5.7g; Fiber: 1g; Sugar: 2.9g; Protein: 42.2g

Mayo Turkey Sandwich

Prep time: 10 minutes | Cook time: 5 minutes | Serves: 2

Ingredients:
- 2 bread slices
- 3 ounces (85 g) turkey breast, cooked and shredded
- 1 tablespoon mayonnaise
- 1 cheese slice

Preparation:
1. On one side of each slice of bread, apply mayonnaise.
2. Place turkey and cheese on one of the bread slices.
3. Top with the last slice of bread.
4. Heat the griddle to a high temperature.
5. Spray the top of the griddle with cooking spray.
6. Cook the sandwich for 5 minutes on a heated griddle top, or until golden brown on both sides.
7. Serve and enjoy.

Per Serving: Calories: 153; Fat: 8.1g; Sodium: 632mg; Carbs: 8.3g; Fiber 0.4g; Sugar: 2.8g; Protein: 11.8g

Itanlian Seasoning Chicken Breasts

Prep time:60 minutes | Cook time: 20 minutes | Serves: 2

Ingredients:
- 2 chicken breasts and boneless
- 2-tablespoon olive oil
- 1-teaspoon Italian seasoning
- 1 ½ cup grape tomatoes, cut in half
- ½ cup olives
- ¼-teaspoon black pepper
- ¼-teaspoon salt

Preparation:
1. Season the chicken with black pepper, salt, and Italian seasoning.
2. Preheat the Griddle by turning all its knob to medium-heat setting.
3. Grease the griddle top with cooking spray.
4. Season the chicken and place it on the hot griddle top.
5. Cook for almost 6 minutes per side. Place the chicken on a serving plate.
6. Cook for 4 minutes on the hot griddle top with the tomatoes and olives.
7. Toss the chicken with the olive and tomato mixture and serve.

Per Serving: Calories: 457; Fat: 28.8 g; Sodium: 712 mg; Carbs: 7.8g; Fiber: 2.9g; Sugar: 3.9g; Protein: 42g

Pepper Chicken Breast Fajita

Prep time: 20 minutes | Cook time: 15 minutes | Serves: 4

Ingredients:
- 1-pound chicken breast, boneless and sliced
- 2-teaspoon olive oil
- 1 onion, sliced
- 2 bell peppers, sliced
- ⅛-teaspoon cayenne
- 1-teaspoon cumin
- 2-teaspoon chili powder
- Pepper
- Salt

Preparation:
1. In a suitable mixing dish, mix well the chicken, onion, and sliced bell peppers.
2. Toss in the cayenne, oil, chili powder, cumin, pepper, and salt.
3. Preheat the Griddle by turning all its knob to medium-heat setting.
4. Grease the griddle top with cooking spray.
5. Pour the egg mixture onto the hot griddle top
6. Transfer the chicken mixture to the hot griddle and cook until chicken is done.
7. Serve and enjoy.

Per Serving: Calories: 186; Fat: 5.8 g; Sodium: 113 mg; Carbs: 8.1g; Fiber: 1.9g; Sugar: 4.3g; Protein: 25.2g

Cheddar Chicken Breasts

Prep time: 20 minutes | Cook time: 25 minutes | Serves: 4

Ingredients:
- 1-pound boneless skinless chicken breasts
- 4 oz. taco seasoning
- 1-teaspoon cayenne pepper
- Kosher salt, to taste
- 2 cloves minced garlic
- 1 chopped small red onion
- 2 chopped red bell peppers
- 15-oz. Can black beans (drained)
- 2 cups shredded cheddar
- ½ cup chopped fresh cilantro

Preparation:
1. Season the chicken with cayenne pepper, salt, and taco seasoning.
2. Preheat the Griddle by turning all its knob to medium-heat setting.
3. Grease the griddle top with cooking spray.
4. Cook it for 6 minutes per side on the hot griddle top.
5. Add the remaining ingredients and cook for another 7 minutes.
6. Garnish and serve.

Per Serving: Calories: 506; Fat: 16.8 g; Sodium: 1011 mg; Carbs: 31.3g; Fiber: 6.3g; Sugar: 4.9g; Protein: 56.7g

Lemon Chicken with Fruit Salsa

Prep time: 20 minutes | Cook time: 20 minutes | Serves: 4

Ingredients:
4 boneless chicken breasts

For the marinade:
- ½ cup fresh lemon juice
- ½ cup soy sauce
- 1-tablespoon fresh ginger, minced
- 1-tablespoon lemon-pepper seasoning
- 2 garlic cloves, minced

For the salsa:
- 1 ½ cups pineapple, chopped
- ¾ cup kiwi fruit, chopped
- ½ cup mango, chopped
- ½ cup red onion, chopped
- 2-tablespoon fresh cilantro, chopped
- 1 small jalapeño pepper, seeded and chopped
- 1 ½-teaspoon ground cumin
- ¼-teaspoon sea salt
- ⅛-teaspoon black pepper
- ½-teaspoon olive oil, more for brushing the griddle

Preparation:
1. In a big sealable plastic bag, mix well the marinade ingredients.
2. Place the chicken in the bag, seal it, and shake it to coat it.
3. Refrigerate for 1 hour to marinate.
4. In a suitable mixing bowl, mix well all of the salsa ingredients.
5. Preheat the Griddle by turning all its knob to medium-heat setting.
6. Grease the griddle top with cooking spray.
7. Cook the marinated chicken for 7 minutes per side.
8. Serve the salsa-topped chicken with your favorite side dishes.

Per Serving: Calories: 391; Fat: 12.3 g; Sodium: 2031 mg; Carbs: 23.9g; Fiber: 3.7g; Sugar: 13.9g; Protein: 46.2g

Spinach and Garlic Turkey Patties

Prep time: 10 minutes | **Cook time:** 10 minutes | **Serves:** 12

Ingredients:
- 3-pound ground turkey
- 3-tablespoon garlic, minced
- 1 onion, chopped
- 5 cups spinach, sautéed
- 3-tablespoon mustard
- Pepper
- Salt

Preparation:
1. Preheat the Griddle by turning all its knob to medium-heat setting.
2. Grease the griddle top with cooking spray.
3. In a suitable mixing bowl, mix well all of the ingredients and stir until well blended.
4. Form the mixture into patties and fry them for 5 minutes per side on the hot griddle top.
5. Serve and enjoy.

Per Serving: Calories: 244; Fat: 13.3 g; Sodium: 144 mg; Carbs: 3g; Fiber: 0.9g; Sugar: 0.7g; Protein: 32.2g

Mayo Turkey Mayo Green Apple

Prep time: 15 minutes | **Cook time:** 4 hrs. 5 minutes | **Serves:** 10

Ingredients:
- 1 Whole turkey (4-lbs., 1.8-kg.)

For the rub
- ½ cup of mayonnaise
- Salt, to taste
- ¾ teaspoon of brown sugar
- ¼ cup of ground mustard
- 2 tablespoons of black pepper, to taste
- 1 teaspoon of onion powder
- 1 ½ tablespoons of ground cumin
- 1 ½ tablespoons of chili powder
- 2 tablespoons of cayenne pepper, to taste
- ½ tablespoon of old bay seasoning
- ½ teaspoon of the filling
- 3 cups of sliced green apples

Preparation:
1. Place salt, brown sugar, brown mustard, black pepper, onion powder, ground cumin, chili powder, cayenne pepper, and old bay seasoning in a suitable bowl, then mix well. Set aside.
2. Next, fill the turkey cavity with sliced green apples, then baste mayonnaise over the turkey skin.
3. Sprinkle the dry spice mixture over the turkey, then wrap with aluminum foil.
4. Marinate the turkey for at least 4 hours or overnight and store it in the fridge to keep it fresh.
5. On the next day, remove the turkey from the fridge and thaw at room temperature.
6. Grease the cooking surface of the griddle with cooking spray.
7. Turn on the 4 burners and turn their knobs to medium-low heat.
8. Let the Griddle preheat for 5 minutes.
9. Unwrap the turkey and place it in the griddle.
10. Smoke the turkey for 4 hours or until the internal temperature has reached 170°F.
11. Remove the smoked turkey from the griddle and serve.
12. Serve.

Per Serving: Calories: 401; Fat: 13g; Sodium: 161mg; Carbs: 10g; Fiber 3.1g; Sugar: 2g; Protein: 25g

Typical BBQ Chicken

Prep time: 15 minutes | **Cook time:** 1 hr. 35 minutes | **Serves:** 6

Ingredients:
- 4 pounds chicken, cut into pieces
- Salt, to taste
- Olive oil
- 1 cup of barbecue sauce

Preparation:
1. Grease the cooking surface of the griddle with cooking spray.
2. Turn on the 4 burners and turn their knobs to medium heat.
3. Let the Griddle preheat for 5 minutes.
4. Rub the chicken with olive oil and salt.
5. Sear chicken skin side down on the griddle for 5-10 minutes.
6. Turn the griddle down to medium-low heat, tent with foil and smoke for 30 minutes.
7. Turn chicken and baste with barbecue sauce.
8. Cover the chicken again and allow it to smoke for another 20 minutes.
9. Baste, cover and then let it cook again for 30 minutes; repeat basting and turning during this time.
10. Baste with more barbecue sauce to serve!

Per Serving: Calories: 421; Fat: 11g; Sodium: 361mg; Carbs: 11g; Fiber 3.1g; Sugar: 2g; Protein: 26g

66 | Chapter 6 Poultry Recipes

Soy Chicken Thighs

Prep time: 10 minutes | **Cook time:** 20 minutes | **Serves:** 4-8

Ingredients:
- 8 boneless, skinless chicken thighs

For the glaze:
- 3 tablespoons dark brown sugar
- 2½ tablespoons soy sauce
- 1 tablespoon fresh garlic, minced
- 2 teaspoons sesame seeds
- 1 teaspoon fresh ginger, minced
- 1 teaspoon sambal oelek
- ⅓ cup scallions, thinly sliced
- non-stick cooking spray

Preparation:
1. In a large mixing basin, combine glaze ingredients; divide and reserving half for serving.
2. Toss the chicken in the bowl to evenly coat it.
3. Heat the griddle to medium-high temperature.
4. Spray with nonstick cooking spray.
5. Cook for 6 minutes on each side or until chicken is cooked through.
6. Arrange the chicken on plates and drizzle with the leftover glaze.

Per Serving: Calories: 309; Fat: 11.3g; Sodium: 1314mg; Carbs: 5.6g; Fiber 0.4g; Sugar: 3.8g; Protein: 43.8g

Chili Smoked Turkey Breast

Prep time: 15 minutes | **Cook time:** 4 hrs. 30 minutes | **Serves:** 8

Ingredients:
- 3-lbs. Turkey breast

For the rub
- ¾ teaspoon of salt
- ½ teaspoon black pepper

For the glaze
- 1 tablespoon of olive oil
- ¾ cup of ketchup
- 3 tablespoons of white vinegar
- 3 tablespoons of brown sugar
- 1 tablespoon of smoked paprika
- ¾ teaspoon of chili powder
- ¼ teaspoon of cayenne powder

Preparation:
1. Score the turkey breast at several places, then sprinkle Black pepper and salt over it.
2. Let the seasoned turkey breast rest for approximately 10 minutes.
3. Grease the cooking surface of the griddle with cooking spray.
4. Turn on the 4 burners and turn their knobs to medium heat.
5. Let the Griddle preheat for 5 minutes.
6. Place the seasoned turkey breast in the griddle and smoke for 2 hours.
7. In the meantime, combine olive oil, ketchup, white vinegar, brown sugar, smoked paprika, chili powder, garlic powder, and cayenne pepper in a saucepan.
8. Wait to simmer, then remove from heat.
9. After 2 hours of smoking, baste the sauce over the turkey breast and continue smoking for another 2 hours.
10. Once the internal temperature of the smoked turkey breast has reached 170°F, remove it from the griddle and wrap it with aluminum foil.
11. Let the smoked turkey breast rest for approximately 15 minutes to 30 minutes, then unwrap it.
12. Cut the smoked turkey breast into thick slices, then serve.

Per Serving: Calories: 317; Fat: 32g; Sodium: 311mg; Carbs: 12g; Fiber 3.1g; Sugar: 4g; Protein: 22g

Chicken Fried Rice and Corn

Prep time: 10 minutes | **Cook time:** 20 minutes | **Serves:** 4

Ingredients:
- 2 chicken breasts,
- 4 cups long grain rice, cooked and allowed to air dry
- ⅓ cup soy sauce
- 1 yellow onion, finely chopped
- 4 cloves garlic, finely chopped
- 1 cups petite peas
- 2 carrots sliced into thin rounds
- ½ cup corn kernels
- ¼ cup vegetable oil
- 2 tablespoons butter

Preparation:
1. Heat the griddle to a medium-high heat.
2. Using vegetable oil, coat the griddle.
3. Add the onion, carrot, peas, and corn when the oil is sizzling.
4. Cook until the vegetables are lightly browned, about a minute.
5. Cook until the chicken is lightly browned, stirring occasionally.
6. In a mixing bowl, combine the rice, soy sauce, garlic, and butter.
7. Continue tossing until the rice is done and the vegetables are slightly softened.
8. Serve immediately.

Per Serving: Calories: 1046; Fat: 26.3g; Sodium: 423mg; Carbs: 160g; Fiber 5.6g; Sugar: 3.8g; Protein: 37.8g

Savory-Sweet Turkey Legs with Mandrain Glaze

Prep time: 15 minutes | Cook time: 5 hrs. | Serves: 4

Ingredients:
- 1 gallon of hot water
- 1 cup of curing salt
- ¼ cup of brown sugar
- 1 teaspoon of black pepper, to taste
- 1 teaspoon of ground cloves
- 1 bay leaf
- 2 teaspoons of liquid smoke
- 4 turkey legs
- Mandarin glaze, for serving

Preparation:
1. In a huge container with a lid, stir together the water, curing salt, brown sugar, pepper, cloves, bay leaf, and liquid smoke until the salt and sugar are dissolved; let come to room temperature.
2. Submerge the turkey legs in the seasoned brine, cover, and refrigerate overnight.
3. When ready to smoke, remove the turkey legs from the brine and rinse them; discard the brine.
4. Grease the cooking surface of the griddle with cooking spray.
5. Turn on the 4 burners and turn their knobs to low heat.
6. Let the Griddle preheat for 5 minutes.
7. Arrange the turkey legs on the griddle, close the lid, and smoke for 4 to 5 hours, or until dark brown and a meat thermometer inserted in the thickest part of the meat reads 165°F.
8. Serve with mandarin glaze on the side or drizzled over the turkey legs.
9. Serve.

Per Serving: Calories: 449; Fat: 21g; Sodium: 421mg; Carbs: 16g; Fiber 2.1g; Sugar: 2.2g; Protein: 27g

Classic Thanksgiving Turkey

Prep time: 15 minutes | Cook time: 4 hrs | Serves: 12

Ingredients:
- 2 cups of butter
- 1 tablespoon of black pepper, to taste
- 2 teaspoons of kosher salt, to taste
- 2 tablespoons of chopped rosemary
- 2 tablespoons of chopped parsley
- 2 tablespoons of chopped sage
- 2 teaspoons of dried thyme
- 6 garlic cloves, minced
- 1 (18 pounds) turkey

Preparation:
1. In a suitable mixing bowl, combine the butter, sage, rosemary, 1 teaspoon of black pepper, 1 teaspoon of salt, thyme, parsley and garlic.
2. Use your fingers to loosen the skin from the turkey.
3. Generously, rub butter mixture under the turkey skin and all over the turkey as well.
4. Season turkey generously with herb mix.
5. Grease the cooking surface of the griddle with cooking spray.
6. Turn on the 4 burners and turn their knobs to low heat.
7. Let the Griddle preheat for 5 minutes.
8. Place the turkey on the griddle and cover and smoke for about 4 hours, or until the turkey thigh temperature reaches 160°F.
9. Take out the turkey meat from the griddle and let it rest for a few minutes. Cut into sizes and serve.
10. Serve.

Per Serving: Calories: 395; Fat: 15g; Sodium: 521mg; Carbs: 14g; Fiber 5.1g; Sugar: 3g; Protein: 27g

Smoked Marinated BonelessTurkey Breast

Prep time: 15 minutes | Cook time: 45 minutes | Serves: 6

Ingredients:
- 1 (5 pounds) boneless chicken breast
- 4 cups of water
- 2 tablespoons of kosher salt, to taste
- **For rub**
- ½ teaspoon of onion powder
- 1 teaspoon of paprika
- 1 teaspoon of salt
- 1 teaspoon of ground black pepper, to taste
- 1 teaspoon of Italian seasoning
- 2 tablespoons of honey
- 1 tablespoon of cider vinegar
- 1 tablespoon of brown sugar
- ½ teaspoon of garlic powder
- 1 teaspoon of oregano

Preparation:
1. In a huge container, combine the water, honey, cider vinegar, Italian seasoning and salt.
2. Add the chicken breast and toss to combine. Cover the bowl and place it in the refrigerator, and chill for 4 hours.
3. Rinse the chicken breast with water and pat dry with paper towels.
4. In another mixing bowl, combine the brown sugar, salt, paprika, onion powder, pepper, oregano and garlic.
5. Generously season those chicken breasts with the rub mix.
6. Grease the cooking surface of the griddle with cooking spray.
7. Turn on the 4 burners and turn their knobs to medium heat.
8. Let the Griddle preheat for 5 minutes.
9. Arrange the turkey breast on the griddle and then let it cook for 20 minutes per side.
10. Serve.

Per Serving: Calories: 397; Fat: 21g; Sodium: 711mg; Carbs: 8g; Fiber 3.1g; Sugar: 4g; Protein: 22g

Buttery Smoked Turkey

Prep time: 15 minutes | Cook time: 4 hrs | Serves: 6

Ingredients:
- 4 lbs. Whole turkey
- **For the brine**
- 2 cans of beer
- 1 tablespoon of salt, to taste
- 2 tablespoons of white sugar
- ¼ cup of soy sauce
- 1 quart of cold water
- **For the rub**
- 3 tablespoons of unsalted butter
- 1 teaspoon of smoked paprika
- 1 ½ teaspoons of garlic powder
- 1 teaspoon black pepper
- ¼ teaspoon of cayenne pepper

Preparation:
1. Pour beer into a container, then add salt, white sugar, and soy sauce, then stir well.
2. Put the turkey into the brine mixture, cold water over the turkey.
3. Make sure that the turkey is completely soaked.
4. Soak the turkey in the brine for at least 6 hours or overnight and store in the fridge to keep it fresh.
5. On the next day, remove the turkey from the fridge and take it out of the brine mixture.
6. Wash and rinse the turkey, then pat it dry. Rub it with the remaining ingredients.
7. Open the beer can, then push it into the turkey cavity.
8. Grease the cooking surface of the griddle with cooking spray.
9. Turn on the 4 burners and turn their knobs to medium heat.
10. Let the Griddle preheat for 5 minutes.
11. Place the seasoned turkey in the griddle and make a tripod using the beer can and the 2 turkey legs.
12. Smoke the turkey for 4 hours or until the internal temperature has reached 170°F.
14. Once it is done, remove the smoked turkey from the griddle and transfer it to a serving dish.
15. Serve.

Per Serving: Calories: 449; Fat: 21g; Sodium: 421mg; Carbs: 16g; Fiber 4.1g; Sugar: 3.2g; Protein: 27g

Smoked Turkey Tabasco in Sauce

Prep time: 15 minutes | Cook time: 4 hrs. 15 minutes | Serves: 8

Ingredients:
- 1 Whole turkey (4-lbs.)
- **For the rub**
- ¼ cup of brown sugar
- 2 teaspoons of smoked paprika
- 1 teaspoon of salt
- 1 ½ teaspoons of onion powder
- 2 teaspoons of oregano
- 2 teaspoons of garlic powder
- ½ teaspoon of dried thyme
- ½ teaspoon of white pepper
- ½ teaspoon of cayenne pepper, to taste
- **For the glaze**
- ½ cup of ketchup
- ½ cup of hot sauce
- 1 tablespoon of cider vinegar
- 2 teaspoons of tabasco
- ½ teaspoon of Cajun spices
- 3 tablespoons of unsalted butter

Preparation:
1. Rub the turkey with 2 tablespoons of brown sugar, smoked paprika, salt, onion powder, garlic powder, dried thyme, white pepper, and cayenne pepper. Let the turkey rest for an hour.
2. Grease the cooking surface of the griddle with cooking spray.
3. Turn on the 4 burners and turn their knobs to low heat.
4. Let the Griddle preheat for 5 minutes.
5. Place the seasoned turkey in the griddle and smoke for 4 hours.
6. Place ketchup, hot sauce, cider vinegar, tabasco, and Cajun spices in a saucepan, then bring to a simmer.
7. Remove the sauce from heat and quickly add unsalted butter to the saucepan. Stir until melted.
8. After 4 hours of smoking, baste the tabasco sauce over the turkey, then continue smoking for 15 minutes.
9. Serve.

Per Serving: Calories: 416; Fat: 31g; Sodium: 501mg; Carbs: 16g; Fiber 2.1g; Sugar: 2.2g; Protein: 28g

Cured Turkey Drumstick

Prep time: 15 minutes | Cook time: 45 minutes | Serves: 3

Ingredients:
- 3 fresh or thawed frozen turkey drumsticks
- 3 tablespoons of olive oil

For the brine
- 4 cups of filtered water
- ¼ cup of kosher salt, to taste
- ¼ cup of brown sugar
- 1 teaspoon of garlic powder
- 1 teaspoon of poultry seasoning
- ½ teaspoon of red pepper flakes
- 1 teaspoon of pink hardened salt

Preparation:
1. Put the salt water ingredients in a 1-gallon sealable bag.
2. Add the turkey drumstick to the salt water and refrigerate for 12 hours.
3. After 12 hours, remove the drumstick from the saline, rinse with cold water, and pat dry with a paper towel.
4. Air-dry the drumstick in the refrigerator without a cover for 2 hours.
5. Remove the drumsticks from the refrigerator and rub a tablespoon of olive oil under and over each drumstick.
6. Grease the cooking surface of the griddle with cooking spray.
7. Turn on the 4 burners and turn their knobs to medium heat.
8. Let the Griddle preheat for 5 minutes.
9. Place the drumstick on the griddle and then let it cook for 20 minutes per side.
10. Cook the turkey drumstick at 325°F until the internal temperature of the thickest part of each drumstick is 180°F with an instant reading digital thermometer.
11. Place a smoked turkey drumstick under a loose foil tent for 15 minutes before eating.
12. Serve.

Per Serving: Calories: 342; Fat: 12g; Sodium: 354mg; Carbs: 24g; Fiber 1.2g; Sugar: 5g; Protein: 28g

Tasty Cornish Game Hen

Prep time: 15 minutes | Cook time: 60 minutes | Serves: 2

Ingredients:
- 1 Cornish game hen
- ½ tablespoons of olive oil
- ¼ tablespoon of poultry seasoning

Preparation:
1. Grease the cooking surface of the griddle with cooking spray.
2. Turn on the 4 burners and turn their knobs to medium-high heat.
3. Let the Griddle preheat for 5 minutes.
4. Brush hen with oil and rub with poultry seasoning.
5. Place hen on preheated griddle top and then let it cook from all the sides until brown.
6. Cover hen with lid or pan and smoke for 60 minutes or until the internal temperature of hen reaches 180°F.
7. Serve.

Per Serving: Calories: 378; Fat: 15g; Sodium: 521mg; Carbs: 14g; Fiber 5.1g; Sugar: 3g; Protein: 27g

Jalapeno Turkey in Broth

Prep time: 15 minutes | Cook time: 3 hrs. 45 minutes | Serves: 4

Ingredients:
- 5 pounds of the whole turkey, giblet removed
- ½ of the medium red onion, peeled and minced
- 8 jalapeño peppers
- 2 tablespoons of minced garlic
- 4 tablespoons of garlic powder
- 6 tablespoons of Italian seasoning
- 1 cup of butter, softened, unsalted
- ¼ cup of olive oil
- 1 cup of chicken broth

Preparation:
1. Place a suitable saucepan over medium heat, add oil and butter, and when the butter melts, add onion, garlic, and peppers and then let it cook for 3 to 5 minutes or until nicely golden brown.
2. Pour in broth, stir well, let the mixture boil for 5 minutes, then remove the pan from the heat and strain the mixture to get just liquid.
3. Inject turkey generously with prepared liquid, then spray the outside of turkey with butter spray and season well with garlic and Italian seasoning.
4. Grease the cooking surface of the griddle with cooking spray.
5. Turn on the 4 burners and turn their knobs to low heat.
6. Let the Griddle preheat for 5 minutes.
7. Place turkey on the griddle, shut with lid, and smoke for 30 minutes, then increase the temperature to medium-low and continue smoking the turkey for 3 hours.

8. Serve.

Per Serving: Calories: 318; Fat: 15g; Sodium: 521mg; Carbs: 14g; Fiber 5.1g; Sugar: 3g; Protein: 27g

Honey-Mustard Chicken

Prep time: 20 minutes | Cook time: 5 minutes | Serves: 4

Ingredients:
- ½ cup Dijon mustard
- 2-tablespoon honey
- 2-tablespoon olive oil
- 1-teaspoon freshly ground black pepper
- 2 pounds chicken tenders
- ½ cup walnuts

Preparation:
1. In a medium mixing bowl, mix well the honey, mustard, olive oil, and black pepper.
2. Toss in the chicken to coat it.
3. Pulse the walnuts in a food processor.
4. Toss the chicken tenders in a thin coating of ground walnuts.
5. Preheat the Griddle by turning all its knob to medium-heat setting.
6. Grease the griddle top with cooking spray.
7. Sear the chicken tenders for 3 minutes per side.
8. Serve.

Per Serving: Calories: 642; Fat: 34.3 g; Sodium: 551 mg; Carbs: 12.9g; Fiber: 2.9g; Sugar: 9.1g; Protein: 70.8g

Sambal-Glazed Chicken Thighs

Prep time: 20 minutes | Cook time: 20 minutes | Serves: 4-8

Ingredients:
- 8 boneless chicken thighs

For the glaze:
- 3-tablespoon dark brown sugar
- 2 ½-tablespoon soy sauce
- 1-tablespoon fresh garlic, minced
- 2-teaspoon sesame seeds
- 1-teaspoon fresh ginger, minced
- 1-teaspoon sambal Oelek
- ⅓ cup scallions, sliced
- Non-stick cooking spray

Preparation:
1. In a suitable mixing bowl, mix well all the glaze ingredients and set aside half for serving.
2. Toss the chicken in the bowl to evenly coat it.
3. Preheat the Griddle by turning all its knob to medium-heat setting.
4. Grease the griddle top with cooking spray.
5. Cook this marinated chicken for 6 minutes.
6. Transfer the chicken to plates and garnish with the remaining glaze.
7. Serve warm.

Per Serving: Calories: 301; Fat: 11.2g; Sodium: 413 mg; Carbs: 4.7g; Fiber: 0.3g; Sugar: 3.5g; Protein: 42.9g

Turkey Cooked in Jerky

Prep time: 15 minutes | Cook time: 4 hrs | Serves: 6

Ingredients:

For marinade
- 1 cup of pineapple juice
- ½ cup of brown sugar
- 2 tablespoons of sriracha
- 2 teaspoons of onion powder
- 2 tablespoons of minced garlic
- 2 tablespoons of rice wine vinegar
- 2 tablespoons of hoisin
- 1 tablespoon of red pepper flakes
- 1 tablespoon of coarsely ground black pepper flakes
- 2 cups of coconut amino
- 2 jalapenos (sliced)

For meat
- 3 pounds of turkey boneless
- skinless breasts, sliced

Preparation:
1. Pour the marinade mixture ingredients in a container and mix until the ingredients are well combined.
2. Put the turkey slices in a gallon-sized zip-lock bag and pour the marinade into the bag. Massage the marinade into the turkey. Seal this bag and refrigerate for 8 hours.
3. Remove the turkey slices from the marinade.
4. Grease the cooking surface of the griddle with cooking spray.
5. Turn on the 4 burners and turn their knobs to medium heat.
6. Let the Griddle preheat for 5 minutes.
7. Remove the turkey slices from the marinade and pat them dry with a paper towel.
8. Arrange the turkey slices on the griddle in a single layer. Smoke the turkey for about 3 to 4 hours.
9. Remove the jerky from the griddle and let it sit for about 1 hour to cool.
10. Serve.

Per Serving: Calories: 317; Fat: 32g; Sodium: 311mg; Carbs: 12g; Fiber 3.1g; Sugar: 4g; Protein: 22g

Roast Pineapple and Chicken Skewers

Prep time: 1hour 10 minutes | Cook time: 15 minutes | Serves 4-5

Ingredients:
- 1 pound (454 g) boneless, skinless chicken breast, cut into 1½ inch cubes
- 3 cups pineapple, cut into 1½ inch cubes

For the marinade:
- ⅓ cup tomato paste
- ⅓ cup brown sugar, packed
- ⅓ cup soy sauce
- ¼ cup pineapple juice
- 2 tablespoons olive oil
- 1½ tablespoons mirin or rice wine vinegar
- 1 large green peppers,
- 1 medium red onion,
- 2 tablespoons olive oil, to coat veggies
- 4 teaspoons garlic cloves, minced
- 1 tablespoon ginger, minced
- ½ teaspoon sesame oil
- ½ teaspoon sea salt
- ½ teaspoon ground black pepper
- 10 wooden skewers, for assembly

Preparation:
1. In a mixing basin, whisk together the marinade ingredients until smooth. ½ cup marinade must be kept in the refrigerator
2. Place the chicken in a sealable plastic bag with the remaining marinade and refrigerate for 1 hour.
3. Soak 10 wooden skewer sticks for 1 hour in water.
4. Preheat the Griddle to a medium heat.
5. Toss red onion, bell pepper, and pineapple in 2 tablespoons olive oil in a mixing dish to coat.
6. Using skewers, skewer pineapple, red onion, bell pepper, and then chicken until all of the chicken is utilized.
7. Place skewers on griddle and take the marinade you saved from the fridge; heat for 5 minutes, then brush with the remaining marinade and rotate.
8. Brush the chicken with the marinade again and sear for another 5 minutes, or until a meat thermometer reads 165°F (74°C).
9. Keep the servings warm.

Per Serving: Calories: 254; Fat: 7.3g; Sodium: 499mg; Carbs: 30.6g; Fiber 3.6g; Sugar: 18g; Protein: 18g

Pineapple, Vegetables and Chicken Skewers

Prep time: 1 hour 10 minutes | Cook time: 15 minutes | Serves 4-5

Ingredients:
- 1 pound (454 g) chicken breast, cut into cubes
- 3 cups pineapple, cut into cubes
- 4 large green peppers, cut into pieces

For the marinade:
- ⅓ cup tomato paste
- ⅓ cup brown sugar, packed
- ⅓ cup soy sauce
- ¼ cup pineapple juice
- 2 tablespoons olive oil
- 1½ tablespoon mirin or rice wine vinegar
- 1 large red onion, cut into pieces
- 2 tablespoons olive oil, to coat veggies
- 4 teaspoons garlic cloves, minced
- 1 tablespoon ginger, minced
- ½ teaspoon sesame oil
- Pinch of sea salt
- Pinch of ground black pepper
- 10 wooden skewers, for assembly

Preparation:
1. In a mixing basin, whisk together the marinade ingredients until smooth. 12 cup of the marinade should be kept in the refrigerator.
2. Refrigerate the chicken for 1 hour in a sealable plastic bag with the remaining marinade.
3. Soak 10 wooden skewer sticks for 1 hour in water.
4. Preheat the griddle to a medium heat.
5. Toss red onion, bell pepper, and pineapple in 2 tablespoons olive oil in a mixing dish to coat.
6. Thread red onion, bell pepper, pineapple, then chicken onto the skewers until all of the chicken is used.
7. Place skewers on griddle and get your marinade out of the fridge; cook for 5 minutes, then brush with remaining marinade and rotate.
8. Brush the chicken with the marinade again and sear for another 5 minutes, or until a meat thermometer reads 165°F (74°C).
9. Serve immediately.

Per Serving: Calories: 338; Fat: 9.3g; Sodium: 469mg; Carbs: 36.5g; Fiber 4.6g; Sugar: 21.8g; Protein: 28g

Spatchcock Turkey

Prep time: 15 minutes | Cook time: 1 hr. 15 minutes | Serves: 6

Ingredients:
- 1 (18 pounds) turkey
- 1 tablespoon of chopped fresh rosemary
- ½ cup of melted butter
- 1 teaspoon of onion powder
- 1 teaspoon of garlic powder
- 1 teaspoon of ground black pepper, to taste
- 2 teaspoons of salt or to taste
- 2 tablespoons of chopped fresh parsley
- 2 tablespoons of chopped fresh thyme
- 2 tablespoons of chopped scallions

Preparation:
1. Remove the turkey giblets and rinse the turkey, in and out, under cold running water.
2. Place the turkey on a working surface, breast side down. Use a poultry shear to cut the turkey along both sides of the backb1 to remove the turkey back bone.
3. Flip the turkey over, back side down. Now, press the turkey down to flatten it.
4. In a suitable mixing bowl, combine the rosemary, parsley, scallions, butter, thyme, pepper, garlic, onion powder and salt.
5. Rub butter mixture over all sides of the turkey.
6. Grease the cooking surface of the griddle with cooking spray.
7. Turn on the 4 burners and turn their knobs to medium-low heat.
8. Let the Griddle preheat for 5 minutes.
9. Place the turkey directly on the griddle top and cover and smoke for 30 minutes.
10. Reduce the heat to 300°F and smoke for an additional 30 minutes, or until the internal temperature of the central part of the thigh reaches 165°F.
11. Take out the turkey meat from the griddle and let it rest for a few minutes. Cut into sizes and serve.
12. Serve.

Per Serving: Calories: 342; Fat: 12g; Sodium: 354mg; Carbs: 24g; Fiber 1.2g; Sugar: 5g; Protein: 28g

Bourbon Turkey

Prep time: 15 minutes | Cook time: 3 hrs | Serves: 8

Ingredients:
- 8 cups of chicken broth
- 1 stick of butter softened
- 1 teaspoon of thyme
- 1 (12 pounds) turkey
- 2 garlic cloves, minced
- 1 teaspoon of dried basil
- 1 teaspoon of pepper
- 1 teaspoon of salt
- 1 tablespoon of minced rosemary
- 1 teaspoon of paprika
- 1 lemon (wedged)
- 1 onion
- 1 apple (wedged)
- 1 orange (wedged)

Maple bourbon glaze
- ¾ cup of bourbon
- ½ cup of maple syrup
- 1 stick of butter (melted)
- 1 tablespoon of lime

Preparation:
1. Under cold running water, wash the turkey meat both inside and out.
2. Place the lemon, onion, apple and orange in the cavity of the turkey.
3. Combine the paprika, butter, thyme, basil, garlic, pepper, salt, and rosemary in a suitable mixing bowl.
4. Brush the butter mixture all over the turkey.
5. In a roasting pan, place a rack and the turkey on the rack. In the bottom of the roasting pan, pour five cups of chicken broth.
6. Grease the cooking surface of the griddle with cooking spray.
7. Turn on the 4 burners and turn their knobs to medium heat.
8. Let the Griddle preheat for 5 minutes.
9. Cook for 1 hour on the griddle using the roasting pan with the cover on.
10. In a suitable mixing bowl, combine all of the ingredients for the maple bourbon glaze. Mix until everything is well blended.
11. Using a glaze mixture, baste the bird. Cove and smoke for another 2 hours, basting the turkey every 30 minutes and adding extra broth as needed, or until the internal temperature is 165°F.
12. Serve.

Per Serving: Calories: 395; Fat: 21g; Sodium: 451mg; Carbs: 17g; Fiber 4.1g; Sugar: 1.2g; Protein: 24g

Blackened Boneless Chicken Breasts

Prep time: 10 minutes | Cook time: 10 minutes | Serves 4

Ingredients:
- 1 pound (454 g) chicken breasts, boneless & skinless
- 2 tablespoons blackened seasoning
- 2 tablespoons butter, melted

Preparation:
1. Rub melted butter and seasoning all over the chicken.
2. Heat the griddle to a high temperature.
3. Spray the top of the griddle with cooking spray.
4. Cook the chicken for 4-5 minutes on each side on a hot griddle.
5. Serve and enjoy!.

Per Serving: Calories: 276; Fat: 14.3g; Sodium: 114mg; Carbs: 0.6g; Fiber 0.1g; Sugar: 1.8g; Protein: 38g

Brine-Marinated Turkey Breast

Prep time: 15 minutes | Cook time: 1 hr. 30 minutes | Serves: 6

Ingredients:
For the brine
1 cup of kosher salt, to taste
1 cup of maple syrup
¼ cup of brown sugar
¼ cup of whole black peppercorns
4 cups of cold bourbon
1 ½ gallons of cold water
1 turkey breast of about 7 pounds
For turkey
3 tablespoons of brown sugar
1 ½ tablespoons of smoked paprika
1 ½ teaspoons of chipotle chili powder
1 ½ teaspoons of garlic powder
1 ½ teaspoons of salt, to taste
1 ½ teaspoons of black pepper, to taste
1 teaspoon of onion powder
½ teaspoon of ground cumin
6 tablespoons of melted unsalted butter

Preparation:
1. Before beginning; make sure that the bourbon; the water, and the chicken stock are all cold
2. Now to make the brine, combine the salt, the syrup, the sugar, the peppercorns, the bourbon, and the water in a large bucket altogether.
3. Remove any pieces that are left on the turkey, like the neck or the giblets.
4. Refrigerate the turkey meat in the brine for about 8 to 12 hours in a resealable bag.
5. Remove the turkey breast from the brine and pat dry with clean paper towels; then place it over a baking sheet and refrigerate for about 1 hour.
6. Grease the cooking surface of the griddle with cooking spray.
7. Turn on the 4 burners and turn their knobs to medium-low heat.
8. Let the Griddle preheat for 5 minutes.
9. In a suitable bowl, mix the paprika with the sugar, the chili powder, the garlic powder, the salt, the pepper, the onion powder and the cumin, mixing very well to combine.
10. Carefully lift the skin of the turkey; then rub the melted butter over the meat
11. Rub the spice over the meat very well and over the skin.
12. Smoke the turkey breast for about 1 ½ hour at a temperature of about 375°F.
13. Slice and serve.
14. Serve.
Per Serving: Calories: 317; Fat: 32g; Sodium: 311mg; Carbs: 12g; Fiber 3.1g; Sugar: 4g; Protein: 22g

Griddle-Smoked Whole Turkey

Prep time: 15 minutes | Cook time: 7 hrs. | Serves: 6

Ingredients:
1 whole turkey of about 12 to 16 lb.
1 cup spice rub
1 cup of sugar
1 tablespoon of minced garlic
½ cup of Worcestershire sauce
2 tablespoons of canola oil

Preparation:
1. Thaw turkey and remove the giblets
2. Pour in 3 gallons of water in a non-metal bucket of about 5 gallons
3. Add the bbq rub and mix very well.
4. Add the garlic, the sugar and the Worcestershire sauce; then submerge the turkey into the bucket.
5. Refrigerate the turkey in the bucket overnight.
6. Grease the cooking surface of the griddle with cooking spray.
7. Turn on the 4 burners and turn their knobs to low heat.
8. Let the Griddle preheat for 5 minutes.
9. Place the griddle on a high smoke and smoke turkey for about 3 hours.
10. Switch the griddling temperature to medium heat; then push a metal meat thermometer into the thickest part of the turkey breast.
11. Cook for about 4 hours until the internal temperature reaches 145 degrees F; then take off the griddle and let rest for about 15 minutes.
12. Slice the turkey, then serve and enjoy your dish!
Per Serving: Calories: 449; Fat: 21g; Sodium: 421mg; Carbs: 16g; Fiber 4.1g; Sugar: 3.2g; Protein: 27g

Balsamic Honey Chicken Thighs

Prep time: 05 minutes | Cook time: 25 minutes | Serves 4

Ingredients:
2 pounds' chicken thighs
1 teaspoons olive oil
1 teaspoon sea salt
½ teaspoon black pepper
¼ teaspoon paprika
¾ teaspoon onion powder
For the marinade:
2 tablespoons honey
2 tablespoons balsamic vinegar
2 tablespoons tomato paste
1 teaspoon garlic, minced

Preparation:
1. Combine the chicken, olive oil, salt, black pepper, paprika, and onion powder in a sealable plastic bag. After sealing and stirring the chicken in spices and oil, set it aside.
2. Combine the balsamic vinegar, tomato paste, garlic, and honey in a mixing bowl. Separate the marinade into two halves. Combine one half with the chicken bag and put the other half in the refrigerator in a covered container.
3. Close the bag and toss the chicken in it to coat it. Refrigerate for 30 to 4 hours before serving.
4. Heat a griddle to medium-high temperature.
5. Toss out the bag and marinade. Cook 7 minutes per side on the griddle, or until juices flow clear and a meat thermometer reads 165°F (74°C).
6. Brush the remaining marinade on top of the chicken thighs during the last minute of cooking
7. Serve as soon as possible.
Per Serving: Calories: 485; Fat: 18.1g; Sodium: 438mg; Carbs: 11g; Fiber 0.5g; Sugar: 9.8g; Protein: 66.1g

Taco Turkey Burger Patties

Prep time: 10 minutes | Cook time: 10 minutes | Serves: 4

Ingredients:
1-pound ground turkey
1-tablespoon taco seasoning
½ cup red peppers, chopped
½ cup green peppers, chopped
Pepper
Salt

Preparation:
1. In a suitable mixing bowl, mix well all of the ingredients and stir until well blended.
2. Preheat the Griddle by turning all its knob to medium-heat setting.
3. Grease the griddle top with cooking spray.
4. Form the mixture into patties and fry them for 4-5 minutes per side on the hot griddle top.
5. Serve and enjoy.
Per Serving: Calories: 324; Fat: 17.8 g; Sodium: 363 mg; Carbs: 8.9g; Fiber: 0.5g; Sugar: 1.9g; Protein: 36.6g

BBQ Boneless Turkey Breast

Prep time: 15 minutes | Cook time: 8 hrs | Serves: 6

Ingredients:
For the brine
2 pounds of turkey breast, deboned
2 tablespoons of ground black pepper, to taste
¼ cup of salt, to taste
1 cup of brown sugar
4 cups of cold water
For the BBQ rub
2 tablespoons of dried onions
2 tablespoons of garlic powder
¼ cup of paprika
2 tablespoons of ground black pepper
1 tablespoon of salt, to taste
2 tablespoons of brown sugar
2 tablespoons of red chili powder
1 tablespoon of cayenne pepper, to taste
2 tablespoons of sugar
2 tablespoons of ground cumin

Preparation:
1. Prepare the brine by combining salt, black pepper, and sugar in a suitable bowl, then adding water and stirring until the sugar has dissolved.
2. Place the turkey breast in it, submerge it well, and refrigerate it for at least 12 hours.
3. Meanwhile, make the BBQ rub by combining all of the ingredients in an appropriate bowl and stirring until well blended. Set aside until needed.
4. Then take the turkey breast from the brine and season well with the barbecue rub you've prepared.
5. Grease the cooking surface of the griddle with cooking spray.
6. Turn on the 4 burners and turn their knobs to medium-low heat.
7. Let the Griddle preheat for 5 minutes.
8. When ready to cook, switch on the griddle, set the temperature to medium and let it preheat for a minimum of 15 minutes.
9. When the griddle has preheated, open the lid, place turkey breast on the griddle grate, shut the griddle, change the smoking temperature to low , and smoke for 8 hours until the internal temperature reaches 160 degrees F.
10. Serve.
Per Serving: Calories: 449; Fat: 21g; Sodium: 421mg; Carbs: 16g; Fiber 4.1g; Sugar: 3.2g; Protein: 27g

Cheddar Chicken Patties

Prep time: 10 minutes | Cook time: 20 minutes | Serves 6

Ingredients:
- 1 egg
- 2 pounds (907 g) ground chicken
- ½ cup cheddar cheese, shredded
- ½ cup onion, diced
- 1 teaspoon garlic, minced
- 1 ounces (28 g) ranch seasoning
- ½ cup breadcrumbs
- ½ teaspoon pepper
- ½ teaspoon salt

Preparation:
1. In a mixing basin, add all of the ingredients and stir until well blended.
2. Preheat the griddle to a medium heat.
3. Spray the top of the griddle with cooking spray.
4. Form 6 patties from the mixture and cook for 6-8 minutes on each side on a hot griddle.
5. Serve and have fun.

Per Serving: Calories: 391; Fat: 15.3g; Sodium: 784mg; Carbs: 7.6g; Fiber 0.7g; Sugar: 1.1g; Protein: 48.8g

Green Cheese Stuffed Chicken

Prep time: 05 minutes | Cook time: 35 minutes | Serves 4

Ingredients:
- 4 boneless, skinless chicken breasts
- 2 tablespoon olive oil
- 2 tablespoons taco seasoning
- ½ red, yellow and green pepper, very thinly sliced
- 1 small red onion, very thinly sliced
- ½ cup Mexican shredded cheese
- guacamole, for serving
- sour cream, for serving
- salsa, for serving

Preparation:
1. Preheat the griddle to medium-high heat.
2. Make tiny horizontal slices across each chicken breast, similar to how hasselback potatoes are cut.
3. Coat the chicken in olive oil and taco seasoning evenly.
4. Fill each cut with a mixture of bell peppers and red onions, then set the breasts on the griddle.
5. Allow 15 minutes for the chicken to cook.
6. When the time is up, top with cheese.
7. Simmer for another 5 minutes, or until the cheese has melted.
8. Remove from the griddle and serve with guacamole, sour cream, and salsa on the side.
9. Servings with your favorite side dishes included!

Per Serving: Calories: 710; Fat: 38.3g; Sodium: 1074mg; Carbs: 26g; Fiber 1.6g; Sugar: 2.8g; Protein: 63.8g

Whole Turkey

Prep time: 15 minutes | Cook time: 7 hrs. 30 minutes | Serves: 10

Ingredients:
- 1 frozen whole turkey, giblets removed, thawed
- 2 tablespoons of orange zest
- 2 tablespoons of chopped fresh parsley
- 1 teaspoon of salt
- 2 tablespoons of chopped fresh rosemary
- 1 teaspoon of ground black pepper, to taste
- 2 tablespoons of chopped fresh sage
- 1 cup of butter, unsalted, softened
- 2 tablespoons of chopped fresh thyme
- ½ cup of water
- Fourteen and a ½-ounce of chicken broth

Preparation:
1. Grease the cooking surface of the griddle with cooking spray.
2. Turn on the 4 burners and turn their knobs to medium heat.
3. Let the Griddle preheat for 5 minutes.
4. Prepare the turkey and for this, tuck its wings under it by using kitchen twine.
5. Place ½ cup of butter in a suitable bowl, add thyme, parsley, and sage, orange zest, and rosemary stir well until combined and then brush this mixture generously on the inside and outside of the turkey and season those external of turkey with black pepper and salt.
6. Place turkey on a roasting pan, breast side up, pour in broth and water, add the remaining butter in the pan, then place the pan on the griddle and shut with lid.
7. Smoke the turkey for 3 hours, then increase the temperature to medium high and continue smoking the turkey for 4 hours or until thoroughly cooked and the internal temperature of the turkey reaches 165 degrees F, basting the turkey with the dripping every 30 minutes, but not in the last hour.
8. When you are done, take off the roasting pan from the griddle and let the turkey rest for 20 minutes.
9. Carve turkey into pieces and serve.
10. Serve.

Per Serving: Calories: 401; Fat: 13g; Sodium: 161mg; Carbs: 10g; Fiber 3.1g; Sugar: 2g; Protein: 25g

Cheese Bacon Chicken Burger Patties

Prep time: 15 minutes | Cook time: 10 minutes | Serves 2

Ingredients:
- ½ pound ground chicken
- ½ cup cheddar cheese, shredded
- ⅓ cup bacon, cooked & chopped
- ½ ounce ranch seasoning mix

Preparation:
1. In a large mixing basin, combine all of the ingredients and stir until well blended. Set the griddle to a high heat.
2. Spray the top of the Griddle with cooking spray.
3. Form patties from the mixture and cook for 5 minutes on each side on a hot griddle.
4. Serve and have fun.

Per Serving: Calories: 373; Fat: 21.3g; Sodium: 428mg; Carbs: 3.2g; Fiber 0.2g; Sugar: 0.3g; Protein: 40.8g

Easy BBQ Chicken

Prep time: 5 minutes | Cook time: 1 hour 45 minutes | Serves 4-6

Ingredients:
- 4 pounds (1.8 kg) of your favorite chicken, including legs, thighs, wings, and breasts, skin-on
- 1 teaspoon salt
- 1 tablespoon olive oil
- ½ cup barbecue sauce

Preparation:
1. Flavor the chicken with salt and olive oil.
2. Heat the griddle to a high temperature.
3. Grill the chicken skin side down for 5-10 minutes.
4. Reduce the heat to low and cook for 30 minutes, tenting the griddle with foil.
5. Flip the chicken and baste it with the barbecue sauce.
6. Return the chicken to the oven and cook for another 20 minutes.
7. Baste, cover, and cook for another 30 minutes, basting and turning once more. When the internal temperature of the chicken pieces reaches 165°F (74°C) and the juices run clear, the chicken is done.
8. To serve, baste with extra barbecue sauce.

Per Serving: Calories: 539; Fat: 11.3g; Sodium: 1044mg; Carbs: 15.6g; Fiber 0.3g; Sugar: 10.8g; Protein: 87g

Simple and Delicious Turkey Legs

Prep time: 15 minutes | Cook time: 5 hrs | Serves: 4

Ingredients:
- 4 turkey legs

For the brine
- ½ cup of curing salt, to taste
- 1 tablespoon of whole black peppercorns
- 1 cup of bbq rub
- ½ cup of brown sugar
- 2 bay leaves
- 2 teaspoons of liquid smoke
- 16 cups of warm water
- 4 cups of ice
- 8 cups of cold water

Preparation:
1. Prepare the brine by filling a large stockpot halfway with heated water, adding the peppercorns, bay leaves, and liquid smoke, stirring in the salt, sugar, and bbq spice, and bringing it to a boil.
2. Remove the saucepan from the heat and allow it to cool to room temperature before adding cold water, ice cubes, and chilling the brine in the refrigerator.
3. Then put the turkey legs in it, completely submerge them, and refrigerate for 24 hours.
4. Grease the cooking surface of the griddle with cooking spray.
5. Turn on the 4 burners and turn their knobs to medium-low heat.
6. Let the Griddle preheat for 5 minutes.
7. Place turkey legs on the griddle grate, cook for 5 hours until nicely browned and the internal temperature reaches 165 degrees F.
8. Serve.

Per Serving: Calories: 397; Fat: 21g; Sodium: 711mg; Carbs: 8g; Fiber 3.1g; Sugar: 4g; Protein: 22g

Roast Turkey in Orange Sauce

Prep time: 15 minutes | Cook time: 2 hrs. 30 minutes | Serves: 2

Ingredients:
1 frozen long island turkey
3 tablespoons of west
1 large orange, cut into wedges
3 celery stems chopped into large chunks
½ a small red onion

For orange sauce
2 orange cups
2 tablespoons of soy sauce
2 tablespoons of orange
marmalade
2 tablespoons of honey
3 teaspoons of grated raw

Preparation:
1. Grease the cooking surface of the griddle with cooking spray.
2. Turn on the 4 burners and turn their knobs to medium-low heat.
3. Let the Griddle preheat for 5 minutes.
4. Remove the giblets from the turkey's cavity and neck and retain or discard it for another use. Wash the duck and pat some dry paper towels.
5. Remove excess; Fat: from the tail, neck and cavity. Use a sharp scalpel knife tip to pierce the turkey's skin entirely so that it does not penetrate the duck's meat, to help dissolve the; Fat: layer beneath the skin.
6. Add the seasoning inside the cavity with 1 cup of rub or seasoning.
7. Season those outside of the turkey with the remaining friction or seasoning.
8. Fill the cavity with orange wedges, celery and onion. Duck legs are tied with butcher twine to make filling easier. Place the turkey's breast up on a small rack of shallow roast bread.
9. To make the sauce, mix the ingredients in the saucepan over low heat and then let it cook until the sauce is thick and syrupy. Set aside and let cool.
10. Cover and smoke the turkey at for 2 hours.
11. After 2 hours, brush the turkey freely with orange sauce.
12. Smoke the orange glass turkey for another 30 minutes.
13. Place turkey under a loose foil tent for 20 minutes before serving.
14. Discard the orange wedge, celery and onion. Serve with ¼ of turkey with poultry scissors.
15. Serve.

Per Serving: Calories: 382; Fat: 21g; Sodium: 451mg; Carbs: 17g; Fiber 4.1g; Sugar: 1.2g; Protein: 24g

Tailgate Smoked Turkey

Prep time: 15 minutes | Cook time: 4 hrs. 30 minutes | Serves: 6

Ingredients:
1 fresh or thawed frozen young turkey
6 glasses of olive oil with roasted
garlic flavor
6 teaspoons poultry seasonings

Preparation:
1. Remove excess; Fat: and skin from turkey breasts and cavities.
2. Slowly separate the skin of the turkey to its breast and ¼ of the leg, leaving the skin intact.
3. Apply olive oil to the chest, under the skin and on the skin.
4. Gently rub or season to the chest cavity, under the skin and on the skin.
5. Grease the cooking surface of the griddle with cooking spray.
6. Turn on the 4 burners and turn their knobs to low heat.
7. Let the Griddle preheat for 5 minutes.
8. Put the turkey meat on the griddle with the chest up.
9. Smoke the turkey for 4 hours at 225°F until the thickest part of the turkey's chest reaches an internal temperature of 170°F and the juice is clear.
10. Before engraving, place the turkey under a loose foil tent for 20 minutes.
11. Serve.

Per Serving: Calories: 416; Fat: 31g; Sodium: 501mg; Carbs: 16g; Fiber 2.1g; Sugar: 2.2g; Protein: 28g

Herbed Spatchcock Turkey

Prep time: 15 minutes | Cook time: 1 hours | Serves 6

Ingredients:
1 (18 pounds / 8.2-kg) turkey
2 tablespoons finely chopped fresh parsley
1 tablespoon finely chopped fresh rosemary
2 tablespoons finely chopped fresh thyme
½ cup melted butter
1 teaspoon garlic powder
1 teaspoon onion powder
1 teaspoon ground black pepper
2 teaspoons salt or to taste
2 tablespoons finely chopped scallions

Preparation:
1. Remove the giblets from the turkey and rinse it thoroughly under cold running water inside and out.
2. Put the turkey breast edge down on a work surface. Cut the turkey along both sides of the backbone with a poultry shear to remove the backbone. Flip the turkey to the other side. Now press down on the turkey to flatten it.
3. Combine the parsley, rosemary, scallions, thyme, butter, pepper, salt, garlic, and onion powder in a mixing dish
4. The butter mixture should be rubbed all over the turkey.
5. Preheat your griddle to high heat for 15 minutes.
6. Cook the turkey for 30 minutes immediately on the griddle.
7. Reduce the heat to medium and continue to cook more, or until the thickest section of the thigh reaches 165°F (74°C).
8. Remove the turkey meat from the carcass.

Per Serving: Calories: 940; Fat: 28.3g; Sodium: 1204mg; Carbs: 32.6g; Fiber 4.6g; Sugar: 28g; Protein:140.8g

Seared Chicken with Kale Caesar Salad

Prep time: 10 minutes | Cook time: 15 minutes | Serves 1

Ingredients:
1 chicken breast
1 teaspoon garlic powder
½ teaspoon black pepper
½ teaspoon sea salt
2 kale leaves, chopped
shaved parmesan, for serving

For the dressing:
1 tablespoon mayonnaise
½ tablespoon dijon mustard
½ teaspoon garlic powder
½ teaspoon Worcestershire sauce
¼ lemon, juice of (or ½ a small lime)
¼ teaspoon anchovy paste
Pinch of sea salt
Pinch of black pepper

Preparation:
1. In a small mixing bowl, combine garlic powder, black pepper, and sea salt. Flavor the chicken with the spice blend.
2. Heat the griddle to medium-high heat.
3. Sear the chicken for 7 minutes on each side, or until a meat thermometer inserted in the thickest portion of the breast registers 165°F (74°C).
4. Combine all of the dressing ingredients in a mixing bowl.
5. Place the kale on a plate and drizzle with the dressing, tossing to mix.
6. Arrange the chicken on top of the salad in a diagonal cut. Serve with a shaved parmesan garnish.

Per Serving: Calories: 284; Fat: 11.3g; Sodium: 13804mg; Carbs: 22.5g; Fiber 3.6g; Sugar: 2.6g; Protein: 28.8g

Honey Turkey Breast

Prep time: 15 minutes | Cook time: 4 hours | Serves 6

Ingredients:
1 (5 pounds / 2.3-kg) boneless chicken breast
4 cups water
2 tablespoons kosher salt
1 teaspoon Italian seasoning
2 tablespoons honey
1 tablespoon cider vinegar

Rub:
½ teaspoon onion powder
1 teaspoon paprika
1 teaspoon salt
1 teaspoon ground black pepper
1 tablespoon brown sugar
½ teaspoon garlic powder
1 teaspoon oregano

Preparation:
1. Combine the water, honey, cider vinegar, Italian spice, and salt in a large container.
2. Toss in the chicken breasts to mix. Chill the basin for 4 hours after wrapper it with plastic wrap.
3. Clean the chicken breasts with paper towels and pat them dry. Combine the brown sugar, salt, paprika, onion powder, pepper, oregano, and garlic in a separate mixing dish.
4. Rub the chicken breasts liberally with the rub mixture.
5. Preheat the griddle to medium-low heat for 15 minutes.
6. Place the turkey breast on a griddle rack and cook. On the griddle, place the griddle rack.
7. Smoke for 3 to 4 hours, or until the turkey breast reaches a temperature of 165°F (74°C).
8. Remove the chicken breasts from the fire and set them aside to cool.
9. When done, serve and enjoy.

Per Serving: Calories: 416; Fat: 8.3g; Sodium: 204mg; Carbs: 22.6g; Fiber 0.6g; Sugar: 18g; Protein: 65.8g

Chapter 7 Beef, Pork and Lamb Recipes

Basic Juicy Strip Steak

Prep time: 15 minutes | Cook time: 15 minutes | Serves: 1

Ingredients:
1 (8-ounce) New York strip steak
Olive oil
Sea salt, to taste
Black pepper, to taste

Preparation:
1. Grease the cooking surface of the griddle with cooking spray.
2. Turn on the 4 burners and turn their knobs to medium heat.
3. Let the Griddle preheat for 5 minutes.
4. Remove the steak from your refrigerator and let it come to room temperature, about 30 to 45 minutes.
5. Warm griddle to medium-high heat and brush with olive oil.
6. Season those steak on all sides with black pepper and salt. Cook steak about 4 to 5 minutes.
7. Flip and then let it cook about 4 minutes more for medium rare steak.
8. Move your steak to a plate then let it rest for 5 minutes before serving.
9. Serve.

Per Serving: Calories: 254; Fat: 7.9g; Sodium: 104mg; Carbs: 6g; Fiber 3.6g; Sugar: 6g; Protein: 18g

Delectable Lamb Chops

Prep time: 15 minutes | Cook time: 15 minutes | Serves: 6

Ingredients:
6 lamb chops
2 tablespoons fresh mint, chopped
½ teaspoon black pepper
2 tablespoons olive oil
½ teaspoon kosher salt, to taste

Preparation:
1. Brush the lamb chops with oil then season by adding pepper and salt.
2. Grease the cooking surface of the griddle with cooking spray.
3. Turn on the 4 burners and turn their knobs to medium heat.
4. Let the Griddle preheat for 5 minutes.
5. Place lamb chops onto the preheated griddle top and then let it cook for 5 minutes.
6. Flip lamb chops and then let it cook for 3 minutes. Garnish with mint.
7. Serve.

Per Serving: Calories: 392; Fat: 31g; Sodium: 501mg; Carbs: 16g; Fiber 2.1g; Sugar: 2.2g; Protein: 28g

Caprese Mignon Fillets

Prep time: 15 minutes | Cook time: 15 minutes | Serves: 4

Ingredients:
4 (6-ounce) Mignon filets
1 teaspoon garlic salt, to taste
Italian olive oil
2 roma tomatoes, sliced
4 ounces fresh buffalo mozzarella, cut into 4 slices
8 fresh basil leaves
Balsamic vinegar glaze, for drizzling
Sea salt, for seasoning
Fresh ground black pepper, to taste

Preparation:
1. Lightly brush each filet, on all sides, with olive oil and rub with garlic salt.
2. Grease the cooking surface of the griddle with cooking spray.
3. Turn on the 4 burners and turn their knobs to medium-high heat.
4. Let the Griddle preheat for 5 minutes.
5. Place steaks on griddle, reduce heat to medium, tent with foil and then let it cook for 5 minutes.
6. Flip, re-tent, and then let it cook for an additional 5 minutes; during the last 2 minutes of cooking top each with a slice of mozzarella.
7. Remove steaks from the griddle and top each with a few tomato slices, 2 basil leaves.
8. Drizzle with balsamic, sprinkle with sea black pepper and salt and serve.
9. Serve.

Per Serving: Calories: 342; Fat: 12g; Sodium: 354mg; Carbs: 24g; Fiber 1.2g; Sugar: 5g; Protein: 28g

Savoury Lamb Loin (Rib Chops)

Prep time: 15 minutes | Cook time: 15 minutes | Serves: 4

Ingredients:
8 (4-ounce) lamb rib or loin chops, 1¼ to 1½ inches thick, trimmed
2 tablespoons olive oil
Black pepper and salt, to taste

Preparation:
1. Rub chops with oil and season by adding black pepper and salt.
2. Grease the cooking surface of the griddle with cooking oil.
3. Turn on the 4 burners and turn their knobs to medium heat.
4. Let the Griddle preheat for 5 minutes.
5. Place chops on griddle and then let it cook until well browned, about 4 minutes per side.
6. Transfer chops to large platter, tent with aluminum foil, and let rest for 5 minutes before serving.
7. Serve.

Per Serving: Calories: 304; Fat: 14.9g; Sodium: 304mg; Carbs: 12g; Fiber 6g; Sugar: 2g; Protein: 21g

Flavorful Beef Stew

Prep time: 15 minutes | Cook time: 5 hrs | Serves: 8

Ingredients:
2-½ lbs. beef stew meat chunks
8 carrots, chopped
3 white onions, quartered
5 white potatoes, quartered
2 cans sweet peas
2 bay leaves
2 beef bouillon cubes
1 tablespoon sugar
1 tablespoon Salt, to taste
¼ tablespoons Thyme
1 tablespoon Black pepper, to taste
¼ cup cornstarch
1 (28-oz.) can whole tomatoes
1 cup water

Preparation:
1. Grease the cooking surface of the griddle with cooking spray.
2. Turn on the 4 burners and turn their knobs to medium-low heat.
3. Let the Griddle preheat for 5 minutes.
4. Pour all the ingredients in a skillet and set on the griddle.
5. Cover and then let it cook for 5 hours, stir once or twice. Serve immediately and enjoy.
6. Serve.

Per Serving: Calories: 318; Fat: 15g; Sodium: 521mg; Carbs: 14g; Fiber 5.1g; Sugar: 3g; Protein: 27g

Teppanyaki Beef

Prep time: 15 minutes | Cook time: 15 minutes | Serves: 6

Ingredients:
For the steak:
2 (1-pound) sirloin steaks
1 tablespoon garlic powder
4 tablespoons soy sauce
1 white onion, sliced
3 zucchinis, sliced
2 cups snap peas
4 tablespoons vegetable oil
3 tablespoons butter
Black pepper and salt, to taste

Preparation:
1. Grease the cooking surface of the griddle with cooking spray.
2. Turn on the 4 burners and turn their knobs to medium heat.
3. Let the Griddle preheat for 5 minutes.
4. Flavor the steak with salt, pepper, and garlic powder.
5. Set your griddle to high heat on one side and medium-high heat on the other side.
6. Add some vegetable oil to the medium-hot side and add the onion rings, zucchini, and snap peas.
7. Season by adding a little Black pepper and salt.
8. Put the steaks to the hot side and then let it cook for 3 minutes.
9. Flip, top with butter and add soy sauce to the steaks. Continue cooking an additional 4 minutes.
10. Remove then slice the steak across the grain before serving.
11. Serve.

Per Serving: Calories: 318; Fat: 15g; Sodium: 521mg; Carbs: 14g; Fiber 5.1g; Sugar: 3g; Protein: 27g

New York Strip Steak

Prep time: 15 minutes | Cook time: 15 minutes | Serves: 2

Ingredients:
2 (1-pound) new york strip steaks, trimmed
For the rub:
1 bunch thyme sprigs
1 bunch rosemary sprigs
1 bunch sage sprigs
1½ teaspoons black pepper
¾ teaspoon sea salt
½ teaspoon garlic powder
2 tablespoons chopped fresh flat-leaf parsley
2 tablespoons olive oil

Preparation:
1. Grease the cooking surface of the griddle with cooking spray.
2. Turn on the 4 burners and turn their knobs to medium heat.
3. Let the Griddle preheat for 5 minutes.
4. Combine rub fixings in a suitable mixing bowl and rub steaks with spice mixture; let rest 10 minutes.
5. Place steaks on griddle and then let it cook 1 minute per side. Turn griddle down to medium heat.
6. Turn steaks and griddle 3 additional minutes per side; or until thermometer registers 135°F (57°C) for medium rare.
7. Remove steaks to a platter. Let rest 5 minutes. Cut steaks across grain into thin slices
8. Serve.
Per Serving: Calories: 378; Fat: 15g; Sodium: 521mg; Carbs: 14g; Fiber 5.1g; Sugar: 3g; Protein: 27g

Rib-Eye Steak

Prep time: 15 minutes | Cook time: 50 minutes | Serves: 4

Ingredients:
1 (24-ounce) bone-in tomahawk rib-eye, 2½ inches thick
Olive oil
Sea salt, to taste
Fresh cracked pepper, to taste
3 tablespoons french butter
½ teaspoon herbed de provence

Preparation:
1. Grease the cooking surface of the griddle with cooking spray.
2. Beat butter with herbs in a suitable mixing bowl, cover and refrigerate until ready to griddle rib-eye.
3. Rub the rib-eye liberally with olive oil, black pepper and salt until entire steak is covered.
4. Wrap lightly with cling wrap and place in the refrigerator to marinate for 12 hours.
5. Preheat the Griddle to high heat on one side and medium low on the other side.
6. Remove the steak from your refrigerator then leave at room temperature during the hour that the griddle is preheating.
7. Put the steak on the center of the hottest side of the griddle.
8. Do this for both sides within 10 minutes.
9. Move the rib-eye to the cooler side of the griddle and then let it cook to rare, about 25 to 30 minutes.
10. Transfer rib-eye to a griddle rack, add herbed butter on top, and lightly tent it with tin foil to rest within 15 minutes before carving. Serve with your favorite sides
11. Serve.
Per Serving: Calories: 416; Fat: 11g; Sodium: 501mg; Carbs: 16g; Fiber 2.1g; Sugar: 2.2g; Protein: 28g

Gribiche Skirt Steak

Prep time: 15 minutes | Cook time: 30 minutes | Serves: 6

Ingredients:
Coriander–ancho rub:
2 tablespoons coriander seeds
4 ancho chiles, stemmed, seeded, and torn
2 teaspoons salt, to taste
1 tablespoon honey
Gribiche
4 hard-boiled eggs, peeled and minced
2 tablespoons minced parsley leaves
2 tablespoons minced shallots
1 lemon, zest and juice
½ cup oil
Black pepper and salt, for seasoning
2 pounds skirt steak

Preparation:
1. Place the coriander and chiles in a skillet over medium heat and stir until toasted and fragrant but not burnt, 3 to 5 minutes.
2. Cool slightly and blend to a fine powder in a suitable blender or food processor. Mix with the salt and honey.
3. To make the gribiche: combine the eggs, parsley, shallots, and lemon zest and juice in a suitable bowl.
4. Slowly add the oil, while whisking constantly. Season by adding black pepper and salt.
5. Gribiche can be covered and refrigerated for up to 8 hours, but should be served on the day it's made.
6. Coat the steaks liberally with the rub.
7. Let them rest uncovered in the refrigerator for at least 1 hour and up to 4 hours.
8. Grease the cooking surface of the griddle with cooking spray.
9. Turn on the 4 burners and turn their knobs to high heat.
10. Let the Griddle preheat for 5 minutes.
11. Place the steak over high heat for about 90 seconds, then turn down 45 degrees F and then let it cook for another 90 seconds. Flip then cooks the other side, for a total of 6 minutes.
12. Move to medium heat and test for doneness by slicing into 1 steak; you don't want it cooked beyond medium-rare.
13. Move the steak to a cutting board then let rest for 5 minutes, then slice against the grain and serve with the gribiche.
14. Serve.
Per Serving: Calories: 376; Fat: 13g; Sodium: 421mg; Carbs: 16g; Fiber 4.1g; Sugar: 3.2g; Protein: 27g

Moink Ball Skewers

Prep time: 15 minutes | Cook time: 1 hr. 15 minutes | Serves: 6

Ingredients:
½ pound of pork sausage, ground
½ pound of ground beef, 80% lean
1 large egg
½ cup of minced red onions
½ cup of parmesan cheese, grated
½ cup of Italian breadcrumbs
¼ cup of parsley, chopped
¼ cup of milk
2 garlic cloves, minced
1 teaspoon of garlic, crushed
1 teaspoon of oregano
½ teaspoon of kosher salt, to taste
½ teaspoon black pepper
¼ cup of barbecue sauce
½ pound of bacon slices, halved

Preparation:
1. Mix up the ground pork sausage, ground beef, breadcrumbs, onion, egg, parsley, parmesan cheese, garlic, milk, oregano, salt, and pepper in a suitable bowl. Whatever you do, don't overwork your meat.
2. Make meatballs of 1½ ounces each. They should be about 1½ in width. Put them on your Teflon-coated fiberglass mat.
3. Wrap up each meatball in ½ a slice of your sliced bacon.
4. Spear your Moink balls, 3 to a skewer.
5. Grease the cooking surface of the griddle with cooking spray.
6. Turn on the 4 burners and turn their knobs to low heat.
7. Let the Griddle preheat for 5 minutes.
8. Smoke the skewered Moink balls for ½ an hour.
9. Turn up the temperature to 350 degrees F, and keep it that way until the internal temperature of your skewered Moink balls hits 175 degrees F, which should take about 40 to 45 minutes, max.
10. When the bacon gets nice and crispy, brush your Moink balls with whatever barbecue sauce you like. Ideally, you should do this in the last 5 minutes of your cook time. Serve the Moink ball skewers while they're hot.
11. Serve.
Per Serving: Calories: 421; Fat: 11g; Sodium: 361mg; Carbs: 11g; Fiber 3.1g; Sugar: 2g; Protein: 26g

Cumin Pork Chops

Prep time: 15 minutes | Cook time: 60 minutes | Serves: 4

Ingredients:
4 pork chops
4 garlic cloves, smashed
2 tablespoons olive oil
⅓ cup lime juice
¼ cup water
1 teaspoon ground cumin
Black pepper and salt, to taste

Preparation:
1. Grease the cooking surface of the griddle with cooking spray.
2. Turn on the 4 burners and turn their knobs to medium heat.
3. Let the Griddle preheat for 5 minutes.
4. Salt the pork chops on both side and sprinkle with the black pepper, then let it cook the chops until lightly browned.
5. Combine the water, garlic, and lime juice in a suitable bowl and whisk until even.
6. Continue cooking the pork chops while basting them with the lime juice mixture.
7. Serve.
Per Serving: Calories: 386; Fat: 13g; Sodium: 421mg; Carbs: 16g; Fiber 4.1g; Sugar: 3.2g; Protein: 27g

Caprese Flank Steak with Balsamic Glaze

Prep time: 15 minutes | **Cook time:** 15 minutes | **Serves:** 4

Ingredients:

- 4 (6-ounce) flank steaks
- Sea salt, for seasoning
- Flakey sea salt, for serving
- Black pepper, to taste
- Olive oil
- 2 roma tomatoes, sliced
- 4 ounces fresh buffalo mozzarella, cut into 4 slices
- 8 fresh basil leaves
- Balsamic vinegar glaze, for drizzling

Preparation:

1. Lightly brush each filet, on all sides, with olive oil and season by adding black pepper and salt.
2. Grease the cooking surface of the griddle with cooking spray.
3. Turn on the 4 burners and turn their knobs to medium heat.
4. Let the Griddle preheat for 5 minutes.
5. Place steaks on griddle, reduce heat to medium, tent with foil and then let it cook for 5 minutes.
6. Flip, re-tent, and then let it cook for an additional 5 minutes; during the last 2 minutes of cooking, top each with a slice of mozzarella.
7. Remove steaks from the griddle and top each with a few tomato slices, 2 basil leaves.
8. Drizzle with balsamic glaze, and sprinkle with flakey salt and a little blacker pepper.
9. Serve.

Per Serving: Calories: 366; Fat: 13g; Sodium: 421mg; Carbs: 16g; Fiber 4.1g; Sugar: 3.2g; Protein: 27g

Dijon Pork Chops

Prep time: 15 minutes | **Cook time:** 35 minutes | **Serves:** 4

Ingredients:

- 4 (10-ounce) bone-in pork rib or center-cut chops, 1 inch thick, trimmed
- ¼ cup sugar
- 1 teaspoon salt
- 1 teaspoon black pepper
- 2 tablespoons cider vinegar
- ½ teaspoon cornstarch
- ¼ cup honey
- 1½ tablespoons dijon mustard
- ½ teaspoon minced fresh thyme
- ⅛ teaspoon cayenne pepper, to taste

Preparation:

1. Pat chops dry using a paper towel then cut 2 slits about 2 inches apart through; Fat: on edges of each chop. Combine sugar, salt, and pepper in bowl, then rub thoroughly over chops.
2. Whisk vinegar and cornstarch together in small saucepan until smooth.
3. Then stir in honey, mustard, thyme, and cayenne.
4. Boil the mixture, then adjust the heat to medium-low and simmer for 5 to 7 minutes.
5. Grease the cooking surface of the griddle with cooking spray.
6. Turn on the 4 burners and turn their knobs to medium heat.
7. Let the Griddle preheat for 5 minutes.
8. Cook the chops on the griddle top for 6 to 10 minutes.
9. Brush tops of chops with glaze, flip glazed side down, and griddle over hotter part of griddle until caramelized, about 1 minute.
10. Transfer chops to platter, tent with aluminum foil, and let rest for 5 to 10 minutes.
11. Brush chops with remaining glaze before serving.
12. Serve.

Per Serving: Calories: 377; Fat: 15g; Sodium: 521mg; Carbs: 14g; Fiber 5.1g; Sugar: 3g; Protein: 27g

Country Ribs

Prep time: 15 minutes | **Cook time:** 2 hrs. and 20 minutes | **Serves:** 6

Ingredients:

- 3 pounds of country-style pork ribs
- 1 cup of low-sugar ketchup
- ½ cup of water
- ¼ cup of onion, chopped
- ¼ cup of cider vinegar or wine vinegar
- ¼ cup of light molasses
- 2 tablespoons of Worcestershire sauce
- 2 teaspoons of chili powder
- 2 garlic cloves, minced

Preparation:

1. Grease the cooking surface of the griddle with cooking spray.
2. Turn on the 4 burners and turn their knobs to medium heat.
3. Let the Griddle preheat for 5 minutes.
4. Mix ketchup, water, onion, vinegar, molasses, Worcestershire sauce, chili powder, and garlic in a saucepan and bring to boil; reduce heat.
5. Simmer, uncovered, for almost 15 minutes or until desired thickness is reached, stirring often.
6. Trim; Fat: from ribs.
7. Place ribs, bone-side down, on the griddle and smoke for 1-½ to 2 hours or until tender, occasionally brushing with sauce during the last 10 minutes of cooking.
8. Serve.

Per Serving: Calories: 376; Fat: 13g; Sodium: 421mg; Carbs: 16g; Fiber 4.1g; Sugar: 3.2g; Protein: 27g

Tuscan-Style Steak and Crispy Potatoes

Prep time: 15 minutes | **Cook time:** 30 minutes | **Serves:** 4

Ingredients:

- 2 bone-in porterhouse steaks
- 1½ pounds small potatoes, halved
- 4 tablespoons olive oil
- Sea salt, to taste
- Black pepper, to taste
- 2 teaspoons red wine
- 1 teaspoon balsamic vinegar
- Pinch red pepper flakes
- 3 fresh rosemary sprigs, needles

Preparation:

1. Put the potatoes to your suitable pot then cover with water, boil over high heat, then adjust the heat to medium-high.
2. Cook until the potatoes for about 10 minutes.
3. Drain, add to a medium mixing bowl, coat with 2 tablespoons olive oil, and set aside.
4. Whisk 2 tablespoons olive oil, rosemary, red wine, vinegar, and pepper flakes; add steaks to marinade and set aside until ready to cook.
5. Grease the cooking surface of the griddle with cooking spray.
6. Turn on the 4 burners and turn their knobs to medium heat.
7. Let the Griddle preheat for 5 minutes.
8. Sprinkle potatoes with black pepper and salt. Add steaks to one side of the griddle and potatoes to the other.
9. Cook steak for 5 minutes, flip and 4 minutes on the other side for medium rare.
10. Add the potatoes to cook for 5 minutes.
11. Transfer steaks to a cutting board and tent with aluminum foil and let rest for 5 minutes while potatoes are cooking.
12. Divide each of your steak into 2 pieces then divide among 4 dinner plates.
13. Spoon some potatoes around the steak.
14. Serve.

Per Serving: Calories: 382; Fat: 21g; Sodium: 451mg; Carbs: 17g; Fiber 4.1g; Sugar: 1.2g; Protein: 24g

Herbed Pork Tenderloin

Prep time: 15 minutes | **Cook time:** 30 minutes | **Serves:** 4

Ingredients:

- 1 pound of pork tenderloin
- 1 tablespoon of olive oil
- ¾ teaspoon of lemon black pepper, to taste
- 2 teaspoons of dried oregano
- 1 teaspoon of garlic powder
- ¼ cup of parmesan cheese, grated
- 3 tablespoons of olive tapenade

Preparation:

1. Put pork on a plastic wrap.
2. Massage the tenderloin with oil, and then sprinkle oregano, garlic powder, and lemon pepper over the entire tenderloin.
3. Wrap the plastic wrap tightly over the tenderloin and refrigerate for around 2 to 4 hours.
4. Transfer pork to a cutting board, remove the plastic wrap, and cut it lengthwise through the center of the tenderloin, opening meat, so it stays flat, but do not cut all the way through.
5. Combine tapenade and parmesan in a suitable mixing bowl; rub into the center of the tenderloin and fold meat back together.
6. Tie together with twine in two-inch intervals.
7. Grease the cooking surface of the griddle with cooking spray.
8. Turn on the 4 burners and turn their knobs to medium heat.
9. Let the Griddle preheat for 5 minutes.
10. Place it on the griddle top cover and let it smoke until the interior temperature at the center of the meat is 145°F.
11. Place the tenderloin on cutting board.
12. Tent it with foil and let it rest for 10 minutes.
13. Remove the twine and cut into quarter-inch-thick slices and serve.
14. Serve.

Per Serving: Calories: 366; Fat: 13g; Sodium: 421mg; Carbs: 16g; Fiber 4.1g; Sugar: 3.2g; Protein: 27g

Chapter 7 Beef, Pork and Lamb Recipes | 75

Texas-Style Beef Brisket

Prep time: 15 minutes | Cook time: 6 hrs. 20 minutes | Serves: 6

Ingredients:
1 (4 ½ lb.) flat-cut beef brisket (about 3 inches thick)
For the rub
1 tablespoon of sea salt
1 tablespoon of dark brown sugar
2 teaspoons of smoked paprika
2 teaspoons of chili powder
1 teaspoon of garlic powder
1 teaspoon of onion powder
1 teaspoon of ground black pepper
1 teaspoon of mesquite liquid smoke

Preparation:
1. Combine the rub ingredients in a suitable mixing bowl.
2. Rinse and pat brisket dry and rub with the coffee mix.
3. Preheat the griddle for cooking; heat one side to 450 degrees F and leaving one side with 210 degrees F.
4. Grease the cooking surface of the griddle with cooking spray.
5. Turn on the 4 burners and turn 2 knobs to medium low heat and other two to medium-high heat.
6. Let the Griddle preheat for 5 minutes.
7. Sear on medium-high side for 3 - 5 minutes on each side or until nicely charred.
8. Move to the other side, tent with foil, and smoke for 6 hours or until a meat thermometer registers 195°F.
9. Remove from griddle. Let stand, covered, 30 minutes.
10. Cut brisket across grain into thin slices and serve.
11. Serve.

Per Serving: Calories: 327; Fat: 22g; Sodium: 421mg; Carbs: 10g; Fiber 4.1g; Sugar: 2g; Protein: 31g

Country Spiced Pork Ribs

Prep time: 10 minutes | Cook time: 2 hours | Serves: 6

Ingredients:
3 pounds (1.4 kg) country-style pork ribs
1 cup low-sugar ketchup
½ cup water
¼ cup onion, chopped
¼ cup cider vinegar or wine vinegar
¼ cup light molasses
2 tablespoons Worcestershire sauce
2 teaspoons chili powder
2 cloves garlic, minced

Preparation:
1. In a suitable saucepan, mix well water, ketchup, vinegar, onion, Worcestershire sauce, chili powder, and garlic; bring to a boil.
2. Cook for almost 10 to 15 minutes with occasional stirring.
3. Preheat the Griddle by turning all its knob to medium-heat setting.
4. Grease the griddle top with cooking spray.
5. Pour the egg mixture onto the hot griddle top
6. Place the ribs on the hot griddle top, and cook for ½ to 2 hours, brushing with sauce.
7. Toss with the remaining sauce and serve.

Per Serving: Calories: 416; Fat: 8.3 g; Sodium: 208 mg; Carbs: 22.9g; Fiber: 0.5g; Sugar: 19g; Protein: 60.6g

Parmesan Pork Tenderloin Pieces

Prep time: 2 hours | Cook time: 30 minutes | Serves: 4

Ingredients:
1 pound pork tenderloin
1 tablespoon olive oil
2 teaspoons dried oregano
¾ teaspoon lemon pepper
1 teaspoon garlic powder
¼ cup parmesan cheese, grated
3 tablespoons olive tapenade

Preparation:
1. Place the pork on a wide plastic wrap sheet.
2. Brush the tenderloin with oil and season generously with garlic powder, oregano, and lemon pepper.
3. Refrigerate for 2 hours after wrapping tightly in plastic wrap.
4. Transfer the pork to a cutting board, remove the plastic wrap, and carve a lengthwise cut through the tenderloin's center, opening it flat.
5. In a suitable mixing bowl, mix well tapenade and parmesan.
6. Rub over the tenderloin's center and fold flesh back together.
7. Tie together in 2-inch intervals using thread.
8. Preheat the Griddle by turning all its knob to medium-heat setting.
9. Grease the griddle top with cooking spray.
10. Sear tenderloin on the griddle top for 20 minutes and flip once cooked halfway though.
11. Remove the tenderloin from the griddle and place it on a chopping board.
12. Cover with foil and set aside for 10 minutes.
13. Remove the string and slice the meat into 14-inch thick pieces to serve.

Per Serving: Calories: 413; Fat: 30.8 g; Sodium: 1279 mg; Carbs: 2.4g; Fiber: 0.5g; Sugar: 1.3g; Protein: 31.6g

Butter Rib Eye Steak

Prep time: 15 minutes | Cook time: 40 minutes | Serves: 1

Ingredients:
1 unpeeled white or red onion
Oil, for coating
1 tablespoon molasses
1 tablespoon butter
Salt, for seasoning and coating
1 (1-pound) bone-in rib eye steak, 1½ inches thick
Black pepper, for coating

Preparation:
1. Grease the cooking surface of the griddle with cooking spray.
2. Turn on the 4 burners and turn their knobs to medium heat.
3. Let the Griddle preheat for 5 minutes.
4. Roast the onion directly onto the griddle until it feels soft when prodded with tongs, about 20 minutes.
5. Move it to a cutting board, remove skin, and chop the flesh finely.
6. Add the onion and then let it cook until it's deep brown.
7. Add the molasses and then let it cook for another 5 minutes, then add the butter, season by adding salt, and keep the sauce warm on a corner of the griddle while you cook the rib eye.
8. Coat the steak generously with black pepper and salt and let sit for 20 to 30 minutes.
9. Place on the griddle top and sear for about 6 minutes per side, turning often, until it's deeply browned.
10. Remove from heat when an instant-read meat thermometer, placed in the thickest part, reads 130 degrees F (54ºC). Transfer to a serving plate and let sit for 10 minutes before eating with the caramelized onions.
11. Serve.

Per Serving: Calories: 342; Fat: 12g; Sodium: 354mg; Carbs: 24g; Fiber 1.2g; Sugar: 5g; Protein: 28g

Easy-to-Make Porterhouse Steak

Prep time: 15 minutes | Cook time: 14 minutes | Serves: 4

Ingredients:
2 porterhouse steaks, 1½ inches thick
Butcher's salt, for coating

Preparation:
1. Grease the cooking surface of the griddle with cooking spray.
2. Turn on the 4 burners and turn their knobs to medium heat.
3. Let the Griddle preheat for 5 minutes.
4. Pat your steaks dry then flavor with the salt. Let sit for 20 to 30 minutes.
5. Place the steaks over high heat.
6. Cook for 7 minutes per side.
7. Serve.

Per Serving: Calories: 392; Fat: 32g; Sodium: 354mg; Carbs: 14g; Fiber 1.2g; Sugar: 5g; Protein: 31g

Fried Lamb Chops with Mint

Prep time: 15 minutes | Cook time: 8 minutes | Serves:6

Ingredients:
6 lamb chops
2-tablespoon fresh mint, chopped
½-teaspoon pepper
2-tablespoon olive oil
½-teaspoon kosher salt

Preparation:
1. Preheat the griddle to medium-high heat.
2. Season the lamb chops with pepper and salt after brushing them with oil.
3. Cook for 5 minutes on a heated griddle top with the lamb chops.
4. Cook for 3 minutes after flipping the lamb chops.
5. Garnish with a sprig of mint.
6. Serve and have fun.

Per Serving: Calories: 199; Fat: 10.9g; Sodium: 259mg; Carbs: 0.6g; Fiber 0.2g; Sugar: 0g; Protein: 24g

Beef Fillets with Pineapple Rice

Prep time: 15 minutes | Cook time: 20 minutes | Serves: 4

Ingredients:
- 4 (4-ounce) beef fillets
- ¼ cup soy sauce
- ½ teaspoon black pepper
- ½ teaspoon garlic powder
- 1 (8-ounce) can pineapple chunks, drained
- 2 scallions, sliced
- 2 (9-ounce) packages pre-cooked brown rice
- 1 teaspoon kosher salt, to taste
- Olive oil, for brushing

Preparation:
1. Grease the cooking surface of the griddle with cooking spray.
2. Turn on the 4 burners and turn their knobs to medium heat.
3. Let the Griddle preheat for 5 minutes.
4. Combine soy sauce, pepper, garlic powder, and beef in a large sealable plastic bag. Seal and massage sauce into beef; let stand at room temperature for 7 minutes, turning bag occasionally.
5. Add pineapple and green onions to griddle and then let it cook 5 minutes or until well charred, turning to char evenly.
6. Remove pineapple mix and brush with additional olive oil. Add steaks and then let it cook 3 minutes on each side, for rare, or until desired temperature is reached.
7. Cook rice according to package instructions. Add rice, pineapple, onions, and salt to a suitable bowl and stir gently to combine. Plate steaks with pineapple rice and serve!
8. Serve.

Per Serving: Calories: 401; Fat: 13g; Sodium: 161mg; Carbs: 10g; Fiber 3.1g; Sugar: 2g; Protein: 25g

Glazed Pork with Fish Sauce

Prep time: 15 minutes | Cook time: 15 minutes | Serves: 8

Ingredients:
- 1 (5-pound) boston butt pork shoulder

Marinade:
- 2 tablespoons garlic, minced
- 1 large piece ginger, peeled and chopped
- 1 cup hoisin sauce
- ¾ cup fish sauce
- ⅔ cup honey
- ⅔ cup shaoxing
- ½ cup chili oil
- ⅓ cup oyster sauce
- ⅓ cup sesame oil

Glaze:
- ¾ cup dark brown sugar
- 1 tablespoon light molasses

Preparation:
1. Put the pork shoulder,; Fat: side down, on your cutting board with a short end facing you.
2. Holding a long sharp knife about 1"–1½" above cutting board, make a shallow cut along the entire length of a long side of shoulder.
3. Continue cutting deeper into your meat, lifting and unfurling with your free hand, until it lies flat.
4. Purée marinade in a suitable blender and reserve 1 ½ cups for glaze, cover and refrigerate.
5. Pour remaining marinade in a large sealable plastic bag.
6. Add pork shoulder to bag and marinate in the refrigerator for 8 hours.
7. Grease the cooking surface of the griddle with cooking spray.
8. Turn on the 4 burners and turn their knobs to medium heat.
9. Let the Griddle preheat for 5 minutes.
10. Remove pork from your marinade, letting excess drip off.
11. Add glaze ingredients to reserved marinade until sugar is dissolved.
12. Sear pork, for 8 minutes, basting and turning with tongs every minute or so, until thick coated with glaze, lightly charred in spots, and warmed through.
13. Move it to your cutting board and slice against the grain, ¼" thick.
14. Serve.

Per Serving: Calories: 382; Fat: 21g; Sodium: 451mg; Carbs: 17g; Fiber 4.1g; Sugar: 1.2g; Protein: 24g

Marinated Flank Steak with Yogurt Sauce

Prep time: 15 minutes | Cook time: 20 minutes | Serves: 4

Ingredients:
- 1 pound flank steak
- 1 white onion, sliced
- 1 roma tomato, sliced

Marinade:
- ¼ cup olive oil
- 1 teaspoon dried oregano
- 1 cucumber, peeled and sliced
- ¼ cup crumbled feta cheese
- 4 (6-inch) pita pockets
- 1 teaspoon balsamic vinegar
- 1 teaspoon garlic powder
- Sea salt, to taste

Sauce:
- 1 cup of plain yogurt
- 2 tablespoons fresh dill, chopped
- Black pepper, to taste
- 1 teaspoon garlic, minced
- 2 tablespoons lemon juice

Preparation:
1. Cut your flank steak into thin strips against the grain.
2. Add the marinade ingredients to a large sealable plastic bag, add the sliced meat, seal, and turn to coat.
3. Put in the refrigerator to marinate within 2 hours or overnight.
4. Grease the cooking surface of the griddle with cooking spray.
5. Turn on the 4 burners and turn their knobs to medium heat.
6. Let the Griddle preheat for 5 minutes.
7. Combine the sauce ingredients in suitable mixing bowl and set aside.
8. Spritz your pitas with a little bit of water, wrap in foil and place in the oven to warm.
9. Brush griddle with olive oil. Add meat to griddle and discard marinade. Cook within 5 minutes.
10. Remove the pitas from your oven, then cut in ½.
11. Arrange the pitas on plates and stuff with cucumber, tomato, onions, and beef.
12. Spoon some yogurt sauce over your meat and top with feta and serve.
13. Serve.

Per Serving: Calories: 385; Fat: 21g; Sodium: 421mg; Carbs: 16g; Fiber 4.1g; Sugar: 3.2g; Protein: 27g

BBQ Baby Back Ribs

Prep time: 15 minutes | Cook time: 45 minutes | Serves: 4

Ingredients:
- 1 tablespoon oil
- 1 white onion, peeled and sliced
- ½ cup chipotle chiles, stemmed and seeded
- 1 cup squeezed orange juice
- 1 cup tamarind paste
- 8 garlic cloves, chopped
- 1 cup vinegar
- 1 cup water
- 2 tablespoons honey
- 1 teaspoon salt
- 4 pounds baby back ribs
- Black pepper and salt, for seasoning

Preparation:
1. Add the onion and then let it cook until softened and slightly caramelized, about 5 minutes.
2. Add the chipotles and then let it cook for another 2 minutes.
3. Stir in orange juice, tamarind paste, garlic, vinegar, water, honey, and salt then cook for 18 minutes.
4. Add more vinegar, honey, or salt, if needed.
5. Grease the cooking surface of the griddle with cooking spray.
6. Turn on the 4 burners and turn their knobs to medium heat.
7. Let the Griddle preheat for 5 minutes.
8. Season those ribs with black pepper and salt.
9. Cook on the griddle top for 10 minutes per side while basting with the prepared sauce.
10. Move it to a cutting board and immediately slice the ribs into two-rib portions.
11. Serve.

Per Serving: Calories: 416; Fat: 11g; Sodium: 501mg; Carbs: 16g; Fiber 2.1g; Sugar: 2.2g; Protein: 28g

Easy Lamb Shoulder Chops

Prep time: 15 minutes | Cook time: 20 minutes | Serves: 4

Ingredients:
- 4 (8- to 12-ounce / 227- to 340-g) lamb shoulder chops (blade or round bone), ¾ to 1 inch thick, trimmed
- 2 tablespoons olive oil
- Black pepper and salt, to taste

Preparation:
1. Grease the cooking surface of the griddle with cooking spray.
2. Turn on the 4 burners and turn their knobs to medium heat.
3. Let the Griddle preheat for 5 minutes.
4. Massage your chops with oil and season by adding black pepper and salt.
5. Put your chops on hotter side of griddle and then let it cook within 2 minutes per side.
6. Slide your chops to cooler side of griddle and continue to cook until meat registers 120 degrees F.
7. Transfer chops to large platter, tent with aluminum foil, and let rest for 5 minutes before serving.
8. Serve.

Per Serving: Calories: 392; Fat: 32g; Sodium: 354mg; Carbs: 14g; Fiber 1.2g; Sugar: 5g; Protein: 31g

Beef and Broccoli Rice

Prep time: 15 minutes | Cook time: 20 minutes | Serves: 4

Ingredients:
- 1 minced garlic clove
- 1 sliced ginger root
- 1 tablespoon olive oil
- 1 teaspoon almond flour
- 1 teaspoon sweetener of choice
- 1 teaspoon soy sauce
- ⅓ cup sherry
- 2 teaspoon sesame oil
- ⅓ cup oyster sauce
- 1 pounds of broccoli
- ¾ pound round steak

Preparation:
1. Remove stems from broccoli and slice into florets. Slice steak into thin strips.
2. Combine sweetener, soy sauce, sherry, almond flour, sesame oil, and oyster sauce together, stirring till sweetener dissolves.
3. Put strips of steak into the mixture and allow to marinate 45 minutes to 2 hours.
4. Grease the cooking surface of the griddle with cooking spray.
5. Turn on the 4 burners and turn their knobs to high heat.
6. Let the Griddle preheat for 5 minutes.
7. Add broccoli and marinated steak to the griddle top.
8. Place garlic, ginger, and olive oil on top and then let it cook 12 minutes
9. Serve with cauliflower rice!

Per Serving: Calories: 327; Fat: 22g; Sodium: 421mg; Carbs: 10g; Fiber 4.1g; Sugar: 2g; Protein: 31g

Flavorful Pork Chops

Prep time: 15 minutes | Cook time: 13 minutes | Serves: 4

Ingredients:
- 4 (½-inch-thick) bone-in pork chops
- 3 tablespoons olive oil
- Kosher salt, to taste
- Black pepper, to taste

For the marinade:
- 1 habanero chili, seeded, chopped fine
- 2 garlic cloves, minced
- ½ cup fresh orange juice
- 2 tablespoons brown sugar
- 1 tablespoon apple cider vinegar

Preparation:
1. Combine marinade ingredients in a large sealable plastic bag.
2. Prick the pork chops all over using a fork and add to bag, seal, and turn to coat.
3. Marinate at room temperature, with occasional stirring, for 30 minutes.
4. Grease the cooking surface of the griddle with cooking oil.
5. Turn on the 4 burners and turn their knobs to medium heat.
6. Let the Griddle preheat for 5 minutes.
7. Remove pork chops from your marinade and pat dry.
8. Sear for 8 minutes, with occasional stirring, until charred and then let it cooked through.
9. Transfer to a plate and let rest within 5 minutes.
10. Serve.

Per Serving: Calories: 449; Fat: 21g; Sodium: 421mg; Carbs: 16g; Fiber 4.1g; Sugar: 3.2g; Protein: 27g

Lime Pork Paillards

Prep time: 15 minutes | Cook time: 10 minutes | Serves: 6

Ingredients:
Marinade:
- 4 cups water
- Juice of 2 limes
- 4 garlic cloves, minced
- ¼ cup sugar
- 2 tablespoons salt, to taste
- 2 teaspoons black peppercorns, cracked
- 2 pounds thin-cut boneless pork shoulder steaks, ¼ inch thick
- Salt, for finishing
- Lemon or lime wedges, for serving

Preparation:
1. Grease the cooking surface of the griddle with cooking spray.
2. Turn on the 4 burners and turn their knobs to medium heat.
3. Let the Griddle preheat for 5 minutes.
4. Mix together the water, lime juice, garlic, sugar, salt, and peppercorns in a suitable bowl.
5. Put the pork to your marinade and let sit at room temperature for 1 hour or refrigerate, covered, for up to 4 hours. Just before cooking, remove the pork from the marinade and pat dry.
6. Cook the pork over high heat for 1 minute, then rotate 45 degrees and then let it cook for another minute.
Flip and repeat on the other side.
7. Transfer to a serving platter in a high pile, sprinkle with salt, and serve with lemon wedges.
8. Serve.

Per Serving: Calories: 381; Fat: 21g; Sodium: 561mg; Carbs: 21g; Fiber 6.1g; Sugar: 5g; Protein: 32g

Pork Ribs with Low-sugar Ketchup

Prep time: 15 minutes | Cook time: 2 hrs | Serves: 6

Ingredients:
- 3 pounds country-style pork ribs
- 1 cup low-sugar ketchup
- ½ cup water
- ¼ cup onion, chopped
- ¼ cup cider vinegar or wine vinegar
- ¼ cup light molasses
- 2 tablespoons worcestershire sauce
- 2 teaspoons chili powder
- 2 garlic cloves, minced

Preparation:
1. Mix the ketchup, water, onion, vinegar, molasses, worcestershire sauce, chili powder, and garlic in a saucepan Let this mixture to a boil then cook for 15 minutes on a simmer with occasional stirring.
2. Grease the cooking surface of the griddle with cooking spray.
3. Turn on the 4 burners and turn their knobs to medium-low heat.
4. Let the Griddle preheat for 5 minutes.
5. Place ribs, bone-side down, on griddle and then let it cook for 1-½ to 2 hours, brushing occasionally with sauce.
6. Serve with remaining sauce and enjoy!

Per Serving: Calories: 392; Fat: 32g; Sodium: 354mg; Carbs: 14g; Fiber 1.2g; Sugar: 5g; Protein: 31g

Garlic Lamb Chops

Prep time: 15 minutes | Cook time: 10 minutes | Serves: 2

Ingredients:
- 1 teaspoon salt
- ½ teaspoon black pepper
- 1 teaspoon minced garlic
- 8 tablespoons butter, room temperature
- 1 pack french lamb ribs
- ¼ cup fresh herbs of your choice, chopped

Preparation:
1. Mix the salt, pepper, garlic, plus butter in a suitable bowl until well combined.
2. Brush all over the lamb.
3. Grease the cooking surface of the griddle with cooking spray.
4. Turn on the 4 burners and turn their knobs to medium heat.
5. Let the Griddle preheat for 5 minutes.
6. Place the lamb on the griddle top.
7. Sear and then let it cook for 5 minutes per side.
8. Serve with chopped herbs.

Per Serving: Calories: 338; Fat: 12g; Sodium: 521mg; Carbs: 14g; Fiber 5.1g; Sugar: 3g; Protein: 27g

Rosemary Flank Steak

Prep time: 15 minutes | Cook time: 20 minutes | Serves: 4

Ingredients:
- 2 (8-ounce) flank steaks

Marinade:
- 1 tablespoon olive oil
- 2 tablespoons fresh rosemary, chopped
- 4 garlic cloves, minced
- 2 teaspoons sea salt, to taste
- ¼ teaspoon black pepper

Preparation:
1. Add marinade fixings to a food processor or blender and pulse until garlic and rosemary are pulverized.
2. Use a fork to pierce the steaks 10 times on each side.
3. Rub each evenly with the marinade on both sides.
4. Put in a covered dish and refrigerate for at least 1 hour or overnight.
5. Grease the cooking surface of the griddle with cooking spray.
6. Turn on the 4 burners and turn their knobs to medium heat.
7. Let the Griddle preheat for 5 minutes.
8. Cook steaks for 5 minutes, flip, tent with foil, and then let it cook for about 3-4 minutes more.
9. Transfer meat to rest on a cutting board, cover with aluminum foil, for about 15 minutes.
10. Slice then serve immediately.

Per Serving: Calories: 416; Fat: 11g; Sodium: 501mg; Carbs: 16g; Fiber 2.1g; Sugar: 2.2g; Protein: 28g

Lamb Burgers in Sauce with Squash Salad

Prep time: 15 minutes | Cook time: 20 minutes | Serves: 4

Ingredients:
Summer squash salad:
Oil, for frying, plus 6 tablespoons
2 pounds (907 g) summer squash, sliced
8 radishes, cut paper-thin
4 jalapeño chiles, stemmed, seeded, and minced
Juice of 1 lemon (about 3 tablespoons)
6 tablespoons oil
1 teaspoon black pepper
½ teaspoon salt
2 tablespoons minced cilantro leaves

Feta–yogurt sauce:
½ cup crumbled feta cheese
½ cup plain whole-milk yogurt
1 garlic clove, minced
Juice and zest of ½ lemon
1 tablespoon minced fennel fronds
1 tablespoon minced parsley leaves
1 teaspoon black pepper
Lamb burgers
Oil, for coating
½ red onion, minced
2 garlic cloves, minced
1 pound (454 g) ground lamb
2 tablespoons chopped fennel fronds
2 tablespoons chopped parsley leaves
1 teaspoon ground cumin
1 teaspoon celery seed
¼ teaspoon ground cinnamon
Salt, for seasoning
4 hamburger buns, toasted

Preparation:
1. Put oil into your small sauté pan to a depth of ¼ inch. Put over high heat until the oil ripples.
2. Put ½ of the zucchini then fry until golden brown.
3. Remove using a slotted spoon then place on a plate lined with paper towels.
4. When it has cooled, add the fried zucchini to a suitable bowl with the remaining raw zucchini, radishes, and jalapeños.
5. Whisk the lemon juice, 6 tablespoons oil with the pepper and salt in a suitable bowl.
6. Put to the salad, tossing to coat. Sprinkle the cilantro on top.
7. To make the sauce, mix the feta and yogurt in a suitable bowl using a fork until smooth.
8. Add the garlic, lemon juice and zest, fennel, parsley, and pepper.
9. To make your burgers, coat the small sauté pan using oil.
10. Set over high heat and add the onion and garlic. Cook until they soften, then move it to a suitable bowl.
11. When your onion and garlic are no longer hot, add the lamb, fennel, parsley, cumin, celery seed, plus cinnamon then mix well with your hands.
12. Divide the mixture into 4 patties.
13. Grease the cooking surface of the griddle with cooking spray.
14. Turn on the 4 burners and turn their knobs to high heat.
15. Let the Griddle preheat for 5 minutes.
16. Cook over high heat within 1½ to 2 minutes per side.
17. Adjust to medium heat and then let it cook to the desired doneness, 2 to 4 minutes more per side.
18. Serve with the salad.

Per Serving: Calories: 327; Fat: 22g; Sodium: 421mg; Carbs: 10g; Fiber 4.1g; Sugar: 2g; Protein: 31g

Vegetables and Ham Hock

Prep time: 15 minutes | Cook time: 2 hrs. 45 minutes | Serves: 6

Ingredients:
1½ pounds smoked ham hocks
Oil, for coating
1 white onion, minced
2 carrots, minced
2 celery stalks, minced
1 pound dried black beans
3-inch-long piece daikon radish
4 bay leaves
1 tablespoon cumin seeds, crushed or ground
10 cups water
Salt, for seasoning

Preparation:
1. Grease the cooking surface of the griddle with cooking spray.
2. Turn on the 4 burners and turn their knobs to high heat.
3. Let the Griddle preheat for 5 minutes.
4. Cook the ham hocks over griddle top until deeply browned, 5 to 10 minutes per side.
5. Add the onion, carrots, and celery and then let it cook until the onions start to brown, about 10 minutes.
6. Transfer the ham hocks, beans, radish (if using), bay leaves, cumin, and water to a pan.
7. Place this pan on one side of the griddle top and switch to medium heat.
8. Cook for at least 2 hours over medium heat, until the beans are very soft.
9. Remove the ham hocks and, when the ham is cool enough, take the meat from the bones, discarding the bones and skin.
10. Return the meat to the pot and season by adding salt.

Per Serving: Calories: 327; Fat: 22g; Sodium: 421mg; Carbs: 10g; Fiber 4.1g; Sugar: 2g; Protein: 31g

Lamb Chops with Spiced New Potatoes

Prep time: 15 minutes | Cook time: 6 minutes | Serves: 4

Ingredients:
2 tablespoons olive oil
1 large clove of garlic, crushed
1 heap cumin seeds, crushed
8 lamb chops
Black pepper and salt to taste
Chopped mint leaves
3 lbs. Cooked potatoes, halved

Preparation:
1. Grease the cooking surface of the griddle with cooking spray.
2. Turn on the 4 burners and turn their knobs to medium heat.
3. Let the Griddle preheat for 5 minutes.
4. Sauté the garlic and cumin seeds on the griddle top until toasted.
5. Add in the lamb chops and sear for 3 minutes on each side.
6. Season by adding black pepper and salt to taste.
7. Garnish with mint leaves and serve with cooked potatoes.

Per Serving: Calories: 381; Fat: 21g; Sodium: 561mg; Carbs: 21g; Fiber 6.1g; Sugar: 5g; Protein: 32g

Paprika Pork Chops

Prep time: 15 minutes | Cook time: 15 minutes | Serves: 4

Ingredients:
4 pork chops
1 tablespoon paprika
½ teaspoon ground cumin
½ teaspoon dried sage
½ teaspoon salt
½ teaspoon black pepper
½ teaspoon garlic powder
¼ teaspoon cayenne pepper, to taste
1 tablespoon butter
1 tablespoon vegetable oil

Preparation:
1. In a medium bowl, combine the paprika, cumin, sage, salt, pepper, garlic, and cayenne pepper.
2. Grease the cooking surface of the griddle with cooking oil and butter.
3. Turn on the 4 burners and turn their knobs to medium heat.
4. Let the Griddle preheat for 5 minutes.
5. Rub the pork chops with a generous amount of the seasoning rub.
6. Place the chops on the griddle and then let it cook for 4 to 5 minutes.
7. Turn the pork chops and continue cooking an additional 4 minutes.
8. Remove the pork chops from your griddle and allow to rest 5 minutes before serving.
9. Serve.

Per Serving: Calories: 392; Fat: 32g; Sodium: 354mg; Carbs: 14g; Fiber 1.2g; Sugar: 5g; Protein: 31g

Tasty Beef Burger Patties

Prep time: 10 minutes | Cook time: 12 minutes | Serves: 6

Ingredients:
2 pounds ground beef
2 tablespoons Worcestershire sauce
¾ cup onion, chopped
½ teaspoon black pepper
½ teaspoon salt

Preparation:
1. In a suitable mixing bowl, mix well all of the ingredients and stir until well blended
2. Preheat the Griddle by turning all its knob to medium-heat setting.
3. Grease the griddle top with cooking spray.
4. Form patties from the mixture and cook for 5 minutes per side on the hot griddle top.
5. Enjoy.

Per Serving: Calories: 292; Fat: 9.4 g; Sodium: 349 mg; Carbs: 2.5g; Fiber: 0.4g; Sugar: 1.6g; Protein: 46.6g

Butter Pork Chops

Prep time: 15 minutes | Cook time: 20 minutes | Serves: 6

Ingredients:
- 4 to 6 pork chops
- 4 garlic cloves, chopped
- ½ cup olive oil
- ½ cup soy sauce
- ½ teaspoon garlic powder
- ½ teaspoon salt
- ½ black pepper, to taste
- ¼ cup butter

Preparation:
1. In a large zipper lock bag, combine the garlic, olive oil, soy sauce, and garlic powder.
2. Put the pork chops then ensure the marinade coats the chops. Set aside for 30 minutes.
3. Put 2 tablespoons of olive oil plus 2 tablespoons of butter to the griddle.
4. Grease the cooking surface of the griddle with cooking spray.
5. Turn on the 4 burners and turn their knobs to medium heat.
6. Let the Griddle preheat for 5 minutes.
7. Add the chops to the griddle at a time, making sure they are not crowded.
8. Put another 2 tablespoons of butter to your griddle and then let it cook the chops for 4 minutes. Cook an additional 4 minutes.
9. Remove the chops from the griddle and spread the remaining butter over them.
10. Serve after resting for 5 minutes.

Per Serving: Calories: 381; Fat: 21g; Sodium: 561mg; Carbs: 21g; Fiber 6.1g; Sugar: 5g; Protein: 32g

Simple Lamb Chops

Prep time: 15 minutes | Cook time: 6 minutes | Serves: 6

Ingredients:
- 6 lamb chops
- 2 tablespoons garlic powder
- 1 tablespoon fresh rosemary
- leaves
- Black pepper and salt to taste
- 2 tablespoons olive oil

Preparation:
1. Place lamb chops in a suitable bowl and season by adding garlic powder, rosemary leaves, salt, and pepper.
2. Grease the cooking surface of the griddle with cooking oil.
3. Turn on the 4 burners and turn their knobs to medium heat.
4. Let the Griddle preheat for 5 minutes.
5. Sear the lamb chops for 3 minutes per side on the griddle top.
6. Serve.

Per Serving: Calories: 318; Fat: 15g; Sodium: 521mg; Carbs: 14g; Fiber 5.1g; Sugar: 3g; Protein: 27g

Oyster Sesame Pork Shoulder

Prep time: 10 minutes | Cook time: 20 minutes | Serves: 6-8

Ingredients:
- 1 (5 pounds) Boston butt pork shoulder
- For the marinade:
- 2 tablespoons garlic, minced
- 1 large piece ginger, peeled and chopped
- 1 cup hoisin sauce
- ¾ cup fish sauce
- For the glaze:
- ¾ cup dark brown sugar
- ⅔ cup honey
- ⅔ cup Shaoxing
- ½ cup chili oil
- ⅓ cup oyster sauce
- ⅓ cup sesame oil
- 1 tablespoon light molasses

Preparation:
1. In a blender, puree the marinade, reserving 1 ½ cup for the glaze, then cover and chill.
2. Pour the remaining marinade into a large plastic bag that can be sealed.
3. Place the pork shoulder in the bag and marinate for 8 hours in the refrigerator.
4. Remove the pork from the marinade and drain any excess.
5. Whisk the glaze ingredients, reserving the marinade, until the sugar is dissolved.
6. Preheat the Griddle by turning all its knob to medium-heat setting.
7. Grease the griddle top with cooking spray.
8. Sear pork for 4 minutes per side while basting with glaze.
9. Transfer to a cutting board and slice 14" thick against the grain then serve.

Per Serving: Calories: 1167; Fat: 82.7 g; Sodium: 2871 mg; Carbs: 54.9g; Fiber: 1g; Sugar: 45.9g; Protein: 51g

Rosemary Lamb Chop Slices

Prep time: 15 minutes | Cook time: 10 minutes | Serves: 8

Ingredients:
- 8 lamb chops
- 1 teaspoon salt
- 1 tablespoon chopped rosemary
- leaves
- 1 tablespoon garlic powder

Preparation:
1. Season those lamb chops with salt, rosemary leaves, and garlic powder.
2. Grease the cooking surface of the griddle with cooking spray.
3. Turn on the 4 burners and turn their knobs to medium heat.
4. Let the Griddle preheat for 5 minutes.
5. Sear the lamb chops on the griddle top for 5 minutes on each side.
6. Allow lamb chops to rest before slicing. Serve.

Per Serving: Calories: 449; Fat: 21g; Sodium: 421mg; Carbs: 16g; Fiber 4.1g; Sugar: 3.2g; Protein: 27g

Rib Roast with Russet Potatoes

Prep time: 15 minutes | Cook time: 3 hrs. minutes | Serves: 8

Ingredients:
- 1 (4-pounds) standing rib roast
- Black pepper and salt, for seasoning
- 1 apple
- 2 large shallots
- 1 large bunch mixed herbs
- 8 large russet potatoes

Preparation:
1. Flavor the roast generously with black pepper and salt and let it sit, covered, at room temperature for 2 hours before cooking.
2. Grease the cooking surface of the griddle with cooking spray.
3. Turn on the 4 burners and turn their knobs to medium heat.
4. Let the Griddle preheat for 5 minutes.
5. Place the roast bone side down over medium heat and put the apple and shallots directly onto the griddle.
6. After about 30 minutes, start turning the roast occasionally, so that every exposed part gets deeply browned
7. As the roast browns and the; Fat: renders from the surface, brush the roast firmly with the herb broom, allowing some of the leaves to fall onto the roast.
8. When the shallot and apple are very soft and almost falling apart, use tongs to rub them all over the roast as it cooks.
9. After about 1 hour, put the potatoes onto the griddle under the roast and then let it cook for 2 hrs.
10. Serve.

Per Serving: Calories: 317; Fat: 32g; Sodium: 311mg; Carbs: 12g; Fiber 3.1g; Sugar: 4g; Protein: 22g

Mayo Filet Mignon Steaks

Prep time: 15 minutes | Cook time: 10 minutes | Serves: 4

Ingredients:
- 4 (8-ounce) filet mignon steaks, 2 inches thick
- Herb mayo:
- ½ cup mixed fresh herbs, minced, such as parsley, basil, and mint
- 2 tablespoons minced fennel fronds
- Black pepper and salt, for coating
- ½ cup butter
- 1 teaspoon lemon zest
- 1 cup mayonnaise
- Salt, for seasoning

Preparation:
1. Grease the cooking surface of the griddle with cooking spray.
2. Turn on the 4 burners and turn their knobs to medium heat.
3. Let the Griddle preheat for 5 minutes.
4. Flavor the steaks generously with black pepper and salt.
5. Put the butter, and when it starts to smell nutty and turn color, add the steaks and turn them in the butter to coat.
6. Sear on all sides until a dark crust forms, 2 to 3 minutes per side.
7. Transfer to the griddle over medium heat and let cook, turning often, until an instant-read meat thermometer, put in the thickest part of 1 steak, reads 125 degrees F (52ºC).
8. Transfer to a platter and let the steaks rest for 10 minutes before serving.
9. While the meat is cooking, make the mayo: in a suitable bowl, mix the herbs, fennel, and lemon zest into the mayonnaise then flavor it with salt. Serve the steaks with the mayo on the side.
10. Serve.

Per Serving: Calories: 395; Fat: 15g; Sodium: 521mg; Carbs: 14g; Fiber 5.1g; Sugar: 3g; Protein: 27g

Pork Loin with Chile and Pineapple Slices

Prep time: 15 minutes | Cook time: 45 minutes | Serves: 8

Ingredients:
- 2 ripe pineapples, peeled
- 2 red onions, peeled, quartered, and sliced
- 8 chiles de árbol
- 2 cups sugar
- 4 cups vinegar
- 1 tablespoon salt
- Salt, for coating
- 1 pork loin roast, boneless (3 pounds)

Preparation:
1. Dice the pineapples into small pieces and add to a large stockpot with the onions, chiles, sugar, vinegar, and salt.
2. Place over medium heat and let the mixture simmer, stirring occasionally for 1 hour.
3. Flavor it with more salt and sugar, if needed.
4. Rub salt all over the pork roast and let it sit, uncovered, in the fridge within 4 hours and up to 24 hours. Remove the roast an hour before you start cooking.
5. Place it over high heat and brown all sides of the meat, 5 to 10 minutes per side.
6. Move to medium heat and then let it cook, with occasional stirring, until an instant-read meat thermometer, placed in the thickest part of your roast, reads 145 degrees F.
7. Move it to your cutting board and let the roast rest for 20 minutes before slicing into serving pieces.
8. Serve with the jam.

Per Serving: Calories: 401; Fat: 13g; Sodium: 161mg; Carbs: 10g; Fiber 3.1g; Sugar: 2g; Protein: 25g

Omelet with Smoky Bacon Strips

Prep time: 15 minutes | Cook time: 15 minutes | Serves: 2

Ingredients:
- 6 strips bacon
- 6 eggs, beaten
- ¼ pound gruyere, shredded
- 1 tablespoon Chives, completely chopped
- 1 teaspoon black pepper
- 1 teaspoon salt

Preparation:
1. Grease the cooking surface of the griddle with cooking spray.
2. Turn on the 4 burners and turn their knobs to medium heat.
3. Let the Griddle preheat for 5 minutes.
4. Sprinkle salt to the beaten eggs and set aside for 10 minutes.
5. Add the bacon strips to griddle and then let it cook until brown then transfer to a plate lined with paper towel.
6. Once the bacon has drained, chop into small pieces. Add the eggs to the griddle in 2 even pools.
7. Cook until the bottom of the eggs starts to firm up stiff.
8. Add the gruyere to the eggs and then let it cook until the cheese has started to melt and the eggs turn out to brown.
9. Place the bacon pieces and use a spatula to flip 1 ½ of the omelet onto the other ½.
10. Remove from the griddle to a platter, season by adding pepper and chives.
11. Serve.

Per Serving: Calories: 395; Fat: 21g; Sodium: 451mg; Carbs: 17g; Fiber 4.1g; Sugar: 1.2g; Protein: 24g

Strip Steak with Worcestershire Sauce

Prep time: 15 minutes | Cook time: 15 minutes | Serves: 6

Ingredients:
- Poblano worcestershire sauce:
- 3 poblano chiles
- 2 white or red unpeeled onions, halved
- Oil and salt, for coating
- 3 tablespoons vinegar
- 2 tablespoons soy sauce
- 1 tablespoon lime juice
- 1 tablespoon roasted garlic
- 1 tablespoon honey
- 2 pounds new york strip steak

Preparation:
1. Grease the cooking surface of the griddle with cooking spray.
2. Turn on the 4 burners and turn their knobs to medium heat.
3. Let the Griddle preheat for 5 minutes.
4. To make the sauce: toss the poblanos and onions in oil and salt.
5. Cook them on the griddle until blackened, for about 10 minutes.
6. Transfer with tongs to a suitable bowl, then tightly cover with plastic wrap to allow them to steam in their own heat and to cool enough to handle.
7. Peel the skin from the chiles with your fingers, but don't worry if some burnt bits remain.
8. Remove and discard the stems and seeds. Cut the peel and root end from the onions.
9. Place the chiles and onions in a suitable blender together with the vinegar, soy sauce, lime juice, garlic, and honey and blend until completely smooth.
10. The sauce can be stored in a covered container in the refrigerator for up to 2 weeks.
11. Coat the steaks generously with the sauce and let them marinate for 1 hour.
12. Place the steaks over high heat and then let it cook about 5 minutes per side.
13. Slice against the grain and serve, passing additional sauce at the table.

Per Serving: Calories: 382; Fat: 21g; Sodium: 451mg; Carbs: 17g; Fiber 4.1g; Sugar: 1.2g; Protein: 24g

Palatable Pork Tenderloins

Prep time: 15 minutes | Cook time: 10 minutes | Serves: 4

Ingredients:
- 2 pork tenderloins, trimmed
- 1 teaspoon annatto powder
- Olive oil

For the marinade:
- 2 oranges, juiced
- 2 lemons, juiced, or more to taste
- 2 limes, juiced, or more to taste
- 6 garlic cloves, minced
- 1 teaspoon ground cumin
- ½ teaspoon cayenne pepper, to taste
- ½ teaspoon dried oregano
- ½ teaspoon black pepper

Preparation:
1. Combine marinade fixings in a suitable mixing bowl and whisk until well-blended.
2. Cut the tenderloins in ½ crosswise; cut each piece in ½ lengthwise.
3. Place pieces in marinade and thoroughly coat with the mixture.
4. Wrap with plastic wrap then refrigerate within 4 to 6 hours.
5. Grease the cooking surface of the griddle with cooking spray.
6. Turn on the 4 burners and turn their knobs to medium-high heat.
7. Let the Griddle preheat for 5 minutes.
8. Transfer pieces of pork from marinade to a paper-towel-lined bowl to absorb most of the moisture.
9. Discard paper towels. Drizzle olive oil and a bit more annatto powder on the pork.
10. Place pieces evenly spaced on griddle; cook 4 to 5 minutes.
11. Turn then cook on the other side within 4 or 5 minutes.
12. Transfer onto a serving platter and allow meat to rest about 5 minutes before serving.
13. Serve.

Per Serving: Calories: 317; Fat: 32g; Sodium: 311mg; Carbs: 12g; Fiber 3.1g; Sugar: 4g; Protein: 22g

Kielbasa with Jalapeño Chiles

Prep time: 15 minutes | Cook time: 25 minutes | Serves: 4

Ingredients:
- 12 jalapeño chiles, stemmed, halved lengthwise, and seeded
- Oil, for coating
- 1 cup vinegar
- 1 tablespoon honey
- 2 teaspoons salt, to taste
- 1½ pounds kielbasa, cut into 5-inch lengths

Preparation:
1. Grease the cooking surface of the griddle with cooking spray.
2. Turn on the 4 burners and turn their knobs to medium heat.
3. Let the Griddle preheat for 5 minutes.
4. Toss the jalapeños with the oil, place over medium heat, and griddle until charred within 2 minutes per side.
5. Using tongs, transfer the jalapeños to a suitable bowl, then tightly cover using a plastic wrap to allow them to steam in their own heat within 15 minutes.
6. Meanwhile, mix together the vinegar, honey, and salt in a suitable bowl until the salt dissolves.
7. Mince the jalapeños and combine with the vinegar mixture.
8. To cook the kielbasa, place over medium heat and then let it cook, turning often, until it is charred and hot throughout, about 10 minutes.
9. Serve with the relish.

Per Serving: Calories: 397; Fat: 21g; Sodium: 711mg; Carbs: 8g; Fiber 3.1g; Sugar: 4g; Protein: 22g

Chapter 7 Beef, Pork and Lamb Recipes | 81

Apricot Jam Lamb Kabobs

Prep time: 15 minutes | Cook time: 10 minutes | Serves: 4

Ingredients:
2 lbs. Lamb, cut into ⅛-inch strips
6 garlic cloves, minced
½ cup olive oil
1 tablespoon Coriander
2 teaspoon Cumin
Zest and juice of 2 lemons
2 tablespoons Fresh mint, chopped
3 teaspoon salt
2 teaspoon black pepper
Apricot jam

Preparation:
1. Mix all of the fixings except for the apricot jam together, and place in the refrigerator overnight.
2. Put all the lamb pieces onto skewers, leaving space between the pieces.
3. Grease the cooking surface of the griddle with cooking spray.
4. Turn on the 4 burners and turn their knobs to medium heat.
5. Let the Griddle preheat for 5 minutes.
6. Sear the skewers for 3–4 minutes per side until cooked through.
7. Brush the apricot jam on the lamb, and griddle for less than 1 minute on each side to set the glaze.
8. Let the meat relax within 5 minutes before serving.
9. Serve.
Per Serving: Calories: 327; Fat: 22g; Sodium: 421mg; Carbs: 10g; Fiber 4.1g; Sugar: 2g; Protein: 31g

Pork Chops with Pineapple and Bacon

Prep time: 15 minutes | Cook time: 60 minutes | Serves: 6

Ingredients:
1 large whole pineapple
6 pork chops
Glaze
¼ cup honey
⅛ teaspoon cayenne pepper, to
12 slices thick-cut bacon

taste

Preparation:
1. Grease the cooking surface of the griddle with cooking spray.
2. Turn on the 4 burners and turn their knobs to medium heat.
3. Let the Griddle preheat for 5 minutes.
4. Slice off the top and bottom of your pineapple, and peel the pineapple, cutting the skin off in strips.
5. Cut pineapple flesh into 6 quarters.
6. Wrap each pineapple section with a bacon slice; secure each end with a toothpick.
7. Brush quarters with honey and sprinkle with cayenne pepper.
8. Put the quarters on the griddle, flipping when bacon is cooked so that both sides are evenly griddleed.
9. While pineapple quarters are cooking, coat pork chops with honey and cayenne pepper. Set on griddle.
10. Tent with foil and then let it cook for 20 minutes.
11. Flip, and continue cooking an additional 10 to 20 minutes or until chops are fully cooked.
12. Serve each chop with a pineapple quarter on the side.
Per Serving: Calories: 339; Fat: 13g; Sodium: 421mg; Carbs: 16g; Fiber 4.1g; Sugar: 3.2g; Protein: 27g

Sweet and Sour Pork Chops

Prep time: 15 minutes | Cook time: 15 minutes | Serves: 4

Ingredients:
¼ cup honey
2 cups warm water
Salt and oil, for coating
4 (12-ounces) bone-in pork rib chops, 1 inch thick

Preparation:
1. Combine the honey and water in a quart jar, cover with a cloth and refrigerate for at least 24 hours.
2. Grease the cooking surface of the griddle with cooking spray.
3. Turn on the 4 burners and turn their knobs to medium heat.
4. Let the Griddle preheat for 5 minutes.
5. Rub the chops well with the salt and oil and let them sit for 30 minutes.
6. Put the pork chops and then let it cook within 2 minutes per side, until deeply browned.
7. Remove the chops to a plate. Deglaze the griddle with the honey vinegar and, then return the pork chops to the pan.
8. Continue reducing the honey vinegar and baste the pork with it, until it reduces to the consistency of maple syrup. Let the pork chops rest within 5 minutes before serving.
9. Serve.
Per Serving: Calories: 385; Fat: 11g; Sodium: 421mg; Carbs: 16g; Fiber 4.1g; Sugar: 3.2g; Protein: 27g

Oregano Lamb Chops

Prep time: 15 minutes | Cook time: 15 minutes | Serves: 4

Ingredients:
8 lamb chops
3 tablespoons lemon juice
4 tablespoons olive oil
3 garlic cloves, minced
2 teaspoon dried oregano
½ teaspoon black pepper
1 teaspoon salt

Preparation:
1. Add garlic, oregano, lemon juice, oil, pepper, and salt in a suitable bowl and mix well.
2. Add lamb chops to the bowl and coat well with marinade and set aside for 30 minutes.
3. Grease the cooking surface of the griddle with cooking spray.
4. Turn on the 4 burners and turn their knobs to medium heat.
5. Let the Griddle preheat for 5 minutes.
6. Place marinated lamb chops on preheated griddle top and then let it cook for 3-4 minutes on each side.
7. Serve.
Per Serving: Calories: 376; Fat: 13g; Sodium: 421mg; Carbs: 16g; Fiber 4.1g; Sugar: 3.2g; Protein: 27g

Honey Boneless Pork Chops

Prep time: 15 minutes | Cook time: 25 minutes | Serves: 6

Ingredients:
6 (4-ounce) boneless pork chops
¼ cup organic honey
1-2 tablespoons soy sauce
2 tablespoons olive oil
1 tablespoon rice mirin

Preparation:
1. Combine honey, soy sauce, oil, and rice mirin and whisk until well-combined.
2. Add sauce and pork chops to a large sealable plastic bag and marinate for 1 hour.
3. Grease the cooking surface of the griddle with cooking spray.
4. Turn on the 4 burners and turn their knobs to medium heat.
5. Let the Griddle preheat for 5 minutes.
6. Cook for 4 to 5 minutes on griddle top, or until the pork chop easily releases from the griddle.
7. Flip and continue to cook until internal temperature reaches 145°F (63°C).
8. Serve.
Per Serving: Calories: 339; Fat: 13g; Sodium: 421mg; Carbs: 16g; Fiber 4.1g; Sugar: 3.2g; Protein: 27g

Pork Chops with Apple and Herbs

Prep time: 15 minutes | Cook time: 25 minutes | Serves: 4

Ingredients:
4 bone-in pork chops
2 honey crisp apples, peeled, cored and chopped
⅓ cup orange juice
1 teaspoon chopped fresh rosemary
1 teaspoon chopped fresh sage
Sea black pepper and salt, to taste

Preparation:
1. Add the apples, herbs and orange juice to a saucepan.
2. Simmer over medium heat until your apples are tender for 10 to 12 minutes.
3. Season pork chops with black pepper and salt.
4. Grease the cooking surface of the griddle with cooking spray.
5. Turn on the 4 burners and turn their knobs to medium heat.
6. Let the Griddle preheat for 5 minutes.
7. Put on the griddle then cook until the pork chop releases from the griddle within 4 minutes.
8. Flip and then cook on the other side within 3 minutes. Transfer to a cutting board and tent with foil.
9. Top with apple compote and serve!
Per Serving: Calories: 395; Fat: 15g; Sodium: 521mg; Carbs: 14g; Fiber 5.1g; Sugar: 3g; Protein: 27g

Mediterranean Pork Tenderloin

Prep time: 15 minutes | Cook time: 30 minutes | Serves: 4

Ingredients:
- 1 pound pork tenderloin
- 1 tablespoon olive oil
- 2 teaspoons dried oregano
- ¾ teaspoon lemon black pepper
- 1 teaspoon garlic powder
- ¼ cup parmesan cheese, grated
- 3 tablespoons olive tapenade

Preparation:
1. Place pork on a large piece of plastic wrap.
2. Rub tenderloin with oil, and sprinkle oregano, garlic powder, and lemon pepper evenly over entire tenderloin.
3. Wrap it tightly in the plastic wrap then refrigerate within 2 hours.
4. Transfer pork to cutting board, remove plastic wrap, and make a lengthwise cut through center of tenderloin, opening meat so it lies flat, but do not cut all the way through.
5. Combine tapenade and parmesan in a suitable mixing bowl; rub into the center of the tenderloin and fold meat back together.
6. Tie together with twine in 2-inch intervals.
7. Grease the cooking surface of the griddle with cooking spray.
8. Turn on the 4 burners and turn their knobs to medium heat.
9. Let the Griddle preheat for 5 minutes.
10. Sear tenderloin for 20 minutes, turning once.
11. Transfer tenderloin to cutting board.
12. Tent with foil; let rest within 10 minutes. Remove string and cut into ¼-inch-thick slices and serve.
13. Serve.

Per Serving: Calories: 318; Fat: 15g; Sodium: 521mg; Carbs: 14g; Fiber 5.1g; Sugar: 3g; Protein: 27g

Lemon Lamb Chops with Apricot

Prep time: 15 minutes | Cook time: 19 minutes | Serves: 4

Ingredients:
- Apricot–chamomile chutney
- Oil, for coating
- 1 white or red onion, chopped
- 1 cup dried apricots, chopped
- 1 tablespoon dried chamomile, plus more for garnish
- 2 whole star anise
- 3 green or white cardamom pods, with seeds removed
- ¼ cup honey, plus more for garnish
- 1 cup water
- 2 tablespoons chopped mint leaves
- 2 tablespoons chopped toasted unsalted almonds
- Juice of 1 lemon (about 3 tablespoons)
- 2½ pounds (1.1 kg) lamb loin chops, at least 1 inch thick
- Salt, for seasoning

Preparation:
1. Grease the cooking surface of the griddle with cooking spray.
2. Turn on the 4 burners and turn their knobs to high heat.
3. Let the Griddle preheat for 5 minutes.
4. Coat a sauté pan with oil and place over medium heat.
5. Put the onion then cook until tender, about 5 minutes.
6. Add the apricots, chamomile, star anise, cardamom, honey, and water.
7. Cook until almost all of its liquid has cooked off and the mixture is thick and syrupy.
8. Discard the star anise. Stir in the mint, almonds, and lemon juice.
9. Score the; Fat:ty edge of each lamb chop by cutting shallow crosshatched slices into it.
10. Salt the chops well, then place them over high heat and sear on all sides about 2 minutes per side.
11. Move to medium heat and then let it cook, turning often, until just past medium-rare for about 5 minutes more in total.
12. Transfer to a serving platter and drizzle with honey, sprinkle with chamomile, and serve with warm chutney alongside.
13. Serve.

Per Serving: Calories: 416; Fat: 11g; Sodium: 501mg; Carbs: 16g; Fiber 2.1g; Sugar: 2.2g; Protein: 28g

Thyme Lamb Racks

Prep time: 15 minutes | Cook time: 35 minutes | Serves: 6

Ingredients:
- 4 teaspoons vegetable oil
- 4 teaspoons minced fresh rosemary
- 2 teaspoons minced fresh thyme
- 2 garlic cloves, minced
- 2 (1¾-pound) racks of lamb, trimmed and frenched
- Black pepper and salt, to taste

Preparation:
1. Grease the cooking surface of the griddle with cooking spray.
2. Turn on the 4 burners and turn their knobs to medium heat.
3. Let the Griddle preheat for 5 minutes.
4. Rub the lamb with oil and all the spices, then place in the griddle.
5. Flip the lamb once cooked halfway through.
6. Serve.

Per Serving: Calories: 317; Fat: 32g; Sodium: 311mg; Carbs: 12g; Fiber 3.1g; Sugar: 4g; Protein: 22g

Seasoned Lamb Patties

Prep time: 15 minutes | Cook time: 15 minutes | Serves: 4

Ingredients:
- 1 lb. Ground lamb
- 5 basil leaves, minced
- 10 mint leaves, minced
- ¼ cup fresh parsley, chopped
- 1 teaspoon dried oregano
- 1 cup feta cheese, crumbled
- 1 tablespoon garlic, minced
- 1 jalapeno pepper, minced
- ¼ teaspoon black pepper
- ½ teaspoon kosher salt, to taste

Preparation:
1. Grease the cooking surface of the griddle with cooking spray.
2. Turn on the 4 burners and turn their knobs to medium heat.
3. Let the Griddle preheat for 5 minutes.
4. Add all the fixings into the mixing bowl and mix until well combined.
5. Make 4 equal shape patties from meat mixture.
6. Place onto the preheated griddle top and then let it cook for 4 minutes on each side.
7. Serve.

Per Serving: Calories: 366; Fat: 13g; Sodium: 421mg; Carbs: 16g; Fiber 4.1g; Sugar: 3.2g; Protein: 27g

Dijon Pork Tenderloin

Prep time: 15 minutes | Cook time: 4 hrs | Serves: 6

Ingredients:
- 2 (1 lb.) Pork tenderloins
- 2 tablespoons dijon mustard
- 1-½ teaspoons smoked paprika
- 1 teaspoon salt
- 2 tablespoons olive oil

Preparation:
1. Combine the mustard and paprika in a suitable bowl.
2. Rub the tenderloins with the mustard mixture, making sure they are evenly coated.
3. Grease the cooking surface of the griddle with cooking spray.
4. Turn on the 4 burners and turn their knobs to medium heat.
5. Let the Griddle preheat for 5 minutes.
6. Place the tenderloins on the griddle and then let it cook until all sides are well browned
7. Remove the tenderloins from the griddle and rest 5 minutes before slicing and serving.
8. Serve.

Per Serving: Calories: 317; Fat: 32g; Sodium: 311mg; Carbs: 12g; Fiber 3.1g; Sugar: 4g; Protein: 22g

Cheese Strip Steak

Prep time: 15 minutes | Cook time: 10 minutes | Serves: 4

Ingredients:
- 1 (24-ounces) dry-aged new york strip steak
- Black pepper and salt, for coating
- ½ cup blue cheese
- 2 tablespoons oil

Preparation:
1. Grease the cooking surface of the griddle with cooking spray.
2. Turn on the 4 burners and turn their knobs to high heat.
3. Let the Griddle preheat for 5 minutes.
4. Pat your steak dry and coat with black pepper and salt. Let sit for 20 to 30 minutes.
5. Place the steak over high heat for 5 minutes, then flip and repeat.
6. Move to medium heat and then let it cook for another 2 to 3 minutes.
7. Combine the cheese and oil in a food processor and blend until smooth and fluffy, about 1 minute.
8. Slice the steak then top with the blue cheese mixture just before serving.
9. Serve.

Per Serving: Calories: 327; Fat: 22g; Sodium: 421mg; Carbs: 10g; Fiber 4.1g; Sugar: 2g; Protein: 31g

Chapter 7 Beef, Pork and Lamb Recipes | 83

Tangy Masala Lamb Chops

Prep time: 15 minutes | Cook time: 10 minutes | Serves: 4

Ingredients:
- 4 lamb chops
- Black pepper and salt, to taste
- 2 tablespoons curry powder
- 1 teaspoon red pepper flakes
- 1 small red onion, chopped
- 1 large tomato, chopped
- 1 cup greek yogurt
- Chopped coriander
- Lemon, sliced

Preparation:
1. Season those lamb chops with salt, pepper, curry powder, and red pepper flakes.
2. Grease the cooking surface of the griddle with cooking spray.
3. Turn on the 4 burners and turn their knobs to medium heat.
4. Let the Griddle preheat for 5 minutes.
5. Sear the lamb chops on griddle top for 3 to 5 minutes on each side.
6. Meanwhile, mix the red onion, tomatoes, yogurt, and coriander in a suitable bowl.
7. Serve your lamb chops with the yogurt mixture and slices of lemon.

Per Serving: Calories: 304; Fat: 14.9g; Sodium: 304mg; Carbs: 12g; Fiber 6g; Sugar: 2g; Protein: 21g

BBQ Lamb Chops

Prep time: 15 minutes | Cook time: 35 minutes | Serves: 4

Ingredients:
- Tomatillo barbecue sauce:
- 10 large tomatillos, peeled and rinsed
- 5 jalapeño chiles
- 2 cups vinegar
- 2 cups water
- ¾ cup sugar
- 1 tablespoon salt, to taste
- 2½ pounds lamb ribs, 1 inch thick
- Salt, for seasoning

Preparation:
1. Grease the cooking surface of the griddle with cooking spray.
2. Turn on the 4 burners and turn their knobs to medium heat.
3. Let the Griddle preheat for 5 minutes.
4. To make the sauce, put the tomatillos and jalapeños over medium heat, with occasional stirring, until slightly charred all over, about 8 minutes total.
5. Transfer to a plate and cut the tomatillos in ½, reserving the juice.
6. Halve the jalapeños lengthwise, remove the stems, and scrape out some of the seeds and veins.
7. Combine the tomatillos and jalapeños together with the vinegar, water, sugar, and salt in a medium saucepan.
8. Simmer over low heat within 20 to 30 minutes, until the sauce is reduced and slightly syrupy.
9. Cool the mixture slightly, transfer to a suitable blender, and blend until very smooth.
10. Salt the chops well, then place them over high heat and sear on all sides about 2 minutes per side.
11. Move to medium heat and then let it cook, turning often, until just past medium-rare.
12. Transfer to a serving platter and let rest for 5 minutes before serving, passing the sauce separately.
13. Serve.

Per Serving: Calories: 317; Fat: 32g; Sodium: 311mg; Carbs: 12g; Fiber 3.1g; Sugar: 4g; Protein: 22g

Tzatziki Lamb Chops

Prep time: 15 minutes | Cook time: 10 minutes | Serves: 6

Ingredients:
- 3 lbs. Lamb chops
- ½ cup olive oil
- ⅓ cup fresh lemon juice
- 3 teaspoon dried oregano
- 2 teaspoon chopped rosemary
- 4 cloves of garlic, minced
- Black pepper and salt to taste
- 1 large red onion, cut into rings
- Tzatziki sauce

Preparation:
1. Combine all the recipe's ingredients except the onions and tzatziki sauce in a ziploc bag and marinate in the fridge for at least 6 hours.
2. Sauté the onion rings until caramelized and golden in a skillet. Set aside.
3. Grease the cooking surface of the griddle with cooking spray.
4. Turn on the 4 burners and turn their knobs to medium heat.
5. Let the Griddle preheat for 5 minutes.
6. Sear the lamb chops on the griddle top and then let it cook for 5 minutes on each side.
7. Allow to rest for 5 minutes then serve with the caramelized onions and tzatziki sauce.

Per Serving: Calories: 395; Fat: 21g; Sodium: 451mg; Carbs: 17g; Fiber 4.1g; Sugar: 1.2g; Protein: 24g

Oregano Zucchini and Beef Skewers

Prep time: 10 minutes | Cook time: 15 minutes | Serves: 4

Ingredients:
- 1 pound beef sirloin tips
- For marinade:
- ¼ cup olive oil
- 1 jalapeno pepper
- ½ tablespoon lime juice
- 1½ tablespoon red wine vinegar
- 1 zucchini, cut into chunks
- 1 teaspoon dried oregano
- 2 garlic cloves
- 1 cup cilantro

Preparation:
1. In a blender, mix well all marinade ingredients and blend until smooth.
2. Into the mixing bowl, pour the mixed mixture.
3. Mix in the beef tips thoroughly and set aside for 30 minutes to marinate.
4. Preheat the Griddle by turning all its knob to medium-heat setting.
5. Grease the griddle top with cooking spray.
6. Thread the skewers with marinated meat tips and zucchini slices alternately.
7. Cook skewers for 7-8 minutes on the hot griddle top.
8. Serve and enjoy.

Per Serving: Calories: 404; Fat: 20.3 g; Sodium: 8 mg; Carbs: 3.4g; Fiber: 1g; Sugar: 1.2g; Protein: 53.4g

Lamb Kofta in Yogurt-Garlic Sauce

Prep time: 15 minutes | Cook time: 25 minutes | Serves: 6

Ingredients:
- Yogurt-garlic sauce:
- 1 cup plain whole-milk yogurt
- 2 tablespoons lemon juice
- Kofte:
- ½ cup pine nuts
- 4 garlic cloves, peeled
- 1½ teaspoons hot smoked paprika
- 1 teaspoon salt
- 1 teaspoon ground cumin
- ½ teaspoon black pepper
- ¼ teaspoon ground coriander
- ¼ teaspoon ground cloves
- 2 tablespoons tahini
- 1 garlic clove, minced
- ½ teaspoon salt
- ⅛ teaspoon ground nutmeg
- ⅛ teaspoon ground cinnamon
- 1½ pounds (680 g) ground lamb
- ½ cup grated onion, drained
- ⅓ cup minced fresh parsley
- ⅓ cup minced fresh mint
- 1½ teaspoons unflavored gelatin

Preparation:
1. Blend all the yogurt sauce ingredients in a suitable bowl for the sauce in a suitable bowl.
2. Add all the ingredients for kofte in a food processor for 2 minutes then make 1 inch meatballs out of it.
3. Grease the cooking surface of the griddle with cooking spray.
4. Turn on the 4 burners and turn their knobs to medium-low heat.
5. Let the Griddle preheat for 5 minutes.
6. Sear the kofte on the griddle top for 10 minutes per side.
7. Serve with the sauce.

Per Serving: Calories: 377; Fat: 15g; Sodium: 521mg; Carbs: 14g; Fiber 5.1g; Sugar: 3g; Protein: 27g

Lamb Kebabs with Lemon Wedges

Prep time: 15 minutes | Cook time: 20minutes | Serves: 6

Ingredients:
- Black pepper and salt, to taste
- 2¼ pounds boneless leg of lamb, diced
- 3 bell peppers, diced
- 1 large red onion, diced
- Lemon or lime wedges (optional)

Preparation:
1. Mix lamb with bell pepper, red onion and seasonings in a suitable bowl.
2. Cover and refrigerate the lamb for 30 minutes the veggies and lamb on the wooden skewers alternately.
3. Grease the cooking surface of the griddle with cooking spray.
4. Turn on the 4 burners and turn their knobs to medium heat.
5. Let the Griddle preheat for 5 minutes.
6. Place the skewers on the griddle and then let it cook for 5 minutes per side.
7. Serve.

Per Serving: Calories: 350; Fat: 13g; Sodium: 421mg; Carbs: 16g; Fiber 4.1g; Sugar: 3.2g; Protein: 27g

Cayenne Pork Chops in Worcestershire Sauce

Prep time: 10 minutes | Cook time: 10 minutes | Serves: 4

Ingredients:
- 4 pork chops
- 1 teaspoon garlic, minced
- ½ teaspoon black pepper
- 2 tablespoons Worcestershire sauce
- ¼ cup soy sauce
- ¼ cup olive oil
- ¼ teaspoon cayenne
- ½ teaspoon salt

Preparation:
1. In a suitable mixing dish, mix well the pork chops and the remaining ingredients.
2. Refrigerate 2-3 hours for marination.
3. Preheat the Griddle by turning all its knob to medium-heat setting.
4. Grease the griddle top with cooking spray.
5. Place pork chops on the hot griddle top and cook for 3-5 minutes per side.
6. Serve and enjoy.

Per Serving: Calories: 382; Fat: 32.5 g; Sodium: 1363 mg; Carbs: 3.2g; Fiber: 0.2g; Sugar: 1.9g; Protein: 19.1g

Griddle-Fried Marinated Flank Steaks

Prep time: 5 minutes | Cook time: 20 minutes | Serves: 4

Ingredients:
- 1 pound flank steak
- 1 white onion, sliced
- 1 roma tomato, sliced
- 1 cucumber, peeled and sliced
- ¼ cup crumbled feta cheese
- 4 6-inch pita pockets

For the marinade:
- ¼ cup olive oil
- 1 teaspoon dried oregano
- 1 teaspoon balsamic vinegar
- 1 teaspoon garlic powder
- ½ teaspoon salt and black pepper

For the sauce:
- 1 cup plain yogurt
- 2 tablespoons fresh dill, chopped
- 1 teaspoon garlic, minced
- 2 tablespoons lemon juice

Preparation:
1. Against the grain, cut the flank steak into thin strips.
2. In a large sealable plastic bag, mix well the marinade ingredients.
3. Add the sliced meat, seal, and shake to coat.
4. Marinate for almost 2 hours or overnight in the refrigerator.
5. Preheat the Griddle by turning all its knob to medium-heat setting.
6. Grease the griddle top with cooking spray.
7. In a suitable mixing bowl, mix well the sauce ingredients and set aside.
8. Spritz the pitas with water, wrap them in foil, and warm them on the griddle top.
9. Drizzle olive oil on the hot griddle top.
10. Place the marinated flank steak on the griddle. Cook for 5 minutes per side,
11. Take the pitas and slice them in half.
12. Place pitas on plates and fill with tomato, cucumber, onions, and beef.
13. Drizzle some yoghurt sauce over the meat and sprinkle with feta cheese.
14. Serve warm.

Per Serving: Calories: 324; Fat: 17.8 g; Sodium: 363 mg; Carbs: 8.9g; Fiber: 0.5g; Sugar: 1.9g; Protein: 36.6g

Cinnamon Pork Tenderloin with Harissa

Prep time: 15 minutes | Cook time: 20 minutes | Serves: 6

Ingredients:
- 2 (1 lb.) pork tenderloins
- 1-teaspoon ground cinnamon
- 1-teaspoon ground cilantro
- 1-teaspoon ground cumin
- 1-teaspoon paprika
- 1-teaspoon sea salt
- 2-tablespoon olive oil

For Creamy Harissa Sauce:
- 1 cup Greek yogurt (8 ounces)
- 1-tablespoon fresh lemon juice
- 1-tablespoon extra-virgin olive oil
- 1-teaspoon harissa sauce
- 1 clove garlic, minced
- Kosher salt and cracked black pepper

Preparation:
1. In a small mixing dish, combine all of the ingredients for the harissa and set aside.
2. Cinnamon, coriander, cumin, paprika, salt, and olive oil are mixed together.
3. Season the pork tenderloins evenly with the seasonings, then cover and chill for 30 minutes.
4. Preheat griddle over high heat and cook tenderloins for 8 to 10 minutes, or until browned.
5. Cook for an additional 8 to 10 minutes on the other side. Transfer the tenderloins to a chopping board and let aside for 10 minutes, covered in foil.
6. Serve with a creamy harissa sauce on the side.

Per Serving: Calories: 373; Fat: 17.8g; Sodium: 421mg; Carbs: 2.6g; Fiber: 0.6g; Sugar: 1.5g; Protein: 45.8g

Garlicky Sirloin Beef with Parmesan

Prep time: 15 minutes | Cook time: 10 minutes | Serves: 8

Ingredients:
- 4-pound Sirloin Beef, Cut into 1-Inch Cubes
- 12 Garlic Cloves, Finely Minced
- ½ Cup Olive Oil
- Sea Salt to Taste
- ½ Cup Grated Parmesan

Preparation:
1. Combine the ingredients in a closed bowl or bag and store in the refrigerator for 3 hours to overnight.
2. Using skewers, attach the meat chunks to the skewers.
3. Preheat the Griddle to high heat and cook the chicken for 3 minutes per side, sprinkle each side with parmesan cheese.
4. Grill for a few minutes longer, or until it's done to your liking.
5. Formerly portion, let the meat to rest for a few minutes.
6. Cook the remaining half of the ingredients with the same steps.
7. Serve and enjoy.

Per Serving: Calories: 542; Fat: 27.1g; Sodium: 225mg; Carbs: 1.6g; Fiber: 0.6g; Sugar: 0.1g; Protein: 65.8g

Butterflied Lamb Leg

Prep time: 15 minutes | Cook time: 30 minutes | Serves: 8

Ingredients:
- 2 to 2½ pounds butterflied leg of lamb (about ½ a leg)
- ½ cup packed fresh cilantro leaves
- 2 garlic cloves, peeled
- 2 teaspoons paprika
- 2 teaspoons ground cumin
- 1 teaspoon black pepper
- 1 teaspoon salt
- ½ teaspoon ground cinnamon
- ½ teaspoon ground ginger
- ½ teaspoon grated nutmeg
- ¼ teaspoon ground cloves
- 2 tablespoons olive oil, or as needed

Preparation:
1. Trim as much surface; Fat: as possible from all sides of the lamb without causing it to fall apart.
2. To make the flavor paste, put the cilantro, garlic, paprika, cumin, pepper, salt, cinnamon, ginger, nutmeg, and cloves in a suitable blender until smooth paste.
3. Rub the lamb with the sauce, cover and marinate for 30 minutes.
4. Grease the cooking surface of the griddle with cooking spray.
5. Turn on the 4 burners and turn their knobs to medium heat.
6. Let the Griddle preheat for 5 minutes.
7. Put the lamb on your griddle and then let it cook within 30 minutes, turning once.
8. Move it to a cutting board and let rest within 5 to 10 minutes.
9. Slice thinly across the grain and serve.

Per Serving: Calories: 327; Fat: 22g; Sodium: 421mg; Carbs: 10g; Fiber: 4.1g; Sugar: 2g; Protein: 31g

Coffee Crusted Steak

Prep time: 10 minutes | Cook time: 20 minutes | Serves: 8

Ingredients:
- ¼ cup coffee beans, ground
- ¼ cup dark brown sugar, firmly packed
- 1½ teaspoon sea salt
- ⅛ teaspoon ground cinnamon
- Pinch cayenne pepper
- 2½ pounds skirt steak, cut into 4 pieces
- 1 tablespoon olive oil

Preparation:
1. To make the rub, mix well the brown sugar, ground coffee beans, cinnamon, salt, and cayenne pepper in a bowl.
2. Rub the steak with oil and spice rub.
3. Preheat the Griddle by turning all its knob to medium-heat setting.
4. Grease the griddle top with cooking spray.
5. Sear the steak on the hot griddle top for 5 minutes per side.
6. Slice and serve.

Per Serving: Calories: 291; Fat: 14.8 g; Sodium: 1363 mg; Carbs: 5.2g; Fiber: 0.5g; Sugar: 4.9g; Protein: 33.6g

Buffalo Beef Mozzarella Filets

Prep time: 10 minutes | Cook time: 10 minutes | Serves: 4

Ingredients:
4 (6 oz.) beef filets
1 teaspoon garlic salt
Italian olive oil
2 Roma tomatoes, sliced
4 oz. fresh buffalo mozzarella, cut into four slices
8 fresh basil leaves
1 tablespoon balsamic vinegar glaze, for drizzling
½ teaspoon sea salt, for seasoning
½ teaspoon fresh ground pepper

Preparation:
1. Lightly brush each beef fillet with olive oil on all sides and season with garlic salt.
2. Preheat the Griddle by turning all its knob to medium-heat setting.
3. Grease the griddle top with cooking spray.
4. Place the steaks on the hot griddle top, and cook for 5 minutes.
5. Flip, and cook for an additional 5 minutes; top each with a mozzarella slice then cook for 2 minutes..
6. Place a few tomato slices and 2 basil leaves on top of each one.
7. Drizzle with salt, balsamic vinegar, and black pepper, and serve.

Per Serving: Calories: 475; Fat: 24.8 g; Sodium: 508 mg; Carbs: 4.1g; Fiber: 0.9g; Sugar: 1.9g; Protein: 58g

Griddle-Cooked Marinated Pork Chops

Prep time: 10 minutes | Cook time: 16 minutes | Serves: 4

Ingredients:
4 pork chops
1 teaspoon dried rosemary
⅛ teaspoon chili flakes
½ teaspoon black pepper
1 teaspoon garlic, minced
2 tablespoons Dijon mustard
3 tablespoons olive oil
½ cup balsamic vinegar
¾ teaspoon salt

Preparation:
1. Place the pork chops in a zip-lock bag with the remaining ingredients.
2. Refrigerate for 4 hours after sealing the bag and shaking it firmly.
3. Preheat the Griddle by turning all its knob to medium-heat setting.
4. Grease the griddle top with cooking spray.
5. Place the marinated pork chops on the hot griddle top and cook for 6-8 minutes per side.
6. Enjoy.

Per Serving: Calories: 360; Fat: 30.8 g; Sodium: 584 mg; Carbs: 1.3g; Fiber: 0.5g; Sugar: 0.2g; Protein: 18.6g

Basil Grilled Filet Mignon

Prep time: 05 minutes | Cook time: 10 minutes | Serves: 8

Ingredients:
8 (12 ounces) filets
2-teaspoon garlic salt
2-teaspoon Italian Olive oil
8 Roma tomatoes, sliced
8 ounces' fresh buffalo mozzarella, cut into four slices
16 fresh basil leaves
Balsamic vinegar glaze for drizzling
Sea salt for seasoning
Fresh ground pepper

Preparation:
1. Brush each fillet with olive oil on all sides and season with garlic salt.
2. Preheat the griddle to high temperature. Place the steaks on the griddle, reduce the heat to medium, and cook for 5 minutes.
3. Cook for an additional 5 minutes after flipping, re-tenting, and topping each with a piece of mozzarella during the last 2 minutes of grilling.
4. Remove the steaks from the griddle and place a few tomato slices and 2 basil leaves on top of each one.
5. Serve with a drizzle of balsamic vinegar and a pinch of sea salt and black pepper.
6. Cook the remaining half of ingredients with the same steps.

Per Serving: Calories: 376; Fat: 19g; Sodium: 684mg; Carbs: 6g; Fiber 0.6g; Sugar: 1.5g; Protein: 45.8g

Greek Cheese Lamb Patties

Prep time: 15 minutes | Cook time: 8 minutes | Serves: 4

Ingredients:
1 lb. ground lamb
5 basil leaves, minced
10 mint leaves, minced
¼ cup fresh parsley, chopped
1-teaspoon dried oregano
1 cup feta cheese, crumbled
1-tablespoon garlic, minced
1 jalapeno pepper, minced
¼-teaspoon pepper
½-teaspoon kosher salt

Preparation:
1. In a mixing bowl, combine all of the ingredients and stir until well blended.
2. Preheat the griddle to medium-high.
3. Coat the top of the griddle with cooking spray.
4. Make four equal-sized patties with the meat mixture and fry them for 4 minutes on each side.
5. When cooked, serve and have fun.

Per Serving: Calories: 330; Fat: 16.6g; Sodium: 807mg; Carbs: 5.6g; Fiber 2.6g; Sugar: 1.7g; Protein: 38.5g

Griddled Lamb Steak

Prep time: 15 minutes | Cook time: 10 minutes | Serves: 6

Ingredients:
2 tablespoons olive oil
1 celeriac, peeled and shaved
3 lbs. lamb steak
Black pepper and salt to taste
1 cup chopped mint

Preparation:
1. Sauté the celeriac with oil in a skillet until caramelized. Set aside.
2. Grease the cooking surface of the griddle with cooking spray.
3. Turn on the 4 burners and turn their knobs to medium heat.
4. Let the Griddle preheat for 5 minutes.
5. Season lamb steak with black pepper and salt.
6. Sear the lamb steak on the griddle top for 3 minutes on each side.
7. Serve with celeriac and chopped mint.

Per Serving: Calories: 386; Fat: 13g; Sodium: 421mg; Carbs: 16g; Fiber 4.1g; Sugar: 3.2g; Protein: 27g

Green Onion and Beef Burger Patties

Prep time: 10 minutes | Cook time: 8 minutes | Serves: 4

Ingredients:
1¼ pounds ground beef
2 pineapple slices, chopped
¼ teaspoon black pepper
1 garlic clove, minced
1 teaspoon ginger, grated
¼ cup green onions, chopped
¼ cup soy sauce
¼ teaspoon salt

Preparation:
1. In a suitable mixing bowl, mix well all of the ingredients and stir until well blended.
2. Preheat the Griddle by turning all its knob to medium-heat setting.
3. Grease the griddle top with cooking spray.
4. Form patties from the mixture and cook for 4 minutes per side on the hot griddle top.
5. Serve and enjoy.

Per Serving: Calories: 634; Fat: 19.6 g; Sodium: 1263 mg; Carbs: 13.1g; Fiber: 1.5g; Sugar: 8.6g; Protein: 96g

Pork Chops Fried in Orange Marinade

Prep time: 30 minutes | Cook time: 10 minutes | Serves: 4

Ingredients:
4½-inch-thick bone-in pork chops
3 tablespoons olive oil, plus more for grill
Kosher salt and freshly ground black pepper

For the marinade:
1 habanero chili, seeded, chopped fine
2 garlic cloves, minced
½ cup fresh orange juice
2 tablespoons brown sugar
1 tablespoon apple cider vinegar

Preparation:
1. In a big sealable plastic bag, mix well the marinade ingredients.
2. Use a fork to pierce the pork chops all over, then place them in the bag, seal it, and turn to coat.
3. Marinate for 30 minutes.
4. Pat the pork chops dry after removing them from the marinade.
5. Preheat the Griddle by turning all its knob to medium-heat setting.
6. Grease the griddle top with cooking spray.
7. Cook for almost 10 minutes per side on the hot griddle top.
8. Serve.

Per Serving: Calories: 1098; Fat: 77.8 g; Sodium: 1693 mg; Carbs: 8.2g; Fiber: 0.1g; Sugar: 7g; Protein: 102.6g

Butter Sirloin Steaks with Vegetables

Prep time: 10 minutes | Cook time: 15 minutes | Serves: 6

Ingredients:
Steak:
2(1 pound) sirloin steaks
1 tablespoon garlic powder
4 tablespoons soy sauce
1 white onion, sliced
3 zucchinis, sliced
2 cups snap peas
4 tablespoons vegetable oil
3 tablespoons butter
½ teaspoon salt and black pepper

Preparation:
1. Sprinkle salt, garlic powder and pepper over the steak.
2. Preheat the Griddle by turning all its knob to medium-heat setting.
3. Grease the griddle top with butter.
4. Add the zucchini, onion rings, salt, black pepper and snap peas to the griddle and cook for 7 minutes.
5. Cook the steaks on the hot griddle top for 2 minutes per side.
6. Top with butter, and season with soy sauce. Continue to cook for another 4 minutes.
7. Serve warm.
Per Serving: Calories: 257; Fat: 17 g; Sodium: 674 mg; Carbs: 13.9g; Fiber: 4.2sugar 5.9g; Protein: 13.6g

Pork, Mushrooms and Bell Pepper Skewers

Prep time: 10 minutes | Cook time: 15 minutes | Serves: 4

Ingredients:
1½ pounds pork loin, cut into 1-inch cubes
2 cups mushrooms
2 cups cherry tomatoes
For marinade:
½ cup vinaigrette
¼ cup Dijon mustard
2 cups onion, cut into pieces
2 cups bell peppers, cut into pieces
½ teaspoon black pepper
½ teaspoon salt

Preparation:
1. In a suitable mixing dish, mix well the pork cubes and marinade ingredients; and set aside for 30 minutes.
2. Thread the skewers with mushrooms, marinated pork cubes, tomatoes, onion, and bell peppers alternately.
3. Preheat the Griddle by turning all its knob to medium-heat setting.
4. Grease the griddle top with cooking spray.
5. Cook the prepared pork skewers for 7 minutes per side on the hot griddle top.
6. Serve and enjoy.
Per Serving: Calories: 629; Fat: 40.5 g; Sodium: 584 mg; Carbs: 16.9g; Fiber: 4.1g; Sugar: 9.3g; Protein: 50.3g

Bell Pepper and Pork with Chimichurri

Prep time: 05 minutes | Cook time: 15 minutes | Serves:8

Ingredients:
Chimichurri Sauce:
2 large red onions, cut into ½-inch slices
4 red bell peppers, cored, seeded, and cut into 1-inch strips
4 yellow bell peppers, cored, seeded, and cut into 1-inch strips
6-tablespoon olive oil
Pork:
4 pounds' pork tenderloin
2-tablespoon olive oil
½-teaspoon salt
4-tablespoon white wine vinegar
Juice 2 lime
2-teaspoon Worcestershire sauce
1-teaspoon red pepper flakes
4-tablespoon chopped fresh parsley leaves

1-teaspoon freshly ground black pepper

Preparation:
1. Getting the ingredients ready.
2. Toss the onion slices and bell pepper strips with 2 tablespoons olive oil to lightly coat them.
3. Preheat the Griddle to high temperature.
4. Grill the onion and peppers for about 6 minutes, until tender and charred, on a hot griddle.
5. In a food processor or with a large sharp knife, finely chop the peppers and onion. Place in a medium mixing basin.
6. Combine the remaining-tablespoon olive oil, vinegar, lime juice, Worcestershire sauce, and red pepper flakes in a large mixing bowl. (The sauce can be refrigerated for up to 2 days if covered with plastic wrap.)
7. Just before serving, add the parsley.
8. Preheat the oven to 350°F. Cut the pork tenderloin into 8 medallions, each about 1-inch-thick, and pound to a 12-inch thickness.
9. Season the pork cutlets with salt and pepper after rubbing them with olive oil. 3 minutes on the oven.
10. Cook the remaining half of the ingredients with the same steps.
11. Serve with the sauce heaped on top.
Per Serving: Calories: 453; Fat: 18.9g; Sodium: 295mg; Carbs: 8.6g; Fiber 1.6g; Sugar: 5g; Protein: 60.8g

Fried Montreal Marinade Pork Chops

Prep time: 6 hours | Cook time: 15 minutes | Serves: 4

Ingredients:
4 pork chops
2 teaspoons Montreal marinade
2 tablespoons soy sauce
¼ cup olive oil

Preparation:
1. Toss the pork chops with the remaining ingredients in a suitable mixing bowl and refrigerate for 6 hours.
2. Preheat the Griddle by turning all its knob to medium-heat setting.
3. Grease the griddle top with cooking spray.
4. Cook pork chops on the hot griddle top for 5-7 minutes per side.
5. Serve and enjoy.
Per Serving: Calories: 368; Fat: 32.8 g; Sodium: 507 mg; Carbs: 0.6g; Fiber: 0.1g; Sugar: 1.1g; Protein: 18.5g

Marinade Citrus Griddle Pork

Prep time: 15 minutes | Cook time: 10 minutes | Serves:2

Ingredients:
2 pork tenderloins, trimmed
1-teaspoon annatto powder
For the marinade:
2 oranges, juiced
2 lemons, juiced, or more to taste
2 limes, juiced, or more to taste
6 cloves garlic, minced
1-teaspoon Olive oil

1-teaspoon ground cumin
½-teaspoon cayenne pepper
½-teaspoon dried oregano
½-teaspoon black pepper

Preparation:
1. In a mixing basin, whisk together the marinade ingredients until thoroughly combined.
2. Cut the tenderloins crosswise in half, then lengthwise in half.
3. Place the pieces in the marinade and coat them completely.
4. Refrigerate for 4 to 6 hours after wrapping in plastic wrap.
5. Remove the pork from the marinade and place it in a paper towel-lined basin to absorb the excess moisture.
6. Paper towels should be discarded. Drizzle the pork with olive oil and a pinch of annatto powder.
7. Lightly oil the griddle and heat it to medium-high heat.
8. Cook for 4 - 5 minutes on a griddle, carefully spacing the pieces. On the other side, cook for another 4 to 5 minutes.
9. Transfer the meat to a serving plate and let aside for 5 minutes before serving.
Per Serving: Calories: 216; Fat: 7.9g; Sodium: 64mg; Carbs: 8.6g; Fiber 2.6g; Sugar: 1.5g; Protein: 25.8g

Griddle-Seared Steaks

Prep time: 15 minutes | Cook time: 10 minutes | Serves:2

Ingredients:
12 oz. steaks (can use 2 6oz. flat iron tenderloin)
1-tablespoon Olive oil
½-teaspoon garlic powder
½-teaspoon onion powder
½-teaspoon black pepper
1 pinch salt (to taste)

Preparation:
1. Close the Griddle Grill and preheat it to medium-high heat.
2. To remove moisture from the steak, pat it with a paper towel once it has reached room temperature.
3. Put salt, pepper, onion, and garlic powder according to taste.
4. Fill your griddle with oil.
5. Allow the steaks to cook for a few minutes before turning them over and repeating the process after the first side is done, then flip and cook for another 3 minutes.
6. Cook for extra 2- 3 minutes on the extra side.
7. Check the steaks to check if they're done to your liking, but they should be brown on all sides.
8. After allowing the steak to cool for a few minutes, slice it and serve it.
Per Serving: Calories: 404; Fat: 17.9g; Sodium: 154mg; Carbs: 1.6g; Fiber 0.6g; Sugar: 5g; Protein: 5.8g

Curry Pork Roast

Prep time: 15 minutes | Cook time: 20 minutes | Serves: 6

Ingredients:
- ½-teaspoon curry powder
- ½-teaspoon ground turmeric powder
- 1 can unsweetened coconut milk
- 1-tablespoon sugar
- 2-tablespoon fish sauce
- 2-tablespoon soy sauce
- 3 pounds' pork shoulder
- Salt and pepper to taste

Preparation:
1. Getting the ingredients ready.
2. Combine all of the ingredients in a bowl and marinate the meat for at least 2 hours in the refrigerator.
3. Preheat the Griddle to high temperature.
4. When the griddle is hot, cook the meat in batches for 20 minutes, flipping the pig after 10 minutes to ensure equal grilling.
5. In the meantime, heat the marinade in a saucepan for 10 minutes, or until the sauce thickens.
6. Before serving, baste the pork with the sauce.

Per Serving: Calories: 454; Fat: 39g; Sodium: 1224mg; Carbs: 7.6g; Fiber 1.6g; Sugar: 5.5g; Protein: 25.8g

Roasted Beef Sirloin Skewers

Prep time: 15 minutes | Cook time: 8 minutes | Serves: 4

Ingredients:
- 2 lbs. beef sirloin, cut into cubes
- 2-teaspoon fresh thyme, minced
- 1-tablespoon fresh parsley, minced
- 1-tablespoon lemon zest
- 4 garlic cloves, minced
- 2-tablespoon fresh lemon juice
- ¼ cup olive oil
- 2-teaspoon dried oregano
- 2-teaspoon fresh rosemary, minced
- Pepper
- Salt

Preparation:
1. In a mixing dish, combine all of the ingredients except the meat and toss thoroughly.
2. Add the meat to the bowl and cover it thoroughly with the marinade.
3. Refrigerate for at least one night.
4. Preheat the griddle to medium-high.
5. Coat the top of the griddle with cooking spray.
6. Using skewers, thread the marinated meat onto the skewers.
7. Cook for 6-8 minutes on the skewers on the hot griddle top. Every 2 minutes, rotate the dish.
8. Serve and have fun.

Per Serving: Calories: 543; Fat: 27.9g; Sodium: 194mg; Carbs: 2.6g; Fiber 1g; Sugar: 0.5g; Protein: 65.8g

Coffee Skirt Steak

Prep time: 15 minutes | Cook time: 20 minutes | Serves: 8

Ingredients:
- ¼ cup coffee beans, finely ground
- ¼ cup dark brown sugar, firmly packed
- 1 ½-teaspoon sea salt
- ⅛-teaspoon ground cinnamon
- Pinch cayenne pepper
- 2 ½ lb. skirt steak, cut into 4 pieces
- 1-tablespoon olive oil

Preparation:
1. Preheat the griddle to high heat.
2. To make the rub, combine coffee, brown sugar, salt, cinnamon, and cayenne pepper in a basin.
3. Remove the steak from the refrigerator and set aside for 15 minutes to come to room temperature. Oil the steak and season it with the spice rub. Rub the spice rub into the meat.
4. 2 to 4 minutes per side, sear until browned and medium-rare. Transfer to a cutting board, cover with foil, and let aside for 5 minutes before slicing thinly across the grain.

Per Serving: Calories: 323; Fat: 16g; Sodium: 460mg; Carbs: 4.6g; Fiber 0g; Sugar: 4.4g; Protein: 35.8g

Fried Pork Chops with Apple Compote

Prep time: 5 minutes | Cook time: 20 minutes | Serves: 4

Ingredients:
- 4 bone-in pork chops
- 2 honey crisp apples, peeled, chopped
- ⅓ cup orange juice
- 1 teaspoon chopped fresh rosemary
- 1 teaspoon chopped fresh sage
- ½ teaspoon sea salt
- ½ teaspoon black pepper

Preparation:
1. In a suitable saucepan, mix well the herbs, apples, and orange juice and cook for 12 minutes.
2. Preheat the Griddle by turning all its knob to medium-heat setting.
3. Grease the griddle top with cooking spray.
4. Sprinkle salt and black pepper over the pork chops.
5. Place the pork chop on the hot griddle top and cook for 4 minutes per side.
6. Slice and serve with apple compote on top!

Per Serving: Calories: 159; Fat: 5.8 g; Sodium: 198 mg; Carbs: 9.5 g; Fiber: 1.1g; Sugar: 7.2g; Protein: 16.6g

Vinegar Pork Tenderloin Cubes

Prep time: 15 minutes | Cook time: 10 minutes | Serves: 6

Ingredients:
- 2 lbs. pork tenderloin, cut into 1-inch cubes
- 3-tablespoon fresh parsley, chopped
- 1-tablespoon garlic, chopped
- 1 onion, chopped
- ½ cup olive oil
- ½ cup vinegar
- Pepper
- Salt

Preparation:
1. Combine vinegar, parsley, garlic, onion, and oil in a big zip-lock bag.
2. Place the meat in the bag and marinate overnight in the refrigerator.
3. Using skewers, thread the marinated meat. Season with salt and pepper.
4. Preheat the griddle to medium-high.
5. Coat the top of the griddle with cooking spray.
6. Cook the meat skewers for 3-4 minutes on each side on the hot griddle top.
7. Serve and have fun.

Per Serving: Calories: 375; Fat: 22.2g; Sodium: 116mg; Carbs: 2.6g; Fiber 0.6g; Sugar: 0.5g; Protein: 39.8g

Palatable Pork Chops with Creole & Parsley

Prep time: 15 minutes | Cook time: 10 minutes | Serves: 2

Ingredients:
- 2 pork chops
- 2-teaspoon creole seasoning
- 2-tablespoon fresh parsley, chopped
- ¼-teaspoon pepper
- Salt

Preparation:
1. Pork chops should be seasoned with Creole spice, pepper, and salt.
2. Preheat the griddle to medium-high.
3. Coat the top of the griddle with cooking spray.
4. Cook the seasoned pork chops for 5 minutes on a heated griddle top.
5. Cook for another 5 minutes after turning the pork chops.
6. Place the pork chops on a serving platter and top with parsley.
7. Serve and have fun.

Per Serving: Calories: 260; Fat: 19.9g; Sodium: 1214mg; Carbs: 0.6g; Fiber 0.6g; Sugar: 0g; Protein: 15.8g

Delicious Pepper Pork Chops

Prep time: 10 minutes | Cook time: 12 minutes | Serves: 4

Ingredients:
- 4 pork chops, boneless

For rub:
- ½ teaspoon ground ginger
- ½ teaspoon ground cumin
- 2 tablespoons brown sugar
- ½ teaspoon dry mustard
- 1 teaspoon black pepper
- 1 teaspoon garlic powder
- 1 tablespoon sugar
- 1½ tablespoons paprika

Preparation:
1. In a suitable mixing dish, mix well the pork chops and rub ingredients.
2. Preheat the Griddle by turning all its knob to medium-heat setting.
3. Grease the griddle top with cooking spray.
4. Cook pork chops for 6 minutes per side on the hot griddle top.
5. Serve and enjoy.

Per Serving: Calories: 319; Fat: 21.2 g; Sodium: 63 mg; Carbs: 14g; Fiber: 3.5g; Sugar: 8.9g; Protein: 19.6g

BBQ Pork Tenderloin Sandwiches

Prep time: 10 minutes | Cook time: 25 minutes | Serves: 6

Ingredients:
- 2 (¾-lb.) pork tenderloins
- 1-teaspoon garlic powder
- 1-teaspoon sea salt
- 1-teaspoon dry mustard
- ½-teaspoon coarsely ground
- pepper
- Olive oil, for brushing
- 6 whole-wheat hamburger buns
- 6-tablespoon barbecue sauce

Preparation:
1. In a small mixing dish, combine the garlic, salt, pepper, and mustard.
2. Rub olive oil all over the pork tenderloins, then season with the seasoning mix.
3. Preheat the griddle to medium-high heat and cook the pork tenderloins for 10 to 12 minutes on each side, or until a meat thermometer inserted into the thickest piece registers 155°F.
4. When cooked, set aside for 10 minutes.
5. Thinly slice the hamburger buns and distribute evenly.
6. Serve each sandwich with barbecue sauce drizzled on top.

Per Serving: Calories: 349; Fat: 19g; Sodium: 124mg; Carbs: 11.6g; Fiber 4.6g; Sugar: 5g; Protein: 15g

Country Ribs in Garlic Sauce

Prep time: 10 minutes | Cook time: 2 hours | Serves: 6

Ingredients:
- 3 pounds' country-style pork ribs
- 1 cup low-sugar ketchup
- ½ cup water
- ¼ cup onion, finely chopped
- ¼ cup cider vinegar or wine vinegar
- ¼ cup light molasses
- 2-tablespoon Worcestershire sauce
- 2-teaspoon chili powder
- 2 cloves garlic, minced

Preparation:
1. In a saucepan, combine ketchup, water, onion, vinegar, molasses, Worcestershire sauce, chili powder, and garlic; bring to a boil.
2. Cook, stirring frequently, for 10 to 15 minutes, or until desired thickness is reached, uncovered.
3. Ribs should be; Fat:-free.
4. Preheat the griddle to medium-high temperature.
5. Place the ribs on the griddle, bone-side down, and cook for 1 ½ to 2 hours, or until tender, brushing with sauce regularly during the last 10 minutes of cooking.
6. Enjoy with the rest of the sauce!

Per Serving: Calories: 316; Fat: 4.3g; Sodium: 104mg; Carbs: 11.6g; Fiber 1.6g; Sugar: 2.8g; Protein: 15.8g

Honey Pork Chops

Prep time: 1 hour | Cook time: 10 minutes | Serves: 6

Ingredients:
- 6 (4 oz.) boneless pork chops
- ¼ cup organic honey
- 1 to 2 tablespoons soy sauce
- 2 tablespoons olive oil
- 1 tablespoon rice mirin

Preparation:
1. Mix well the soy sauce, honey, oil, and white vinegar until blended.
2. In a big sealable plastic bag, mix well the sauce and pork chops and refrigerate for 1 hour.
3. Preheat the Griddle by turning all its knob to medium-heat setting.
4. Grease the griddle top with cooking spray.
5. Sear the pork chop for 4 to 5 minutes per side.
6. Serve and enjoy.

Per Serving: Calories: 267; Fat: 15.2 g; Sodium: 479 mg; Carbs: 13.9g; Fiber: 0.1g; Sugar: 12.9g; Protein: 20.6g

Glazed Pork Shoulder Fried in Sauce

Prep time: 15 minutes | Cook time: 8 minutes | Serves: 8

Ingredients:
- 1 (5 lbs.) Boston Butt pork shoulder

For the marinade:
- 2-tablespoon garlic, minced
- 1 large piece ginger, peeled and chopped
- 1 cup hoisin sauce
- ¾ cup fish sauce
- ⅔ cup honey
- ⅔ cup Shaoxing
- ½ cup chili oil
- ⅓ cup oyster sauce
- ⅓ cup sesame oil

For the glaze:
- ¾ cup dark brown sugar
- 1-tablespoon light molasses

Preparation:
1. Place the pork shoulder on a chopping board,; Fat: side down, with the short end facing you. Make a shallow cut along the full length of a long side of the shoulder with a long sharp knife held approximately 1"–1½" above the cutting board.
2. Continue cutting into the meat with your free hand, lifting and unfurling it until it lies flat.
3. In a blender, puree the marinade, reserving ½ cups for the glaze cover, and refrigerate.
4. Fill a large sealable plastic bag halfway with the leftover marinade.
5. Add the pork shoulder to the bag and marinate for 8 hours in the refrigerator.
6. Preheat the griddle to medium heat (the thermometer should read 350° with the cover covered). Remove the pork from the marinade and drain any excess.
7. Reserving the marinade, stir in the glaze ingredients until the sugar is dissolved.
8. Grill pork for 8 minutes, basting and flipping with tongs every minute or so, until thickly coated in glaze.
9. An instant-read thermometer put into the thickest part should register 145°F when lightly browned in spots and warmed through.
10. To serve, transfer to a cutting board and slice 14" thick against the grain.
11. Enjoy!

Per Serving: Calories: 1080; Fat: 62.9g; Sodium: 2804mg; Carbs: 59.6g; Fiber 1g; Sugar: 46.5g; Protein: 75.8g

Smoked Flat Beef Brisket

Prep time: 10 minutes | Cook time: 6 hours 20 minutes | Serves: 6

Ingredients:
- 1 (4 ½ pounds) flat cut beef brisket (3 inches thick)

For the rub:
- 1 tablespoon sea salt
- 1 tablespoon dark brown sugar
- 2 teaspoons smoked paprika
- 2 teaspoons chili powder
- 1 teaspoon garlic powder
- 1 teaspoon onion powder
- 1 teaspoon ground black pepper
- 1 teaspoon mesquite liquid smoke

Preparation:
1. In a small mixing dish, mix well the rub ingredients.
2. Rinse the brisket and pat it dry before rubbing it with the coffee mixture.
3. Preheat the Griddle by turning all its knob to high-heat setting.
4. Grease the griddle top with cooking spray.
5. Sear for 3 to 5 minutes per side on high heat until charred.
6. Reduce to a low heat setting and cook for 6 hours.
7. Slice the brisket across the grain and serve.

Per Serving: Calories: 324; Fat: 17.8 g; Sodium: 363 mg; Carbs: 8.9g; Fiber: 0.5g; Sugar: 1.9g; Protein: 36.6g

Pork Tenderloin with Creamy Harissa Sauce

Prep time: 40 minutes | Cook time: 20 minutes | Serves: 6

Ingredients:
- 2 (1 pound) pork tenderloins
- 1 teaspoon ground cinnamon
- 1 teaspoon ground cilantro
- 1 teaspoon ground cumin
- 1 teaspoon paprika
- 1 teaspoon sea salt
- 2 tablespoons olive oil

For creamy harissa sauce:
- 1 cup Greek yogurt (8 oz.)
- 1 tablespoon fresh lemon juice
- 1 tablespoon olive oil
- 1 teaspoon harissa sauce
- 1 clove garlic, minced

Preparation:
1. In a small mixing dish, mix well all of the ingredients for the harissa sauce and set aside.
2. Mix the coriander, cinnamon, paprika, cumin, salt, and olive oil in a suitable mixing bowl.
3. Season the pork tenderloins with the seasonings; cover and refrigerate for 30 minutes.
4. Preheat the Griddle by turning all its knob to medium-heat setting.
5. Grease the griddle top with cooking spray.
6. Cook tenderloins for 10 minutes per side until browned.
7. Slice and serve with a creamy harissa sauce.

Per Serving: Calories: 248; Fat: 11.8 g; Sodium: 421 mg; Carbs: 2.2g; Fiber: 0.4g; Sugar: 1.5g; Protein: 33.3g

Chapter 7 Beef, Pork and Lamb Recipes | 89

Vinegar-Marinated Pork Chops

Prep time: 15 minutes | Cook time: 15 minutes | Serves: 4

Ingredients:
- 4 ½-inch-thick bone-in pork chops
- 3-tablespoon olive oil
- Kosher salt and freshly ground black pepper

For the marinade:
- 1 habanero chili, seeded, chopped fine
- 2 garlic cloves, minced
- ½ cup fresh orange juice
- 2-tablespoon brown sugar
- 1-tablespoon apple cider vinegar

Preparation:
1. In a big sealable plastic bag, combine the marinade ingredients.
2. Pork chops should be pierced all over with a fork before being placed in the bag, sealed, and turned to coat.
3. Preserve for 30 minutes at room temperature, rotating irregularly.
4. Preheat the griddle to medium-high heat.
5. Using a brush, coat the griddle with oil.
6. Take the pork chops out of the marinade and blot them dry. Drizzle with the salt and ground black pepper.
7. Sear for 8 minutes, until blackened and cooked through, flipping once.
8. Place on a platter and set aside to cool for 5 minutes.
9. Serve with your favorite side dish.

Per Serving: Calories: 338; Fat: 25.2g; Sodium: 373mg; Carbs: 8.2g; Fiber 0.6g; Sugar: 7g; Protein: 22.8g

Cayenne Pork Chops

Prep time: 10 minutes | Cook time: 15 minutes | Serves: 8

Ingredients:
- 8 pork chops
- 2-tablespoon paprika
- 1-teaspoon ground cumin
- 1-teaspoon dried sage
- 1-teaspoon salt
- 1-teaspoon black pepper
- 1-teaspoon garlic powder
- ½-teaspoon cayenne pepper
- 2-tablespoon butter
- 2-tablespoon vegetable oil

Preparation:
1. Combine the paprika, cumin, sage, salt, pepper, garlic powder, and cayenne pepper in a medium mixing bowl.
2. Heat the butter and oil in the griddle over medium-high heat.
3. Season the pork chops generously with the spice rub.
4. Cook for 4 to 5 minutes on the griddle with the chops. Cook for a further 4 minutes after turning the pork chops.
5. Allow 5 minutes for the pork chops to rest after removing them from the griddle.
6. Use the same steps to cook the remaining half of the ingredients.
7. Serve and enjoy.

Per Serving: Calories: 320; Fat: 27.9g; Sodium: 368mg; Carbs: 1.6g; Fiber 0.8g; Sugar: 0.3g; Protein: 18.5g

Rosemary-Coconut Pork Chops

Prep time: 05 minutes | Cook time: 15 minutes | Serves: 8

Ingredients:
- 8 pork chops, boneless
- 4-tablespoon fresh rosemary, chopped
- ¼ cup Dijon mustard
- ¼ cup coconut aminos
- 4-tablespoon olive oil
- ½-teaspoon salt

Preparation:
1. In a bowl, combine rosemary, coconut aminos, olive oil, Dijon mustard, and salt.
2. Toss the pork chops in the basin and coat thoroughly.
3. Refrigerate for 1 hour after covering with plastic wrap.
4. Preheat the griddle to medium-high heat.
5. Coat the top of the griddle with cooking spray.
6. Cook for 5 minutes on each side on a hot griddle top with marinated pork chops.
7. Serve and have fun.

Per Serving: Calories: 200; Fat: 17.9g; Sodium: 2004mg; Carbs: 9.6g; Fiber 4.6g; Sugar: 5g; Protein: 5.8g

Garlicky Pork Chops

Prep time: 15 minutes | Cook time: 15 minutes | Serves: 4

Ingredients:
- 4 to 6 pork chops
- 4 cloves garlic, finely chopped
- ½ cup olive oil
- ½ cup soy sauce
- ½-teaspoon garlic powder
- ½-teaspoon salt
- ½ black pepper
- ¼ cup butter

Preparation:
1. Combine the garlic, olive oil, soy sauce, garlic powder, salt and black pepper in a big zipper-lock bag.
2. Place the pork chops in the marinade and make sure they are well coated. Allow 30 minutes for preparation.
3. Preheat the griddle to medium-high. 2-tablespoon olive oil and 2-tablespoon butter, melted on the griddle
4. Place the chops on the griddle one at a time, being careful not to crowd them. Cook the chops for another 4 minutes on the griddle with 2-tablespoon butter. After that, cook for another 4 minutes.
5. Remove the chops from the griddle and brush them with the remaining butter. After 5 minutes of resting, serve.

Per Serving: Calories: 596; Fat: 56.9g; Sodium: 2224mg; Carbs: 3.6g; Fiber 0.6g; Sugar: 0.5g; Protein: 20.8g

Roast Cumin Steak

Prep time: 10 minutes | Cook time: 25 minutes | Serves: 2

Ingredients:
- 1 lb. hanger steak or shirt steak
- ¼ cup olive oil
- 1 lime, juiced
- 1 orange, juiced
- 1 garlic clove, finely chopped
- ½-teaspoon cumin
- ¼-teaspoon salt
- ¼-teaspoon ground pepper
- A handful of fresh cilantro, chopped

Preparation:
1. In a big sealable plastic bag, combine all of the ingredients.
2. Chill for 1 t- 2 hours to marinate.
3. Cook for 3 minutes on each side or until just cooked through on medium/high heat.
4. Allow to rest for 10 minutes on a chopping board.
5. Serve by slicing against the grain.

Per Serving: Calories: 392; Fat: 20.9g; Sodium: 594mg; Carbs: 36g; Fiber 1.6g; Sugar: 4.5g; Protein: 15.8g

Rosemary Pork Chops with Sage Apple

Prep time: 05 minutes | Cook time: 15 minutes | Serves: 4

Ingredients:
- 4, bone-in pork chops
- 1 honey crisp apples,
- ⅓ cup orange juice
- 1-teaspoon chopped fresh
- rosemary
- 1-teaspoon chopped fresh sage
- Sea salt
- Black pepper

Preparation:
1. In a saucepan, combine the apples, herbs, and orange juice; cook, stirring occasionally, until the apples are soft and the juices have thickened to a thin syrup, about 10 to 12 minutes.
2. Pork chops should be seasoned with salt and pepper.
3. Place the pork chop on the griddle and cook for 4 minutes over high heat, or until it releases from the griddle.
4. Cook for 3 minutes slower on the other side.
5. Transfer to a chopping board and tent with foil.
6. Serve with a compote of apples on top!

Per Serving: Calories: 202; Fat: 5.9g; Sodium: 165mg; Carbs: 9.6g; Fiber 1.6g; Sugar: 7.5g; Protein: 25.8g

Garlic Soy Pork Chops in Soy Sauce

Prep time: 45 minutes | Cook time: 10 minutes | Serves: 4-6

Ingredients:
- 4 to 6 pork chops
- 4 cloves garlic, chopped
- ½ cup olive oil
- ½ cup soy sauce
- ½ teaspoon garlic powder
- ½ teaspoon salt
- ½ black pepper
- ¼ cup butter

Preparation:
1. Mix well the garlic, olive oil, soy sauce, and garlic powder in a big zipper lock bag.
2. Place the pork chops in the marinade and mix well to coat.
3. Keep them aside for 30 minutes for marination.
4. Preheat the Griddle by turning all its knob to medium-heat setting.
5. Grease the griddle top with 2 tablespoons olive oil and 2 tablespoons butter.
6. Place the chops on the hot griddle top and cook the chops for 4 minutes per side.
7. Serve.

Per Serving: Calories: 398; Fat: 37.8 g; Sodium: 1463 mg; Carbs: 2.5g; Fiber: 0.2g; Sugar: 0.5g; Protein: 13.6g

Glazed Pork Chops with Pineapple Quarter

Prep time: 15 minutes | Cook time: 1 hour | Serves: 6

Ingredients:
- 1 large whole pineapple
- 6 pork chops
- 12 slices thick-cut bacon
- Toothpicks, soaked in water

For the glaze:
- ¼ cup honey
- ⅛-teaspoon cayenne pepper

Preparation:
1. Turn both sides of the Griddle to medium-high heat, then turn one side off and the remaining burners down to medium after about 15 minutes.
2. Remove the top and bottom of the pineapple, then peel it, cutting the skin away in strips.
3. The pineapple flesh should be cut into six quarters.
4. Wrap a bacon slice around each pineapple chunk and fasten with a toothpick at each end.
5. Drizzle honey over the quarters and season with cayenne pepper.
6. Place the quarters on the griddle and heat until the bacon is equally browned on both sides.
7. While the pineapple quarters are cooking, rub honey and cayenne pepper onto pork chops. Place the pan on the griddle.
8. Cook for 20 minutes after tenting with foil. Cook for a further 10 to 20 minutes, or until chops are completely done.
9. Each chop should be served with a pineapple quarter on the side.
10. When ready, enjoy.

Per Serving: Calories: 453; Fat: 30.9g; Sodium: 437mg; Carbs: 15.3g; Fiber 0.4g; Sugar: 14.3g; Protein: 25.8g

Vinegar Flank Steak with Oregano

Prep time: 5 minutes | Cook time: 20 minutes | Serves: 4

Ingredients:
- 1 pound flank steak
- 1 white onion, sliced
- 1 Roma tomato, sliced
- 1 cucumber, peeled and sliced
- ¼ cup crumbled feta cheese
- 4 6-inch pita pockets

For the marinade:
- ¼ cup olive oil
- 1 teaspoon dried oregano
- 1 teaspoon balsamic vinegar
- 1 teaspoon garlic powder
- Salt and black pepper, to taste

For the sauce:
- 1 cup plain yogurt
- 2 tablespoons fresh dill, chopped
- 1 teaspoon garlic, minced
- 2 tablespoons lemon juice

Preparation:
1. Against the grain, cut the flank steak into thin strips.
2. In a suitable sealable plastic bag, mix well the marinade ingredients.
3. Add the sliced meat, seal, and turn to coat.
4. Marinate for 2 hours or overnight in the refrigerator.
5. In a small mixing dish, mix well the sauce ingredients and put aside.
6. Preheat the Griddle by turning all its knob to medium-heat setting.
7. Grease the griddle top with cooking spray.
8. Spritz the pitas with water, wrap them in foil, and warm them on the griddle top.
9. Remove the meat from the marinade and place it on the griddle.
10. Cook for almost 5 minutes per side until golden.
11. Take the pitas out of the oven and slice them in half.
12. Stuff the pitas with tomato, cucumber, onions, and beef and arrange on plates.
13. Drizzle some yoghurt sauce over the meat and sprinkle with feta cheese.
14. Serve warm.

Per Serving: Calories: 1291; Fat: 27.8 g; Sodium: 1608 mg; Carbs: 188.9g; Fiber: 9.8g; Sugar: 12.9g; Protein: 65.6g

Cumin Cuban Pork Chops

Prep time: 30 minutes | Cook time: 1 hour 30 minutes | Serves: 4

Ingredients:
- 4 pork chops
- 4 cloves garlic, smashed
- 2 tablespoons olive oil
- ⅓ cup lime juice
- ¼ cup water
- 1 teaspoon ground cumin
- Salt and black pepper

Preparation:
1. Preheat the Griddle by turning all its knob to medium-heat setting.
2. Grease the griddle top with cooking spray.
3. Cook the pork chops on the hot griddle top until lightly browned on both side.
4. In a suitable mixing bowl, whisk together the garlic, water, and lime juice until smooth.
5. While the pork chops are cooking, baste them with the lime juice mixture.
6. Garnish with more sauce, salt and black pepper.
7. Serve warm.

Per Serving: Calories: 325; Fat: 27 g; Sodium: 58 mg; Carbs: 2.2g; Fiber: 0.2g; Sugar: 0.2g; Protein: 18.3g

Herbed Pork Patties

Prep time: 10 minutes | Cook time: 10 minutes | Serves: 8

Ingredients:
- 1 pound ground pork
- ⅛ teaspoon red pepper, crushed
- ¾ teaspoon black pepper
- ½ teaspoon onion powder
- 1 teaspoon garlic powder
- ⅛ teaspoon ground nutmeg
- ½ teaspoon dried thyme
- ¾ teaspoon ground sage
- ¾ teaspoon fennel seeds
- ½ teaspoon salt

Preparation:
1. In a suitable mixing bowl, mix well all of the ingredients and stir until well blended.
2. Preheat the Griddle by turning all its knob to medium-heat setting.
3. Grease the griddle top with cooking spray.
4. Form patties from the mixture and cook for almost 5 minutes per side on the hot griddle top.
5. Serve and enjoy.

Per Serving: Calories: 123; Fat: 3.1 g; Sodium: 195 mg; Carbs: 0.6g; Fiber: 0.2g; Sugar: 0.1g; Protein: 2.1g

Honey Vinegar Boneless Pork Chops

Prep time: 2 hours | Cook time: 10 minutes | Serves: 6

Ingredients:
- 6 pork chops, boneless
- 1 tablespoon vinegar
- 2 tablespoons olive oil
- 1 tablespoon soy sauce
- ¼ cup honey
- ½ teaspoon black pepper
- ½ teaspoon salt

Preparation:
1. Mix well the pork chops and the remaining ingredients in a zip-lock bag and mix thoroughly.
2. Shake the sealed bag well before placing it in the refrigerator for 2 hours.
3. Preheat the Griddle by turning all its knob to medium-heat setting.
4. Grease the griddle top with cooking spray.
5. Pour the egg mixture onto the hot griddle top
6. Cook pork chops for 5 minutes per side on the hot griddle top.
7. Serve and enjoy.

Per Serving: Calories: 341; Fat: 24.6 g; Sodium: 401 mg; Carbs: 12g; Fiber: 0.1g; Sugar: 11.9g; Protein: 18.6g

Roasted Basil Pork Tenderloin

Prep time: 15 minutes | Cook time: 1 hour | Serves: 4

Ingredients:
- 1 (3-pound) pork tenderloin
- 2-tablespoon extra-virgin olive oil
- 2 garlic cloves, minced
- 1-teaspoon dried basil
- 1-teaspoon dried oregano
- 1-teaspoon dried thyme
- Salt
- Pepper

Preparation:
1. Getting the ingredients ready.
2. Drizzle olive oil over the pork tenderloin.
3. Rub the tenderloin with garlic, basil, oregano, thyme, and salt & pepper to taste.
4. Preheat the Griddle to high temperature. Place the tenderloin on the heated griddle and cook for 45 minutes.
5. To check for doneness, use a meat thermometer. Cook the pork tenderloin on the other side. Cook for a total of 15 minutes more.
6. Remove the cooked pork from the pan and set aside for 10 minutes before slicing.

Per Serving: Calories: 551; Fat: 19g; Sodium: 233mg; Carbs: 0.9g; Fiber 0.3g; Sugar: 0g; Protein: 89.8g

Conclusion

The Outdoor Gas Griddle is a great and very functional grill that among the search button for years. With this griddle, you can fix the food on it quickly and easily. This is a very useful grill that can make any food you cooked to be delicious. The Outdoor Gas Griddle is one of the most fired grills you can find. This grill is easy to clean and this makes it a perfect griddle for your grilling needs. This is also an essential tool for your BBQ cooking because it is very useful when cooking food. Pair it with this cookbook that contains healthy and delicious recipes comes from different categories like breakfast, poultry, pork, beef, lamb, seafood, fish, side dishes, vegetables, snacks and more, hope you have a great culinary journey.

Appendix 1 Measurement Conversion Chart

VOLUME EQUIVALENTS (LIQUID)

US STANDARD	US STANDARD (OUNCES)	METRIC (APPROXIMATE)
2 tablespoons	1 fl.oz	30 mL
¼ cup	2 fl.oz	60 mL
½ cup	4 fl.oz	120 mL
1 cup	8 fl.oz	240 mL
1½ cup	12 fl.oz	355 mL
2 cups or 1 pint	16 fl.oz	475 mL
4 cups or 1 quart	32 fl.oz	1 L
1 gallon	128 fl.oz	4 L

TEMPERATURES EQUIVALENTS

FAHRENHEIT(F)	CELSIUS(C) (APPROXIMATE)
225 °F	107 °C
250 °F	120 °C
275 °F	135 °C
300 °F	150 °C
325 °F	160 °C
350 °F	180 °C
375 °F	190 °C
400 °F	205 °C
425 °F	220 °C
450 °F	235 °C
475 °F	245 °C
500 °F	260 °C

VOLUME EQUIVALENTS (DRY)

US STANDARD	METRIC (APPROXIMATE)
⅛ teaspoon	0.5 mL
¼ teaspoon	1 mL
½ teaspoon	2 mL
¾ teaspoon	4 mL
1 teaspoon	5 mL
1 tablespoon	15 mL
¼ cup	59 mL
½ cup	118 mL
¾ cup	177 mL
1 cup	235 mL
2 cups	475 mL
3 cups	700 mL
4 cups	1 L

WEIGHT EQUIVALENTS

US STANDARD	METRIC (APPROXINATE)
1 ounce	28 g
2 ounces	57 g
5 ounces	142 g
10 ounces	284 g
15 ounces	425 g
16 ounces (1 pound)	455 g
1.5 pounds	680 g
2 pounds	907 g

Appendix 2 Recipes Index

A

Almond Vanilla Pancakes 8
Apricot Jam Lamb Kabobs 82
Arugula and Mushroom Burgers 25
Asparagus with Butter and Pepper 20
Avocados Chicken Fajitas with Corn Tortillas 61

B

Bacon Brussels Topped with Blue Cheese 21
Bacon Burrito 8
Bacon Chicken Breast with Chipotle 63
Bacon Egg Sandwich with Cheese Slices 11
Bacon Gruyere Omelet 15
Bacon Omelet with Gruyere 10
Bacon Scallops 57
Bacon, Egg and Cheese Sandwich 12
Balsamic Honey Chicken Thighs 70
Banana and Strawberry Pizza 32
Banana Chocolate Peanut Chips 41
Banana Pancakes 7
Basic Juicy Strip Steak 73
Basil Grilled Filet Mignon 86
Basil Halibut Fillets 53
Basil Salmon Fillets with Broccolini 52
Basil Tomato and Zucchini Ratatouille 26
Basil Tomato Omelet 14
Basil Tomatoes with Cheese 27
Basil Veggie Salad with Cheese 23
BBQ Baby Back Ribs 77
BBQ Boneless Turkey Breast 70
BBQ Lamb Chops 84
BBQ Pork Tenderloin Sandwiches 89
Beef & Corn Burgers 17
Beef and Broccoli Rice 78
Beef Fillets with Pineapple Rice 77
Bell Pepper and Pork with Chimichurri 87
Blackened Boneless Chicken Breasts 69
Blackened Cod 57
Boneless Salmon Fillets 51
Bourbon Turkey 69
Brine-Marinated Turkey Breast 70
Brioche Apricots with Ice Cream 37
Brioche Toast with Maple Syrup 39
Broccoli Omelet 8
Broccoli Onion Hash with Cheddar Cheese 13
Buffalo Beef Mozzarella Filets 86
Bulgur Beet Burgers 17
Butter Almond Cauliflower Patties 11
Butter Cheese Sandwiches 11
Butter Pork Chops 80
Butter Pumpkin Seeds with Cinnamon 38
Butter Rib Eye Steak 76
Butter Salmon Fillets with Broccolini 50
Butter Sirloin Steaks with Vegetables 87
Butterflied Lamb Leg 85
Buttermilk Biscuits 41
Buttery Smoked Turkey 67

C

Cabbage Bacon Pancake 25
Cajun White Fish Fillets 44
California Seared Chicken Breast 61
Caprese Flank Steak with Balsamic Glaze 75
Caprese Mignon Fillets 73
Caramel Bananas 34
Carrot Coleslaw 26
Cauliflower and Zucchini Fritters 37
Cauliflower Patties 6
Cayenne Pork Chops in Worcestershire Sauce 85
Cayenne Pork Chops 90
Celery Onion Corn Bread 24
Cheddar Chicken Breasts 65
Cheddar Chicken Patties 71
Cheese and Tomato Burgers 17
Cheese Bacon Chicken Burger Patties 71
Cheese Buffalo Turds 28
Cheese Butter Sandwich 7
Cheese Cauliflower Cakes 30
Cheese Cauliflower Patties 9
Cheese Coconut Pancakes 11
Cheese Halibut with Parsley 54
Cheese Ham Omelet 9
Cheese Kale Omelet 8
Cheese Omelet with Olives 8
Cheese Pepperoni Chicken Sandwich 40
Cheese Pistachio Shrimp 57
Cheese Strip Steak 83
Cheese Tomato Omelet 10
Cheesy Potato Hash Brown 10
Cherry Tomato Omelet with Mozzarella Cheese 7
Chicken Breasts Fried Rice with Veggies 63
Chicken Burger Patties 42
Chicken Drumsticks with Sauce 62
Chicken Fried Rice and Corn 66
Chicken Fritters with Dill 59
Chicken Thighs Cooked in Root Beer 59
Chicken Zucchini Pepper Stir Fry 63
Chili Chicken Wings 58
Chili Crab Legs 49
Chili Lime Chicken with Sesame Seed 58
Chili Pineapple Slices 41
Chili Smoked Turkey Breast 66
Chipotle Salmon Fillets 46
Chocolate Bacon Pecan Pie 35
Chocolate Marshmallows Dip 34
Chocolate Marshmallows Toast 33
Chorizo Scramble Greens 14
Cinnamon Apple Pie 33
Cinnamon Cheese Pancakes 7
Cinnamon Chocolate Pancake 6
Cinnamon Pork Tenderloin with Harissa 85
Cinnamon Pumpkin Pancakes 10
Cinnamon Pumpkin Seeds 34
Cinnamon Seed Eggplant 24
Cinnamon Toast Sticks 8
Classic Thanksgiving Turkey 67
Cocoa Vanilla Pies 31
Coconut Chicken with Almond Butter Sauce 62
Coconut Chocolate Brownies 38
Coconut Spinach Pancakes 9
Coconut-Rum Shrimp and Pineapple Skewers 56
Cod Fish Fillets 43
Coffee Crusted Steak 85
Coffee Skirt Steak 88
Colada Tacos 32
Collards Greens Stew in Chicken Stock 22
Corn Tilapia Fillets 53
Cotija Vegetable Scrable 20
Country Ribs in Garlic Sauce 89
Country Ribs 75
Country Spiced Pork Ribs 76
Cranberry Jalapeño Stuffed Sausage 22
Creamy Berries Cake 35
Creamy Vanilla Fruit Skewers 38
Crispy Bacon Potato Hash 12
Crispy Cooked Potatoes 19
Crispy Seasoned Eggplant Bites 35
Croque Ham Cheese Buegers 17
Cumin Cuban Pork Chops 91
Cumin Pork Chops 74
Cured Turkey Drumstick 68
Curried Chicken Kebabs 65
Curry Pork Roast 88
Delectable Crab Legs 47
Delectable Egg Fried Rice with Green Onion 27

D

Delectable Lamb Chops 73
Delectable Turkey Burger 42

Delicious Bacon-Wrapped Scallops 45
Delicious Crab Cakes 47
Delicious Pepper Pork Chops 88
Delicous Pepper Butternut Squash 22
Dijon Lump Crab Cakes 44
Dijon Mustard Chicken Wings 64
Dijon Pork Chops 75
Dijon Pork Tenderloin 83
Dijon-ginger Glazed Salmon 57
Doughnut with Vanilla Ice Cream 33

E

Easy BBQ Chicken 71
Easy Lamb Shoulder Chops 77
Easy Pumpkin Pancake 6
Easy Scallops 49
Easy-to-Make Broccoli Omelet 7
Easy-to-Make Porterhouse Steak 76
Egg Scrambled with Tomato and Chili 14

F

Fennel Clam and Shrimp Bouillabaisse 49
Flavored Buttermilk Pancakes 13
Flavorful Beef Stew 73
Flavorful Cornish Hen 64
Flavorful Pork Chops 78
Flavorful Tilapia 44
Fluffy Blueberry Pancakes with Maple Syrup 6
Fluffy Vanilla Pancakes 14
French Crepes 7
French Fruit Stuffed Toast 32
French Toast with Maple Syrup 12
Fried Brussels Sprouts and Dried Cranberries 20
Fried Fish with Cilantro Mixture 43
Fried Green Tomatoes with Parsley 19
Fried Lamb Chops with Mint 76
Fried Montreal Marinade Pork Chops 87
Fried Pork Chops with Apple Compote 88
Fruits Pound Cake 34

G

Garlic Cabbage in Soy Sauce 29
Garlic Cauliflower and Broccoli Patties 15
Garlic Cauliflower in BBQ Sauce 29
Garlic Cauliflower Skewers 31
Garlic Cheese Pizza 18
Garlic Chicken Breast on Tortillas 59
Garlic Chicken Breast with Kale Caesar Salad 62
Garlic Chicken Thighs and Vegetable Skewers 60
Garlic Eggplant 23
Garlic Lamb Chops 78
Garlic Lemon Zucchini Slices with Parsley 27
Garlic Parsley Cheese Sandwiches 17
Garlic Potato Cubes with Corn and Black Beans 26
Garlic Shrimp with Lime Juice 47
Garlic Soy Pork Chops in Soy Sauce 90
Garlic Thyme Mushrooms 28
Garlic Tofu with Cilantro 26
Garlic Turkey Patties 63
Garlicky Pork Burgers 16
Garlicky Pork Chops 90
Garlicky Sirloin Beef with Parmesan 85
Garlicky Tomatoes 28
Garlicky Tuna Steaks 45
Ginger Coleslaw Egg Rolls 22
Ginger Salmon 57
Glazed Chicken Wings 59
Glazed Pork Chops with Pineapple Quarter 91
Glazed Pork Shoulder Fried in Sauce 89
Glazed Pork with Fish Sauce 77
Gochujang Chicken Wings 59
Gold Potato Hobo Packs 28
Golden Banana Coconut Fritters 33
Golden Potato Hash Browns 13
Golden Zucchini Patties 38
Golden Zucchini Tuna Patties 48
Gorgonzola Pear Bowls with Craisins 31
Greek Cheese Lamb Patties 86
Green Beans Pancetta 21
Green Beans with Sesame Seed 29
Green Cheese Stuffed Chicken 71
Green Onion and Beef Burger Patties 86
Gremolata Swordfish Skewers 43
Gribiche Skirt Steak 74
Griddle-Baked Stuffed Apple 33
Griddle-Cooked Marinated Pork Chops 86
Griddle-Cooked Potatoes and Carrots 36
Griddled Lamb Steak 86
Griddle-Fried Marinated Flank Steaks 85
Griddle-Seared Steaks 87
Griddle-Smoked Whole Turkey 70
Grilled Bell Pepper and Zucchini 27
Grilled Bok Choy 25
Grilled Dijon Artichokes 29
Grilled Jumbo Shrimp 54
Grilled Soy Salmon 54
Grilled Squash 30
Grilled Teriyaki-glazed Coho Salmon Fillets 51
Grilled Thyme Zucchini 28

H

Halibut Dill with Herbs and Olives 54
Halibut Fillets with Spinach 44
Hawaiian Chicken Kabob 60
Healthy Basil Wine Zucchini and Eggplant Salad 26
Herb Roasted Turkey in Chicken Broth 61
Herbed Cheese Omelet 11
Herbed Pork Patties 91
Herbed Pork Tenderloin 75
Herbed Potatoes 39
Herbed Spatchcock Turkey 72
Herded Broccoli Rice 23
Homemade Caribbean Jerk Vegetables 20
Homemade Cheese Omelet 9
Honey Boneless Pork Chops 82
Honey Cornish Hen 64
Honey Nectarines Topped with Blackberries 31
Honey Peaches Apricots 34
Honey Peaches with Vanilla Ice Cream 35
Honey Pork Chops 89
Honey Turkey Breast 72
Honey Vinegar Boneless Pork Chops 91
Honey Walnut Figs 31
Honey-Glazed Pineapple Slices 39
Honey-Lime Tilapia 46
Honey-Mustard Chicken 68

I

Itanlian Seasoning Chicken Breasts 65

J

Jalapeno Chicken Thighs 62
Jalapeno Corn Cakes 39
Jalapeno Turkey in Broth 68

K

Kale Omelet with Parmesan Cheese 14
Kielbasa with Jalapeño Chiles 81

L

Lamb amd Cucumber Burger 16
Lamb Burgers in Sauce with Squash Salad 79
Lamb Chops with Spiced New Potatoes 79
Lamb Kebabs with Lemon Wedges 84
Lamb Kofta in Yogurt-Garlic Sauce 84
Lemon Butter Shrimp 53
Lemon Butter Tilapia 56
Lemon Chicken with Fruit Salsa 65
Lemon Lamb Chops with Apricot 83
Lemon Mushrooms 25
Lemon Oysters with Spiced Tequila Butter 44
Lemon Pepper Salmon 55
Lemon Pepper Scallops 49
Lemon Pepper Vegetables 29

Lemon Scallops   51
Lemon Seafood Salad   52
Lemon Spinach Halibut   50
Lemon Strawberry Shortcake   40
Lemon Trout   56
Lemon Wilted Spinach   30
Lime Corn Tilapia   50
Lime Pineapple with Maple Walnut Ice Cream   34
Lime Pork Paillards   78
Lobster Salad with Vinaigrette   49
Lobster Tails with basil Butter   47
Lobster Tails   46

M

Maple Glazed Green Beans Fried Bacon and Onion   23
Maple-Glazed Bananas with Vanilla Ice Cream   39
Marinade Citrus Griddle Pork   87
Marinated Chicken Breast with Salsa Verde   58
Marinated Chicken Thighs   60
Marinated Chicken with Veggie and Brown Rice Bowls   62
Marinated Flank Steak with Yogurt Sauce   77
Marinated Portobello Cheese Burgers   17
Mayo Filet Mignon Steaks   80
Mayo Mussels with Italian Bread   48
Mayo Potato Skewers   40
Mayo Salmon Patties   53
Mayo Turkey Mayo Green Apple   66
Mayo Turkey Sandwich   65
Mayonnaise Bacon Patties   32
Mayonnaise Corn Fritters   22
Mediterranean Pork Tenderloin   83
Mexican Shrimp   55
Mint Five-Spice Oranges   42
Moink Ball Skewers   74
Mozzarella Broccoli Fritters   37
Mozzarella Vegetable Pizza   18
Mustard Crab Panko Cakes   50
Mustard Pork Tenderloin Sandwiches   16

N

New York Strip Steak   74

O

Octopus with Lemon and Oregano   54
Olive BBQ Chicken   58
Omelet with Smoky Bacon Strips   81
Onion and Tomato Sandwich   26
Oregano Boneless Chicken   59
Oregano Lamb Chops   82
Oregano Shrimp Skewers   56
Oregano Spinach Turkey Burgers   39
Oregano Vegetable Frittata   27

Oregano Zucchini and Beef Skewers   84
Oyster Sesame Pork Shoulder   80

P

Pain Perdu Strawberries   37
Palatable Cod Patties   47
Palatable Pork Chops with Creole & Parsley   88
Palatable Pork Tenderloins   81
Paprika Cheese Ears Corn   25
Paprika Crab Cakes   52
Paprika Lemon Eggplant   29
Paprika Pork Chops   79
Paprika Potatoes   30
Paprika Salmon with Parsley   52
Paprika Shrimp   51
Parmesan Cauliflower Hash Browns   9
Parmesan Pork Tenderloin Pieces   76
Parmesan Zucchini   19
Parsley Parmesan Ravioli with Sauce   24
Peach Apple Pie   42
Peanut Butter Chips with Banana   35
Peanut Butter Pancake   40
Pepper Chicken Breast Fajita   65
Pepper Shrimp with Parsley   50
Pepper Swordfish   55
Pinapple and Ham Sandwich   16
Pine Nuts Shrimp   52
Pineapple and Shrimp Skewers   46
Pineapple and Strawberry Sundae   36
Pineapple Chunks and Shrimp with Sauce   56
Pineapple, Vegetables and Chicken Skewers   69
Pita Bread   21
Pop-Open Clams with Horseradish Sauce   48
Pork Chops Fried in Orange Marinade   86
Pork Chops with Apple and Herbs   82
Pork Chops with Pineapple and Bacon   82
Pork Loin with Chile and Pineapple Slices   81
Pork Ribs with Low-sugar Ketchup   78
Pork Tenderloin with Creamy Harissa Sauce   89
Pork, Mushrooms and Bell Pepper Skewers   87
Potatoes Hash Browns   10

Q

Quick Halibut   48
Quick Shrimp   53
Quick-Cooking Shrimp   45

R

Radish Bell Pepper   23
Raspberry Cobbler   33

Rib Roast with Russet Potatoes   80
Rib-Eye Steak   74
Roast Cumin Steak   90
Roast Pineapple and Chicken Skewers   69
Roast Turkey in Orange Sauce   72
Roasted Basil Pork Tenderloin   91
Roasted BBQ Hen   64
Roasted Beef Sirloin Skewers   88
Rosemary Bread   20
Rosemary Cauliflower Bites   37
Rosemary Cheese Tomatoes   42
Rosemary Flank Steak   78
Rosemary Honey Chicken Tenders   63
Rosemary Lamb Chop Slices   80
Rosemary Pork Chops with Sage Apple   90
Rosemary Potatoes   21
Rosemary Red Potatoes   28
Rosemary Skinless Salmon   55
Rosemary-Coconut Pork Chops   90
Rum-Soaked Pineapple with Vanilla Ice Cream   40

S

S'mores Toast   31
Salmon Fillets with Broccolini   54
Salmon Patties   47
Salmon Zucchini Patties   56
Salty Sweet Potatoes   29
Sambal-Glazed Chicken Thighs   68
Sausage and Cheese Balls   36
Sausage Scramble Vegetable   12
Sautéed Savoury Green Beans   19
Sautéed Zucchini and Carrots   22
Savory Candied Sweet Potatoes   21
Savory-Sweet Turkey Legs with Mandrain Glaze   67
Savoury Lamb Loin (Rib Chops)   73
Savoury Plantains   24
Savoury Red Snapper Fillets   45
Scallion Cauliflower Pancakes   10
Scallops with Lemony Salsa Verde   48
Scrambled Bean with Cheese   13
Scrambled Egg with Tomato   6
Scrambled Eggs with Cilantro   14
Scrambled Eggs with Spinach and Mushroom   10
Seared Chicken with Kale Caesar Salad   72
Seared Fruits with Berries   42
Seared Spicy Boneless Chicken Thighs   58
Seasoned Chicken Breast Stuffed with Cheese   60
Seasoned Chicken Wings with Buffalo Sauce   61
Seasoned Lamb Patties   83
Seasoned Rainbow Trout   43
Seasoned Sirloin Pieces and Eggs   9

Seasoning Salmon Fillets 48
Sesame Pineapple Fried Rice 27
Shrimp and Pineapple Skewers 51
Shrimps with Cherry Tomatoes Asparagus Salad 51
Simple Almond Pancakes 6
Simple and Delicious Turkey Legs 71
Simple Cooked Ears Corn 30
Simple French Crepes 9
Simple Garlic Haddock 43
Simple Grouper 44
Simple Lamb Chops 80
Simple Omelet with Cheddar Cheese 11
Simple Toad in a Hole 12
Sizzling Chicken Breasts with Tortillas 64
Smoked Flat Beef Brisket 89
Smoked Marinated BonelessTurkey Breast 67
Smoked Turkey Tabasco in Sauce 67
Snapper with Mango Salad 47
Soft Blueberry Pancakes 13
Sour and Sweet Shrimp 55
Soy Chicken Thighs 66
Spatchcock Turkey 69
Spice Popcorn Shrimp 55
Spiced Snapper with Mango Salsa and Lime Wedges 56
Spicy Amberjack Fillets 45
Spicy Bacon Vegetable Tortillas 12
Spicy Chicken Breasts 65
Spicy Chicken with Blue cheese 63
Spicy Cod Fillets 44
Spicy Onion Patties 23
Spicy Shrimp 46
Spicy Squid in Sauce 45
Spinach and Garlic Turkey Patties 66
Spinach Pepper Egg Scramble 8
Sriracha Chicken Thighs 61
Star Fruit Skewers with Orange-Clove Syrup 41
Steamed Bell Peppers with Vinaigrette 25
Steamed Carrots in Ranch Dressing 19
Stir Fry Chicken Breast and Broccoli 63
Stir-Fried Shrimp and Veggie 53
Strip Steak with Worcestershire Sauce 81
Stuffed Chicken Breast 58
Sugared Peaches with Ginger Ice Cream 32
Sweet and Sour Pork Chops 82
Sweet and Sour Watermelon 35
Sweet Apple Bowls 34
Sweet Apple Cobbler 37
Sweet Chocolate Bread 36
Sweet Cinnamon Peaches 37
Sweet Pear Crisp 38
Sweet Potato Black Bean Burritos 21
Sweet Potato Fries 41
Sweet Potato Pancakes 41
Sweet Potato Snapper Apple Ceviche 46
Sweet Yogurt Flatbread 24
Swordfish Skewers 53

T

Taco Turkey Burger Patties 70
Taco-Seasoned Chicken Drumsticks 41
Tailgate Smoked Turkey 72
Tangy Masala Lamb Chops 84
Tasty Bacon Cheese Serrano Wraps 16
Tasty Balsamic Chicken 64
Tasty Beef Burger Patties 79
Tasty Ceviche 43
Tasty Cornish Game Hen 68
Tasty Herb-Seasoned Fish 45
Tasty Mushrooms with Herbs 38
Tasty Oregano Chicken Bites 62
Teppanyaki Beef 73
Texas-Style Beef Brisket 76
Thyme Lamb Racks 83
Thyme Lemon Cabbage 24
Thyme Mushroom Skewers 39
Tomato Crab-stuffed Trout 50
Tomato Omelet 13
Turkey Burger Patties 64
Turkey Cooked in Jerky 68
Tuscan-Style Steak and Crispy Potatoes 75
Typical BBQ Chicken 66
Typical Denver Omelet 7
Tzatziki Lamb Chops 84

V

Vanilla Butter Blackberry Pie 36
Vanilla Chocolate Bread Pudding 36
Vanilla Chocolate Chip Cookies 38
Vanilla Oatmeal Pancakes 15
Vanilla Peanut Butter Sundae 33
Vanilla Pineapple Sundae 35
Vanilla Toast Sticks 8
Vegetable Fried Rice 20
Vegetables and Ham Hock 79
Veggie Pesto Flatbread with Mozzarella Cheese 16
Vinegar Coleslaw with Mayo Dressing 27
Vinegar Flank Steak with Oregano 91
Vinegar Pork Tenderloin Cubes 88
Vinegar-Marinated Pork Chops 90

W

Walnut Chocolate Chip Cookies 40
Whitefish with Garlic Mayonnaise 57
Whole Turkey 71

Y

Yogurt Oatmeal Pancake 11
Yummy Jumbo Shrimp 49

Z

Zucchini Basil Crusted Chicken 60
Zucchini Squash Mix 19
Zucchini Turkey Patties 61

Made in the USA
Columbia, SC
27 November 2022